DATE DUE

4 2008

The Economic Costs and Consequences of Terrorism

The Economic Costs and Consequences of Terrorism

Edited by

Harry W. Richardson, Peter Gordon and
James E. Moore II

*School of Policy, Planning and Development,
University of Southern California, USA*

Edward Elgar
Cheltenham, UK • Northampton, MA, USA

Published by
Edward Elgar Publishing Limited
Glensanda House
Montpellier Parade
Cheltenham
Glos GL50 1UA
UK

Edward Elgar Publishing, Inc.
William Pratt House
9 Dewey Court
Northampton
Massachusetts 01060
USA

A catalogue record for this book
is available from the British Library

Library of Congress Cataloguing in Publication Data

The economic costs and consequences of terrorism / edited by Harry W.
Richardson, Peter Gordon and James E. Moore II.
    p. cm.
  Includes bibliographical references and index.
    1. Terrorism—Economic aspects—United States. 2. Infrastructure
(Economics)—United States. 3. Electric utilities—United States. 4.
Transportation—Effect of terrorism on—United States. 5. Terrorism—United
States—Prevention. I. Richardson, Harry Ward. II. Gordon, Peter, 1943–
III. Moore, James Elliott.
  HV6432.E34 2006
  363.325–dc22   2006008419

ISBN 978 1 84542 734 4 (cased)

Printed and bound in Great Britain by MPG Books Ltd, Bodmin, Cornwall

Contents

Contributors

Jay Apt, Electricity Industry Center, Carnegie Mellon University, Pittsburgh, PA

Niyazi Onur Bakir, CREATE, University of Southern California, Los Angeles, CA

Matthew P. Drennan, UCLA

Bruno S. Frey, Institute for Empirical Research in Economics, University of Zurich, Switzerland

Peter Gordon, School of Policy, Planning and Development, University of Southern California, Los Angeles, CA

Soojung Kim, School of Policy, Planning and Development, University of Southern California, Los Angeles, CA

Howard Kunreuther, Risk Management and Decision Processes Center, The Wharton School, University of Pennsylvania, Philadelphia, PA

Lester B. Lave, Electricity Industry Center, Carnegie Mellon University, Pittsburgh, PA

Shu-Yi Liao, National Chung Hsing University, Taichung, Taiwan

Richard G. Little, Director, Keston Institute for Infrastructure, University of Southern California, Los Angeles, CA

Simon Luechinger, Institute for Empirical Research in Economics, University of Zurich, Switzerland

Erwann Michel-Kerjan, Risk Management and Decision Processes Center, The Wharton School, University of Pennsylvania, Philadelphia, PA

Hamid Mohtadi, Professor, Department of Economics, University of Wisconsin, Milwaukee, WI and Adjunct Professor, Department of Applied Economics, University of Minnesota, St Paul, MN

James E. Moore II, School of Policy, Planning and Development, University of Southern California, Los Angeles, CA and Viterbi School of Engineering

Granger Morgan, Electricity Industry Center, Carnegie Mellon University, Pittsburgh, PA

Antu Panini Murshid, Assistant Professor, Department of Economics, University of Wisconsin, Milwaukee, WI

Gbadebo Oladosu, Oak Ridge National Laboratory, Oak Ridge, TN

Qisheng Pan, Associate Professor, Texas Southern University

Jiyoung Park, School of Policy, Planning and Development, University of Southern California, Los Angeles, CA

Larry Parkinson, Deputy Assistant Secretary of Law Enforcement and Security, United States Department of the Interior, Washington DC.

Robert W. Poole, Jr., Director of Research, Reason Foundation, Los Angeles, CA

Carlos E. Restrepo, New York University

Harry W. Richardson, School of Policy, Planning and Development, University of Southern California, Los Angeles, CA

Adam Rose, CREATE and School of Policy, Planning and Development, University of Southern California, Los Angeles, CA

Richard E. Schuler, P.E., Ph.D., Professor of Economics and Civil and Environmental Engineering, Cornell University, Ithaca, NY

Jeffrey S. Simonoff, New York University

Thomas F. Stinson, National Center for Food Protection and Defense Department of Applied Economics, University of Minnesota, Minneapolis, MN

Lanlan Wang, School of Policy, Planning and Development, University of Southern California, Los Angeles, CA

Rae Zimmerman, New York University

Preface and acknowledgments

Since 2004 the United States Department of Homeland Security has established six university research centers dealing with different issues related to homeland security and counterterrorist approaches. The first of these centers was established at the University of Southern California. As its name implies, CREATE (the Center for Risk and Economic Analysis of Terrorism Events) is devoted to two themes, risk assessment and economic modeling. It is a joint enterprise of two academic units, the Viterbi School of Engineering and the School of Policy, Planning and Development, and is directed by Professor Detlof von Winterfeldt. It also involves researchers from other universities. Among CREATE's many activities, its Economic Modeling Group organizes an annual workshop which brings together CREATE and other researchers to discuss a variety of topics related to the economic aspects of homeland security. The origins of the chapters in this book were papers first presented at the second Economics workshop held in August 2005.

Although the research in this book was supported by the United States Department of Homeland Security through CREATE, grant number EM-2004-GR-0112, any opinions, findings and conclusions or recommendations in the book are those of the authors and do not necessarily reflect views of the United States Department of Homeland Security.

PART I

Introduction

1. Introduction

Harry W. Richardson, Peter Gordon and James E. Moore II

This book is the second edited volume in a series about the economic consequences of terrorist attacks. The first was published in 2005, *The Economic Impacts of Terrorist Attacks* (Edward Elgar Publishing). It consisted (in addition to the Introduction) of 15 chapters by economists and others with expertise on terrorist issues, some but not all of them associated with CREATE (the Center for Risk and Economic Analysis of Terrorism Events) at the University of Southern California and sponsored by the US Department of Homeland Security. The book covered a variety of topics: transnational terrorism, air baggage security, electricity supply, biological attacks, homeland security communications, terrorist threat impacts on land values, container inspections, port security, radiological bomb attacks and destruction of bridges at the ports, the bombing of major highway bridges and modeling research (cost–benefit analysis and computable general equilibrium analysis). This volume returns to some of the same topics and some of the same authors, but also expands the range of both topics and authors.

Deterrence has been a crucial element in fighting terrorism. But in some cases there may be superior strategies to deterrence. In chapter 2, Frey and Luechinger suggest three policies, which could easily be compatible with the existing constitutions of democratic and rule-based countries. Two policies are based on diminishing the marginal benefit of terrorist acts for prospective terrorists. This can be done by decentralizing various parts of the economy or by diverting attention from terrorists, once a terrorist act has been committed. Another policy is to raise the opportunity cost, rather than the material cost, to terrorists. The effectiveness of positive incentives is substantiated by a discussion of the peace process in Northern Ireland and an overview of the empirical literature on the relationship between terrorism and political freedoms.

The Kunreuther and Michel-Kerjan chapter (chapter 3) focuses on the Terrorism Risk Insurance Act (TRIA) passed in 2002 as a temporary measure to increase the availability of commercial coverage for terrorist acts. The chapter discusses terrorism risk insurability in the context of homeland security with a focus on the design of TRIA and impediments to free markets for terrorism risk management, including state regulation. The chapter attempts to measure the impact of TRIA loss-sharing from a terrorist attack by victims, insurers, all commercial policyholders and taxpayers. It draws on two large data-sets: first, the premia and surpluses of the 451 largest insurance firms operating in the US property and casualty and workers' compensation markets; and second, scenarios of different types of terrorist attacks against 477 high-rise buildings in the country. The focus is on Los Angeles alongside comparisons with New York and Houston. The conclusion of the analysis is that taxpayers are unlikely to be liable for losses below $15 billion. For a $25 billion loss, insurers and policyholders would handle between 80 and 100 percent of the loss depending on the property take-up rate. Only for terrorist attacks where insured losses were $100 billion or more, would taxpayers have to pay 50 percent or more of the claims.

Robert Poole argues in chapter 4 that the legislation that created the Transportation Security Administration (TSA) and the current approach to aviation security, though well intentioned, was poorly thought out and is fundamentally flawed. It mandated costly changes in some aspects of aviation security, without any analysis of relative risks, costs or benefits. Consequently, it has wasted passengers' time and absorbed large sums of money that could have done more to improve security if used in other ways. With recent changes in leadership at the TSA and its parent agency, the Department of Homeland Security, the time is ripe for rethinking how the USA approaches airport security.

There are three basic flaws in the current model. First, the law presumes that all air travelers are equally likely to be a threat, and mandates equal attention (and spending) on each – which is very wasteful of scarce security resources. Second, the TSA operates in a highly centralized manner, which is poorly matched to the wide variation in sizes and types of passenger airports. Third, the law puts the TSA in the conflicted position of being both the airport security policymaker and regulator, and the provider of some (but not all) airport security services.

Department of Homeland Security Secretary Chertoff has repeatedly called for reorienting security policies along risk-based lines. At the same time, the General Accounting Office has found that today's very costly airport screening is little better than what existed prior to 'federalization' of this function. Also, the performance-contracting approach implemented on a pilot program basis at five airports appears to have worked slightly better than TSA-provided screening. Both factors set the stage for fundamental reform.

The chapter calls for three major reforms to address the three key flaws in the current approach. First, to remove the inherent conflict of interest, the TSA should be phased out of performing airport screening services. Instead, its role should become purely policy-making and regulatory (and better balanced among all transportation modes). Second, the screening functions should be devolved to each individual airport under TSA oversight. Third, screening and other airport security functions should be redesigned along risk-based lines to target resources better on identifying dangerous people rather than dangerous objects.

Devolving screening responsibilities to airports would mean that each airport could decide to meet the requirements either with its own workforce or by hiring a TSA-approved screening contractor. This model has been used successfully in Europe and Israel since the 1980s, and has worked very well. Funding would be reallocated to airports on a monthly (or at least quarterly) basis, rather than annually as at present. This would permit a much better match of screener numbers to actual passenger throughput in the rapidly changing airline environment.

If the funding was managed at the airport level, airport managers would have strong incentives to finance the upgrading of baggage-screening systems to make them less labor-intensive. At most larger airports, this would mean replacing lobby-based EDS (explosive detection systems) machines with automated, in-line EDS systems. At smaller airports, it would replace labor-intensive ETD (electronic trace detection) installations with EDS machines transferred from larger airports. These changes alone would save over $700 million per year in screener staffing costs nationwide.

A risk-based model would separate passengers into three groups: low-risk, high-risk and ordinary. Low-risk travelers would be those who qualify for Registered Traveler status. They would get expedited checkpoint processing and their bags could usually bypass EDS screening. This change would cut future EDS acquisition costs by $1–2 billion, and would yield another $200 million annual savings in baggage screener costs. High-risk travelers would receive mandatory body-scans and explosive-detection inspection of both checked and carry-on baggage.

These changes would free resources to use for increased security in lobby areas and on the tarmac, as well as improved control of access by non-passengers to secure areas. Overall, this set of risk-based changes would put much greater emphasis on guarding against the threat of explosives (as opposed to just weapons) getting onto planes, as well as the threat of suicide bombers in terminals and on planes.

In addition, by putting all airport security functions under the control of the airport (instead of dividing them between the airport and the TSA, as today), and putting all these functions under arm's-length TSA regulation, overall airport security would be more integrated and more effective, and the whole program would be more accountable. Freeing almost $1 billion a year from screening would provide the resources for reconfiguring passenger checkpoints and beefing up the other aspects of airport security.

As the United States has regrouped in the years since the attacks of 11 September 2001, the question of how best to protect our cities from future acts of terrorism has been a topic of continuing discussion. However, despite a rational concern with terrorist vehicle-bomb attacks and other threat scenarios, a coherent, cost-effective strategy for protecting buildings and facilities while maintaining full and free access to them has yet to emerge. As a result, building owners and managers have been forced to implement ad hoc approaches targeted more at generic vulnerabilities than at actual threats – not necessarily an effective, let alone cost-effective approach to urban terrorism. Richard Little's chapter (chapter 5) explores basic risk management principles as a means for building owners, alone or in groups, and in partnership with municipal and federal authorities, to develop responses that balance actual threats, available resources, and a consensus level of risk tolerance.

Onur Bakir analyzes in chapter 6 how the risks posed by the import of illegal weapons and explosives to launch attacks in the US homeland have grown significantly in recent years. Sea borders remain vulnerable because it is very costly to inspect every vessel that sails in American waterways. He examines the inspection strategies that the United States Coast Guard (USCG) should adopt, given the level of risk and cost of operations that could deter commercial or personal vessel owners from collaborating with terrorists. The critical question is how the optimal strategy changes with respect to critical factors that affect the decision to collaborate with terrorists. Two cases are analyzed. First, all small vessels are assumed to pose the same level of terrorism risk. Some insights are provided into the impact of risk aversion on optimal strategy. He then extends the initial model to include two different risk types. The model shows that the USCG should allocate more resources to high-risk small vessels while maintaining some minimal level of deterrence on both risk types.

Larry Parkinson in chapter 7 examines the problems facing the Department of the Interior and the National Park Service (NPS) in protecting national iconic monuments (such as the Statue of Liberty, the Liberty Bell, the National Mall and the St Louis Arch) against terrorist attacks. Given that no extra security funds are provided, the NPS has to consider risks, threats and deterrence. The chapter uses the Statue of Liberty, the Liberty Bell and Independence Hall as case-studies of risk assessment and management. The key issue is how, under severe fiscal constraints, to draw a balance between security and freedom of access.

There is no universal solution because that balance has to be drawn in the context of the specifics of the individual iconic site, taking account of history, tradition, aesthetics, community preferences, budget constraints and symbolism.

Tom Stinson focuses in chapter 8 on the macroeconomic impacts of terrorist attacks. He does not consider the psychological and emotional consequences of an attack, but instead measures the direct economic losses (the value of the lives and income lost and the business activity lost by firms in the industries and communities directly affected by any attack) associated with terrorist actions. He suggests that although these losses can be catastrophic for the individuals and firms affected, and while substantial at the micro level, they are likely to be small when viewed in the context of the US economy as a whole.

The long-term impacts of a terrorist attack on the economy as a whole may be much larger than the direct losses associated with an attack. A modest slowdown in national consumer spending, a slight increase in interest rates, a brief slump in the stock market, and a small increase in the value of the dollar will all slow the US economy only slightly in the short run. But even a small, temporary decline in the growth rate in an $11 trillion economy is likely to dwarf the direct losses caused by a terrorist act.

For example, in the long run, any future terrorist attack will require many firms to increase the resources they devote to security. Productivity losses will be very costly, even after appropriately discounting future reductions in output to present values, because the amounts lost will not be recovered over a few years but will continue to grow, uninterrupted, into the future.

This chapter is one of the first attempts to provide a measure of the scale of the national economic losses resulting from a catastrophic terrorist event. Its focus is on the broad, spillover effects of such an attack on the national economy, not on the direct losses suffered by the victims of the attack. The research was motivated by concerns about the impact of a major food terrorism incident, but the value assigned to the indirect economic loss estimates by this study is indicative of the indirect economic impact of other large-scale, catastrophic terrorist events. The chapter analyzes six real-world attacks occuring after 1970. Three were major events: the 9/11 aircraft hijackings that led to the destruction of the World Trade Center's Twin Towers; Iraq's invasion of Kuwait in August 1990; and the Iranian Embassy hostage situation which began in October 1979. Three were lesser events: the original World Trade Center bombing attempt in February 1993; the Embassy bombings in Africa of July 1998; and the attack on the USS *Cole* in September 2000. He uses these examples to predict the five-year macroeconomic impact of a hypothetical attack occurring in 2005.

A terrorist act of the scale hypothesized would also create significant losses at the personal, firm and industry levels, but those losses were outside the scope of this analysis. No adjustments are made to reflect the value of the lives lost or the direct losses suffered by economic sectors. Estimates of the productivity losses which may follow attacks, almost certainly larger than the short-term indirect losses estimated, were also not included.

Matthew Drennan focuses in chapter 9 on whether shocks to local economies (in this case, New York City after 9/11) result in temporary or permanent dislocations. This question has received considerable attention since New York's experience of 9/11. His argument is that agglomeration economies are difficult to destroy but that they are more network- than space-based. After the destruction of the World Trade Center, the firms that had occupied one-half of the destroyed space of all large tenants chose to relocate elsewhere downtown despite the fact that they could have paid much lower rents by relocating across the river in urban New Jersey. Thus, the spatial advantages and the business networks linking downtown firms with each other, with midtown, the region and the world, were not eliminated.

Nevertheless, spatial advantages and place-specific business networks and agglomeration economies can be eroded because of changes in technology and shifts in national and international demand. Drennan uses the historical example of the flood of 1972 in Elmira, New York, to show that a negative shock to a stagnant economy can have a permanent effect. On the other hand, despite its relative poverty, Homestead recovered quite quickly from the effects of Hurricane Andrew in the 1990s, primarily because of its location within the dynamic metropolitan region of Miami. A question of some concern is whether the slow decline of New Orleans over the 25 years before Hurricane Katrina may imply that the adverse economic effects of the flooding could be permanent.

Hamid Mohtadi and Antu Panini Murshid address a very different issue in chapter 10. Using a data-set constructed about terrorist activity involving the use of chemical, biological or radionuclear (CBRN) agents, they calculate the likelihood of a catastrophic event of this nature. Assuming a continuation of recent trends in the use of CBRN agents, an attack of the same magnitude as that on the Tokyo subway in 1995 could be expected to occur by 2009. Consistent with pronounced non-stationary patterns in these data, the 'reoccurrence period' for such an attack decreases every year. Similar trends are evident in a broader data-set which is non-specific as to the methods or means of attack. For instance, an attack that results in the deaths of 1000 people could be expected to occur within the next ten years. However an attack of the same magnitude as the September 11 tragedy, when nearly 3000 people died, is not expected in the near future.

Relying on a wide array of data sources, Park et al. specify and apply an operational multi-regional input–output (MRIO) model for the United States in chapter 11. The National Interstate Economic Model (NIEMO) provides results for 47 major economic sectors (called the 'USC sectors', developed to reconcile these models and all the different databases) for all 50 states, the District of Columbia, and a residual (or leakage) region, 'The Rest of the World'. NIEMO is used to estimate industry and state-level impacts from the short-term loss of the services of three major US seaports – Los Angeles/Long Beach, New York/Newark and Houston – as a consequence of terrorist attacks. The attacks on the three port complexes are treated as alternatives rather than as simultaneous events. A one-month loss of the services of the Los Angeles/Long Beach port costs the US economy approximately $21 billion. Corresponding impacts for the ports of New York/New Jersey and Houston are $14.4 billion and $8.4 billion, respectively. State-by-state impacts are a function of state size and distance from the site of attack.

Richardson et al. also use the NIEMO (National Interstate Economic Model) model in chapter 12 to trace the interregional economic effects of attacks on major theme parks (11 individual parks plus two geographical clusters) located in a modest number of states (eight). The theme parks are identified by state but not by smaller geographical units, to avoid identifying individual parks. A key assumption of some of the major scenarios is that an attack on one theme park will be perceived as an attack on all (this is called 'spillover'). However, the chapter also examines a more conservative assumption, that an attack on one park will not affect attendances at others. It also takes account of the probability that even a major terrorist attack on a theme park will not eliminate American vacations, but rather result in shifts to safer destinations. One possible scenario is examined: substituting visits to national parks for theme parks.

The results are easily summarized. In the spillover cases, the range of estimates of business interruption is between $19 billion and $23 billion plus up to $12 billion of air revenue losses. Without spillovers, the impacts are much smaller, between $500 million and $11.3 billion. These numbers combined may be in the same neighborhood as the costs of the 9/11 disaster. In diversion scenarios (for example, substitution of national parks for theme parks), there are economic losses because some people will stay at home, increase their savings and postpone decisions. Of course, there are offsets. In the national parks example, Florida and California are net losers (despite having important national parks), while states such as Arizona, Utah and Wyoming gain.

The economic impact estimates in this study certainly justify more expenditures on prevention. The problem is in spillover scenarios: how can the smaller theme parks afford the costs of more prevention? Perhaps the answer is a combination of local, state and/or subsidies and a co-insurance scheme among theme park owners.

The last four chapters deal with interruptions to electricity supply as a result, either explicitly or implicitly, of a terrorist attack. However, the virtue of protections for the electricity system is that they have a dual function. Not only do they guard against or mitigate terrorist acts they also protect against natural disasters, weather-related events and massive equipment failure.

Lester Lave and his colleagues point out in chapter 13 that the American economy and our lifestyles are dependent on reliable, low-cost electricity. Unfortunately, natural hazards and human error frequently leave us in the dark. Blackouts cost the economy billions of dollars and threaten health and safety. Parts of the electricity system are highly vulnerable to attack. The combination of high cost of disruptions and extreme vulnerability has led disgruntled workers, environmental extremists and landowners to target the electricity system. Paradoxically, there is an important side benefit from the facts that natural hazards and human error have posed major challenges to the electricity system; the efforts to reduce the disruption and to speed recovery from these challenges have made it easier to cope with a terrorist threat.

With thought and design, major steps can be taken to accomplish simultaneously improvements in reliability and protection of the system against natural hazards, human error and human attack. The chapter stresses the importance of interactions among the three types of threats since the benefits of improving any one might be too small to justify taking action, while the benefits of mitigating the effects of all three threats might generate several times the benefit of any one and justify taking action. In particular, recognizing the interactions among the three may easily justify steps to improve the reliability of electricity delivery beyond current levels.

The general goal is to improve the resiliency of the US electricity system. The chapter explores 11 ways of enhancing resilience: improving operator training and communication; developing multiple transmission lines for service delivery; erecting physical barriers for protecting key substations; diversification of fuel supply and generation technology; on-site fuel storage; decentralized generation with intelligent control; automated distribution; back-up generators; promoting the ability to shed individual loads automatically; improved, secure information and control systems including the use of autonomous distribution agents; and building up the inventories of portable high-voltage transformers. Each of these approaches should be subjected to detailed cost–benefit analysis.

Rae Zimmerman, Carlos Restrepo and the rest of their research team (chapter 14) estimate the loss of service that might result from terrorist attacks on electric power grids using the New York City area as an exemplar scenario. The model is based on electricity interruptions resulting from factors other than terrorist attacks. The mean value of gross domestic product (GDP) for each American is estimated at $112 per person per day, the social loss from a premature death used is US Environmental Protection Agency's (EPA) estimate (adjusted to current dollars) of $5.8 million, and the value of time lost from transportation-related congestion resulting from a blackout is half the average wage. Using these parameters and combining them with outputs from a statistical analysis of outage events, the chapter estimates the losses from hypothetical blackouts caused by a storm or crime, and so on. For example, a winter blackout in New York that lasts 20 hours and affects 2.6 million people is estimated to cost $245 million in business losses, $870 million in death and injury, and $117 million in congestion, resulting in a total loss of $1.2 billion. Although these estimates are uncertain because the scenario is not defined in detail, the method can be used to estimate the social costs of a range of disruption scenarios from terrorist attacks on electric power for any other area of the country.

Adam Rose and his group (chapter 15) explore lifeline interruptions as a result of terrorism at the local level, more specifically water supply interruption in Los Angeles. The chapter develops and applies a computable general disequilibrium model to estimate the business interruption impacts of an attack on the water supply system serving Los Angeles County. The model has several attributes: it was especially designed to incorporate engineering and spatial aspects of the water supply system in the context of the regional economy, to reflect the several types of disequilibria that a water supply disruption would bring about, to include the various inherent and adaptive resilience responses at the individual, market and economy-wide levels, and to capture both partial and general equilibrium effects. The simulation of a two-week total water outage in LA County amounts to a business interruption loss of $20.7 billion without any resilience adjustment, and $2.3 billion with the inclusion of several types of resilience, most prominently the rescheduling (recapture) of production after water supply is restored. The results indicate that inherent aspects of the water–economy relationship (for example, input substitution) and adaptive behavioral responses (for example, conservation, water storage) can reduce the potential disruption impacts by 88 percent.

There are two key caveats to the analysis. First, many of the resilience factors are rough estimates, and more empirical work is needed to refine them. However, the model serves the useful purpose of identifying the many important considerations affecting the impacts and the relative sensitivity of the results to these various factors. This provides a guide to setting priorities for further conceptual and empirical research. Second, the chapter measures only one, although likely the major, aspect of water supply disruption – business interruption. This result could be supplemented by crude estimating factors for household impacts, property damage and casualties. The next priority would be to extend the model to estimate household impacts, given the sizeable portion of the market represented by this customer group.

One final conclusion has a great bearing on future policy and is especially poignant in light of Hurricane Katrina. In the aftermath of the September 11 terrorist attacks, no politician wanted to admit that the government could not protect its people from a major threat. Likewise, in the case of utility outages, no matter what the cause, US citizens have looked to utilities to protect them. This chapter indicates how customers can protect themselves and contribute to the national war on terrorism by enhancing resilience to disasters in general. It identifies several ways this can be accomplished and the relative effectiveness of each type of resilience response at the individual, market and regional economy levels. There is a strong indication that people learn from disaster experiences, and that options implemented for one type of disaster apply to others (for example, purchase of back-up electric generators in the aftermath of the Northridge Earthquake). Thus, there is some cause for optimism that resilience to disasters will increase over time.

Richard Schuler (chapter 16) suggests that high-voltage electricity systems may become more reliable under market-based dispatch than they were under cost-based, regulated assignments if customers are faced with real-time prices. As an example, in Australia where all electricity is transacted through a spot energy market without any regulatory price caps, retail suppliers and large customers have installed frequency-sensing devices to turn off or reduce power to designated loads when the system's frequency falls below a pre-set level. While most of these relay installations were required by the grid managers, some of the automated load-shedding is also purchased as a market service. These mechanisms were put to the test in summer 2004 when the system suddenly lost 3100 MW of generation. Sufficient load was shed automatically so the system restabilized within 30 seconds. In periods when demand exceeds the system's supply capability, either because of unexpected high demand or supply disturbances, there is an inverse relationship between frequency and the price of electricity. So automatic load-shedding devices could also help buyers avoid price spikes.

While there is little experience in the United States with widespread direct customer participation in electricity markets, economic experiments have been conducted at Cornell University with human subjects. These trials of full two-sided electricity markets are cleared subject to the laws of physics over Cornell's PowerWeb, 30 bus, 6 generator, simulated AC power network. The results demonstrate the ability of a small portion (20 percent) of active customers to mute the market power exercised by sophisticated players representing the generators, all without regulated price caps or strictures against withholding capacity. Furthermore, simulations of electrical flows on individual lines suggest that the capacity needs of the system per MW of overall demand are up to 10 percent smaller with active customer participation, compared to a regulated regime, and that would provide more breathing room for existing facilities. Those line flows are also more predictable when customers are actively engaged in power markets, making the job of dispatching and controlling the system easier. So if we want to reap the full benefits of markets for power in the US, including enhanced reliability and robust rapid responses to natural or terrorist-inflicted assault, we need to get the customers into the game as full participants.

A wide range of topics has been explored in this book, but there are many more being currently researched or to be addressed in the future. These include MANPADS (for example, portable rocket propelled grenade) attacks on airplanes, more attacks on downtown office buildings (using methods other than suicide aircraft bombers), terrorist-induced Foot and Mouth attacks on the animal population and other types of biological attacks (many of them impacting humans), more border security issues, and the mother of all attacks – a terrorist-based nuclear attack. Also, the close relationship between terrorist (that is, manmade) and natural disasters should not be ignored. By the time that this book appears, CREATE will have held a conference on the impacts of Hurricane Katrina. Lessons should be learned from that terrible event that will have repercussions for emergency response, prevention and other issues related to terrorism.

PART II

General issues

2. Terrorism: considering new policies

Bruno S. Frey and Simon Luechinger

Politics focuses almost exclusively on deterrence in its fight against terrorism. In striking contrast to the prominence given to deterrence, the evaluation of this strategy by many renowned terrorism experts is unfavorable. Hoffman (1998, p. 61), for example, claims that countless times 'attempts by the ruling regime to deter further violence . . . backfired catastrophically'.

In this chapter we argue that there are superior strategies to deterrence. In contrast to raising the direct costs of terrorism, as is the case with a deterrence policy, terrorists can be effectively dissuaded from attacking either if the utility of committing an attack to the terrorists is lowered or if the opportunity costs are raised.

We propose three strategies to deal with terrorism, the first two aiming at lowering the utility of terrorism to terrorists, the third attempting to raise the opportunity costs:

1. Polycentricity. A system with many different centers is more stable than a more centralized one. When one part of the system is negatively affected, one or several other parts can take over. A prospective target of terrorist attacks can reduce its vulnerability by decentralizing the economy, the polity and the society. Terrorists are aware of this reduced vulnerability and are, therefore, dissuaded from attacking.
2. Diffusing media attention. The relationship between terrorists and the media can be described as 'symbiotic'. Both want to make news. One way to ensure that terrorists derive lower benefits from terrorism would be for the government to ascertain that a particular terrorist act is not attributed to a particular terrorist group. This prevents terrorists receiving credit for the act, and thereby gaining full public attention for having committed it. The government must see to it that no particular terrorist group is able to monopolize media attention.
3. Positive incentives. Positive incentives can be offered to actual and prospective terrorists not to engage in violent acts. Offering valuable alternatives raises the opportunity costs of terrorism. Two specific strategies are suggested: reintegrating terrorists and providing access

to the political process, and welcoming repentants. The interaction between terrorists and government is transformed into a positive-sum game: both sides benefit. The proposals break the organizational and mental dependence of persons on the terrorist organizations. In contrast, deterrence policy locks prospective and actual terrorists into their organization and provides them with no alternatives but to stay on. The strategy proposed here undermines the cohesiveness of the terrorist organization. The incentive to leave is an ever-present threat to the organization. With good outside offers available to the members of a terrorist group, its leaders tend to lose control. The terrorist organization's effectiveness is thereby reduced. Although positive incentives may be insufficient to affect the hard core of the terrorist organization, they may still be effective in dissuading the sympathizers and supporters from supporting the terrorists.

The three strategies proposed here are not confined to, nor primarily aimed at, combating Islamic terrorism. It should be realized that this is only one, though today topical, form of terrorism. Unfortunately, there have always been terrorist movements all over the world. Examples are the Basque Country (ETA), Northern Ireland (IRA), Palestine and Israel (PFLP, PLO, Hamas and so on), Kurdistan (PKK), Sri Lanka (LTTE), Columbia (FARC), or RAF in Germany and the Brigate Rosse in Italy.

Below, we present the polycentricity strategy and the diffusion of media attention strategy. We then present the positive incentives strategy and provide evidence for the effectiveness of this strategy based on (1) the Northern Ireland conflict, and (2) empirical analyses on the relationship between terrorism and civil democracy.

THE POLYCENTRICITY STRATEGY

Terrorists seek to destabilize the polity and damage the economy (see Frey et al., 2004a, 2004b for a survey on the economic consequences of terrorism and an estimate of the overall consequences of terrorism in France, the UK and Ireland). One way to immunize a country against terrorist attack and therewith provide disincentives for terrorists is to decentralize various aspects of the society (see more fully Frey and Luechinger, 2004).

Making Prospective Targets Safer

A system with many different centers is more stable than a more centralized one. When one part of the system is negatively affected, one or several other parts can take over. The more centers of power there are in a country, the less the damage caused in the case of an attack.

The increased resilience of a system due to decentralization is emphasized in many contributions to this volume, for example by Lave et al. in chapter 13 for electricity systems, and by Little in chapter 5 for protection against urban terrorism and vehicle bombings. According to Lave et al. electricity systems are highly vulnerable to terrorist attacks, but this vulnerability can be reduced by decentralized generation, diversified fuel supply and generation technology, and a multiplicity of transmission lines to deliver electricity. Spreading risk by choosing multiple locations for certain activities is also one of several options discussed by Little for managing the risk of vehicle bomb attack.

The terrorists anticipate that less damage will be caused in a decentralized society and have, for this reason, a lower incentive to attack in the first place. In contrast, in a centralized system, most decision-making power with respect to the economy, polity and society takes place in one location. This central power is an ideal target for terrorists, and therefore runs a greater risk of being attacked.

In the following, polycentricity in the economy, polity and other parts of society are discussed.

Market polycentricity
A market economy is based on an extreme form of decentralization of decision-making and implementation. Under competitive conditions, the suppliers are able to substitute completely for one other. If one of them is eradicated due to a terrorist attack, the other suppliers are able to fill the void. They are prepared, and have an incentive, to step in. No special governmental plans have to be set up for such substitution. The more an economy functions according to market principles, the less vulnerable it is to terrorist attacks. According to Rose et al. (chapter 15 in this volume), market economies are inherently resilient to adverse shocks not only because of substitution (in their case energy input substitution) but also because price signals initiate the relocation of resources.

The resilience of a market economy may be illustrated by 9/11. Though this was so far the gravest terrorist attack on the USA, the economic system as a whole was hardly affected. Due to its decentralized market economy, the United States' economy was only very marginally hit; the many other centers of economic activity were not directly affected at all. Even in Manhattan, the recovery was remarkably quick (see Drennan, chapter 9 in this volume, for evidence on Manhattan's post 9/11 recovery). This does not, of course, mean that there were no human or material losses. But the point is that even this dreadful blow was not able seriously to damage a decentralized economy like the American one. Many of the high costs were the result of the political response to the attack, and not the result of the attack itself. Viewed from this perspective, the attack was far from being a victory to the terrorists, but rather demonstrated the strength of a decentralized economic system.

Political Decentralization

Political polyarchy may take two forms: horizontal decentralization or separation of powers, and vertical decentralization or federalism:

1. Separation of powers: political authority is distributed over a number of different political actors. Most important is the classical separation of power between government, legislature and courts.
2. Federalism: political power can also be spatially decentralized and be divided over various levels of government.

Spatial decentralization and polycentric society

The high population density typical for large urban areas makes them ideal targets for terrorists and other aggressors. The spatial decentralization of the population is of particular importance in cases where terrorists use biological and chemical weapons. In areas of very dense population, viruses (such as smallpox) introduced by terrorists spread quickly, leading to many casualties in a short period of time.

The danger of physical centralization has been demonstrated by the two terrorist attacks on New York's Twin Towers. The first attack in 1993 destroyed a central command post of the emergency services. Nevertheless, the Mayor of New York, Rudolph Giuliani, ordered the establishment of a new central Office of Emergency Management in a building next to the World Trade Centre. On 11 September 2001, this office, which was intended to coordinate all police and support units in the event of a catastrophe, including terrorist attacks, was again destroyed and proved to be useless.

The Tendency to Centralize

When faced with terrorism, most countries have an overwhelming urge to centralize decision-making powers. One example is the United States. The mega-merger of various bodies into the new Department of Homeland Security is a move in the wrong direction and increases the vulnerability of these authorities. Any terrorist group able to attack this Department, for example by interfering with its electronic system, can inflict considerable damage. Moreover, as the response of the TSA to 9/11 with respect to passenger screening demonstrates, such overcentralization is also questionable on efficiency grounds (Poole, chapter 4 in this volume).

More constitutionally, the separation of powers switched in favor of the executive branch (Cole and Dempsey, 2002, p. 149). The ability of the public, the press and even Congress to gain access to information necessary in order to hold the executive accountable for their actions has been restricted (Chang, 2002, p. 124). But such reactions can also be observed in many other countries. According to a study of six countries – Canada, France, Germany, India, Israel and the United Kingdom – a common structural approach in the fight against terrorism is the centralization of decision-making (Perl, 2000).

Why does such a centralizing policy reaction occur, despite the fact that it may be counter-productive? Two reasons may be adduced. First, deterrence and a 'strong central command' visibly demonstrates politicians' determination to fight terrorism. Second, government politicians and public bureaucrats exploit the special situation created by terrorist threats to extend their own competencies. It is, therefore, all the more important to safeguard political and economic decentralization at the constitutional level.

THE STRATEGY OF DIFFUSING MEDIA ATTENTION

In this section, another anti-terrorism policy based on reducing the marginal benefits of terrorism to terrorists is discussed. The policy aims at reducing the publicity terrorists can get from committing violent acts (Frey, 1988, 2004).

Symbiosis of Terrorism and the Media

Dramatic terrorist actions receive huge media coverage. The most impressive example is 9/11. The event completely dominated the American news for weeks and was relayed to billions of TV viewers worldwide

Terrorists have become very skilled in using the media to achieve maximum publicity. Moreover, the media share a common interest with the terrorists: to make news and to ensure the longevity of the 'story'. Journalists are pressed to enlarge upon incidents of potential interest to the viewers. This multiplies the effect of a particular terrorist act.

It is sometimes argued that publicity is secondary to Islamic terrorist organizations in general and al-Qaida in particular, their main goal being the destruction of the infidel. However, we think there is plenty of evidence to the contrary. The attacks of 9/11 were orchestrated to assure maximum media attention and al-Qaida often makes great efforts to claim responsibility for terrorist attacks, as the videotaped message of al-Qaida's deputy leader in the aftermath of the London attacks exemplifies. Publicity is vital for fundraising and recruiting purposes. Beside the destruction of the infidel, another stated goal of al-Qaida is the formation of a caliphate in the Islamic world. Terrorism is in this context often seen as an exported civil war and a means to expand the support base in the Islamic world. Also in this context, the terrorists crucially depend on publicity. Finally, terrorist attacks are not primarily aimed at direct damage and destruction but rather at terrorizing the targeted society and at having far-reaching psychological repercussions beyond the immediate victim or target. Therefore, terrorism, including Islamic terrorism, essentially depends on publicity.

Reducing Media Attention

Terrorists can be prevented from committing violent acts if they benefit less from them. A specific way to ensure that terrorists derive lower benefits from terrorism consists of the government ascertaining that a particular terrorist act is not attributed to a particular terrorist group. This prevents terrorists receiving credit for the act, and thereby gaining full public attention for having committed it. The government must see to it that no particular terrorist group is able to monopolize media attention. Therefore, several scholars advocate media censorship, statutory regulations or voluntary self-restraint (Wilkinson, 2000). All information on who committed a particular terrorist act is then suppressed. But in an open and free society, it is impossible to withhold the type of information which the public is eager to know. Further, such intervention does not bind the foreign press and news media. Any news about the occurrence of a terrorist act and the likely perpetrators is therefore very likely to leak out. Terrorists seeking publicity can easily inform foreign news agencies. This first strategy must therefore be rejected as being ineffective and incompatible with democracy as the freedom of the press is seriously limited.

We propose an alternative way of diffusing media attention without infringing on the freedom of the press. Media attention can be dispersed by supplying more information to the public than would be wished by the perpetrators of a particular violent act. This can be done by making it known that several terrorist groups could be responsible for a particular terrorist act. The authorities have to reveal that they never know with absolute certainty which terrorist group may have committed a violent act. Even when it seems obvious which terrorist group is involved, the authorities can never be sure. They have to refrain from attributing a terrorist act with any degree of certainty to a particular group, as long as the truth of the matter has not been established. In a lawful country, based on the separation of power, this is the privilege of the courts, but not of the executive branch.

In the case of many spectacular terrorist events, no credible claims by the perpetrators have ever been made. Examples are the sarin nerve-gas attack in Tokyo (1995) or the bombing of the Federal Office Building in Oklahoma City (1995). Although the perpetrators were later identified and are known today, such knowledge did not exist when the events occurred. At that time, many different terrorist groups might have been credible aggressors. In many cases, however, several groups claim to have committed a particular terrorist act. For example, in the terrorist attack on the discotheque La Belle in Berlin in 1986, the Anti-American Arab Liberation Front, the RAF, and an offshoot of the RAF, the Holger Meins Commando, all claimed responsibility for the blast.

The government has to stress that any one of the groups claiming responsibility may be the one responsible. As a consequence, the media disperses public attention to many different, and possibly conflicting, political groups and goals. When only one group claims to have committed the terrorist act, the authorities responsible have to point out that such a claim is not necessarily substantiated.

The information strategy of refusing to attribute a terrorist attack to one particular group has systematic effects on the behavior of terrorists. The benefits derived from having committed a terrorist act decrease for the group having undertaken it. The group does not reap the public attention it hoped to get. This reduction in publicity makes the terrorist act (to a certain degree) pointless. The terrorists become frustrated and will either desist from further activities, or increasingly expose themselves to ordinary counter-terrorist methods by the police. The amount of terrorism will decrease; the dissatisfaction with existing political and social conditions will be expressed in different, less violent ways.

THE STRATEGY OF POSITIVE INCENTIVES

Positive sanctions can consist of providing people with previously nonexistent or unattainable opportunities to increase their utility. Similarly, they consist of offering non-violent alternatives to address terrorists' political goals. In economic terminology, the opportunity costs of being a terrorist are raised. In the following, we advance concrete anti-terrorist policies based on opening up alternatives, namely reintegrating terrorists and providing access to the political process, and welcoming repentants (see also Frey and Luechinger, 2003; Frey, 2004).

Two Forms of Positive Incentives

In the following, two specific policies for reintegrating potential and actual terrorists are discussed.

Reintegrating terrorists and access to the political process

One of the most fundamental of human motivations is the need to belong. This also applies to terrorists. In most cases, former relationships are completely severed when joining a terrorist group. The isolation from other social entities strengthens the terrorist group, because it has become the only place where the sense of belonging is nurtured.

An effective way of overcoming terrorism is to break up this isolation. Interaction between groups tends to reduce extremist views (Hardin, 2002). Stopping the vicious circle of segregation and extremism can be expected to lower terrorists' inclination to participate in violent activities. The terrorists need to experience that there are other social bodies able to give them a sense of belonging which, if that can be achieved, reduces the power of the terrorist leaders.

Further, terrorists can be granted access to the normal political process. This lowers the costs of pursuing the political goal by legal means and hence raises the opportunity costs of terrorism. There are various ways to motivate terrorists to interact more closely with other members of society and to pursue their political goals by legal means:

1. The terrorists, and in particular their supporters and sympathizers, can be involved in the institutionalized political process. As will be discussed later, this approach was effective in the case of the Northern Ireland conflict.
2. The terrorists can be involved in a discussion process, which takes their goals and grievances seriously and which tries to see whether compromises are feasible. There is strong evidence from experimental research in game theory that communication and personal contacts between players increases cooperation. A meta-analysis of hundreds of social-dilemma experiments concludes that 'the experimental evidence shows quite clearly that discussion has an extremely positive effect on subjects' willingness to cooperate' (Sally, 1995, p. 61).

Welcoming repentants

Persons engaged in terrorist movements can be offered incentives, most importantly reduced punishment and a secure future, if they are prepared to leave the organization they are involved with and are ready to talk about it and its objectives. The prospect of being supported raises a member's opportunity costs of remaining a terrorist. Such an approach has indeed been put into practice with great success. In Italy, a law introduced in 1982, the *legge sui pentiti* (law on repentents), left it up to the discretion of the courts to reduce sentences quite substantially, on condition that convicted terrorists provide tangible information leading to the arrest and conviction of fellow-terrorists. The implementation of this principal witness programme turned out to be an overwhelming success (Wilkinson, 2000). It provided the police with detailed information, which helped to crack open the Brigate Rosse cells and columns.

Application: The case of Northern Ireland

The strategy of offering positive incentives to terrorists to relinquish violence has been used with good results by the British and Irish government in the bloody Northern Ireland conflict. According to the article 'Mainstreaming Terrorists' in *The Economist* (2005, p. 14):

> . . . offer such people [terrorists] a legitimate way to get what they care about most and they drop the most extreme aims, and give up terrorism too. It has more or less worked with Sinn Fein in Northern Ireland . . .

This evaluation is buttressed by Neumann (2003) in his extensively documented and careful study of how the Republican Army and Sinn Fein were induced to engage in the peace process. His main conclusion is:

> . . . it seems certain that the peace process of the 1990s will go down in history of the conflict as a profoundly significant event, not least because it was the first successful attempt to include representatives of paramilitary groups in a political settlement. In fact, compared to previous political initiatives, which had been exclusive in that only constitutional parties participated, the peace process of the 1990s appeared to set a precedent well beyond Northern Ireland in showing that the main insurgent group – the Republican movement, consisting of the Provisional Irish Republican Army (IRA) and its political front, Sinn Fein – could be persuaded to abandon its military campaign in exchange for nothing but a place at the negotiating table (Neumann, 2003, p. 154).

Indeed, one can even talk of a 'British tradition of inclusiveness' (Neumann, 2003, pp. 157–61). Many different British governments of both parties had a strong belief that 'men of violence' could be converted into 'men of peace', and that such conversion towards peaceful politics should be actively supported. It has been maintained that the British government even offered to help with public relations in case the Republicans decided to stand for election (O'Brien, 1999). The basic idea was that the British government was convinced that ongoing peace talks were an incentive that attracted the Republicans into the political process, thus forcing them to take a decision in favor of abandoning their military activities.

Nobody can argue that the Northern Irish conflict has been settled and that total peace reigns. However, the scale of terrorist activities has greatly diminished, as can be seen from Figure 2.1. Guelke (2005, p. 6) observes that 'despite the political deadlock, no breakdown of the peace occurred. Indeed, fatalities as a result of political violence fell to their lowest level since 1969 in 2004, when only four people died in political violence.' In 2005, the IRA leadership declared an end to the armed conflict, and weapons decommissioning started.

It is interesting to note that after the IRA declared a ceasefire in 1997 new Republican dissident groups continued the armed conflict. But because they could not enjoy a significant urban support base (Tonge, 2004, p. 674), their effectiveness was rather small. This demonstrated that positive incentives, even if not able to influence the hard core of the terrorists, can still undermine their vigor by depriving them of the support of sympathizers and supporters.

Application: Relationship between Civil Liberties, Political Rights and Terrorism

If terrorists' and their supporters' inclination to participate in violent activities can be lowered by offering them non-violent alternatives to address their grievances, one should observe less terrorism in countries with extensive political rights and civil liberties. This stands in stark contrast to the widely held belief of a trade-off between civil liberties and security. As Cole and Dempsey (2002, p.178) observe '(t)he premise of this argument – so unquestioningly accepted that it often goes unstated – is that antiterrorism measures infringing civil liberties will work.' However, Leone and Anrig (2003, p. ix) point out that 'there has been a disturbing absence of information and debate about the genuine and imagined trade-offs between liberty and security'. A growing body of cross-country studies is providing evidence on the relationship between political rights, civil liberties and terrorism.

Most of the empirical research is based on two competing theoretical hypotheses. The first hypothesis is largely congruent with our hypothesis on the effectiveness of positive incentives: The granting of extensive political rights and civil liberties decreases terrorism by decreasing the price of non-violent legal activity and therefore increasing the price of terrorism ('political access school'). The other hypothesis ('strategic school') posits the opposite: Freedom of speech, movement and association facilitate terrorism as they permit parochial interests to get organized and reduce the costs of conducting terrorist activities.

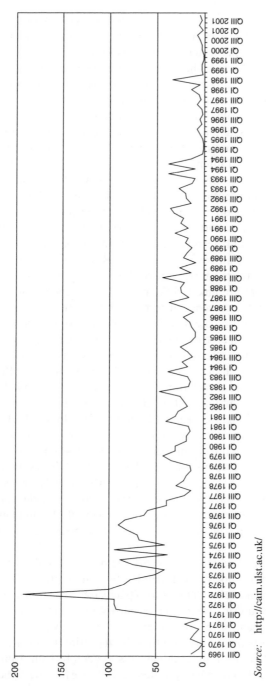

Source: http://cain.ulst.ac.uk/

Figure 2.1 Fatalities in the Northern Ireland conflict: 1968–2000

In a pioneering study, Eubank and Weinberg (1994) analyze the relationship between terrorism and democracy. They construct a dichotomous variable indicating whether a country hosts a known terrorist group or not. Calculating the odds-ratio, they conclude that regime type does discriminate in a meaningful way between countries with and without terrorist groups: the likelihood of terrorist groups occurring in democracies is three and a half times greater than their occurring in non-democracies. The main objections raised in response to their research (Hewitt, 1994; Miller, 1994; Sandler, 1995) are that their variables cannot capture the huge variation in the scale and intensity of terrorist campaigns, that they do not control for possibly confounding factors and that their results may be a statistical artifact or 'optical illusion' caused by the reporting bias. Rulers in autocratic regimes often deliberately bias their reporting to fake security and stability. The reporting bias may be especially severe in the case of directories that list only terrorist groups whose names are known, information that authoritarian governments can easily keep quiet. In two following articles, the authors address one of the critical points raised (Weinberg and Eubank, 1998; Eubank and Weinberg, 2001). Instead of the dichotomous variable on the presence of terrorist groups, they make use of event count data. The authors calculate the average number of terrorist incidents per country in a given type of regime. The idea is that, if the occurrence of terrorist events was unaffected by the type of government or the degree of freedom, the events should occur at the same rate across different categories. The results are depicted in Table 2.1. For the years 1994 and 1995, the highest number of terrorist incidents is reported for democracies or countries with the highest degree of political freedom. No clear pattern emerges for the other regime types. However, countries with an intermediate degree of political freedom seem to be the least terrorist-ridden. For the period 1980–87, Eubank and Weinberg (2001, p. 160) summarize their results as 'the more democracy, the more terrorism'. However, this only holds if one looks at the absolute number of terrorist incidents per type of regime. If one weighs the number of incidents with the number of countries per regime type, incomplete or partial democracies experience the most terrorism.

It is questionable whether the short periods, especially the two single years, chosen by Weinberg and Eubank (1998) are representative for other years. Further, event count data are also plagued by the reporting bias. In an unpublished manuscript, we try to replicate the results for a longer period of time, 1980–2000, and with data on fatal incidents only (Luechinger, 2002). This analysis rests on the premise that the reporting bias is less severe for fatal incidents than for non-fatal incidents. As can be seen from Table 2.1, only the result for 1994 can be replicated. In 1995, we find the highest number

Table 2.1   Political freedom and terrorism; battlefields

Weinberg and Eubank (1998)[1]			Eubank and Weinberg (2001)[6]
Regime type[2]	Average number of incidents per country		Average number of incidents per country [f]
	1994[4]	1995[5]	1980–1987[7]
Democracy	3.06	1.14	20.93
Insecure democracy	1.48	0.52	13.42
Partial democracy	2.56	0.08	23.22
Limited authoritarianism	0.96	0.32	3.75
Absolutism	2.19	0.08[c]	2.21
Number of countries	167	161	159
Chi^2-test[a]	$p < 0.01$	$p < 0.01$[d]	$p < 0.01$

Weinberg and Eubank (1998)[1]			Luechinger (2002)[8]		
Political freedom[3]	Average number of incidents per country		Average number of fatal incidents per country and year		
	1994[4]	1995[5]	1994[9]	1995[9]	1988–2000[9]
Free	2.13	0.55[e]	2.88	0.92	1.82
Partly free	1.19	0.30	4.71	1.61	13.16
Not free	1.91[b]	0.36	0.08	0.05	3.09
Number of countries	173	173	188	188	178
Chi^2-test [a]	$p < 0.1$	$p < 0.01$[d]	$p < 0.05$	$p > 0.1$	$p < 0.01$

Notes: [a] If the occurrence of terrorist events is unaffected by the degree of freedom, the events should occur at the same rate across the different categories; the results are tested against the null of a uniform distribution with a chi^2 goodness-of-fit test. [b] 1.19 in Table 3a of Weinberg and Eubank (1998). [c] 1.16 in Table 2 of Weinberg and Eubank (1998). [d] The value of the test statistic reported in Weinberg and Eubank (1998) cannot be replicated. The percentages of terrorist events that occur in the different categories of regime type do not sum to 100 percent. However, qualitatively we get the same result. [e] 0.69 in Table 3b of Weinberg and Eubank (1998). [f] Eubank and Weinberg (2001) do not report these results; calculations are based on information provided in the text and Table 1.

Source: [1] Weinberg und Eubank (1998), Tables 1–3; [6] Eubank and Weinberg (2001), Table 1; [8] Luechinger (2002).

Original data source: [2] Wesson (1987); [3] Freedom House (various years); [4] Rand-St Andres Chronology of International Terrorism for 1994 provided by Hoffmann and Hoffmann (1995); [5] *Pattern of Global Terrorism* for 1995 of the US Department of State (various years); [7] ITERATE (see for example Mickolus et al., 1989); [9] Terror Attack Database of the International Policy Institute for Counter-Terrorism (2002).

of fatal incidents in countries with an intermediate degree of political freedom. This pattern is even more pronounced for the whole period. This result is compatible with the finding of Eubank and Weinberg (2001) that partial democracies experience the highest number of incidents per country in the period 1980–87. Therefore, both analyses spanning a longer period of time find evidence of an inverted U-shaped relationship between political freedom and terrorism.

To address the problem of confounding factors, several authors use regression analyses. Most of them, however, are conceptually or methodologically flawed (Eyerman, 1998; Testas, 2004; Li, 2005); an exception is Abadie (2004) discussed below. All studies discussed so far rely on measures of international terrorism. This is problematic insofar as international terrorism is only a small fraction of overall terrorist activities. Moreover, most studies are likely to be plagued by the reporting bias. As an alternative measure, Abadie (2004) uses country-level ratings on terrorist risk from an international risk agency that are used by international investors to evaluate specific types of country risk. This measure captures the intensity of terrorist campaigns, it captures both domestic and international terrorism, and is less susceptible to the reporting bias. In OLS regressions, freedom is shown to explain terrorism in a non-monotonic way. As depicted in Figure 2.2, countries with an intermediate degree of political rights are more prone to terrorism than countries with high levels of political freedom or countries with highly authoritarian regimes. The result is robust to variations in the specification and still holds if GDP per capita is instrumented by geographical variables.

The majority of results points to an inverted u-shaped relationship between political freedom and democracy. This is evidence for countervailing effects as posited in the literature. For a more direct test of the two theoretical effects, more differentiated analyses and analyses based on micro-data instead of macro-data are needed:

1. Direct costs mainly determine in which countries attacks take place, whereas opportunity costs determine from which countries terrorists originate. Differentiating between origin and target countries may, therefore, help to disentangle the two effects.
2. Different electoral systems may affect the inclusiveness of the political system and therewith the opportunity costs of violence for minority groups, without affecting the direct cost of violence. In particular, proportional systems are said to be more inclusive than majoritarian systems. Differences in the electoral system allow for analysis of the effect of increasing the opportunity costs, independent of the effect of the direct costs.

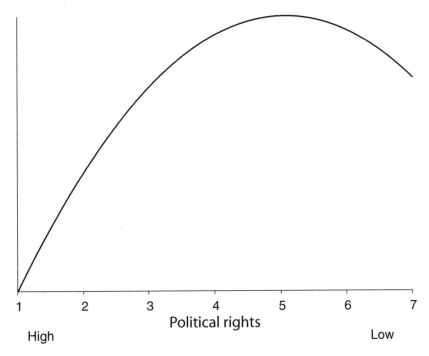

Source: Abadie (2004), Figure 1d, Table 3.

Figure 2.2   *Non-monotonic relationship between terrorism and political rights*

3. A lack of opportunities for pursuing political aims by legal means may to a large extent influence preferences for revolutionary actions, whereas execution of revolutionary actions depends on both preferences and costs. Micro-data on individuals' revolutionary preferences can therefore provide further evidence.

Instead of attributing attacks to a country on the basis of where it took place, Eubank and Weinberg (2001) and Krueger and Laitin (2003) assign the attacks to countries based on the perpetrators' citizenship and the victims' citizenship. Eubank and Weinberg (2001) report the total number of incidents per regime type and the number of countries per type of regime. This allows for the calculation of the average number of attacks perpetrated by, or targeted against, citizens of a country for the different types of regime. Krueger and Laitin (2003) calculate the average number of incidents per person in either the origin or target country according to three degrees of civil liberties and political rights. The average number of attacks assigned based on perpetrators' citizenship, is directly related to our hypothesis that offering access to the legal political process lowers the incentives to undertake terrorist attacks. For the sake of completeness, all results are shown in Table 2.2. The results based on Eubank and Weinberg (2001) provide mixed evidence for the positive incentive hypothesis. Weighted by the number of countries per type of regime, most incidents are perpetrated by terrorists originating from partial democracies. However, the results of Krueger and Laitin (2003) strongly support the positive incentive hypothesis: Countries with a lower level of civil liberties or political rights have, on average, a higher participation rate in terrorism.

Further evidence for the pacifying effect of inclusiveness is provided by Li's (2005) analysis of the effect of different electoral systems on terrorism. He finds that proportional systems, commonly considered more inclusive than other systems, are less prone to terrorism than either mixed or majoritarian systems.

Finally, there is also evidence for the positive incentive hypothesis from micro-data. MacCulloch and Pezzini (2002) analyze the determinants of revolutionary preferences of respondents in three surveys conducted over three time periods between 1981 and 1997, containing the answers of 130 000 people living in 61 countries. Revolutionary preferences are elicited by agreement or disagreement to the following statement: 'The entire way our society is organized must be radically changed by revolutionary action.' The effect of political freedom on support of revolutionary actions is analyzed with a probit regression controlling for individual characteristics, macroeconomic variables, country and time fixed-effects. The coefficient on Freedom House's composite index of political freedom is negative and significant. An individual living in a country that loses one degree of freedom on the three-point scale experiences an increase in their probability of supporting a revolt by 3 to 4 percentage points, depending on the specification. Similarly, civil liberties and political rights both have negative and significant effects on revolutionary tastes. Hence, denial of civil liberties and political freedom increases the propensity to undertake terrorist acts. This is shown by individuals' behavior (Krueger and Laitin, 2003) and stated preferences (MacCulloch and Pezzini, 2002).

What Lessons can be Learned from this Literature Overview for the Actual Fight against Terrorism?

First, and most important, the empirical literature indicates that positive incentives work. In contrast to conventional wisdom, there is no trade-off between liberty and security. The empirical results strongly support the

Table 2.2   *Political freedom and terrorism; perpetrators and victims*

Eubank and Weinberg (2001)[1]

Regime type[2]	Average number of incidents per country[a, 5]			
	Origin[a]	Target[a]		
Democracy	14.36	23.25	Number of countries	159
Insecure democracy	7.65	8.65	Period	1980–87
Partial democracy	18.44	7.72	Chi²-test; origin[b]	$p < 0.01$
Limited authoritarianism	4.73	3.54	Chi²-test; target[b]	$p < 0.01$
Absolutism	4.28	3.64		

Krueger and Laitin (2003)[3]

Civil liberties[4]	Average number of incidents per person (in either origin or target country)[6]			
	Origin	Target		
High	0.02	0.12	Number of countries	159
Medium	0.27	0.38	Period	1997–2002
Low	0.42	0.19	Chi²-test; origin[c]	$p < 0.01$
			Chi²-test; target[c]	$p < 0.01$

Political rights[4]	Average number of incidents per country)[6]			
	Origin	Target		
High	0.13	0.38	Chi²-test; origin[c]	$p < 0.01$
Medium	0.30	0.14	Chi²-test; target[c]	$p < 0.01$
Low	0.39	0.12		

Notes: [a] Eubank and Weinberg (2001) do not report these results; calculations are based on information provided in Table 2. From Table 2, it is not entirely clear which numbers are related to the origins and which to the targets of an attack. [b] If the occurrence of terrorist events is unaffected by the degree of freedom, the events should occur at the same rate across the different categories; the results are tested against the null of a uniform distribution with a chi² goodness-of-fit test. [c] Krueger and Laitin (2003) compute each test by estimating a separate negative binominal regression. with log population as an additional control variable, constraining the coefficient on log population to equal one.

Source: [1] Eubank and Weinberg (2001), Table 2; [3] Krueger and Laitin (2003), Table 5.

Original data source: [2] Wesson (1987); [4] Freedom House (various years); [5] ITERATE (see for example Mickolus et al., 1989); [6] *Patterns of Global Terrorism* of the US Department of State (various years).

effectiveness of providing positive incentives and granting terrorists access to the normal political process to pursue their goals.

Second, the empirical literature gives a rough idea about the size of the negative consequences of a badly chosen anti-terrorism policy and the area where it might be counter-productive. For example, if one takes the results of Abadie (2004) at face value, in countries such as the USA or most Western European countries with the highest degree of political freedom (that is, a value of 1 in Figure 2), infringing upon these freedoms backfires. Restricting political freedoms is counter-productive for all countries having less political rights than countries such as Bahrain, Morocco, Russia or Singapore. But even highly authoritarian countries such as Burma, China, Cuba, North Korea, Libya, Saudi Arabia or Turkmenistan have, on average, a higher risk of terrorism than the USA or Western European countries. Infringing civil liberties selectively, that is, for minorities, may also be counter-productive. MacCulloch and Pezzini (2002) find that people from a Christian or Muslim minority react more strongly to the denial of freedom than if they were part of the majority, with Muslims reacting twice as strongly as Christians to the denial of rights.

CONCLUDING REMARKS

Politics, as well as rational choice analysis, have always been committed to fighting terrorism by deterrence. We argue that the application of the rational choice approach offers a wider range of anti-terrorism policies. A first alternative to deterrence is to reduce terrorist attacks by making them less attractive to terrorists. This can be done be immunizing targets through decentralization, or by diffusing media attention once an attack has taken place. Another strategy is to raise the opportunity cost to terrorists. Specifically, we suggest reintegrating terrorists and providing access to the political process, welcoming repentants and offering valued opportunities. The strategy of offering positive incentives to terrorists to relinquish violence has been used with good results by the British and Irish governments in the bloody Northern Ireland conflict. Further evidence on the effectiveness of this approach comes from cross-country studies on the relationship between civil liberties, political rights and terrorism. Terrorists often originate from countries with regimes that suppress the political rights and civil liberties of their citizens. Moreover, countries with an intermediate level of political rights and civil liberties face the highest terrorism risk.

The three policies against terrorism outlined in this chapter support the view that 'there is no contradiction between a robust application of constitutional rights and an effective counterterrorism strategy' (Cole and

Dempsey, 2002, p. 15). On the contrary, extensive separation of powers is the cornerstone of the constitution in all democratic countries, a federalistic structure in many. Publicity for terrorists can be reduced without infringing on the freedom of the press, but by the rigid application of the principle that someone is considered innocent until proven guilty. Finally, no trade-off exists between civil liberty (and political rights) and security.

REFERENCES

Abadie, Alberto (2004), 'Poverty, Political Freedom, and the Roots of Terrorism', Faculty Research Working Paper Series No. 04-043, John F. Kennedy School of Government, Harvard University.

Chang, Nancy (2002), *Silencing Political Dissent: How Post-September 11 Anti-Terrorism Measures Threaten Our Civil Liberties*, New York: Seven Stories Press.

Cole, David and James X. Dempsey (2002), *Terrorism and the Constitution. Sacrificing Civil Liberties in the Name of National Security*, New York: New Press.

Drennan, Matthew P. (2007), 'The Economic Cost of Disasters: Permanent or Ephemeral?', Chapter 9 of this volume.

The Economist (2005), 'Democracy in the Middle East: Mainstriming Terrorists', 25 June, pp. 14–15.

Eubank, William L. and Leonard B. Weinberg (1994), 'Does Democracy Encourage Terrorism?', *Terrorism and Political Violence*, 6(4): 417–43.

Eubank, William L. and Leonard B. Weinberg (2001), 'Terrorism and Democracy: Perpetrators and Victims', *Terrorism and Political Violence*, 13(1): 155–64.

Eyerman, Joe (1998), 'Terrorism and Democratic States: Soft Targets or Accessible Systems', *International Interactions*, 24(2): 151–70.

Freedom House (various years), *Freedom in the World. The Annual Survey of Political Rights and Civil Liberties*, New York: Freedom House.

Frey, Bruno S. (1988), 'Fighting Political Terrorism by Refusing Recognition', *Journal of Public Policy*, 7: 179–88.

Frey, Bruno S. (2004), *Dealing with Terrorism: Stick or Carrot?*, Cheltenham, UK and Northampton, MA, USA: Edward Elgar.

Frey, Bruno S. and Simon Luechinger (2003), 'How to Fight Terrorism: Alternatives to Deterrence', *Defence and Peace Economics*, 14(4): 237–49.

Frey, Bruno S. and Simon Luechinger (2004), 'Decentralization as a Disincentive for Terror', *European Journal of Political Economy*, 20(2): 509–15.

Frey, Bruno S., Simon Luechinger and Alois Stutzer (2004a), 'Calculating Tragedy: Assessing the Costs of Terrorism', CESifo Working Paper No. 1341, Munich: CESifo.

Frey, Bruno S., Simon Luechinger and Alois Stutzer (2004b), 'Valuing Public Goods: The Life Satisfaction Approach', CESifo Working Paper No. 1158, Munich: CESifo.

Guelke, Adrian (2005), 'Whither the Peace Process in Northern Ireland', ISP/NSC Briefing Paper No. 05/01, Royal Institute of International Affairs, Chatham House.

Hardin, Russel (2002), 'The Crippled Epistemology of Extremism' in Albert Breton, Gianluigi Galeotti, Pierre Salmon and Ronald Wintrobe (eds), *Political*

Extremism and Rationality, Cambridge, UK and New York, USA: Cambridge University Press, pp. 143–60.

Hewitt, Christopher (1994), 'Some Skeptical Comments on Large Cross-National Studies', *Terrorism and Political Violence*, 6(4): 439–41.

Hoffman, Bruce (1998), *Inside Terrorism*, New York: Columbia University Press.

Hoffman, Bruce and Donna K. Hoffman (1995), 'The Rand–St Andrews Chronology of International Terrorism, 1994', *Terrorism and Political Violence*, 7(4): 178–229.

International Policy Institute for Counter-Terrorism (2002), 'Terror Attack Database', www.ict.org.il/, accessed 16 April.

Krueger, Alan B. and David D. Laitin (2003), 'Kto Kogo? A Cross-Country Study of the Origins and Targets of Terrorism', Mimeo, Princeton University.

Lave, Lester, Jay Apt and Granger Morgan (2007), 'Worst-Case Electricity Scenarios: The Benefits and Costs of Prevention', Chapter 13 of this volume.

Leone, Richard C. and Greg Anrig, Jr. (eds) (2003), *The War on Our Freedoms: Civil Liberties in an Age of Terrorism*, Public Affairs: New York.

Li, Quan (2005), 'Does Democracy Promote or Reduce Transnational Terrorist Incidents?', *Journal of Conflict Resolution*, 49(2): 278–97.

Little, Richard G. (2007). 'Cost-Effective Strategies to Address Urban Terrorism: A Risk Management Approach', Chapter 5 of this volume.

Luechinger, Simon (2002), 'Über den Zusammenhang zwischen Polyarchie, Marktwirtschaft und Terrorismus', Lizentiatsarbeit, University of Zurich.

MacCulloch, Robert and Silvia Pezzini (2002), 'The Role of Freedom, Growth and Religion in the Taste for Revolution', Mimeo, London: London School of Economics and Political Science.

Mickolus, Edward F., Todd Sandler, Jean M. Murdock and Peter Fleming (1989), *International Terrorism: Attributes of Terrorist Events, 1978–1987 (Iterate 3)*, Dunn Loring, VA: Vinyard Software.

Miller, Abraham H. (1994), 'Comment on Terrorism and Democracy', *Terrorism and Political Violence*, 6(4): 435–9.

Neumann, Peter R. (2003), 'Bringing in the Rogues: Political Violence, the British Government and Sinn Fein', *Terrorism and Political Violence*, 15(3): 154–71.

O'Brien, Brendan (1999), *The Long War: The IRA and Sinn Fein (Irish Studies)*, 2nd edn. Syracuse, NY: Syracuse University Press.

Perl, Raphael (2000), 'Terrorism: Threat Assessment in a Changing Global Environment', Paper prepared for Statement before the House Committe on Government Reform, Subcommittee on National Security, Veterans Affairs, and International Relations, Washington, DC, 16 July.

Poole, Robert W. (2007), 'Airport Security: Time for a New Model', Chapter 4 of this volume.

Rose, Adam, Gbadebo Oladosu and Shu-Yi Liao (2007), 'Regional Economic Impacts of a Terrorist Attack on the Water System of Los Angeles: A Computable General Disequilibrium Analysis', Chapter 15 of this volume.

Sally, David (1995), 'Conversation and Cooperation in Social Dilemmas. A Meta-Analysis of Experiments from 1958 to 1992', *Rationality and Society*, 7(1): 58–92.

Sandler, Todd (1995), 'On the Relationship between Democracy and Terrorism', *Terrorism and Political Violence*, 7(4): 1–9.

Testas, Abdelaziz (2004), 'Determinants of Terrorism in the Muslim World: An Empirical Cross-Sectional Analysis', *Terrorism and Political Violence*, 16(2): 253–73.

Tonge, Jonathan (2004), ' "They Haven't Gone Away, You Know". Irish Republican "Dissidents" and "Armed Struggle" ', *Terrorism and Political Violence*, 16(3): 671–93.

US Department of State (various years), *Patterns of Global Terrorism*, Washington, DC: US Department of State.

Weinberg, Leonard B. and William L. Eubank (1998), 'Terrorism and Democracy: What Recent Events Disclose', *Terrorism and Political Violence*, 10(1): 108–18.

Wesson, Robert (ed.) (1987), *Democracy: A Worldwide Survey*, New York: Praeger.

Wilkinson, Paul (2000), *Terrorism Versus Democracy: The Liberal State Response*, London, UK and Portland, OR, USA: Frank Cass.

3. An empirical analysis of the Terrorism Risk Insurance Act (TRIA)*

Howard Kunreuther and Erwann Michel-Kerjan

SETTING THE STAGE

Prior to 11 September 2001 terrorism exclusions in commercial property and casualty policies in the US insurance market were extremely rare (outside of ocean marine insurance) because losses from terrorism had historically been small and, to a large degree, uncorrelated. Attacks of a domestic origin were isolated, carried out by groups or individuals with disparate agendas. Thus the country did not face a concerted domestic terrorism threat, as did countries such as France, Israel, Spain and the UK.

Even the first attack on the World Trade Center (WTC) in 1993[1] and the Oklahoma City bombing of 1995[2] were not seen as threatening enough for insurers to consider revising their view of terrorism as a peril worth considering when pricing a commercial insurance policy. Since insurers and reinsurers felt that the likelihood of a major terrorist loss was below their threshold level of concern, they did not pay close attention to their potential losses from terrorism in the United States (Kunreuther and Pauly, 2005).[3]

The terrorist attacks of 11 September 2001 killed over 3000 people from over 90 countries and injured about 2250 others. The attacks inflicted damage currently estimated at nearly $80 billion, about $32.4 billion of which was covered by about 120 insurers and reinsurers (Hartwig, 2004).[4] Of the total insured losses, those associated with property damage and business interruption are estimated at $22.1 billion. Reinsurers (most of them European) were responsible for a large portion of the claims from 9/11 (Dubois, 2004).[5] Coming on top of a series of catastrophic natural disasters over the previous decade and portfolio losses due to stock market declines, their capital base was severely hit. Furthermore, their appetite for new capital to provide reinsurance against terrorism risk was sharply curtailed. Hence most reinsurers decided to reduce drastically their exposure to terrorism, or even stopped covering this risk. The few that marketed policies charged extremely high rates for very limited protection. This directly affected insurance supply. Most insurers stopped covering terrorism in areas they perceived to be high risk unless they were forced to include it in their policies, as was the case with workers' compensation. When coverage was offered, the prices were likely to increase significantly over what they were prior to 9/11, and coverage limits were reduced.

Take the case of insuring Chicago's O'Hare Airport. Prior to 9/11, the airport had $750 million of terrorism insurance coverage at an annual premium of $125 000. After the terrorist attacks, insurers only offered the airport $150 million of coverage at an annual premium of $6.9 million. The airport was required to purchase this coverage (Jaffee and Russell, 2003).[6] Golden Gate Park in San Francisco, CA was unable to obtain terrorism coverage after 9/11 and its non-terrorism coverage was reduced from $125 million to $25 million. Yet the premiums for this reduced amount of protection increased from $500 000 in 2001 to $1.1 million in 2002 (Smetters, 2004).[7]

Insurers warned that another event of comparable magnitude to 9/11 could seriously strain the capacity of the industry.[8] Furthermore, they contended that the uncertainties surrounding large-scale terrorism risk were so significant that the risk was uninsurable by the private sector alone. In other countries, similar reactions were observed. Deprived of reinsurance at an affordable price, most insurers decided to stop covering terrorism risk and turned to the government to fill the gap (Michel-Kerjan and Pedell, 2005; OECD, 2005).[9]

At the end of 2002 Congress passed the Terrorism Risk Insurance Act (TRIA) as a temporary measure to increase the availability of risk coverage for terrorist acts.[10] TRIA is based on risk-sharing between the insurance industry and the federal government. The Act was due to expire on 31 December 2005, but was renewed at the last minute. Today it is unclear what type of terrorism insurance program, if any, will emerge in the US government's long-term overall plan for dealing with the economic and social consequences of terrorist attacks.

This chapter undertakes an empirical analysis of the financial impact of TRIA on the different stakeholders following a terrorist attack, and suggests ways of improving the public–private partnership between insurers and the federal government. The next two sections discuss the nature of terrorism risk insurability issues and impediments to a free market for terrorism insurance. We then describe the design of TRIA, focusing on the loss-sharing process between the insurers, policyholders and taxpayers. The empirical analysis of loss-sharing between the key stakeholders in the following section focuses on Los Angeles. We then suggest several long-term options for private–public partnerships for providing terrorism coverage. The final section highlights future research that is required for examining alternative strategies in this regard.

TERRORISM AS AN EXTREME EVENT: INSURABILITY ISSUES

Role of Catastrophe Models and Exceedance Probability Curves

Before insurance providers are willing to offer coverage against an uncertain event they feel they must be able to identify and quantify, or at least partially estimate, the chances of the event occurring and the extent of losses likely to be incurred. Such estimates can be based on past data (for example, loss history of the insurer's portfolio of policyholders, loss history in a specific region) coupled with data on what experts know about a particular risk through the use of catastrophe models. Based on the outputs of a catastrophe model, the insurer can construct an exceedance probability (EP) curve that specifies the probabilities that a certain level of losses will be exceeded. The losses can be measured in terms of dollars of damage, fatalities, illness or some other unit of analysis.

To illustrate with a specific example, suppose one were interested in constructing an EP curve for an insurer with a given portfolio of insurance policies covering wind damage from hurricanes in a south-eastern US coastal community. Using probabilistic risk assessment, one would combine the set of events that could produce a given dollar loss and then determine the resulting probabilities of exceeding losses of different magnitudes. Based on these estimates, one can construct a mean EP curve, such as the one depicted in Figure 3.1. The x-axis measures the loss to insurer in dollars and the y-axis depicts the probability that losses will exceed a particular level. Suppose the insurer focuses on a specific loss L_i. One can see from Figure 3.2 that the likelihood that insured losses exceed L_i is given by p_i.

An insurer utilizes its EP curve for determining how many structures it will want to include in its portfolio given that there is some chance that there will be hurricanes causing damage to some subset of its policies during a given year. More specifically, if the insurer wanted to reduce the probability of a loss from hurricanes that exceeds L_i to be less than p_i it will have to determine what strategy to follow. The insurer could reduce the number of policies in force for these hazards, decide not to offer this type of coverage at all (if permitted by law to do so) or increase the capital available for dealing with future hurricanes that could produce large losses.

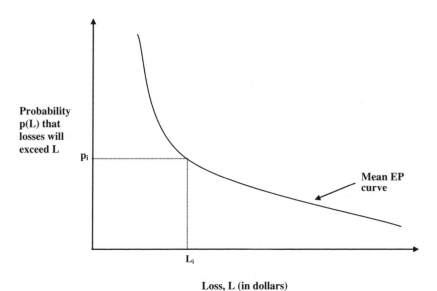

Figure 3.1   Sample Mean Exceedance Probability Curve

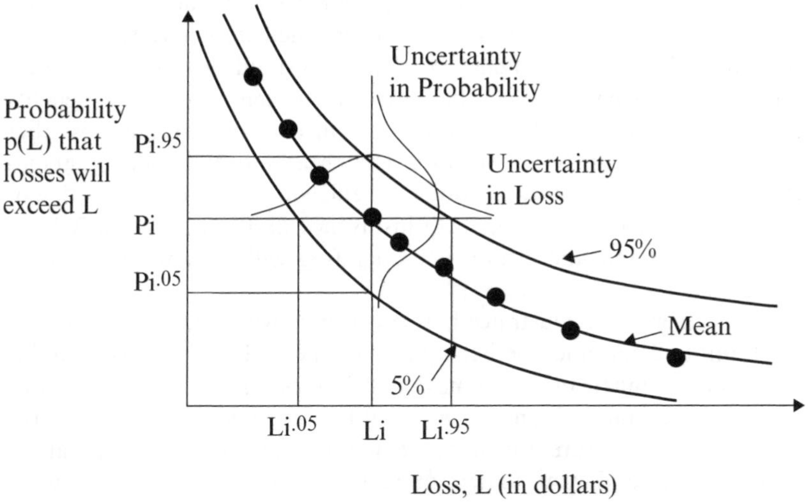

Figure 3.2   Confidence intervals for a mean exceedance probability (EP) curve

The uncertainty associated with the probability of an event occurring and the magnitude of dollar losses of an EP curve is reflected in the 5 percent and 95 percent confidence interval curves in Figure 3.2. The curve depicting the uncertainty in the loss shows the range of values, L_i^{05} and L_i^{95} that losses can take for a given mean value, L_i, so that there is a 95 percent chance that the loss will be exceeded with probability p_i. In a similar vein one can determine the range of probabilities, p_i^{05} and p_i^{95} so that there is 95 percent certainty that losses will exceed L_i. For low-probability, high-consequence risks, the spread between the 5 percent and 95 percent confidence intervals depicted in Figure 3.2 shows the degree of indeterminacy of these events.

The EP curve serves as an important element for evaluating risk management tools. It puts pressure on experts to make explicit the assumptions upon which they are basing their estimates of the likelihood of certain events occurring and the resulting consequences.

Determining Whether to Provide Coverage

In his study on insurers' decision rules as to when they would market coverage for a specific risk, Stone (1973)[11] develops a model whereby firms maximize expected profits subject to satisfying a constraint related to the survival of the firm.[12] An insurer satisfies its 'survival constraint' by choosing a portfolio of risks with an overall expected probability of a total claims payments greater than some predetermined amount (L^*) that is less than some threshold probability, p_1. This threshold probability is determined by the insurer to reflect the trade-off between the expected benefits of another policy and the costs to the firm of a catastrophic loss that reduces their surplus by L^* or more. This threshold probability bears no necessary relationship to what would be efficient for society. The value of L^* is determined by concerns with insolvency and/or a sufficiently large loss in surplus that the insurer's credit rating will be downgraded by a rating agency.

A simple example illustrates how an insurer would utilize its survival constraint to determine whether a particular portfolio of risks is insurable with respect to hurricanes. Assume that all homes in a hurricane-prone area are equally resistant to damage such that the insurance premium, z, is the same for each structure. Further assume that an insurer has A dollars in current surplus and wants to determine the number of policies it can write and still satisfy its survival constraint. Then, the maximum number of policies, n, satisfying the survival constraint is given by:

$$\text{Probability } [\text{Claims Payments } (L^*) > (n \cdot z + A)] < p_1 \qquad (3.1)$$

The insurer will use the survival constraint to determine the maximum number of policies it is willing to offer, with possibly an adjustment of the amount of coverage and premiums and/or a transfer of some of the risk to others in the private sector (for example reinsurers or capital markets) or it will rely on state or federal programs to cover catastrophic losses.

Special Features of Terrorism Risk

Terrorism presents a set of very specific problems that makes its insurability by the private market problematic. These include the potential for catastrophic losses, the existence of interdependencies and the dynamic uncertainty associated with terrorism. These factors make it difficult to estimate the likelihood and consequences of the risk and increase the amount of capital insurers must hold to support terrorism coverage. The associated cost of holding that capital increases the premiums they would need to charge. The fact that government actions are likely to influence both the will and capacity of terrorist groups to attack (foreign policy, counterterrorism) and on the level of potential losses poses additional challenges.

Following the 9/11 events, insurers have been concerned with the possibility that catastrophic losses from future terrorist attacks may have a severe negative impact on surplus and may possibly lead to insolvency. Empirical evidence provided by experts on terrorism threats supports their concern. There are an increasing number of extremist terrorist groups grounded in religious fundamentalism and fueled by other agendas, many of whom advocate mass casualties and directly target US interests.

Attacks using chemical, biological and radiological (CBR) weapons have the potential to inflict large insured losses, especially on workers' compensation and business interruption lines. Plausible scenarios elaborated by Risk Management Solutions, one of the three leading modeling firms examining catastrophe risks, indicate that large-scale anthrax attacks on New York City could cost between $30 and $90 billion in insured losses (Towers Perrin, 2004).[13] Nuclear attacks could have a much more severe impact.

The vulnerability of one organization, critical economic sector and/or country depends to some extent not only on its own choice of security investments, but also on the actions of other agents. This concept of 'interdependent security' implies that failures of a weak link in a connected system could have devastating impacts on all parts of it, and that as a result there may be suboptimal investment in the individual components (Kunreuther and Heal, 2003; Heal and Kunreuther, 2005).[14] The existence of such interdependencies provides another challenge in determining how much terrorism coverage to offer and what premium to charge.

Terrorists may respond to security measures by shifting their attention to more vulnerable targets. Keohane and Zeckhauser (2003)[15] analyze the relationships between the actions of potential victims and the behavior of terrorists.

Since terrorists are likely to design their strategies as a function of their own resources and their knowledge of the vulnerability of the entity they want to attack, the nature of the risk is continuously evolving. The likelihood and consequences of a terrorist attack are determined by a mix of strategies and counter-strategies developed by a range of stakeholders and changing over time. This 'dynamic uncertainty' makes the likelihood of future terrorist events extremely difficult to estimate (Michel-Kerjan, 2003).[16] A factor that is associated with dynamic uncertainty is the timing of an attack. Given the eight years that separated the first World Trade Center bombing in 1993 and the large-scale terrorist attacks during the morning of 11 September 2001, one may conclude that terrorist groups program their attacks far in advance and perpetrate them when the public's attention and concern with terrorism have receded.

An important feature of terrorism is how knowledge of risk is managed and by whom. The sharing of information on terrorism risk is clearly different to the sharing of information regarding other potentially catastrophic events. Data on terrorist groups' activities and current threats are normally kept secret by federal agencies for national security reasons. From an economic perspective, one justification for government intervention in insurance markets relates to the asymmetry of information between buyers and sellers and the problems this may cause, such as adverse selection. In the case of terrorism, there is a very peculiar case of symmetry of non-information of the risk for both insureds and insurers, where the government is the most informed party (Michel-Kerjan, 2003). Combined with dynamic uncertainty, this presents special challenges for insurers who need information in order to establish predictability regarding the likelihood and consequences of a particular risk for at least one year, but preferably over a period of years in order to price their product.

Finally, there are also more fundamental aspects of the threat of terrorism. International terrorism has always been viewed as a matter of national security as well as of foreign policy. It is obvious that the government can influence the level of risk of future attacks through appropriate counter-terrorism policies and international cooperation as well as through adequate crisis management to limit consequences should an attack occur. Some decisions made by a government as part of their foreign policy can also affect the will of terrorist groups to attack this country or its interests abroad (Lapan and Sandler, 1988; Lee, 1988; Pillar, 2001).[17]

Utilizing a Scenario-Based Approach for Terrorism

Given the challenges in modeling terrorism risk, it is extremely difficult for insurers and other interested parties to construct exceedance probability curves as has been done with respect to natural hazards. Experts utilize a scenario-based approach to estimate direct consequences (for example physical damage, lives lost) as well as indirect impacts (for example business interruption loss) from a range of terrorism-related events. However, in using scenarios, one cannot generate a sufficiently rich set of outcomes to represent the full range of possible terrorism threats. Thus, unlike natural hazards, estimating recurrence times and probabilities of scenario-based events is problematic.

The focus of attention by insurers has been on the outcomes of deterministic scenarios on potential losses, such as the consequences of an explosion of a 5–6-ton truck-bomb in an urban area. Insurers and reinsurers pay careful attention to their aggregate exposure to risk in relation to their current policyholder surplus.[18] How the exposure is diversified geographically and across industries also plays a key role. For example, a $1 billion exposure in a given city should not be viewed as equal to ten risks of $100 million in ten different cities.

Even though there is a reluctance to utilize explicit probabilities in estimating terrorism risks, insurers are concerned that their losses will exceed a prespecified level. In this sense they will evaluate the impact of different coverage strategies on their survival constraint and use this as one of their guides as to how much terrorism insurance capacity they should provide in different parts of the country.[19]

IMPEDIMENTS TO FREE MARKETS IN TERRORISM RISK MANAGEMENT

Economic analysis as to whether government intervention in private markets is economically efficient naturally focuses on whether there exists significant market failure compared to a competitive market, and if so, whether government intervention to address that failure is likely to produce benefits that outweigh the costs.[20]

It is not easy to answer these questions in a world where government intervention represents the outcome of a political process that reflects interest group pressure. Perceived market failures may reflect private sector responses to existing government regulation and constraints that undermine rather than enhance economic efficiency.

Federal Disaster Assistance

Federal disaster assistance creates a type of Samaritan's dilemma: providing large amount of assistance *ex post* (after hardship) reduces parties'
incentives to manage risk *ex ante* (before hardship occurs).[21] Indeed, to
the extent that parties expect to receive such government assistance after a
loss – a form of free or low-cost insurance – they might have less incentive
to engage in mitigation or buy insurance before a disaster occurs. Because
less insurance is purchased, more victims have to deal with their entire
losses on their own, which amplifies the pressure on government to provide
them with some type of assistance. This problem has been widely discussed
in the context of federal aid following natural catastrophes, such as hurricanes and floods.[22] Federal assistance has reached a new record in the aftermath of Hurricane Katrina with the federal government voting nearly $60
billion of aid within two weeks following the disaster.

Corporate Income Taxes

US federal tax policy increases the costs of private sector arrangements for
spreading catastrophe risk, thus reducing the supply of insurance and alternative risk-spreading vehicles. Insurers cannot establish tax-deductible
reserves for events that have not occurred. Premiums are taxed up front,
leading to high taxes in years where losses from extreme events are relatively
low, with limited write-offs from net loss carryback and carryforward provisions when losses are high. More important, providing insurance against
rare but potentially enormous losses actually requires insurers to hold large
amounts of equity (non-debt) capital, which is primarily invested in mar-
ketable securities.

   When held by an insurer to back the sale of its policies, the returns are
taxed twice, at the corporate level and personal level, because insurers
cannot hold such capital in tax-deferred accounts. In order for the securities to be used to back policies, the premiums must therefore be high
enough to compensate investors for the extra layer of taxes. The total cost
can be very large for the amounts of capital that must be invested to back
the sale of insurance for rare but potentially extreme events, such as large
losses from terrorist attacks.

Mandatory Insurance Coverage and Insurance Rate Regulation

Existing state requirements and regulation significantly affect the demand
and supply of terrorism insurance in a variety of ways that reduce the
private sector's ability to manage terrorism risk. Two major forms of state

regulation significantly impede the ability of firms and insurers to manage terrorism risk through the private market alone:

- Mandatory requirements, including compulsory coverage of workers' compensation claims caused by terrorism (including chemical, biological, radiological and nuclear attacks) in all states. In 16 states fire losses due to a terrorist attack are covered for those purchasing a fire insurance policy, whether they have purchased terrorism insurance or not.
- A few states – California, Florida, Georgia, New York and Texas – also prohibit terrorism exclusions in their property insurance policies.

Prior approval and other regulatory controls of rates are required for property/casualty insurance covering losses caused by terrorism.

THE TERRORISM RISK INSURANCE ACT OF 2002 (TRIA)

The lack of availability of terrorism insurance soon after the 9/11 attacks led to a call from some private sector groups for federal intervention. For example, the US Government Accountability Office (GAO, formally General Accounting Office) reported in 2002 that the construction and real estate industries claimed that the lack of available terrorism coverage delayed or prevented several projects from going forward because of concerns by lenders or investors (US GAO, 2002).[23] In response to such concerns, the Terrorism Risk Insurance Act of 2002 (TRIA) was passed by Congress and signed into law by President Bush on 26 November 2002.[24]

Eligibility for Coverage

Under TRIA, insurers are obliged to offer terrorism coverage to all their commercial policyholders, but these firms are not required to purchase this insurance unless mandated by state law, as with workers' compensation. The stated coverage limits and deductibles must be the same as for losses from other events covered by the firm's current policy.[25] This implies that if there are restrictions on a standard commercial insurance policy, then terrorism coverage will also exclude losses from these events. Thus the risks related to a terrorist attack using chemical, biological, radiological and nuclear (CBRN) weapons of mass destruction are covered under TRIA only if the primary policy includes such coverage.

Commercially insured losses are eligible for coverage under TRIA only if the event is certified by the Treasury Secretary (in concurrence with the Attorney-General and Secretary of State) as an 'act of terrorism'. One of the conditions for certification is that total losses from the attack must be greater than $5 million. Moreover, according to TRIA, an 'act of terrorism' has to be 'committed by an individual or individuals acting on behalf of any foreign person or foreign interest, as part of an effort to coerce the civilian population of the US or to influence the policy or to affect the conduct of the US Government by coercion' (TRIA, 2002). Therefore, an event like the Oklahoma City bombing of 1995, which killed 168 people and had been the most damaging attack on domestic soil prior to 9/11, would not be covered under TRIA because it would be considered 'domestic terrorism'.[26]

Structure of the Partnership

Under TRIA's three-year term that was scheduled to end 31 December 2005, there is a specific risk-sharing arrangement between the federal government and insurers for a certified event. Figure 3.3 depicts the public–private loss-sharing for one insurer when total insured losses are less than $100 billion. Should the loss suffered by an insurance company be below its deductible level as specified by TRIA, it does not receive any

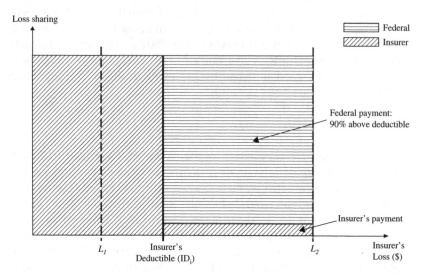

Figure 3.3   Loss-sharing under TRIA between insurer and federal government

reimbursement from the federal government. This situation is illustrated by an insured loss of L_1 in Figure 3.3 where the insurer's payment is represented by the oblique lines. When the insured loss due to a certified terrorist attack is above its deductible, as depicted by L_2 in Figure 3.3, the federal government will reimburse the insurer for 90 percent of the losses above its deductible, and the insurer will end up paying only 10 percent of it up front. The federal payment is represented by horizontal lines in the figure. This federal backstop provision is equivalent to free upfront reinsurance above the deductible. As discussed below, the federal government will recoup part or all of this payment from all commercial policyholders.

The insurer's deductible is determined as a percentage of its total direct commercial property and casualty earned premiums of the preceding year for TRIA lines and not just the premiums of clients that purchase TRIA coverage. If an attack had occurred in 2005, insurers would have been responsible for losses equal to 15 percent of the direct commercial property and casualty earned premiums in 2004.[27] This deductible plays a very important role in determining loss-sharing between insurers and the federal government and can be very large for many insurers. Using data provided by A.M. Best on their estimates of TRIA retentions for major publicly held insurance companies for 2005, we determined this deductible to be $3.6 billion for AIG and $2.5 billion for St Paul Travelers. Four other companies in the top ten insurers based on TRIA-line direct earned premiums (DEP) (Zurich, Liberty, Chubb and ACE) had TRIA deductibles between $800 million and $2.1 billion in 2005.

If the insurance industry suffers terrorism losses that require the government to cover a portion of their claims, then these outlays shall be fully or partially recouped *ex post*. More specifically, the federal government will recoup the portion of its payment between the total insurers' outlays and a market aggregate retention amount, which is defined by the law ($15 billion in 2005); that is called the 'mandatory recoupment'.[28] This amount will be recouped by levying a surcharge on all commercially insured policyholders. Taxpayers will pay insured losses between $15 billion and $100 billion. Should the insured losses exceed $100 billion during the year, then the US Treasury determines how the losses above this amount will be covered.[29]

Figure 3.4 depicts the repayment schedule in 2005 between the insurers (the area comprised of oblique lines), all commercial policyholders (solid gray area) and the taxpayers (area comprised of horizontal lines) after the federal government has reimbursed all insurers for 90 percent of their claims payments above their deductible level (for those suffering loss above their TRIA deductible). In the example we consider here, since the total insured loss L is greater than $15 billion but total payments by insurers are below the market aggregate retention of $15 billion, the government

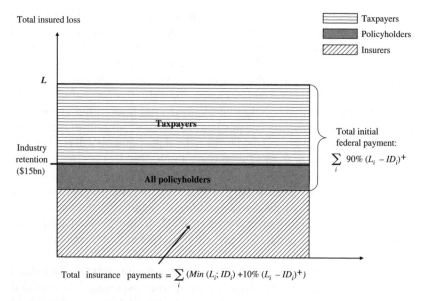

*Figure 3.4   Loss-sharing under TRIA between insurance industry, all
             policyholders and taxpayers in 2005*

recoups a portion of the payments from commercial policyholders with the
remaining amount paid by US taxpayers.

LOSS-SHARING WITH AND WITHOUT TRIA: AN EMPIRICAL ANALYSIS

The empirical analyses in this section focus on loss-sharing between those
directly targeted by a terrorist attack, their insurers and other interested
parties such as commercial policyholders and US taxpayers based on
insurer behavior under TRIA today and if TRIA is a permanent policy. The
analyses undertaken in this section are based on data provided by A.M. Best
and Risk Management Solutions, and informed by extended discussions
with key interested parties concerned with terrorism insurance and by
responses to a questionnaire designed by the Wharton Risk Center and distributed to insurers by the American Insurance Association (AIA) and the
Property Casualty Insurers Association of America (PCIAA).[30]

Constructing Scenarios

Due to the difficulty in estimating the likelihood of a terrorist attack, insurers utilize scenarios to determine their maximum exposure to a range of possible attacks that vary by location and mode of attack. However, few insurers consider the likelihood of these scenarios in determining their exposure, as illustrated by the following responses to the question posed by a Wharton Risk Center questionnaire sent to insurers in the spring of 2005: 'Do you take estimates of the likelihood of the various known scenarios into account when making underwriting decisions?':

> 'Not really. There is little historical data to predict future events.'

> 'Likelihood is very unpredictable for terrorist acts.'

> 'Our company does not believe that estimates of the frequency of terrorism attacks are credible at a country, regional or specific property level.'

Given insurers' focus on deterministic scenarios, we examined the impact of a series of terrorist attacks on financial losses between the non-insured victims, the insurers and the taxpayers under TRIA and if the program were made permanent. We also utilized these scenarios to analyze the impact on the distribution of losses if TRIA had not been renewed so that the private market (that is, insurers, property owners and/or employers) would have been responsible for all the losses.

Most insurers focus on damage from 2–10-ton truck-bombs in determining the losses they will suffer from a terrorist attack.[31] Hence we have used data provided by Risk Management Solutions (RMS) to the Wharton Risk Center on the impact of a 5-ton truck-bomb exploding in each of the 447 largest commercial high-rise buildings in the country on property damage and workers' compensation losses.[32]

Figure 3.5 describes the methodology for allocating losses from a specific scenario to the potential victims as well as the insurers and federal government immediately after a terrorist attack. The loss allocation process can be divided into several steps:

- Step 1: identify the nature of the terrorist attack (for example, 'certified' or non-certified event).
- Step 2: determine losses covered by insurance.
- Step 3: determine what proportion of losses is assumed by each of the affected parties.

Figure 3.6 provides the distribution of loss for each of 447 commercial high-rise buildings on two major insurance lines covered by TRIA:

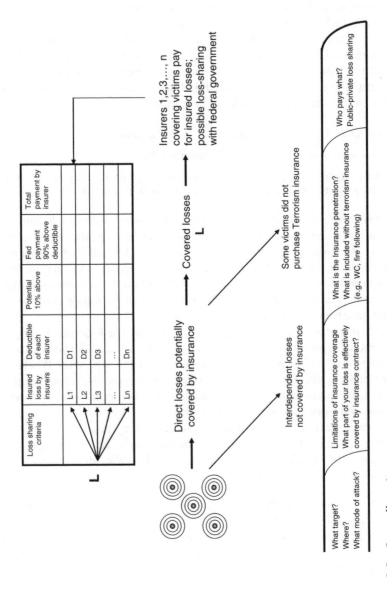

Figure 3.5 Loss allocation process

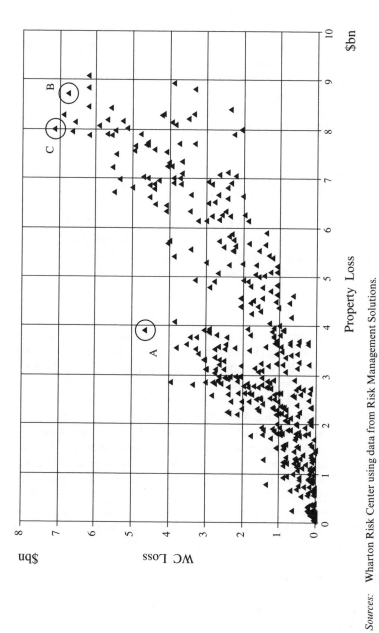

Sources: Wharton Risk Center using data from Risk Management Solutions.

Figure 3.6 Property losses and workers' compensation losses from 5-ton bomb attacks to 447 high-rise buildings in the United States

property (including business interruption) and workers' compensation. The explosion of a 5-ton truck-bomb would inflict disastrous damage to the specific building that terrorists want to target, but also to other adjacent structures. The impact on property would then mainly depend on the nature of the building and the number of employees in the building.[33] As shown in Figure 3.6 a 5-ton truck-bomb attack on Building A would inflict $4.7 billion in losses on workers' compensation and $3.9 billion in property loss. An attack on Building B in a different city could inflict $6.8 billion in workers' compensation (WC) losses and $8.7 billion in property loss. The maximum combination of property and WC losses is estimated to be between $15 billion and $16 billion for a single event, as shown by Buildings B or C.

IMPACT OF LOCATION, ATTACK SIZE AND INSURANCE TAKE-UP RATE UNDER TRIA

How would losses from foreign terrorist attacks on US soil be distributed across the relevant affected parties? This section examines this question under different risk-sharing scenarios that vary with respect to location, magnitude of damage and terrorism risk insurance take-up rate.

Assumptions

We have utilized market shares of insurers to allocate losses from a terrorist attack between the 451 largest insurers that comprise 97 percent of the market with respect to 2004 TRIA-line direct earned premiums (DEP).[34] Property insurance lines have been separated from workers' compensation lines. In the case of property coverage we have utilized premiums written for commercial coverage on a nationwide basis. With respect to workers' compensation (WC) coverage we had access to insurers' market shares in the relevant states and so have allocated losses using these data. It is worth noting that in each of the three states on which we focus our analysis, there are major competitive WC insurers: New York State Insurance Fund, State Compensation Insurance Fund of California and Texas Mutual Insurance Company. The State Compensation Insurance Fund of California covers half of WC lines in the state while the major insurers in New York and Texas cover 40 percent and 20 percent respectively of the total WC coverage in their states.

A Comparative Analysis for 2005 under TRIA

Consider the loss distribution between the affected parties as one varies location, level of loss and take-up rate under a scenario where the terrorist attacks took place in 2005 with TRIA in place. Insurers would pay their entire loss up to their TRIA deductible D (15 percent of the TRIA-lines direct earned premium in 2004) and then an additional 10 percent above D with the federal government paying the other 90 percent.[35] Under TRIA the federal government would levy a surcharge against all policyholders purchasing commercial insurance to recoup part of its payment within the total insurers' payments and the insurance industry retention ($15 billion in 2005) ('mandatory recoupment').

Impact of location

Table 3.1 examines the impact of two 5-ton truck-bomb attacks in one of the major cities in each of the three states under the assumption that the total property loss is $15 billion and workers' compensation (WC) loss is $10 billion in each of the locations we study (Los Angeles for California, New York City for New York, and Houston for Texas); that is, a total $25 billion loss. We also assume that half of the property damage to commercial enterprises in the buildings are covered by either terrorism insurance or fire following a terrorist attack, and that all the WC losses are covered by insurance. This results in a $17.5 billion insured loss out of the $25 billion total loss.

For this scenario the insurers and policyholders would absorb $15 billion of the $17.5 billion insured loss in each of the three cities. However, the

Table 3.1   *$25 billion losses due to two 5-ton truck-bombs (50% insurance for property coverage; 100% insurance for WC)*

City Comparison	Non-insured[a]	Loss-sharing			
		Total insured	Insurers' payments	All policyholders[b]	Final fed. gov. taxpayers
Los Angeles, CA	$7.5bn	$17.5bn	$13.1bn	$1.9bn	$2.5bn
% total insured			75%	11%	14%
New York, NY	$7.5bn	$17.5bn	$13.27bn	$1.73bn	$2.5bn
% total insured			76%	10%	14%
Houston, TX	$7.5bn	$17.5bn	$14.5bn	$0.5bn	$2.5bn
% total insured			83%	3%	14%

Notes:
[a] Retained by policyholders who suffered the losses but were not covered against terrorism.
[b] The federal government recoups the 90 percent portion of the insured loss it initially paid above insurers' payments up to an industry aggregate of $15 billion in 2005 (see above on TRIA design).

distribution of payments between insurers and all policyholders differ
across metropolitan areas (due to different WC market share). In both
California and New York there are two or three large insurers providing a
very large portion of WC coverage for the entire state, so that they would
have a much higher loss relative to their TRIA deductible than WC insurers in Texas where there is less concentration of coverage in one company.
Hence, the federal government would initially pay more in California and
New York (the 90 percent portion above the deductible of the few key WC
insurers), and then recoup part of that payment against all policyholders.
In all three cities the federal government covers $2.5 billion of the loss,
which is shared by all US taxpayers.[36]

Impact of size of loss in Los Angeles, California
Table 3.2 shows how changing the size of the loss from $0.5 billion to $100
billion affects the distribution of payments in Los Angeles using the same
assumptions as above regarding coverage: half of the property damage to
commercial enterprises in the buildings are covered by either terrorism
insurance or by fire following a terrorist attack, and all the WC losses are
covered by insurance. We consider seven cases: total losses of $500 million,
$5 billion, $15 billion, $25 billion and $40 billion (two sub-cases depending on what line of coverage is most affected by the attacks, property
or workers' compensation). Finally, we consider the extreme case of a
$100 billion loss.

The figures reveal that if losses from terrorist attacks do not exceed
$15 billion the insurance companies and policyholders will bear all of the
losses. Analyzing two cases where the total loss is $40 billion brings inter-
esting findings. In Case 1 property loss is $28 billion and WC is $12 billion.
In Case 2 the dollar figures are reversed: property loss is $12 billion and
WC is $28 billion. Even if the total loss is the same, the loss-sharing differs
considerably between these two cases. While taxpayers would end up
paying $5.65 billion in Case 1, they would pay $15.1 billion in Case 2. The
difference is due to both the level of insured loss and the distribution of loss
among insurers who have different deductibles under TRIA. In other
words, a $1 billion loss due to property damage is shared differently to a $1
billion loss of WC because the insurers will be different. Should the terrorist attacks lead to losses of $100 billion, then the US taxpayers would bear
52 percent of the total insured losses.

Impact of insurance coverage
Turning now to the impact of the percentage insured on the distribution of
payments, we again focus on Los Angeles where a terrorist attack causes
total property losses of $15 billion and WC losses of $10 billion. All

Table 3.2 *Impact of varying losses from 5-ton truck-bomb attacks on Los Angeles, California (50% insurance for property coverage; 100% insurance for WC)*

Los Angeles California	Non-insured	Insured loss-sharing			
		Total insured	Insurers' payments	All policyholders[a]	Final fed. gov. taxpayers
Scenarios (total loss)					
Total: $0.5bn Property:$0.25bn WC: $0.25bn	$125mi	$375mi	$375mi	$0	$0
% total insured			100%	0%	0%
Total: $5bn Property: $2.5bn WC: $2.5bn	$1.25bn	$3.75bn	$3.675bn[b]	$75mi	$0
% total insured			98%	2%	0%
Total: $15bn Property: $9bn WC: $6bn	$4.5bn	$10.5bn	$8.5bn	$2bn	$0
% total insured			71%	19%	0%
Total: $25bn Property: $15bn WC: $10bn	$7.5bn	$17.5bn	$13.1bn	$1.9bn	$2.5bn
% total insured			75%	11%	14%
Total: $40bn Property: $28bn WC: $12bn	$14bn	$26bn	$20.35bn	$0	$5.65bn
% total insured			78%	0%	22%
Total: $40bn Property: $12bn WC: $28bn	$6bn	$34bn	$18.9bn	0$	$15.1bn
% total insured			56%	0%	44%

Table 3.2   (continued)

Los Angeles California	Non-insured	Insured loss-sharing			
		Total insured	Insurers' payments	All policyholders[a]	Final fed. gov. taxpayers
Total: $100bn Property: $50bn WC: $50bn	$25bn	$75bn	$35.8bn	$0	$39.2bn[c]
% total insured			48%	0%	52%

Notes:
[a] The federal government is assumed to recoup the portion of insured loss it initially paid above insurers' payments up to an industry aggregate of $15 billion in 2005.
[b] Including $1.2 billion paid by the State Comp Insurance Fund of CA for workers' compensation.
[c] Including $21.8 billion that would represent the 90 percent federal payment above the State Compensation Insurance Fund of California's TRIA deductible.

employees are protected against WC losses; the percentage of commercial enterprises insured against property damage is now varied from 0 percent to 100 percent.

Table 3.3 shows that insurers and policyholders would absorb all of the losses if 25 percent or less of the commercial enterprises purchase property insurance. Even when 50 percent or more of those at risk are insured against terrorism losses, three-quarters or more of the property and WC losses from the terrorist attack would be covered by the insurance industry.

Summary of findings
The above analyses provide the following insight into the distribution of losses under TRIA should a terrorist attack have occurred in 2005: the US taxpayers will cover a relatively small proportion of the losses if half of the property losses are covered by insurance unless there is a terrorist attack that produces extreme losses of $100 billion or more (see Table 3.2).

Even if all property is protected by insurance, the US taxpayers would absorb only 17.5 percent of the total loss under TRIA from a terrorist attack inflicting a $25 billion loss in Los Angeles (see Table 3.3). This is due to the high deductible associated with TRIA. It is interesting to note that Congressional bills introduced in 2004 specified higher deductibles in 2006 (D = 17.5 percent) and 2007 (D = 20 percent).

Table 3.3 *Impact of varying percentage insured against property and workers' compensation losses in Los Angeles, California ($25 billion losses due to two 5-ton truck-bombs; 100% insurance for WC)*

Los Angeles California	Non-insured	Insured loss sharing			
		Total insured	Insurers' payments	All policyholders[a]	Final fed. gov. taxpayers
Take-up rate					
0%	$15bn	$10bn	$5.8bn	$4.2	$0
% total insured			58%	42%	0%
25%	$11.25bn	$13.75bn	$9.47bn	$4.28bn	$0
% total insured			69%	31%	0%
50%	$7.5bn	$17.5bn	$13.1bn	$1.9bn	$2.5bn
% total insured			75%	11%	14%
75%	$3.75bn	$21.25bn	$16.85bn	$0	$4.4bn
% total insured			79.4%	0%	20.6%
100%	$0	$25bn	$20.5bn	$0	$4.5bn
% total insured			82%	0%	18%

Note:
[a] The federal government is assumed to recoup the portion of insured loss it initially paid above insurers' payments up to an industry aggregate of $15 billion in 2005.

Who bears the loss if TRIA is eventually abolished?

What would be the severity of the losses to insurers if they continued to provide the same amount of terrorism coverage for property and workers' compensation as they are currently doing, TRIA is eventually abolished, and insurers would be responsible for the entire loss from both foreign and domestic terrorist attacks? Another series of analyses show that if insurers maintained their current book of business, some would have loss–surplus ratios exceeding 1 following a 5-ton truck-bombing, implying that they would become insolvent.

A closer look at the data from the scenarios of terrorist attacks in Los Angeles, California reveals that most of the 90 percent quota-share above the deductible would be paid by the federal government to a few large workers' compensation insurers in the state if TRIA were in place. If TRIA were eventually abolished then this federal backstop would be removed and insurers whose book of business was primarily workers' compensation would be in a highly vulnerable situation.[37]

ISSUES FOR FUTURE RESEARCH

In this concluding section, we highlight a set of open issues that call for both conceptual and empirical research before a long-term terrorism insurance program is designed. As we have advocated recently,[38] Congress and the White House should consider establishing a national commission on terrorism risk coverage to examine the most effective and sustainable way for the nation to recover from future terrorism and the role that insurance can and should play in this process.

Possible Federal Pre-Emption of Certain State Regulations and Requirements

As noted above, a variety of state regulations constrain private parties' ability to enter into optimal contracts in the presence of terrorism risk. Workers' compensation insurance coverage must include coverage for worker injuries caused by terrorism. About a third of the states continue to require property insurance policies to cover fire losses from terrorism. Rate regulation remains prevalent, especially for workers' compensation insurance, and it could be used to prevent necessary increases in premium rates with or without a federal terrorism insurance backstop.

Consideration should be given to federal pre-emption of state regulation of terrorism insurance rates as part of any long-term federal involvement in terrorism insurance markets. Consideration should also be given to federal pre-emption of state requirements that fire insurance policies cover fire losses following terrorism, as there is no economic basis for such selective restrictions on private contracting. An analysis should be undertaken as to whether there is a need for mandatory coverage of terrorism losses in workers' compensation insurance and possible alternatives to this requirement.

Considering Covering Both Domestic and Foreign Terrorism[39]

TRIA stipulates that a terrorist attack would be certified as an act of terrorism only if it is perpetrated by 'an individual or individuals acting on behalf of any foreign person or foreign interest, as part of an effort to coerce the civilian population of the United States or to influence the policy or affect the conduct of the United States Government by coercion'. Consideration should be given as to whether it is desirable to include domestic terrorism as part of the events covered in a national terrorism insurance program, for the following reasons.

First, the evolution of international terrorist activities from more locally organized and even national groups to global organization makes it difficult to distinguish between domestic and foreign terrorism as illustrated by the July 2005 bombings in London, UK.[40] Some of these terrorists had been trained to kill in Pakistan. Should one thus conclude that they were 'acting on behalf of a foreign person or foreign interest'? On the other hand, they had been living in England for years, studying or working there. Should one conclude they acted on behalf of their own ideology? In that case, should we conclude that the nearly 800 casualties were victims of domestic terrorism? Had these events been more devastating and occurred in the US, would they have qualified for TRIA coverage? Today this gray zone is likely to inflict legal costs on both victims and insurers, and considerably delay claims payments to victims of the attacks.

Second, the decision to exclude domestic terrorism from TRIA because it was not considered a serious threat needs to be re-evaluated in the light of the current threats posed by extremist groups in the United States.[41] Data on domestic terrorism from the US Federal Bureau of Investigation reveal that over 350 acts of domestic terrorism have been perpetrated on the US soil during the period 1980–2001. Although the annual number of such attacks decreased during the 1980s and mid-1990s, it started increasing again in the past ten years, averaging 15 attacks a year nationwide during the period 1996–2001 (FBI, 2002).[42] It is likely that this increase has been galvanized by anti-globalization imperatives.

Gaining Knowledge of Terrorism Premiums Collected

There is great uncertainty associated with the likelihood of any specific terrorist attack occurring during a specific period of time in a specific location. In fact, it is almost impossible to establish such a probability, as the terrorism threat is continuously evolving. If one knew the premiums an insurer collected for a given amount of terrorism coverage for a particular structure in a given location, it would be possible to calculate a range for the implicit probability that an insurer associates with terrorism attacks, as long as reasonable assumptions could be made about the capital costs (charges) included in the premiums. The same logic applies at an industry level.

To date no one has collected and made public the total premiums for terrorism coverage levied by insurers over the period of operation of TRIA. Such information would be very useful to have available so one can do a more detailed analysis of the impact of TRIA and possibly alternative long-term programs on the determinants of terrorism insurance rates.

NOTES

*   This chapter is based on a longer report 'TRIA and Beyond' completed by a Wharton Risk Center team and available at http://grace.wharton.upenn.edu/risk/downloads/ TRIA%20and%20Beyond.pdf.

   We thank Neil Doherty, Esther Goldsmith, Scott Harrington, Paul Kleindorfer, Mark Pauly, Irv Rosenthal Peter Schmeidler and Kent Smetters for insightful comments on different aspects of the analyses provided here.

1. The 1993 bombing of the WTC killed 6 people and caused $725 million in insured damages. See Swiss Re (2002), *Focus Report: Terrorism – Dealing with the New Spectre*, Zurich: Swiss Re, February.

2. Prior to September 11, the Oklahoma City bombing of 1995, which killed 168 people, had been the most damaging terrorist attack on domestic soil, but the largest losses were to federal property and employees and were covered by the government.

3. Kunreuther, H. and M. Pauly (2005), 'Terrorism Losses and All-perils Insurance', *Journal of Insurance Regulation*, 23(4): 3–20.

4. Hartwig, R. (2004), 'The Fate of TRIA: Is Terrorism an Insurance Risk?' New York: Insurance Information Institute. This estimate keeps changing as a result of new claims settlements and court rulings. For example, a federal jury ruled in December 2004 that the 9/11 attacks against the World Trade Center's towers constituted two separate 'occurrences' under certain insurance policies, entitling the World Trade Center lease-holder Silverstein Properties to collect $2.2 billion from nine insurers. This is twice the amount of coverage Silverstein carried for a single occurrence from these nine insurers. See Bagli C. (2004), 'Tower's Insurance Must Pay Double', *New York Times*, 7 December, p. A1.

5. Testimony of Jacques Dubois, Chairman and CEO Swiss Re America, on behalf of Swiss Re before the United States Senate on Banking, Housing, and Urban Affairs, 18 May 2004.

6. Jaffee, D. and T. Russell (2003), 'Market Under Stress: The Case of Extreme Event Insurance' in R. Arnott, B. Greenwald, R. Kanbur and B. Nalebuff (eds), *Economics for an Imperfect World: Essays in Honor of Joseph E. Stiglitz*, Cambridge, MA: MIT Press.

7. Smetters, K. (2004), 'Insuring Against Terrorism: The Policy Challenge', in R. Litan and R. Herring (eds), *Brookings-Wharton Papers on Financial Services*, Brookings Institution, Washington, DC, and The Wharton School of Finance, University of Pennsylvania, Philadelphia. pp. 139–82.

8. As stated by the US Government Accountability Office, 'ISO found that from 1990 through 2003 industry equity capital increased from $194.8 billion to $347 billion on an inflation-adjusted basis. The insurance industry equity capitals (financial resources available to cover catastrophic risk and other types of claims that exceed premium and investment income) commonly are used to assess capacity to cover catastrophic risk. It is difficult [however] to determine whether the growth in insurer equity capital has resulted in material increase in the industry's relative capacity to pay claims. Insurers may also face significant financial exposure in areas prone to catastrophe, which could partially offset the increase in insurer capital over the years.' US GAO (2005), *Catastrophe Risk, US and European Approaches to Insure Natural Catastrophe and Terrorism Risks*, Appendix III, GAO-05-199, Washington, DC, 28 February.

9. Michel-Kerjan, E. and B. Pedell (2005), 'Terrorism Risk Coverage in the Post- 9/11 Era: A Comparison of New Public–Private Partnerships in France, Germany and the US', *Geneva Papers on Risk and Insurance*, 30(1): 144–70. See also Organization for Economic Cooperation and Development (2005), *Terrorism Insurance in OECD Countries*, Paris: OECD, 5 July.

10. US Congress (2002), *Terrorism Risk Insurance Act of 2002*, HR 3210, Washington, DC, 26 November.

11. Stone, J. (1973), 'A Theory of Capacity and the Insurance of Catastrophic Risks: Part I and Part II', *Journal of Risk and Insurance*, 40: 231–43 (Part I) and 40: 339–55 (Part II).

12. Stone also introduces a constraint regarding the stability of the insurer's operation. However, insurers have traditionally not focused on this constraint in dealing with catastrophic risks.

13. Towers Perrin (2004), 'Workers' Compensation Terrorism Reinsurance Pool Feasibility Study', March, New York.

14. Kunreuther, H. and G. Heal (2003), 'Interdependent Security', *Journal of Risk and Uncertainty*, 26(2/3): 231–49; Heal, G. and H. Kunreuther (2005), 'IDS Models for Airline Security', *Journal of Conflict Resolution*, 49(2): 201–17.

15. Keohane, N. and R. Zeckhauser (2003), 'The Ecology of Terror Defense', *Journal of Risk and Uncertainty*, 26(2/3): 201–29.

16. Michel-Kerjan, E. (2003), 'Large-scale Terrorism: Risk Sharing and Public Policy', *Revue d'Economie Politique*, 113(5): 625–48.

17. Lapan, H. and T. Sandler (1988), 'To Bargain or Not to Bargain: That is The Question', *American Economic Review*, 78(2): 16–20; Lee, D. (1988), 'Free Riding and Paid Riding in the Fight Against Terrorism', *American Economic Review*, 78(2): 22–6; Pillar, P. (2001), *Terrorism and US Foreign Policy*, Washington, DC: Brookings Institution Press.

18. Insurer capital represents the net worth of the company (assets minus liabilities) and is traditionally referred to as 'policyholders' surplus'. Despite the connotation of the term 'surplus', there is nothing superfluous about it – it is, in fact, an essential component supporting the insurance promise. The cost of that capital is an insurer expense that must be considered in pricing insurance, along with expected losses, sales and administrative expenses for policies written.

19. Although providing terrorism insurance is mandatory under TRIA, an insurer can decide not to cover more than *n* businesses in a specific area to limit its aggregate exposure there.

20. See Breyer, S. (1981), *Regulation and Its Reform*, Cambridge, MA: Harvard University Press.

21. Kunreuther, H., R. Ginsberg, L. Miller, P. Sagi, P. Slovic, B. Borkan and N. Katz (1978), *Disaster Insurance Protection: Public Policy Lessons*, New York: Wiley; Kaplow, L. (1991), 'Incentives and Government Relief for Risk', *Journal of Risk and Uncertainty*, 4: 167–75; Harrington, S. (2000), 'Rethinking Disaster Policy', *Regulation*, Spring: 40–46; Browne, M.J. and R.E. Hoyt (2000), 'The Demand for Flood Insurance: Empirical Evidence', *Journal of Risk and Uncertainty*, 20(3): 291–306; Ganderton, P.T., D.S. Brookshire, M. McKee, S. Stewart and H. Thurston (2000), 'Buying Insurance Disaster-Type Risks: Empirical Evidence', *Journal of Risk and Uncertainty*, 20(3): 271–89; Moss, D. (2002), *When All Else Fails: Government as the Ultimate Risk Manager*, Cambridge, MA: Harvard University Press.

22. In a study published in 2001, Kenneth Froot indicated that 'Since the late 70's the Federal government has spent annually an average of $8 billion (current) on disaster assistance. This is far greater than the average annual loss borne by reinsurers on US catastrophe coverage.' See Froot, K. (2001), 'The Market for Catastrophe Risk: A Clinical Examination', *Journal of Financial Economics*, 60: 529–71.

23. US General Accounting Office (GAO) (2002), 'Terrorism Insurance: Rising Uninsured Exposure to Attacks Heightens Potential Economic Vulnerabilities', Testimony of Richard J. Hillman before the Subcommittee on Oversight and Investigations, Committee on Financial Services, House of Representatives, 27 February.

24. The complete version of the Act can be downloaded at: http://www.treas.gov/offices/domestic-finance/financial-institution/terrorism-insurance/claims_process/program.shtml

25. In most instances, this 'make available' requirement means that insurers are required to offer a policy without a terrorism exclusion or limitation. Once an insurer has satisfied this offer requirement, the insurer is permitted to offer other terrorism coverage options, such as a policy with a sub-limit.

26. The distinction between what would be a 'certified' event covered by TRIA and a so-called 'domestic' terrorist event may difficult to establish. For example, would attacks on

US soil similar to those perpetrated in London on 7 July 2005 be considered domestic or international?

27. In 2003 the deductible under TRIA was 7 percent of direct commercial property and casualty earned premiums the previous year and 10 percent in 2004.

28. The law is ambiguous on what would happen should the total insurers' outlays be above $15 billion.

29. The TRIA legislation states that 'If the aggregate insured losses exceed $100,000,000,000, (i) the Secretary shall not make any payment under this title for any portion of the amount of such losses that exceeds $100,000,000,000; and (ii) no insurer that has met its insurer deductible shall be liable for the payment of any portion of that amount that exceeds $100,000,000,000. Congress shall determine the procedures for and the source of any payments for such excess insured losses.' §103(e)(2)(A).

30. We thank Debra Ballen of AIA and Greg Heidrich of PCIAA for their helpful suggestions in constructing the questionnaire and distributing it to their members.

31. More specifically, 90 percent of the Wharton questionnaire indicated that they were using that type of scenario in evaluating their exposure: seven of the ten insurers responding to the questionnaire indicated that they used 5-ton bomb scenario and two insurers indicated they were using a 2-ton truck-bomb scenario.

32. We are grateful to Andrew Coburn from Risk Management Solutions who provided us with these data.

33. The attack was assumed to occur at a time when most employees would be in the building (10 a.m. on a Wednesday).

34. Since data are not available on individual insurers' terrorism exposure, market share appears to be the most reasonable proxy for analyzing loss-sharing across the affected parties.

35. We are assuming that insurers have not purchased reinsurance. Had they done so, then the amount of their loss would be somewhat reduced. We assume a zero deductible for the policyholder on their terrorism insurance policy. This assumption simplifies the analysis but does not affect the qualitative results.

36. Treasury has the authority to collect the $2.5 billion through surcharges should it elect to do so, but here we only allow a recoupment for losses between the insurer's payments and the $15 billion market retention in 2005.

37. For details on the analysis should TRIA be abolished, see Wharton Risk Management and Decision Processes, *TRIA and Beyond: Terrorism Risk Financing the US*, Sect. 6.4, August 2005.

38. See Kunreuther, H. and Erwann Michel-Kerjan (2005), 'Terrorism Insurance 2005. Where Do We Go from Here?' *Regulation. The Cato Review for Business and Government*, Washington, DC: Cato Institute, Spring 2005. pp. 44–51.

39. We appreciated discussions on this domestic terrorism issue with James O. Ellis III (Memorial Institute for the Prevention of Terrorism in Oklahoma City), Mark Potok (Southern Poverty Law Center) and with Henry Schuster (CNN).

40. For an insightful analysis of the London bombing in that regard, see the series of articles in *The Economist* (2005), 'In Europe's Midst', 16 July.

41. For discussions on the nature of these groups and their operation, see Ellis III, J. 'Terrorism in the Homeland: A Brief Historical Survey of Violent Extremism in the United States', Memorial Institute for the Prevention of Terrorism, Oklahoma City; Hoffman, B. (1998) *Inside Terrorism*, New York: Columbia University Press; Stern, J. (2003), *Terror in the Name of God: Why Religious Militants Kill*, New York: Harper Collins; Potok, M. (2004), 'The American Radical Right: The 1990s and Beyond', in R. Eatwell and C. Mudde (eds), *Western Democracies and the New Extreme Right Challenge*, New York: Routledge; Chalk, P. Hoffman, R. Reville and A-B. Kasupski (2005), *Trends in Terrorism*, Santa Monica, CA: Rand Corporation, June.

42. US Department of Justice, Federal Bureau of Investigation (2002), 'Terrorism 2000/2001', FBI, Counterterrorism division, Publication 0328.

PART III

Security

4. Airport security: time for a new model

Robert W. Poole, Jr.

Two months after the 9/11 attacks, Congress enacted the Aviation and Transportation Security Act (ATSA) of 2001. This law created the Transportation Security Administration (TSA), initially as part of the Department of Transportation but later folded into the newly created (in 2002) Department of Homeland Security (DHS). The law is perhaps best known for 'federalizing' airport security, by creating a large federal workforce of passenger and baggage screeners to replace the private contract screeners previously employed by airlines to staff passenger screening checkpoints at airport concourses. As part of this federalization, Congress mandated that all checked bags be inspected for explosives by 31 December 2002 (later extended to 31 December 2003). Built into this federalization were two unstated assumptions: that all passengers are equally suspicious and should receive the same scrutiny, and that the principal purpose of airport security is to keep dangerous objects off airplanes.

This chapter will argue that, though well intentioned, much that was legislated in ATSA was poorly thought out and ill-advised. The law, as implemented by the TSA, has wasted large sums of taxpayers' money and passengers' time while doing little to increase aviation security. The DHS plans to shift some functions from the TSA to other parts of the DHS. It needs to rethink TSA's role in airport security, as well, beginning with the underlying, unexamined premises about equal risk.

TSA'S BASIC FLAWS

Broadly speaking, there are three basic flaws with the current approach to airport security, each of which will be discussed here. First is the equal-risk model, which has produced a number of harmful consequences. Second is the TSA's very centralized approach to interpreting its charge under ATSA, which is at odds with the great variation in size, design and function of America's more than 400 commercial-service airports. And third, because of its legislated role as the principal provider of airport screening services, the TSA is in the conflicted position of being both the aviation security policymaker and regulator, and the provider of some (but not all) airport security services.

The Equal-Risk Model

The unstated assumption that every passenger poses the same risk of being a threat to aviation security lies behind the legislated mandate that every checked bag be screened for explosives before being loaded on a plane. The equal-risk assumption was never applied quite as stringently to passenger screening itself, though it did lead to the basic model of everyone, including the flight crew, receiving the same level of passenger screening (removal of shoes and jackets, removal of cameras and laptops, X-ray screening of carry-ons, and magnetometer walk-through of the person). From the outset, however, two subsets of passengers were selected for additional 'secondary' screening (wanding, possible pat-downs, examination of carry-ons) in addition to the basics. One subset was randomly selected and another subset was flagged by the pre-9/11 computer system called CAPPS (Computer-Assisted Passenger Pre-Screening). With respect to the latter subset, at least, a modest element of estimated risk was taken into account in deciding what resources to apply to a few passengers.

The consequences of these assumptions, especially given the tight implementation deadlines imposed by Congress, were several: a much larger TSA screening workforce than anyone had anticipated, long checkpoint lines, and a huge investment in baggage-screening equipment.

Long lines resulted from the significantly increased processing time per passenger, due to the new, more stringent checkpoint screening process (shoe and jacket removal, more banned objects for screeners to look for, greater sensitivity levels of the magnetometers, many more secondary screenings, and so on), combined with limited space in terminals to add checkpoint lanes and (despite a large increase) limitations on the numbers of screeners.

The huge investment in checked-baggage screening equipment – $2.5 billion as of September 2004 (GAO, 2005b) – stemmed from the low throughput and high error rate of the costly explosive detection system (EDS) machines, which required them to be purchased in much larger numbers than Congress had anticipated. And because of the tight deadlines, only a handful of airports were able to reconfigure their entire baggage-processing systems to permit the EDS machines to be installed in baggage areas, fed by conveyor belts, where throughput rates could be optimized (so-called 'in-line' installations). Instead, most airports had to make do with installing these minivan-sized machines in their ticket lobbies, to which passengers would have to transport their suitcases for hand-feeding by baggage screeners, an inherently slow and labor-intensive process.

Manual (piecework) loading of EDS machines led to an unexpectedly large number of baggage screeners being hired by the TSA, in addition to the unexpectedly large number of passenger screeners. At one point, the total screening workforce approached 60000, compared with a pre-9/11 screener force of under 20000 (Quinn, 2005). Balking at the cost, the House Transportation Appropriations Subcommittee imposed a cap of 45000 full-time screeners in 2003, which, while holding down budgetary costs, imposed a cost on travelers in terms of slower processing of bags and people.

In addition to creating unexpected consequences, the law's mandates on passenger checkpoints and checked-baggage screening focused most of the TSA's attention on those two areas. But when outside analysts stepped back and assessed the larger screening picture, they pointed out glaring inconsistencies in this model. First, the very costly 100 percent inspection of checked bags is not matched by equally rigorous inspection of carry-on bags. In Europe, checked bags are screened by various high-speed X-ray systems, but those are rejected by the TSA as not accurate enough for use in this country. Yet those systems are actually more advanced than the X-ray machines used to screen carry-on luggage at US airports. And given the large size of many wheeled carry-on bags these days, it is not credible to defend current practice by claiming that carry-ons are too small to contain enough explosives to cause harm.

The second inconsistency is that the vast majority of passengers are screened solely for metallic objects. Yet a terrorist bent on either blowing up or taking over a plane could wear body-conformal plastique or carry a variety of non-metallic lethal weapons. Yet the equal-risk model does not inspect every passenger's body or clothing for such objects – only for metallic ones.

Complaints about these inconsistencies, especially in high-profile speeches and articles by people such as House Aviation Subcommittee Chair John Mica (Republican, Florida), led the TSA to test such devices as walk-though explosive-detection 'puffer' booths and back-scatter X-ray machines (which can see through clothing) at selected airports. But the former take significantly longer to process each passenger than a magnetometer, and the latter pose serious privacy concerns. Hence, despite much testing, no decision to mandate their use for all passengers seems at all likely.

Overcentralization

From the outset, TSA has been plagued by the conflict between centralization and decentralization. Part of the rationale for 'federalizing' airport security was to provide a consistently high level of security nationwide, regardless of the myriad differences among airports (which range from huge to tiny, from primarily origin and destination – O&D – to primarily transfer hubs, and from centralized terminals to multiple terminals). These differences crucially affect numerous aspects of both passenger and baggage processing. Early on, TSA officials verbally acknowledged this vast diversity by repeatedly saying, 'If you've seen one airport, you've seen one airport.' But their highly centralized approach does not fully take this diversity into account.

One example is how the TSA allocates screeners among the 446 airports it is responsible for. Once a year, it reallocates the screening workforce, to take into account changes in airline activity, using a confidential algorithm called REGAL. These allocations may be tweaked occasionally during the course of a year, but airport directors have no idea how the algorithm works and have little ability to influence the allocations. Members of Congress sometimes go to bat for an airport in their district where long lines have been a particular problem, and their intervention is believed to have some effect. And TSA maintains a mobile screener force that can provide temporary relief of some screener shortages (but cannot address surpluses of screeners at airports with reduced traffic).

The problem is that commercial aviation is an inherently dynamic industry. As one indication, Table 4.1 shows how much variability there is in annual passenger numbers at the 100 largest US airports (comparing 2004 with 2003). As can be seen, 26 of the top 100 airports experienced increases of 11 to 50 percent, while three had declines of from 5 to 35 percent. For smaller airports, the fraction of double-digit percentage changes is even

Table 4.1   Percentage change in US airport passengers 2004 vs 2003 (top 100 airports)

Percent change	Number of airports
−35% to −11%	1
−10% to −5%	2
−4% to 0%	2
1% to 5%	27
6% to 10%	41
11% to 15%	17
16% to 20%	8
21% to 35%	1
36% to 50%	1

Source: Airports Council International North America.

greater, affecting 40 percent of airports ranking 101–150 in size (not shown in the figure). And the relative impact of not getting more screeners can be much greater at a small airport like Peoria (#146) when it experiences 23 percent passenger growth, or Newburgh, NY (#142) with 34 percent growth. When a single airline begins serving, or withdraws from serving, such an airport, the change can happen in a matter of a month or two, but it may take the TSA six months or more to catch up with it (if it is under sufficient pressure to make a change prior to the next annual screener real-location). During those many months, the airport will operate with too few or too many screeners.

A second example is the highly centralized way in which the TSA has interpreted the provision in ATSA that allowed five airports to opt out of TSA-provided screening as a pilot program to test TSA-certified security firms as an alternative (see Box 4.1). What airports expected, and what most people would assume to be the way to implement such a program, would be for the TSA to define criteria for such firms, certify those that met the criteria, define the rules for airports to implement outsourced screening, and then let those airports with acceptable plans issue RFPs (requests for proposals) and select the firm (from those on the TSA's list) submitting the best proposal. The airport would then contract with the firm, under the supervision of the TSA's Federal Security Director who oversees all other security operations at that airport.

BOX 4.1   THE 5-AIRPORT PILOT PROGRAM

The 2001 ATSA legislation authorized the TSA to permit five air-ports – one in each size category – to obtain their passenger and baggage screening from TSA-certified private screening com-panies. Interested airports applied to the TSA, and the agency selected San Francisco, Kansas City, Rochester, Jackson Hole and Tupelo as what became known as the PP5 airports. The idea was to test whether outsourcing this function with strong perform-ance standards and federal oversight (both lacking under the pre9/11 outsourcing of passenger screening by airlines) could produce results as good as or better than directly provided federal (TSA) screening.

Congress asked the GAO* to assess the performance of screen-ing at the PP5 airports (GAO, 2004), and the TSA itself hired BearingPoint to make a similar assessment (BearingPoint, 2004). Both reports were released in April 2004. Both broadly concluded that, within the limitations of a very small sample size and very narrow bounds for deviation from the TSA model, the private screening operations worked as well as or better than TSA-provided screening.

The BearingPoint assessment looked at security effectiveness, cost, and customer and stakeholder impact. On security effectiveness, Kansas City was judged to be outperforming comparable airports while the other four PP5 airports performed at the same level as comparables. This was measured by covert testing, the use of Threat Image Projection (TIP) data, and recertification testing. The costs to the government were not significantly different from the estimated cost of a TSA operation at the same airport (which is not surprising, given how severely ATSA and the TSA constrained the private operations). On overall customer satisfaction, the results were mixed, with no general pattern. On customer complaints, there were no significant differences. And on wait time, San Francisco and Kansas City had significantly shorter wait times for passenger screening; insufficient data were available for the smaller airports.

The GAO study focused more on the limitations of the PP5 design. Not only was the sample size too small (just one airport in each of the five size categories, out of a total of more than 400 airports mandated to have federally imposed screening) but, 'TSA provided the screening contractors with little opportunity to demonstrate innovations, achieve efficiencies, and implement initiatives that go beyond the minimum requirements of [ATSA]'. In those limited cases where the TSA did provide some operational flexibility, the GAO found that, 'These practices have enabled the private screening contractors to achieve efficiencies that are not currently available at airports with federal screeners.' These included such things as hiring baggage handlers to move bags from one location to another rather than tying up more highly trained screeners with this task, screening job applicants before they are hired through TSA assessment centers, and selecting screening supervisors from within the screener workforce rather than relying on the decisions of the TSA's hiring contractors. Within the limits of the performance data the GAO was able to obtain, the agency concluded that 'in general, private and federal screeners performed similarly'.

That was not how TSA implemented the pilot program, however. While it did certify a number of firms, it did not allow airports to issue RFPs, select their preferred bidder, or enter into a contract. Rather, after the TSA selected the five airports that would participate as the pilot sites, it assigned one of its certified firms to each airport. The TSA itself entered into a contract with each firm and directly supervised its operation at each airport. Moreover, when the November 2004 date specified by ATSA approached, after which point all airports would be free to opt out of TSA-provided screening in favor of contract operations, the TSA defined its Screening Partnership Program along the same highly centralized lines (TSA, 2004).

And the centralization does not stop there. As the General Accounting Office noted in an April 2004 assessment of the pilot program, because the TSA runs the program in such a centralized manner, 'private screening contractors have had little opportunity to demonstrate and achieve efficiencies.' (GAO, 2004) Among other things, the GAO report notes that the contractors lack the authority to determine staffing levels and conduct hiring. And actual hiring by the contractors must be coordinated through TSA headquarters. Before new staff can be hired by a contractor, the TSA must authorize this, and it must set up an assessment center in the area, using the TSA's national assessment contractor. According to the GAO, this process typically takes several months. Their report notes a case at one of the pilot program airports where a staff shortage went on for months, waiting for the TSA's process. The inability to hire screeners during this time 'contributed to screener performance issues, such as absenteeism or tardiness, and screener complacency, because screeners were aware that they are unlikely to be terminated due to staffing shortages'.

GAO also reported that Federal Security Directors (FSDs) at non-pilot program airports expressed similar frustrations at TSA's centralization of hiring and training. In a survey of all 155 FSDs, the GAO found that 'the overwhelming majority . . . reported that they needed additional [local] authority to a great or very great extent'.

Conflict of Interest

Congress decided to 'federalize' airport screening after concluding that the prior institutional arrangements included both regulatory failure and conflict of interest. Prior to 9/11, the Federal Aviation Administration (FAA) was in charge of airport security, and its rules required that access to airport concourses be limited to those who cleared a basic screening process at checkpoints. The FAA delegated this screening responsibility not to the airports (which own the premises) but rather to the airline that had the largest presence on each concourse (generally a 'signatory' airline that had signed a long-term use and lease agreement with the airport). The structural failure was that the airlines had no real incentive to make security a priority. Since operating this function was a cost item for airlines, and airlines operate in a very competitive business, their interest was to meet whatever requirements the FAA laid down at minimal cost. Over time, that led to the well-documented situation in which the airline-selected screening companies paid not much more than minimum wage, did only modest amounts of training, and suffered turnover rates sometimes in excess of 100 percent per year.

The regulatory failure was that the FAA essentially set no standards for hiring and training of screeners. Moreover, the FAA was de facto satisfied with the relatively low level of performance of those screeners, when challenged by 'Red Teams' that attempted to get prohibited items past the screeners. The GAO called for implementation of performance standards for screening in 1987 (GAO, 1987), but the agency failed to act. In the 1996 FAA Reauthorization Act, Congress required FAA to 'certify companies providing security screening and to improve the training and testing of security screeners through development of uniform performance standards'.[1] Three years later, in January 2000, FAA issued a proposed rule, Certification of Screening Companies, which would have held companies to minimum performance standards. When the rule had not been finalized by November 2000, Congress directed the FAA to issue a final rule no later than 31 May 2001.[2] The FAA failed to meet this deadline, so Congress then required it to report twice a year on the status of each missed statutory deadline. That was the situation as of 11 September 2001.

In response, Congress took responsibility for aviation security away from the FAA and gave it to the newly created TSA, an appropriate response to the FAA's regulatory failure. But in response to the structural failure, instead of doing as nearly every other country in the world does – making each airport responsible for securing its operations under national regulatory supervision – Congress instead vested in the TSA not only the regulatory responsibility but also the service provision duties of airport screening. Note that the TSA was not required to take over access control or perimeter patrols or law enforcement functions at the airports. Those security functions were still the airport's responsibility, under the watchful eye of the TSA's Federal Security Director (FSD) assigned to that airport. But for baggage and passenger screening, the TSA was to be both the regulator and the operator.

This dual role is a potentially serious conflict of interest. As one airport director said to a *Chicago Tribune* reporter in the early days of the TSA, 'The problem inherent in the federally controlled screening process is that you end up having a federal agency sitting in the middle of your terminal, essentially answerable to nobody.' This point was underscored in BearingPoint's report on the five pilot-program airports. 'Because the screeners at a private contractor [pilot program] airport are not government employees, the FSD is able to take a more objective approach when dealing with screener-related issues raised by stakeholders such as airport management or air carriers' (BearingPoint, 2004).

The classic example of a federal agency with this kind of dual-role conflict was the Atomic Energy Commission (AEC), created after World War II to encourage peaceful uses of nuclear power. In carrying out this mission, the AEC became both a promoter of nuclear energy (funding research and development, doing educational and marketing work, and so on) and the regulator of all civilian nuclear reactor operations. Eventually, public criticism of the conflict of interest – that the AEC could not serve as an objective regulator if it was also the chief promoter of nuclear power – led Congress to split those functions. It created a purely regulatory body, the Nuclear Regulatory Commission, for that role. And it shifted the R&D functions into the newly created Department of Energy.

RETHINKING THE TSA

Early in 2005 separate reports were made to Congress, one by the DHS Inspector General's Office (DHS, 2005) and the other by the GAO (GAO, 2005a). Based on testing of airport screening operations, both concluded that there was no evidence that screening performance today, several years after the TSA took over, is better than it was prior to the TSA putting its own screeners into airports. In other words, this new agency with a budget of $5.5 billion per year, more than half of which is devoted to baggage and passenger screening, has not led to demonstrably improved protection of planes from dangerous objects.

This sobering finding ought to lead to a serious reassessment of the premises that underlie ATSA, and the TSA as it was created and as it has evolved. One of the most important premises is that we should continue spending $2.5 billion per year to keep dangerous objects off planes. In point of fact, there have been no further attempts to hijack US airliners since 9/11. Many aviation and security experts believe that the policy changes that led to strengthened and always-locked cockpit doors, a greatly expanded sky marshall program, and revised crew protocols for dealing with hijackers have made hijacking essentially impossible, regardless of knives or guns that might somehow get past screening checkpoints. At the very least, this proposition should lead us to question the massive expenditure on keeping such objects off airplanes.

The GAO report also found that the limited covert testing that was done showed that performance of screeners at the five pilot-program airports was slightly better than that of TSA screeners (though the GAO also noted that there were not enough data to draw broad conclusions). Given that

TSA provision of screening services entails a conflict of interest, those limited findings serve to strengthen the case for separating such service provision from the TSA's inherently governmental role as security policy-maker and regulator in aviation. That would permit the actual provision of airport security to be devolved to each airport, as it is in Europe and most of the rest of the world, under TSA oversight via the FSDs. Airports would be free to provide those services either in-house, with their own workforces, or by contracting with a TSA-certified security company.

Finally, a revamped approach would scrap the equal-risk premise in favor of a risk-based approach to dealing with passengers and their bags. To the extent that passengers can be separated into high-risk, ordinary and low-risk groups, security resources can be adjusted proportionally, thereby getting more bang for the buck from whatever level of airport security budgets Congress decides to set. The guiding principle should be to identify dangerous people and keep them off planes, rather than trying to keep all dangerous objects off planes.

Separating Policy-Making and Regulation from Operations

The need for legislation

The dual-role nature of the TSA stems directly from the ATSA legislation. Thus, this problem can only be corrected by new legislation to overhaul the TSA in the interest of improving its performance, thereby increasing aviation security. Is such a change conceivable in the real world of Washington politics?

Certainly the TSA, as it now exists, is subject to considerable critical commentary. In a widely discussed commentary, *Washington Post* columnist Anne Applebaum cited the evidence that TSA-type screening is little better than what existed before, and called the creation of the TSA a mistaken use of $5.5 billion (per year) that would have been better spent beefing up intelligence on terrorism (Applebaum, 2005).

The Bush Administration's FY2006 budget proposal called for shifting several key programs out of the TSA into a new Screening Coordination and Operations Office within the DHS that would include:

- Secure Flight (the successor to CAPPS);
- Registered Traveler;
- Transportation Worker Identity Credential (TWIC).

This change, not yet approved by Congress, would 'strip the TSA of its biggest and most high-profile programs and leave it largely as a manager of 45 000 security screeners' (Goo, 2005a). A subsequent news report speculated that, with the dismissal of David Stone as the TSA's director, the agency itself was slated for dismantling. 'The agency's very existence, in fact, remains an open question, given that the legislation creating the Department of Homeland Security contains a clause permitting the elimination of TSA as a "distinct entity" after November, 2004' (Goo, 2005b). The same article noted that even the TSA's remaining airport screening role 'could diminish as private screening companies increasingly seek a comeback at US airports'. Despite the referenced clause in the DHS legislation, ATSA still calls for the federal government to provide airport screening services, except for those airports that choose to opt out after November 2004. So it would still appear necessary for Congress to remove the agency from screening operations, in order to resolve the conflict-of-interest issue. But without the above list of programs and without its major current role in operating screening, the remaining policy-making, R&D and regulatory roles for the TSA would be a tiny fraction of its current responsibilities. It would no longer seem to warrant the designation as an 'administration' within the DHS, and would probably best be configured as an 'office' comparable to the one proposed for Secure Flight, Registered Traveler, and the other information-centered programs.

How Europe handles airport screening

Europe began confronting hijackings and terrorist attacks on airports in the late 1960s. Risk analysis identified the need for a comprehensive approach that included background checks of airport personnel, passenger and baggage screening, and airport access control. The initial approach in most nations was to use national government employees to beef up airport security, either from the transport agency or the justice agency. But beginning in the 1980s, European airports began developing a performance contracting model, in which government set and enforced high performance standards and airports carried them out – usually by hiring security companies, but occasionally with their own staff. Belgium was the first to adopt this model, in 1982, followed by The Netherlands in 1983 and the United Kingdom in 1987, when BAA was privatized. The 1990s saw a new wave of conversions to the public–private partnership model, with Germany switching in 1992, France in 1993, Austria and Denmark in 1994, Ireland and Poland in 1998, and Italy, Portugal, Spain and Switzerland in 1999.

Table 4.2 provides a breakdown of outsourced passenger and baggage screening at 33 large European airports as of late 2001. Of these, only Zurich and Lisbon airports were not using the performance contracting model, and in both nations, efforts to shift to this model were under way.

The GAO visited five nations in 2001 to examine their security screening practices – Canada and four European nations: Belgium, France, The

Table 4.2   Outsourced passenger and baggage screening in europe

Rank by total int'l pass[1]	City (airport code)	Passenger & hand baggage screening[2]	Private screeners?	Hold baggage screening	Private screeners?
1	London (LHR)	BAA	Y	ADI Initial, SIS (CIVAS)	Y
2	Paris (CDG)	SIFA/Brinks /ICTS	Y	ICTS/ASA/SIFA	Y
3	Frankfurt/ Main (FRA)	FRAPORT	Y	FRAPORT and others[3]	Y
4	Amsterdam (AMS)	Group 4 Falk	Y	Randon Securicor-ADI & Group 4 Falk	Y
5	London (LGW)	BAA	Y	ICTS; Initial	Y
6	Brussels (BRU)	Securair	Y	Securair	Y
7	Zurich (ZRH)	State Police		State Police[4]	See note 4 below
8	Copenhagen (CPH)	Copenhagen Airport Security	Y	Copenhagen Airport Security	Y
9	Manchester (MAN)	Manchester Airport plc	Y	Securicor/ADI	Y
10	Madrid (MAD)	Vinsa, State Police	Y	State Police	
11	Munich (MUC)	SGM (Airport Company)	Y	various private companies[3]	Y
12	Rome (FCO)	Aeroporto di Roma; physical searches handled by police	Y	Aeroporto di Roma	Y
13	Dusseldorf (DUS)	ADI	Y	ADI	Y
14	Milan (MXP)	SEA; physical searches handled by police	Y	SEA	Y
15	Dublin (DUB)	Aer Rianta (Airport Authority)	Y	Aer Rianta (Airport Authority)	Y
16	Stockholm (ARN)	Group 4 Falk	Y	Group 4 Falk	Y
17	Vienna (VIE)	VIASS	Y	VIASS and others[3]	Y

Table 4.2   (continued)

Rank by total int'l pass[1]	City (airport code)	Passenger & hand baggage screening[2]	Private screeners?	Hold baggage screening	Private screeners?
18	Paris (ORY)	ASA, SIFA	Y	ICTS, Brinks	Y
19	Barcelona (BCN)	Prosegur, State Police	Y	Prosegur,State Police	Y
20	London (STN)	BAA	Y	ADI (Securicor)	Y
21	Lisbon (LIS)	State Police[5]	See note 5 below	State Police[5]	See note 5 below
22	Oslo (OSL)	ADECCO, Olsten	Y	ADECCO, Olsten	Y
23	Malaga (AGP)	80% Securitas/20% State Police	Y	80% Securitas/20% State Police	Y
n/av	Geneva (GVA)	Airport Authority	Y	ICTS	Y
n/av	Athens (ATH)	ICTS/ Wackenhut/3D	Y	Hermis/Civas	Y
n/av	Nice (NCE)	ICTS, SGA	Y	ICTS, SGA	Y
n/av	Helsinki (HEL)	Securitas	Y	Securitas	Y
n/av	Birmingham (BHX)	ICTS & AAS	Y	ICTS & AAS	Y
n/av	Berlin (BER)	Securitas	Y	Securitas	Y
n/av	Stuttgart (STR)	FIS	Y	FIS	Y
n/av	Cologne (CGN)	ADI	Y	ADI	Y
n/av	Hamburg (HAM)	FIS	Y	FIS	Y
n/av	Hanover (HAJ)	FIS	Y	FIS	Y

Notes:
1   Based on 1999 Int'l Airport Traffic Statistics from ACI.
2   As of October 2001.
3   These airports do not have centralized baggage screening, but airlines hire private companies to X-ray bags.
4   Public/private partnership under way.
5   Legislation proposed to permit public/private sector partnership.

Source: Aviation Security Association.

Netherlands and the United Kingdom (GAO, 2001). Its report focused on
the superior performance of the European airports, all of which use the
performance contracting model. The GAO reported significant differences
between their screening practices and that of then-current US airports in
four areas:

- Better overall security system design (allowing only ticketed passengers past screening, stationing law enforcement personnel at or near checkpoints, and so on).
- Higher qualifications and training requirements for screeners (for example 60 hours in France vs. 12 hours as then required by the FAA).
- Better pay and benefits, resulting in much lower turnover rates.
- Screening responsibility lodged with the airport or national government, not with airlines.

Most of these lessons were incorporated by Congress into the ATSA.
What was largely ignored, however, was the fact that under the European
conditions of high standards and oversight, performance contracting
(hiring private security firms, paying them adequately and holding them
accountable for results) is the model adopted by nearly all European airports over the past two decades. Israel and a number of other nations in the
Caribbean and the Far East also use this model.

Companies that do not meet the standards or perform effectively are not
simply fined but actually have their contracts cancelled. Since these are typically long-term (for example, up to six-year) contracts, losing such a contract is a serious loss of business, creating a strong incentive for high
performance. Companies often bid on a whole package of security services,
not just passenger screening, paid for via a single monthly charge. This
avoids undue cost pressures being put on any one element.

Standards are set and enforced by a national government agency, typically either a civil aviation authority or a justice or interior ministry. The
performance standards and enforcement process focus on four areas:

- Certification of the security companies, in which the government agency reviews the financial fitness of each firm, as well as the backgrounds of its officers and directors.
- Licensing of individual employees, initially as a trained security officer and then as a specialized aviation security agent.
- Standards for compensation and benefits, to ensure that people of sufficient caliber are recruited, and that they are motivated to remain with the company.

- Training, both initial and recurring, of both managers and operating personnel. The government develops goals and objectives for the training, and companies devise the curriculum, which the government must approve before it can be used.

Government oversight includes periodic audits of the qualifications and training of managers and staff. It conducts random, unannounced testing at the screening sites. It also conducts audits to be sure that the training has been conducted. Two main sanctions are used instead of fines: termination of specific contracts and revocation of the company's license to provide aviation security services. Individual screeners can have their licenses suspended or terminated for failing to perform properly.

Political feasibility
When Congress debated what became the ATSA legislation, the Senate version passed on 11 October 2001, by 100:0, calling for a complete 'federalization' of airport security. There was no fact-finding testimony, just bipartisan speeches attacking the private screening companies and assuring the worried public that a new federal workforce would be replacing them 'as soon as practicable' (Brill, 2003). By contrast, the House took more time, and with the support of the GOP leadership, passed a bill allowing airports to choose private screeners under new federal supervision, by a vote of 218:214. But when White House Chief of Staff Andrew Card conceded that the President would sign a bill that federalized all screening, the balance of power in the conference committee went with federalization, and the Senate's approach largely prevailed. As a concession to the House bill, the final version of ATSA allowed for the five-airport pilot program using private contractors and for all airports to be able to opt out after November 2004.

What has changed since then is the creation of the DHS, the actual and potential removal of a number of functions from the TSA, and a growing number of critical reports about the TSA from the GAO, the DHS Inspector General, and most recently a scathing audit on TSA spending by the Defense Contract Audit Agency (Higham and O'Harrow, 2005). Thus, as of 2005, the original sanctity of the TSA as originally conceived has certainly worn off. But given how partisan the original House vote on 'federalization' was, it is not clear how viable a proposal to shift that function to a new model of private provision would be. Opponents of the current opt-out provision repeatedly characterize such a move (as proposed by Representative Mica) as 'going back' to the pre-9/11 model, even though it is nothing of the sort.

The alternative recommended here is not 'privatization' – which would be the case if all airports were required to use private contractors. Rather, it is devolution. The idea would be to remove the TSA's conflict of interest by devolving the actual provision of screening to the airport level, which is where all other aspects of airport security (such as access control and perimeter protection) already reside. Airports would then have the option of complying with federal screening requirements either with their own TSA-approved screening workforce or by hiring a TSA-certified screening contractor. This approach has strong support among airport directors, and is also embraced by the leading congressional champion of TSA reform, Representative John Mica (Republican, Florida), chairman of the House Aviation Subcommittee. Mica has called for 'a decentralized screening program with federal oversight', citing the TSA's conflict of interest as a case of 'the regulator regulating itself'.

The stage was set for making basic changes in the TSA by DHS Secretary Michael Chertoff's call for reform in mid-July 2005. Contrary to some expectations, the proposed overhaul did not call for abolishing the TSA, and actually gave back to it responsibility for the Federal Air Marshal Service. The TSA will also continue to have responsibility for security for all modes of transportation, not just aviation. Since some of Chertoff's proposed changes will require legislation, there will be an opportunity to revise ATSA's mandate that the TSA both regulate and operate airport screening. If US airlines via their trade association, the Air Transport Association, and the airport community, via the American Association of Airport Executives and the Airports Council International North America, coalesced around devolution of airport screening, it could well prove to be a politically viable approach, as part of overall reform of the TSA and the DHS.

Airport-Centered Security

How would devolution work? This section outlines some of the key features of a devolved, airport-centered approach to security, of which screening would become an integral part. As in Europe, the Airport Director would be in charge of securing the airport premises, under the supervision of the TSA Federal Security Director (FSD) assigned to that airport. (Note that large airports have their own FSD, whereas for smaller airports, a single FSD may supervise several within a geographic region.)

Make-or-buy authority
The most fundamental aspect of devolution is that the responsibility for carrying out the screening of baggage and passengers would be shifted from the TSA to each individual airport. And as with all other airport services, it would be up to the airport to decide how to carry out the screening

functions. Like most businesses, airports outsource some services and perform others using their own paid staff. In the case of screening, as with other security functions, the operations would have to comply with all TSA requirements. But with the TSA no longer being in the business of screening, its requirements would have to be reconfigured for the new circumstances. To gain the flexibility advantages that go along with devolution, the hiring and training of screeners should be devolved rather than being centralized in Washington and carried out by a national TSA contractor. Rather, the TSA would provide training requirements and a core curriculum which could be used by airports, TSA-certified screening contractors, and TSA-certified screener training firms operating on a decentralized basis in various parts of the country.

Funding allocations
Under current law, passenger and baggage screening are paid for by the TSA, whether provided by its own workforce or by TSA-certified contractors. This funding would presumably continue under devolution, but in order to take advantage of the flexibilities provided by devolution, two key changes should be made in how the funding is done. First, the allocations should be made far more frequently than once a year; ideally every month but at least quarterly. This should be done in accordance with a transparent workload formula arrived at with significant input from the airport organizations (AAAE and ACI-NA) and the air carriers. Second, each airport should receive a lump sum amount which it can use as it sees fit for TSA-approved screening operations. The airport would be subject to reporting and audit requirements to ensure that the funds were spent solely on airport security purposes.

Why monthly allocations rather than the current more-or-less annual allocation? The idea is to match resources better with workload. Today's dynamic, highly competitive airline industry is characterized by rapid change. US Airways downsizes its hub at Pittsburgh; JetBlue orders 100 new larger-size regional jets to add service to many smaller airports; America West and US Airways merge, very likely leading to further cutbacks at some airports; and one or more legacy carriers may well liquidate (Chapter 7 bankruptcy), leading to significant changes in service. Tables 4.3 and 4.4 are drawn from a database of monthly enplaned passengers at the top 100 airports. For the sample 2003, the tables illustrate the month-to-month volatility in passenger numbers at these airports, which account for the lion's share of passengers and screeners. A screener staffing allocation decided a year in advance is simply not a good fit for this dynamic airline environment. With funding allocations adjusted every month among the 446 airports with screeners, and the local flexibility to increase and decrease

Security

Table 4.3   *Monthly changes in enplaned passengers, top 100 US airports, 2003*

Month	No. airports with +/−10%	No. airports with +/−15%	Airport with greatest change	Amount of change
January	77	54	Pensacola	−26%
February	7	1	San Juan	−19%
March	95	81	Myrtle Beach	76%
April	24	6	Salt Lake City	−18%
May	29	15	Palm Springs	−37%
June	20	7	Anchorage	57%
July	19	10	Islip	26%
August	11	0	Wichita	−15%
September	82	56	San Juan	−38%
October	64	35	Palm Springs	39%
November	23	9	St Louis	−47%
December	14	3	Myrtle Beach	−22%

Source: US DOT T-100 carrier reports.

Table 4.4   *Examples of Monthly Airport Enplanement Volatility, 2003 (% change)*

Airport	Jan	Feb	Mar	Apr	May	Jun	Jul	Aug	Sep	Oct	Nov	Dec
Ft. Myers	7	8	38	−11	−32	−20	3	−8	−23	38	28	6
Seattle	−21	−4	17	1	9	16	11	2	−25	−4	−4	12

Source: US DOT T-100 carrier reports.

staffing as needed, there will be a much better match of screening workforce to actual workloads.

In addition to keeping funding in pace with passenger flow, the devolved system should leave the funds unencumbered by many of the current requirements. Currently, TSA screeners are paid on a national wage scale, regardless of local living costs. And TSA-certified screening contractors must, per ATSA, pay identical wages and benefits to their screeners. While the intent of these provisions in ATSA was to prevent a return to minimum-wage screeners with high turnover, that was a brute-force solution to a problem caused by the lack of FAA standards for screener selection, training and performance. With hiring and operations under the control of each airport, the airport or its contractor should be free to innovate, using whatever mix of job functions and compensation approaches will best get the job done, while meeting all TSA training and performance standards. Thus, especially at smaller airports, the same employee might do passenger screening during peak morning hours and do access-control or perimeter patrol during the remainder of their shift. Some airports (or their contractors) might develop workable split-shift approaches to cover morning and afternoon peaks without paying for a lot of unproductive time in between. The point is to let airports and their contractors decide on the best use of the screening money, to get the most value for money.

Incentives for in-line baggage systems

The imposition, in ATSA, of extremely tight deadlines for implementing 100 percent explosive-detection inspection of all checked baggage also led to brute-force solutions. Large and medium-sized airports mostly installed huge EDS machines in their ticket lobbies or in available spaces in their baggage areas; in either case, they had to be loaded by hand, one bag at a time. (Each EDS machine also requires an electronic trace detection – ETD – machine to be used for resolving alarms, also by hand.) Between the inherently slow processing time and this hand-feeding, processing rates are often as low as 100 bags per hour. Hence, in order to prevent massive delays, large numbers of $1 million apiece EDS machines were required. Smaller airports were equipped mostly with ETD machines as their primary means of compliance with the inspection mandate. In addition, as noted, thousands of ETDs were installed at large and medium-sized airports for secondary screening of bags identified as suspicious by EDS. As of June 2004, some 1228 EDS and 7146 ETD machines had been installed at US airports (GAO, 2005a).

These brute-force approaches are very labor-intensive. If EDS machines are integrated into a conveyor-fed baggage processing system (called 'in-line systems'), and especially if go–no-go assessments are made at a remote display terminal (called 'on-screen resolution'), the bag processing rates go way up and the labor involved goes way down. The latest GAO report on the subject cites TSA findings that when installed in-line, an EDS can process up to 425 bags per hour compared with 180 bags per hour when used in a stand-alone mode. And replacing an ETD operation with stand-alone EDS changes throughput from 36 bags per hour to 180 bags per hour. (GAO, 2005b). These changes, if carried out, would mean the number of EDS machines at larger airports could be cut in half, with the excess machines shifted to smaller airports to replace ETD-only systems.

The savings in labor would be very impressive. According to the GAO report, a typical lobby-based EDS installation has one EDS plus three ETDs, requiring a workforce of 19 screeners. This can be replaced by an in-line EDS requiring just 4.25 screeners – a 78 percent reduction. For the nine large airports that have implemented in-line systems, TSA's retrospective analysis found a reduction in bag screeners and supervisors of 78 percent. Similar GAO calculations analyzed replacing a three- to five-unit ETD installation with one stand-alone EDS plus one ETD for alarm resolution. The former would require between 12.3 and 20.5 screeners, while the latter needs only 6.75. If we take the intermediate case of a four-unit ETD installation, the reduction in staff from 16.4 to 6.75 is 59 percent.

Because of numbers like these, several airports that have switched from stand-alone, lobby-based EDS to in-line systems with on-screen resolution have reported a payback period of little more than one year. The TSA's analysis of nine airports shifting to in-line systems reached a similar conclusion, the GAO reported. In other words, the one-time investment in in-line EDS quickly pays for itself in reduced payroll costs. It should be noted that the GAO's review of the TSA's aggregated analysis found that the results held true for eight of the nine airports; modification costs were so high at Seattle's SEA-TAC that there were no net cost savings from the conversion (GAO, 2005b).

In order to estimate overall labor savings from optimal revision of baggage screening systems (from stand-alone EDS to in-line EDS for larger airports, and from all-ETD to EDS plus ETD at smaller airports), we need to know how many baggage screeners are involved at each type of airport. Unfortunately, the TSA does not release this information, but we will make a guess that the equivalent of 50 percent of the 45 000 TSA screeners are de facto dedicated to baggage screening. Using data on baggage flow per year at the top 100 airports from Leigh-Fischer Associates (Dickey, 2005), and estimates for airports in the smaller categories, we have the comparative bag processing workloads shown in Table 4.5. Assuming that baggage screeners are distributed proportionally to workload, we then estimate how the 22 500 baggage screeners are distributed among the five categories of airports. Then, using the TSA–GAO calculation of 78 percent savings for shifting from stand-alone to in-line systems at large airports, we estimate a reduction of 9477 bag screeners at Category X airports. For small, all-ETD airports, we assume that Category IV airports do not have enough workload to justify an EDS+ETD solution, so we assume zero reductions there. For Category III, we use the GAO estimate of 59 percent. And for the Category I and II airports, which are intermediate in size, we use the average of 78 and 59 percent, which is 68.5 percent. Altogether, that produces a total reduction in the need for baggage screeners of 16 173.

In point of fact, as the GAO pointed out, there will be a few airports where for specialized, local reasons, these revisions are not cost-effective. So, to be conservative, we assume that one out of nine airports (11 percent)

Table 4.5   Potential labor savings from optimized bag-screening systems

Airport category	No. of airports	Average bags per year (M)	Workload (bags x airports)	% of total	No. of screeners	% Reduced	No. reduced
X	21	15	315	54	12 150	78	9477
I	61	3	183	31	6975	68.5	4778
II	50	1	50	9	2025	68.5	1387
III	124	0.2	25	4	900	59	531
IV	190	0.05	9	2	450	0	0
Total	446		582	100	22 500		16 173

Source: Author's calculations from TSA data in GAO-05-365.

will not change bag-screening systems, thereby reducing the workforce saving from 16 173 to 14 394. Based on FY 2005 TSA budget data reported by the GAO, the screening workforce budget was $2.424 billion. Averaged over 45 000 screeners, that equates to $53 867 apiece. But assuming that 5–6 percent of the budget is management that would not be eliminated by reducing the need for baggage screeners, we can use $50 000 per screener as the approximate annual payroll savings from optimizing the baggage screening along these lines. Applied to 14 394 positions, that means annual savings of $720 million.

If TSA screening funds were devolved to airports as proposed above, it would clearly be in an airport's interest to finance the investment in new screening systems so as to achieve these ongoing savings. And once the costs of the equipment and facility modernization were paid off, the savings could (with TSA consent) be used for other security improvements, such as more passenger screening lanes and screeners, if needed. Over time, as overall screening costs came down, smaller annual allocations from the TSA would be needed, thereby producing federal budget savings.

Liability
One of the issues that has held back many airports from participating in the post-November 2004 opt-out program (which the TSA calls the Screening Partnership Program) is liability. With the TSA as their provider of screening services, if a terrorist incident having any connection with passenger or baggage screening occurs at the airport, then the TSA is the party most likely to be at risk for lawsuits. But if the airport opts for a TSA-certified contractor, and such an incident occurs, there has been concern that the airport might be at greater risk for not having gone with the standard approach.

This liability issue arose first in connection with EDS machines and other technologies needed in security protection. In response, Congress passed the Support Anti-terrorism by Fostering Effective Technologies Act, better known as the SAFETY Act. It provides a process by which companies providing homeland security technologies or services can become certified by the DHS and win a limit on their liability. FirstLine and Covenant, two of the leading private screening companies, have recently received this designation.

However, if the TSA withdraws from the provision of screening services and this function is devolved to airports, the same liability concern could arise on the part of the airports. Under that new set of alternatives, it would maintain more of a level playing field between in-house and contracted screening services if airports were made eligible to receive the same extent of SAFETY Act protection as designated screening companies. Congress took a step in that direction via language included in the Homeland Security Appropriations Conference Report that passed both houses and was signed by the President in October 2005. Sec. 547 amends Sec. 44920 of Title 49, USC, by making airport operators not liable for any claims for damages relating to their decision to opt out of TSA-provided screening.

Risk-Based Model

The basic principle suggested here is that the equal-risk assumption embedded in ATSA be replaced with a risk-based approach to airport security. The new principle would be to allocate security resources in proportion to the risk posed. In fact, this is how most other federal security policy is done – for example, air cargo, truck and rail cargo, and sea cargo do not have anything like 100 percent physical inspection. Instead, various procedures have been devised to identify those containers, trailers or packages most likely to be dangerous, and those are physically inspected. And for people crossing US borders, a number of programs (including FAST, INSPASS, NEXUS, PAL and SENTRI) give expedited processing to subsets of travelers who have registered in advance and undergone some kind of background checking, thereby getting designated as lower risk (Poole, 2003).

On 13 July 2005, the relatively new DHS Secretary Michael Chertoff announced a sweeping reorganization of the agency, shifting priorities in what appeared to be a more risk-based approach to security. The former DHS Inspector General, Clark Kent Ervin, praised the new approach, characterizing it as 'a threat-based, risk-based, consequence-based approach'. And new TSA Administrator Kip Hawley has said that '(t)he federal government must focus resources on the basis of consequences, threat and vulnerability assessments, and the prioritization of risks.'

The discussion below suggests how such an approach could be implemented for airport security.

Three-tiered approach for air travelers

The basic approach was outlined in this author's report on risk-based airport security (Poole, 2003). It is based on the premise that the task of airport security is to identify and isolate dangerous persons, not dangerous objects per se. The challenge is to keep those persons from causing harm, either in the terminal area or to the planes themselves. There are many ways in which terrorists can cause great harm in connection with airports: getting on board with the aim of hijacking, getting on board as a suicide bomber, putting explosives into checked luggage but not getting on board, or targeting large concentrations of passengers in terminals. The TSA's current emphasis seems to devote the lion's share of its airport resources to just one of these threats: preventing would-be hijackers from boarding with weapons. Yet since the completion of the program that installed strengthened, locked cockpit doors (along with changing protocols for how crews deal with hijack threats), most experts consider the hijack threat to be greatly reduced. Far less money and effort is spent on securing airport terminal lobby areas and the ramp area where planes park. Thus, current policy de facto downplays the threat of suicide bombers targeting crowds at checkpoints and lobby-based EDS installations, and the threat of bombs being smuggled onto planes from the ramp (as opposed to the terminal).

Our proposed risk-based approach would shift the focus to identifying dangerous people. This could include greater security guard presence in terminal lobby areas and outside the terminal, in ramp areas and around the airport perimeter. And within the terminal, from the checkpoint onwards, it requires separating passengers into at least three TSA-defined groups, based on the quantity and quality of information about each:

- low-risk passengers, about whom a great deal is known;
- high-risk passengers, based either on no knowledge or on specific, negative information;
- 'ordinary' passengers, mostly infrequent flyers and leisure travelers.

A different approach to both passenger screening and bag screening would be applied to each group.

Low-risk passengers are defined as those who possess a current federal security clearance or who have been accepted into a Registered Traveler program by passing a background check and being issued a biometric identity card. Passengers in this group would go through express lanes at checkpoints, with something like pre-9/11 protocols (for example, no shoe or jacket removal, not having to remove laptops or video cameras, and so on). Their checked bags would not have to be EDS screened. The whole point is to not waste the system's resources or those passengers' time on procedures that add very little value to airport security. As a safeguard against the small probability that a dangerous person might slip into this category, a certain percentage of these people and bags would be randomly selected for 'ordinary passenger' screening.

High-risk passengers include those with no paper trail, about whom so little is known that the safest thing to do is to assume the worst and do a thorough screening of both person and bags (both checked and carry-on). Everyone in this group, in other words, would receive a more rigorous version of today's 'secondary' screening, to include both explosive-detection screening of their carry-ons and bodies, and either see-through scanning to detect non-metallic objects or a thorough pat-down search. The same protocol would apply to those whose names appear on government-maintained watch lists. Some of those in the latter category – those on the No-Fly List – would in most cases be detained rather than being put through a screening process.

Ordinary travelers are those in between the other two risk categories. These people would receive something like today's level of passenger screening (but with a much-reduced list of banned objects such as lighters, nail files, and razors). A fraction of this group would be randomly selected for secondary screening, as described above.

Identifying low-risk passengers
Aviation experts Michael Levine and Richard Golaszewski suggested the idea of separating out low-risk travelers and expediting their processing at airports in an article published two months after 9/11 (Levine and Golaszewski, 2001). It was first subject to detailed analytical scrutiny by a team of graduate students in operations research at Carnegie Mellon University in 2003 (Foster et al., 2003). They first created a model of passenger checkpoint processing, based on data from Pittsburgh International Airport (PIT). Next they created a design for a Registered Traveler program called SWIFT and simulated its operations using the model. Based on data from two surveys of airline passengers, they estimated that 40 percent of originating passengers would sign up for and be accepted into the system. Based on their simulation, first-class and elite frequent flyers (who already had a priority line at PIT) would see their average throughput time cut nearly in half, from 2.5 minutes down to 1.35. Coach passengers joining the program would have their average time slashed from 19.5 to 1.35 minutes. But those still using the regular lanes would also benefit. Since 40 percent

fewer people would be using the regular lanes, their average processing time would drop from 19.5 to 12.1 minutes. The paper estimates that first-year benefits would exceed first-year costs by $2 million.

In 2004, TSA launched a five-airport pilot program to test a watered-down version of the Registered Traveler concept. At each airport (Poole, 2005a), enrollment was limited to frequent flyers of a single airline, with a maximum of 10 000 participants nationwide. There was no shortage of volunteers signing up, even though the members still had to endure the identical checkpoint processing (though bypassing the long lines and normally being exempt from secondary screening). Initial expectations were that after testing this model on a limited basis, the TSA would roll it out to a much larger number of airports and airlines. But instead of doing that, in 2005 the agency decided to open the field to private-sector firms, as recommended in Reason's 2003 study (Poole, 2003).

The first private-sector offering came from Verified Identity Pass, which was selected in spring 2005 by Orlando International Airport over a competing proposal from Unisys to provide a 'known traveler' program open to all airlines and intended to be expanded nationwide. Enrollment began on June 21, 2005. Verified handles the enrollment process, except for the background check and clearance decision, which is done by the TSA. The company will initially charge members $79.95 per year, and it is working out co-marketing agreements with airline frequent-flyer programs. Because participating airports must make room for express lanes and special kiosks (to verify the members' identity biometrically), Verified shares a percentage of its revenue with each participating airport.

At this point, it is not clear which checkpoint requirements (for example, shoe and laptop removal) the TSA might be willing to waive for members of the program. But if the TSA approves something like the Carnegie Mellon model, the time-saving benefits for both members and non-members should be significant. There should also be some reduction in checkpoint screening personnel requirements, depending on what proportion of average daily passengers shifts from regular lines to the express lines requiring less screener interaction with passengers (fewer inexperienced travelers to coach, much less use of secondary screening).

Separating ordinary and high-risk passengers

Once low-risk passengers have been self-selected out of the mix, the remaining task is to use all feasible information to separate high-risk passengers from all the rest. One tool for doing this is a government-maintained watch list, continuously updated, against which all airline passenger reservations would be checked by the TSA in real time. Despite significant efforts among a number of federal agencies to create and maintain such a unified list, nearly four years after 9/11 this watch list still leaves a great deal to be desired, as discussed in many recent articles.

A second approach is to assess what is known about each passenger, based on information provided at the time of ticket purchase. This is the function of the pre 9/11 CAPPS, which actually flagged some, but not all, of the 9/11 hijackers. The idea of such risk-screening systems is to use various algorithms to (1) verify the passenger's identity, and (2) look for patterns that might suggest high risk. TSA's proposed Secure Flight system is intended to do this, replacing CAPPS.

The original CAPPS, still in use because its replacement has been repeatedly delayed, uses rather crude algorithms, some of whose parameters have become well known (paying cash, buying a one-way ticket, and so on) and can hence be avoided by those seeking to do harm. It apparently does not make use of travel-history data maintained in airline industry databases, linked to the passenger name record (PNR). An exercise carried out in 2003 for Reason Foundation by R.W. Mann & Company tested several different algorithms using only 5 million travel records (no names) for the two-month period before and after 11 September 2001. One query identified 13 sets of travelers fitting a pattern that closely matched those of the actual 9/11 hijackers; this set of records included all of the actual hijackers (Poole, 2003).

To supplement the above tools, and to deal with lobby-area persons not holding tickets (and therefore not passing through the screening checkpoints), a technique called 'behavioral profiling' is being used at Israeli airports (Davis et al., 2002), Boston's Logan Airport (Airports, 2002), and Las Vegas casinos (Poole, 2005b). The general idea is unobtrusively to monitor people's behavior, looking for suspicious activities, to be followed up by questioning by security personnel.

Redesigning passenger checkpoints

Security checkpoints for a risk-based system would be different from those at today's airports. First, there would be two different sets of lanes, one set for Registered Travelers and the other for all others. The proportion of each would have to be varied over time, depending on the fraction of daily originating passengers who were Registered Traveler (RT) program members. Space would be required on the approach to the RT lanes for kiosks at which members would insert their biometric identity cards to gain admission to the line for these lanes. These kiosks might be combined with common-use boarding-pass kiosks, saving RT members without bags to check in from having to stop at two different kiosks.

On the sterile side of the checkpoint, additional space would be required for secondary screening portals to check the bodies and carry-on bags of selectees for explosives and potential weapons. All high-risk passengers (except those on the No Fly List, who would be detained) would automatically go through secondary screening. Boarding passes would be coded electronically, not visibly, so that a selectee would not know whether they had been selected by Secure Flight or at random.

It is likely that meeting this set of requirements would need somewhat more square footage than is now allocated for checkpoints, though this remains to be determined. On the one hand, added space would be needed for RT kiosks and for expanded secondary screening equipment for selectees. On the other hand, significant RT enrollment should reduce the length of waiting lines (and hence reduce the area needed for that purpose). And a smaller total number of selectees (as the TSA has promised for the more sophisticated Secure Flight, when it replaces CAPPS) would lead to a smaller secondary screening area than if current percentages of passengers continued to be selected.

Redesigning baggage screening
The risk-based model would reduce the size and cost of checked baggage screening. The bags of RT members could be screened via high-speed X-ray machines, reducing the load on (and hence number of) EDS machines. RAND Corporation has done a number of studies of the impact that an RT program (which RAND refers to as 'positive profiling') could have on the size and cost of EDS installations at large and medium-sized airports. In a 2004 report, one representative result from a simulation modeling exercise used the following parameters: size the system to ensure that bags get to the intended flight 99 percent of the time, assume 90 percent reliability (up-time) of the EDS machines, and assume that 50 percent of all bags are exempted from EDS screening. For this particular set of assumptions, the RAND team estimated the total cost to the flying public of various levels of EDS deployment, where cost includes both the capital and operating costs (screener payroll) of the EDS machines and the extra time currently wasted by passengers getting to the airport early enough to ensure that their flight is not delayed due to slow bag processing. In the absence of an RT program, the optimal number of EDS machines under these assumptions (nationwide) was found to be 6000. But with an RT program that exempts 50 percent of all bags from screening (defined as screening all bags of non-members plus one-sixth of the bags of the 60 percent of passengers who are RT members), the optimal number of EDS machines declines to about 2500. That's an enormous difference in both the space required at airports and also in the capital and operating costs. As a ballpark estimate, we could say that under a reasonable set of assumptions, an RT program could cut costly EDS deployment by up to 50 percent.

Cost implications

The risk-based approach would produce significant cost savings, in both capital and operating costs, while targeting those funds spent on airport security toward the passengers most likely to pose threats to people and property. And those savings, in turn, could be devoted partially to expanded security in other areas and partially to reducing the cost burden on passengers, airlines, airports and taxpayers.

As shown in the previous subsection, the risk-based approach would reduce the scale of EDS deployment, potentially by about 50 percent. GAO reports that the TSA has not done a detailed assessment of the cost of adding in-line EDS systems at all the remaining airports where it would make sense, but has provided a broad estimate that the cost would be $3 to 5 billion (GAO, 2005b). A system needing half as many EDS machines would probably not be 50 percent less costly, due to some factors that do not scale downwards as much (facility modifications, conveyor systems, overheads, and so on). So a safer estimate of capital cost savings would be 40 percent. Hence, those one-time savings would be in the range of $1.2 to 2 billion, reducing the cost of the remaining in-line systems to $1.8 to 3 billion.

In a previous section, we saw that optimizing EDS and ETD systems would produce dramatic reductions in the number of baggage screeners needed, eliminating 14 394 of the estimated 22 500 now in place and saving $720 million per year in payroll costs. That 8106-person workforce could be further reduced by the risk-based resizing of EDS systems. Another 50 percent reduction would reduce the bag screening workforce to 4053, saving another $202.65 million per year in payroll costs. Thus, the total payroll savings, from both in-line systems and risk-based resizing, would be $923 million.

Some of the capital cost savings could be used for expanding passenger checkpoints and/or for beefing up terminal access control and airport perimeter control. The latter two uses aim at protecting planes on the ramp from unauthorized persons. And some of the payroll cost savings could be used to increase passenger checkpoint screener numbers, to add security personnel in lobby areas, and to add staff for access control and perimeter control, as necessary.

The risk-based approach should produce significant savings in passenger time, by speeding up baggage screening and passenger screening alike. While the modeling necessary to quantify such savings is beyond the scope of this chapter, the ultimate impact would be that people would not have to arrive at airports as early as they have learned to do in the post-9/11 era, reclaiming that time for personal or business purposes.

SUMMING UP: BENEFITS OF REFORM

This chapter has argued for three basic changes in the model of airport security that has been employed in the United States since the passage of the ATSA legislation in 2001. Those changes are: (1) to remove the TSA's conflict of interest by making it the policy-maker and regulator, but not the provider, of airport screening; (2) to devolve screening responsibility to the airport level, under the supervision of the TSA's Federal Security Director in each case; and (3) to shift the paradigm from an equal-risk model to a seriously risk-based model for airport security.

Those changes would improve airport security in several ways. They would target more of the available resources (of people and equipment) toward those passengers who pose relatively greater risk of harm, thereby getting more value for money. By making all on-airport security functions the responsibility of the airport, this approach would lead to a more integrated approach, with the FSD supervising everything. Removing EDS and ETD installations from ticket lobbies and reducing the extent of lines at passenger checkpoints would reduce large concentrations of people that could be targets for suicide bombers.

The proposed changes in passenger and baggage screening should have the effect of significantly reducing the average passenger waiting time to get through security and also the unpredictable variability of those times. An analysis carried out by *USA Today*, using TSA data from 2004–2005, found that at the 15 busiest airports, although average waits were seldom more than five minutes, the maximum wait could be as long as 133 minutes (Los Angeles), 120 minutes (Atlanta) or 100 minutes (Fort Lauderdale). This kind of extreme variability forces passengers to arrive at the airport far earlier than is usually necessary, wasting a huge amount of people's time.

Removing the TSA's conflict of interest, and making the airport responsible for all aspects of security (as in Europe) should also increase accountability for results.

Finally, as discussed above, this approach should produce meaningful cost savings, both in one-time capital costs for additional baggage system improvements and in annual payroll costs for screening functions. This will free up scarce airport security resources for other security needs besides screening, as well as creating the possibility of savings for airlines, airports, passengers and taxpayers. Over time, those savings may permit the TSA and the DHS to spend relatively more on protecting vital non-aviation infrastructure.

NOTES

*   GAO The General Accounting Office became the Government Accountability Office in July 2004.
1.   Sec. 302, P.L. 104–264.
2.   Sec. 3, P.L. 106–528.

REFERENCES

Airports (2002), 19 November, p. 4.

Applebaum, Anne (2005), 'Airport Security's Grand Illusion', *Washington Post*, 15 June.

BearingPoint (2004), 'Private Screening Operations Performance Evaluation Report', Transportation Security Administration, 16 April.

Brill, Steven (2003), *After: How America Confronted the September 12 Era*, New York: Simon & Schuster.

Davis, Ann, Joseph Pereira and William M. Bulkeley (2002), 'Security Concerns Bring Focus on Translating Body Language', *Wall Street Journal*, 15 August.

Department of Homeland Security (DHS), Office of Inspector General (2005), 'Follow-Up Audit of Passenger and Baggage Screening Procedures at Domestic Airports (Unclassified Summary)', OIG-05-16, March.

Dickey, Rodger L. (2005), 'Inline Lite – Inline Right?', *Airport Magazine*, May/June.

Foster, Catharine David Hamond, Mike Kaufman, Timothy Lo, Don Ojoko-Adams, Matthew Ragan, Jordan Schreck, David Stopp and Ryan Wilson (2003), 'Enhancing Aviation Security with the SWIFT System (Short-Wait Integrated Flight Travel)', Systems Synthesis Project, H. John Heinz III School of Public Policy and Management, Carnegie Mellon University, 18 May.

General Accounting Office (GAO) (1987), 'Aviation Security: FAA Needs Preboard Passenger Screening Performance Standards', GAO-RCED-87-182, Washington, DC, 24 July.

General Accounting Office (GAO) (2001), 'Aviation Security: Terrorist Acts Demonstrate Urgent Need to Improve Security at the Nation's Airports', Testimony of Gerald L. Dillingham before the Senate Commerce, Science, and Transportation Committee, 20 September.

Goo, Sara Kehaulani (2005a), 'Proposed Budget Would Strip TSA of its Biggest Programs', *Washington Post*, 9 February.

Goo, Sara Kehaulani (2005b), 'TSA Slated for Dismantling', *Washington Post*, 8 April.

Government Accountability Office (GAO) (2004), 'Aviation Security: Private Screening Contractors Have Little Flexibility to Implement Innovative Approaches', Testimony of Norman J. Rabkin, GAO-04-505T, 22 April.

Government Accountability Office (GAO) (2005a), 'Aviation Security: Systematic Planning Needed to Optimize the Deployment of Checked Baggage Screening Systems', GAO-05-365, Washington, DC, March.

Government Accountability Office (GAO) (2005b), 'Aviation Security: Screener Training and Performance Measurement Strengthened, but More Work Remains', GAO-05-457, May. (The classified version is GAO, 'Results of Transportation Security Administration's Covert Testing for Passenger and

Checked Baggage Screening for September 2002 through September 2004',
GAO-05-437C.)

Higham, Scott and Robert O'Harrow, Jr. (2005), 'The High Cost of a Rush to
Security', *Washington Post*, 30 June.

Levine, Michael E. and Richard Golaszewski (2001), 'E-ZPass for Aviation',
Airport Magazine, November/December.

Mica, John L. (2005), 'Screening Reform', *Aviation Week and Space Technology*,
6 June.

Poole, Robert W. (2003), Jr., 'A Risk-Based Airport Security Policy', Policy Study
No. 308, Los Angeles: Reason Foundation, May.

Poole, Robert W., Jr. (2005a), 'Finally, Airport Screening Relief for Frequent
Flyers', *Aviation Security Newsletter*, 14, Reason Foundation, June (available at
www.reason.org).

Poole, Robert W., Jr. (2005b), 'Vegas Casinos: A Different Approach to Security',
Aviation Security Newsletter, 14, Reason Foundation, June (available at www.
reason.org).

Quinn, Kenneth (2005), personal communication, 19 July.

Shaver, Russell and Michael Kennedy (2004), 'The Benefits of Positive Passenger
Profiling on Baggage Screening Requirements', DB-411-RC, RAND Corporation,
September, www.rand.org/pubs/documented_briefings/2004/RAND_DB411.pdf.

Transportation Security Administration (TSA) (2004), 'Guidance on Screening
Partnership Program', June, www.tsa.gov/interweb/assetlibrary/SPP_OptOut_
Guidance_6.21.04.pdf.

5. Cost-effective strategies to address urban terrorism: a risk management approach

Richard G. Little

Following the terrorist attacks of 11 September 2001, the civilian and military branches of the United States federal government intensified ongoing efforts to develop comprehensive standards to enhance the physical security of federal buildings and protect those who work in and visit these facilities. These standards apply to essentially all federally occupied space in the United States, whether it is located in buildings owned by the government or in leased commercial space, and require that buildings be able to withstand the effects of an explosion (typically assumed to be delivered as a car or truck bomb) and reduce casualties from building collapse, glass and debris, and other causes. These requirements can be met through a combination of site design features, structural enhancements, window improvements, and increased setbacks from roads and parking areas. At present few, if any, commercial buildings, particularly those in urban locations, conform to these standards, but increasingly, commercial owners are considering the hardening[1] of portions of their buildings. According to the US General Services Administration (2005), the federal government leases almost 4 million square feet of space in approximately 400 buildings located in the eight-county area consisting of Kern, Ventura, Los Angeles, Orange, Riverside, San Bernardino, San Diego and Imperial. As these leases become due, building owners will be faced with the prospect of renovating to satisfy the ISC or UFC requirements or risk losing federal tenants.

The federal guidelines are based on many years of research, testing, analysis and observation into the effects of vehicle bombs on typical commercial building construction. They propose a variety of management and engineering interventions that could prove effective in reducing the effects of an explosion. While not inexpensive, these methods can provide enhanced protection against vehicle bomb attack. However, the inventory of buildings that theoretically could require protection is quite large.

It will be shown later in this chapter that protecting just hundreds of buildings could result in an overall cost of several billion dollars. Even if these funds were made available, it is questionable whether this would be a wise expenditure in light of the large number of buildings potentially at risk compared to the relatively small number of vehicle bomb attacks that have actually occurred in the USA. Potential targets vary from general-purpose office buildings to shopping centers to federal court-houses to iconic civilian structures, and each of them has a unique set of mission objectives, design considerations, site characteristics, threat profiles, risk tolerance and budgetary limitations. Under these circumstances, it is both illogical and inefficient to prescribe security design requirements that are not risk-based. The remainder of this chapter will present a case for a risk management approach to the question of how best to manage resources to protect our cities and their inhabitants from vehicle bomb attack.

ASSESSING AND MANAGING RISK

Risk can be expressed conceptually as the product of the probability of an event and its consequences or $R = P \times C$. Risk assessment systematically incorporates consideration of adverse events, vulnerabilities, and event probabilities and consequences. It has classically been defined by three questions Kaplan and Garrick (1981):

1. What can go wrong?
2. What is the likelihood that it would go wrong?
3. What are the consequences of failure?

In the context of this chapter, the threat of concern (What can go wrong?) is taken to be persons using vehicle bombs to inflict harm on buildings and the people within them. The likelihood of this occurring, while not available statistically, can be subjectively estimated from a combination of historic frequency, intelligence information and expert opinion (Keeney and von Winterfeldt, 1991; Paté-Cornell, 2002). However, as will be shown later in this chapter, the ability to specify the probability of a terrorist attack against a specific structure or geographic area is not necessary to make informed and pragmatic decisions regarding countermeasure strategies. Finally, the consequences of failure (that is, a successful attack) are discussed in human and economic terms.

WHAT CAN GO WRONG?

Despite the devastation caused by the terrorist attacks of September 11, their very success has probably ensured that this mode of attack will not easily be repeated. The vehicle-bomb employing conventional explosives still appears to be the most likely threat confronting public buildings and spaces in the United States. Vehicle-bombs of damaging size are relatively easy to manufacture and deliver and enable the terrorist to make a large statement at relatively low cost. This is borne out by the very large number of such attacks that are currently occurring in Iraq. Table 5.1 presents statistics from selected vehicle-bombings around the world.

Although there is no theoretical limit on the size of an explosive device or the location in which it might be placed, there are practical implications of size and weight on explosive devices that could constitute a terrorist weapon. The density of common high-energy explosives, such as ammonium nitrate and fuel oil (ANFO), TNT and C4, is on the order of 100 pounds per cubic foot. Based on this, the explosive capacities of various delivery devices ranging from a small suitcase bomb to a large truck can be calculated. Examples of various bomb types are shown in Table 5.2.

Explosive materials are designed to release a large amount of energy in a very short time. Part of the energy is released as heat and part travels as shock waves through the air and ground. The shock wave in air, or airblast, radiates at supersonic speed in all directions from the explosive source and diminishes in intensity as the distance from the source increases. In a general sense, the blast energy experienced by a building is related to the amount of explosive used and the distance of the building from the explosion. As will be shown in subsequent discussions, this physical relationship drives much of the planning and design for building protection. The ability to limit the size of a bomb through vehicle control and inspection and to enforce stand-off[2] distances from possible targets through perimeter security are two of the most important and readily available tools for those charged with protecting people and buildings from bomb damage.

Buildings experience the effects of explosions in several stages. The first stage coincides with the arrival of the initial blast wave that typically shatters windows and causes other damage to the building façade. The second stage is when the blast wave enters the building and exerts pressure on internal parts of the structure. When directed upwards, this pressure may be extremely damaging to the slabs and columns which are designed to resist gravity loads acting in a downward direction.

The windows and façade are a building's first real defense against the effects of a bomb. The behavior of glazing material in the first few milliseconds following an explosion will determine the extent of injuries and death caused by

Table 5.1   Some major terrorist vehicle-bomb attacks[a] (1946–2003)

Location	Year	Size of bomb (kg TNT equivalent)	Casualties (# killed)
St David Hotel* Jerusalem	1946	350	91
US Marine Barracks* Beirut	1982	5550	242
US Embassy Beirut	1983	1000	63
St Mary Axe London	1992	350	0[b]
World Trade Center New York	1993	900	8[c]
Jewish Community Center* Buenos Aires	1994	275	26
Alfred P. Murrah Building* Oklahoma City	1995	1800	169
Khobar Towers Dharan, Saudi Arabia	1996	2300	20
U.S. Embassy Nairobi	1998	275	213
Sari Club Bali	2002	750–1000	202
Marriott Hotel Jakarta	2003	220	12
Military Hospital Mozdok, Chechnya	2003	1000	50
HSBC Bank Istanbul	2003	200	15

Notes:
[a] Information on the size of bombs and the numbers of casualties was developed from a variety of published sources and may not agree in all cases with 'official' figures.
[b] The bomb was detonated near midnight when few people were in the vicinity.
[c] The bomb was detonated in the parking garage in an attempt to collapse the building. Those killed were in the immediate vicinity of the blast.
* Partial structural collapse

glass shards and whether large amounts of blast energy enter occupied spaces. Considerable progress has been made in designing blast-resistant window panes that reduce shattering – generally employing laminated glass, extra-thickness tempered glass, or anti-shatter film. Although breakage occurs, the potential for the production of deadly shards is reduced. Ultimately, the injury and damage risk posed by many small shards must be weighed against that of a single large sheet (National Research Council, 2002).

Table 5.2   Explosive capacity of some typical bomb delivery methods

Delivery method	Explosive capacity (pounds/kilograms)
Mail bomb	5/2.3
Suitcase bomb	50/23
Automobile	500–1000/225–450
Van	4000/1800
Truck	10 000–30 000/4500–13 500
Semi-trailer	40 000/18 000

Source: Technical Support Working Group (1999).

Collapse is a principal, if not the leading, cause of injury and death in building failures, regardless of the source of the loading (for example, bomb, earthquake, internal explosion) (Sevin and Little, 1998). Progressive structural collapse occurs when the loss of load-bearing capacity (for example, through the destruction of one or more columns, or of load-bearing walls) results in localized structural failure that leads to further loss of support and, ultimately, collapse of all or part of the structure. The extent of total damage is disproportionate to the original cause. For this reason, designing to prevent the progressive collapse of a building that is the target of terrorist attack is a critical element of building defense.

WHAT IS THE LIKELIHOOD THAT IT WILL GO WRONG?

Ideally in risk calculation, a probability distribution function (pdf) is available, or can be developed, to assign likelihood to hazardous events of various magnitudes. However, the relative infrequency of attacks is compounded by the fact that they are carried out by intelligent and adaptable agents which makes it difficult to develop such a relationship empirically. In these cases, expert opinion can be used to assign probabilities (Keeney and von Winterfeldt, 1991) or values based on modeling (Paté-Cornell and Guikema, 2002), or subjective estimates can be applied (Paté-Cornell, 2002). For example, Reagan et al. (1989) assigned numerical ranges to verbal expressions of probability that can be quite helpful in populating simple decision matrices such as depicted in Figure 5.1. If decision-makers can agree that, for their purposes, a 'highly probable' event can be expressed as $p = 0.80$ and an 'improbable' one as $p = 0.001$, an ordinal ranking of risk can be determined. Such guidance, based on the verbal specification of

Consequence

Likelihood	Catastrophic 1	Very serious 2	Serious 3	Not serious 4
Certain A	1A	2A	3A	4A
Highly probable B	1B	2B	3B	4B
Probable C	1C	2C	3C	4C
Improbable D	1D	2D	3D	4D

Risk level	Action indicated
1A,1B,1C,2A,2B,3A	These are unacceptable risks. Action must be taken to eliminate or reduce them.
1D,2C,2D,3B,3C	These may be unacceptable risks. These risks may be acceptable as part of a comprehensive risk management strategy.
3D,4A,4B,4C,4D	These risks are usually acceptable as part of a comprehensive risk management strategy.

Figure 5.1   A risk management decision matrix

event probabilities and their estimated consequences, can permit rational defensive action to be taken even if the actual probability of an attack is unknown (Paté-Cornell, 2002).

Return periods for large vehicle bomb attacks can be developed for estimation purposes even though the occurrence of an attack cannot be predicted with the same level of confidence as say floods, windstorms or even earthquakes. For example, including the attacks of 11 September 2001 (but not the current Iraq insurgency), during the last 20 years there have been at least ten significant attacks against US interests domestically and overseas, on average one every two years. On this basis, the probability of terrorist attack in any year could be construed to be as high as 0.5. However, this information alone provides little basis for action as the inventory of buildings owned by the US government is estimated to be at least 500 000; if all potential non-governmental targets in the US and overseas are included, the total is much greater. In any event, using just the figure of 500 000 buildings yields a probability of attack against any building in a given year of about 4×10^{-6} $(1 \div 0.5 \times 5 \times 10^5)$. In reality, much of the building inventory cannot be considered a legitimate target due to its location, lack of significance or other factors, so the actual probability of attack will no doubt be higher. However, even reducing the number of potential targets by a factor of 100 yields a probability of only 4 in 10 000; still not a likely event (Little, 2002, pp. 49–56). Therefore, while it is surely possible to bound the likelihood of an attack through more sophisticated analysis than the simplistic examples presented here, it will be demonstrated later that is not really necessary to do so to evaluate potential countermeasure strategies.

WHAT ARE THE CONSEQUENCES?

The primary consequences of vehicle-bomb attacks against occupied buildings are human suffering, economic loss and some level of social and political destabilization.

People exposed to explosions are subject to death and injury from several sources. Most immediate is the intense heat and pressure generated at the site of the detonation where temperatures can range up to 3000°C – 4000°C and pressures to several hundred times atmospheric. The extremely high pressures damage the major organs, blood vessels, eyes and ears, resulting in serious injury or death. However, because even modest pressure waves are reflected off walls, floors and ceilings, forming a series of harmful pressure pulses, special care needs to be taken to minimize the opportunity for blast pressures from outdoor explosions to enter occupied spaces, and to protect such spaces from even small explosive devices (Cooper, 1996).

Medical reports of past bombings and recent suicide bombing attacks cite shock and organ trauma as leading causes of death (Brismar and Bergenwald, 1982; Rivkind, 2002; Weightman and Gladish, 2001). Physical translations, debris injury and blunt trauma from furniture, accessories and non-structural building components such as overhead lighting and duct-work that become detached from their moorings are other causes of injury and death. Studies of the attack on the US embassy in Nairobi found that substantial injuries can result even if structural collapse does not occur:

> The damage to the embassy was massive, especially internally. Although there was little structural damage to the five story reinforced concrete building, the explosion reduced much of the interior to rubble – destroying windows, window frames, internal office partitions and other fixtures on the rear side of the building. The secondary fragmentation from flying glass, internal concrete block walls, furniture, and fixtures caused most of the embassy casualties (US Department of State, 1999).

Analysis of the 1995 Oklahoma City bombing (Mallonee et al., 1996) showed that building collapse was the primary cause of death in that incident. In the 1996 bombing of the Khobar Towers residential complex in Saudi Arabia, the structure did not collapse and the number of fatalities was far less than in Oklahoma City.

Economic losses are of several types. First are direct losses attributable to premature death and injury and damage to buildings and infrastructure. Secondary economic losses arise from lost income because businesses are disrupted or forced to close. Total direct and indirect economic losses for the September 11 attacks in New York exceeded $38 billion (Dixon and Stern, 2004). Additional losses which are more difficult to capture are what might be termed 'avoidance' losses from people who stay away from a city or urban district out of fear or other psychological reasons.

Risk Management

Although the risk assessment process is useful because it identifies those situations that demand priority attention, it provides little insight into what countermeasures or other mitigation strategies might be most appropriate in a specific application. For this, risk management is necessary. Risk management builds on the risk-assessment process by seeking answers to a second set of questions (Haimes, 2002):

4. What can be done and what options are available?
5. What are the associated trade-offs in terms of all costs, benefits and risks?
6. What are the impacts of current management decisions on future options?

WHAT CAN BE DONE AND WHAT OPTIONS ARE AVAILABLE?

Ellingwood (2005) has defined the probability of structural failure over the collectively exhaustive universe of n mutually exclusive hazards, H_i, as: $P_f = \Sigma \ P(F|H_I) \ P(H_I)$ where $P \ (F|H_I)$ is the conditional probability of failure due to hazard H_I (failure in this case being human casualties and/or other descriptors of loss), and $P(H_I)$ is the probability of the hazard occurring. Putting this in terms of terrorist attack it can be seen that overall risk can be reduced either by avoiding or minimizing the likelihood of attack (controlling $P(H_I)$) or by designing the structure to resist the effects of attack (reducing $P(F|H_I)$ to some acceptable level). It was shown earlier that if a terrorist vehicle-bomb attack occurs in close proximity to an unhardened structure, a large glass and fragment load will be produced and building collapse may occur. If the building is occupied at the time of the attack, many of the occupants will be killed or injured – $P(F|H_I)$ will be high and unacceptable. Therefore, unless the probability of attack, $P(H_I)$ can be reduced to some acceptably low value (Paté-Cornell, 2002, suggests 10^{-7}/year as a *de minimis* risk threshold where society is indifferent) some intervention is indicated. The action taken may be to acquire additional land for stand-off, provide hardening features, limit vehicular access and parking, or assign security personnel to patrol the area. It could even entail relocating personnel and operations to another location. The following list shows several options for managing the risk of vehicle-bomb attack:

- Avoiding the risk by locating somewhere else. (This is not always an option for many place-based industries or iconic structures.)
- Reducing the risk by taking countermeasures. (The focus of this chapter.)
- Spreading the risk by choosing multiple redundant locations for certain activities. (The New York Stock Exchange and many businesses in New York and elsewhere have taken this approach.)
- Transferring the risk by buying insurance. (The viability of this option will depend on permanent reauthorization of the Terrorism Risk Insurance Act of 2002 and the willingness of the insurance industry to underwrite terrorism risk at rates the real estate industry is able and willing to pay.)
- Retaining the risk. (In light of the preceding points, building owners may have no choice but to accept a portion of the consequences of terrorist acts.)

Countermeasures for Vehicle-Bomb Attack

Based on experience with blast effects on buildings and people, there are several basic tenets of physical protection for buildings that have evolved over time. These are:

- preventing the glazing and façade materials from shattering and entering occupied spaces;
- keeping the blast energy outside the building;
- protecting the occupants from injury by fragments and larger objects, blast pressure, or physical translation;
- preventing structural collapse, both global and progressive.

The building security standards discussed at the beginning of this chapter typically seek to accomplish these objectives by:

- maintaining safe separation of attackers and targets through vehicle control and perimeter security;
- providing strong, resilient construction to protect people and key building assets.

Because of the basic physics of an explosion, the importance of stand-off distance cannot be overemphasized. Despite the great strides that have been made in developing new materials and innovative strengthening techniques that will reduce building damage and occupant injury in the event of a bombing attack, the enormous amount of energy generated by even modest amounts of high explosives will still cause extensive building damage and personal injury if detonated at close range. If adequate stand-off distance can be established and maintained, the tenets of building protection described above become realistically achievable. However, if perimeter security cannot be established and reliably enforced, a combination of active site security, operational procedures and building improvements must be provided.

A comprehensive strategy to achieve this might include armed security personnel involved in active perimeter control, together with landscaping, earthworks and appropriately designed street furniture, planter boxes, bollards and plinths to control vehicular access. The building itself may have a range of blast-resistant features such as additional structural reinforcing details, composite fiber wraps to strengthen columns and slabs, and high-performance glazing materials which do not produce lethal shards.

It should be noted that these measures address the physics of a bombing attack. They attempt to protect people and assets by keeping an attacker at bay through perimeter security, and if that fails, building features that resist the energy released in an explosion. These protective features are, in essence, the manifestation on the ground of the solution to a blast physics problem. Although these measures are vitally important in reducing casualties and damage in the event of an attack, their overall cost-effectiveness must be considered as well – particularly in commercial buildings.

WHAT ARE THE ASSOCIATED TRADE-OFFS IN TERMS OF ALL COSTS, BENEFITS AND RISKS?

Those responsible for protecting people and buildings must also consider the cost of providing a given level of safety. The cost that must be considered is not only the direct economic cost of defensive features but also the lost opportunity cost of the invested capital as well as economic losses that may accrue over time to businesses with reduced access and clientele. Ultimately, a choice must be made as to whether an investment nominally to reduce risk to those potentially affected is of greater benefit than expending the funds for some other purpose. There are also non-monetary and perhaps non-quantifiable costs, such as the loss of public access and a possible deadening of architectural spirit, to be considered as well.

Because of the difficulty in determining the likelihood of an attack, and hence the risk, building protection standards tend to emphasize the vulnerabilities of various building elements to blast loadings. As discussed earlier, perimeter control, stand-off distance and structural enhancements are all solutions to a blast physics problem. If an appropriately prepared building is attacked, the likelihood that the occupants will be killed or injured and the building seriously damaged will be reduced. However, these features will be effective only if the threat and design intersect. Otherwise, they will constitute what amounts to a modern-day Maginot Line – formidable but ineffective defenses (Little, 2004). In some sense, this approach resembles the Precautionary Principle which has as its basic premise that one should not wait for conclusive evidence of an environmental or health risk before putting control measures in place (Gollier and Treich, 2003). Although prudent when resources are unlimited or the potential harmful effects so devastating that society directs that they be prevented at any cost, what amounts to a precautionary approach to building protection from vehicle-bomb attack demands some economic scrutiny.

For the purposes of this chapter, a marginal cost of $15–$20 per square foot[3] of building area for blast-resistant features (that is, glazing, façade, structural members) is assumed, as is a land value of $75 per square foot. Thus for a 300 000 square foot building with an additional 25-foot set-back (approximately 0.5 acre) provided around the building, the marginal cost of security features would be in the range of $7 million for the example building. If this hypothetical building was attacked, in an ideal case the expected number of deaths and injuries would be reduced to zero. The direct benefits in this case would be the deaths, injuries, and property damage prevented.

In economic terms, many values for a statistical life have been determined. Vicusi and Aldy have probably done the most complete assessment and their analysis predicted a mean value from $5.5 to $7.6 million (Viscusi and Aldy, 2003). Values used by US agencies in setting policy range from $3.0 million for the Federal Aviation Administration to $6.2 million for the Environmental Protection Agency. Benefits paid to the survivors of civilians killed in the World Trade Center attacks averaged $3.1 million (Dixon and Stern, 2004). For the purpose of this analysis, $5 million will be assumed to represent the value of a statistical life. Although the value of injury has been reported in the range $20 000–$70 000 (Viscusi and Aldy, 2003), this seems low in comparison with the severity of injuries incurred in bombing attacks. Therefore, a value of $125 000 is assigned to each injury.

At this point, it will be useful to revisit the risk management decision matrix presented earlier but with quantitative (albeit self-selected) values defined for the categories of 'Catastrophic', 'Very Serious', 'Serious' and 'Not Serious' as shown in Table 5.3. Applying nominal values for 'Highly Probable', 'Possible' and 'Improbable' categories of 'Likelihood' of 0.8, 0.5 and 0.001, respectively, provides a rough yardstick with which to measure the expected economic benefits of the hardening features incorporated into

Table 5.3   Assumed consequences of event categories

Category of event	Consequences
Catastrophic	≥50 lives lost ≥200 seriously injured ≥$250 million in damage
Very serious	10–49 lives lost 50–199 seriously injured $100–$250 million in damage
Serious	5–9 lives lost 25–49 seriously injured $25–$100 million in damage
Not serious	<5 lives lost <25 seriously injured <$25 million in damage

Category of event

		Catastrophic	Very serious	Serious	Not serious
Likelihood	Highly probable p = 0.8	$420	$125–$420	$42.5–$125	<$42.5
	Possible p = 0.5	$262.5	$78.1–$262.5	$26.6–$78.1	<$26.6
	Improbable p = 0.001	$0.525	$0.156–$0.525	$0.053–$0.156	<$0.053

Figure 5.2   Expected values of consequences avoided ($10^6)

the hypothetical building described earlier. These potential benefits are assumed to be the consequences avoided as summarized in Figure 5.2.

At first glance, the $7 million cost for hardening appears to be a very good investment. However, even this simplistic analysis highlights some important questions that need to be considered. First, the expected benefits are not realized until a building is attacked; if an attack never occurs the sunk costs of hardening are not recovered. Additionally, if an entire city, urban district or large building inventory is protected on a building-by-building basis, the costs of hardening increase as a factor of the number of buildings while the expected benefits remain the same. Thus, the case for hardening 50 potential targets for $350 million does not look so compelling. In fact, it only begins to become cost-effective if it is known (or can be reasonably assumed) that there is a roughly 50:50 chance that an attack will occur against a building in that group. This leads to the second concern. That is, unless the probability of attack against a specific building is quite high, the expected benefits are not likely to offset the cost of protecting multiple targets. This is not intended to dismiss physical hardening as a countermeasure but rather to point out that because it results in immediate and large sunk costs, it needs to be used judiciously. There are buildings whose mission or iconic status makes them highly likely targets of terrorist attack and this risk will probably justify the cost of hardening.[4] However, there are far too many buildings that could be considered potential targets to embark on a precautionary program of vulnerability reduction without a full understanding of the costs and benefits of such a program. In addition, the bombings of public transportation as have occurred in Madrid and London may represent an evolution of terrorist tactics away from vehicle-bomb attacks. If this is indeed the case, hardening individual targets may become less cost-effective. However, only time will tell if this represents a true change in tactics or an expansion to all targets of opportunity.

In this regard, it is illustrative to compare the estimated cost of a statistical life saved through the hypothetical $350 million investment in building protection to other regulations of the federal government. It was assumed that protective features would be fully effective and that 50 deaths would be avoided. Converting the initial investment of $350 million to a series of ten equal annual payments at a discount rate of 2.5 percent (Office of Management and Budget, 2005) yields an annual cost per life saved of $800 000,[5] well below the $5 million value of a statistical life used in the earlier analysis. Morrall has reported on the opportunity costs per statistical life saved of various risk-reducing regulations and $0.8 million per statistical life saved is greater than steering column protection ($0.2 million), passive restraints in automobiles ($0.5 million) and head impact protection ($0.7 million) but less than seat cushion flammability in aircraft ($1.0 million), children's sleepwear flammability ($2.2 million) and asbestos protection for workers ($5.5 million) (Morrall, 2003). Therefore, compared to the cost of previously enacted regulations, the opportunity costs per statistical life saved of the hypothetical building protection program described above do not appear excessive. However, it would seem reasonable that given the potential magnitude of the total nationwide costs,[6] a serious discussion of the policy implications of this aspect of homeland security is in order. In this regard, the *Washington Post* noted in a 2004 editorial that:

> Despite the creation of a vast new Department of Homeland Security and despite the billions of dollars the government has poured into homeland security over the last three years, there has been little hard discussion in Congress, in the media or elsewhere about just what the nation's long-term homeland security priorities should be (*Washington Post*, 2004).

The importance of open policy discussion and meaningful stakeholder involvement in this process cannot be overemphasized. Given the high cost of implementing effective physical security strategies, the participation and knowledge of all affected parties, including law-enforcement officials, building owners and occupants, planners, architects, engineers and security specialists is required. Such debate on security that has occurred has tended to be unproductive because some believe that security must be maximized regardless of the cost or consequences for design or accessibility, while others demand attractive, accessible architecture with minimal concern for security. This debate fails to recognize the distinct differences between the technical aspects of physical protection (that is, the physics problem) and other public needs and values. A balance must be achieved if workable strategies are to be developed and implemented.

WHAT ARE THE IMPACTS OF CURRENT MANAGEMENT DECISIONS ON FUTURE OPTIONS?

This final question is particularly relevant because actions since September 11 have shown that all too often, what were labeled as 'temporary' security measures have become de facto permanent solutions. Targeting generic vulnerabilities rather than perceived but undetermined threats does allow action to be taken promptly. However, in addition to the lost opportunity cost, this precautionary approach to terrorist attack carries the collateral risk of making cities far less viable and attractive places while not necessarily increasing safety in a meaningful way (Little, 2004). A more effective (and economical) alternative to building-by-building defense may be to manage urban security at a neighborhood or district scale, as was done in London during the IRA bombings of the 1990s (Coaffee, 2003). For example, restricting trucks from parts of the city at certain times of the day, or requiring a physical inspection (or explosives detection screening) before they could enter, would initially be disruptive and probably costly. However, it would be a far greater deterrent to terrorist attack than merely providing perimeter security and enhanced construction features at a few buildings. For example, at the present time, there are a number of different explosive detection technologies available or in development that promise a high rate of detection with a minimum of false positives and claims of 'acceptable' throughput rates. These are available at estimated costs ranging from 10^5 up to 10^7. Pulsed Fast Neutron Analysis, the most sophisticated, potentially effective, and costly of the technologies, is estimated to cost upwards of $10 million in operational form. Limiting truck traffic to an average of five portals for 50 cities at a cost of $15 million each would cost about $3.75 billion, or about half the cost of target hardening estimated earlier in this chapter. This approach would also lessen the impact of the widespread militarization of the urban landscape – a consequence of implementing target-hardening measures more broadly than suggested by actual risks and which could take decades to undo.

SOME FINAL THOUGHTS

September 11 made it clear that there are no safe havens from terrorism. Tragedy can strike anyone, anywhere, at any time. As we have moved beyond the immediate aftermath of those events, building occupants have rational concerns regarding the ability of buildings to protect them from possible future attacks. Despite the terrible loss of life, the World Trade Center towers and the Pentagon actually performed extremely well under circumstances far more severe than anything anticipated when they were designed – demonstrating that buildings can make a real difference in saving lives. In the case of the Pentagon, hardened structural features played a role, while in the case of the World Trade Center, no specific structural hardening was provided. However, although over \$2 billion was spent on security upgrades at the World Trade Center following the 1993 bombing (Karpiloff, 2000), none of these features were effective against the attack that actually occurred. Despite the fact that much is known regarding the nature of the terrorist vehicle-bomb threat, it has been demonstrated that implementing effective countermeasures is not a straightforward technical exercise. Although people expect buildings to provide some measure of protection in the event of an attack, no consensus exists on how this can best be achieved. The government and individual building owners clearly have some responsibility to provide for the safety of building occupants. However, when considering appropriate protection levels for buildings and the means of providing it, the cost of providing protection must also be considered. Many physical responses to the threat of terrorist attack are driven more by the desire to protect people and assets from what could happen rather than what is likely to happen. In other words, these measures address the vulnerability of people and buildings to certain types of attack and are not a true assessment of the risk of that attack. This approach essentially removes the public from the decision process and eliminates from consideration any willingness on the part of the public to accept some portion of that risk. Given the high cost of providing security to buildings and public spaces, in terms of both cost and the impact on our built environment, this is a policy discussion that should be informed by sound risk-management principles and reasonably should include representatives of the public at large and not be limited to just government agencies and building owners.

NOTES

1. Hardening of a structure refers to all measures that are taken, either in the design phase of a new building, or in subsequent (retrofit) actions to reduce or eliminate the effects of an explosion.
2. 'Stand-off' is generally understood to be the distance between the detonation point of a bomb and the target building.
3. This is for new construction. Although the cost of retrofitting a structure for blast resistance would be expected to be higher, if the retrofit was done at the same time as other scheduled renovations or upgrades, this figure is probably acceptable for retrofit, at least for this level of analysis.
4. The structural upgrades installed at the Pentagon prior to the September 11 attacks performed as designed and are credited with saving lives, reducing injuries, and limiting damage to the building (Mlakar, et al., 2003, pp. 58–9).
5. \$350 000 000/8.75 (PWF, 2.5 percent, ten years)/50 lives = \$800 000 per life per year.

6. For example, if it is assumed that there are 1000 potential targets (50 cities with 20 targets each) to be protected at a hypothetical cost of $7 million each, the total cost would be $7 billion. A detailed, nationwide inventory of public and private buildings to which security measures should be applied would probably yield a larger number.

REFERENCES

Brismar, B. and L. Bergenwald (1982), 'The Terrorist Bomb Explosion in Bologna, Italy, 1980: An Analysis of the Effects and Injuries Sustained', *Journal of Trauma*, 3: 216–20.

Coaffee, J. (2003), *Terrorism, Risk and the City: The Making of a Contemporary Urban Landscape*, Aldershot: Ashgate Publishing.

Cooper, P.W. (1996), *Explosives Engineering*, New York: Wiley-VCH.

Dixon, L. and R.K. Stern (2004), *Compensation For Losses From the 9/11 Attacks*, Santa Monica, CA: Rand Corporation.

Ellingwood, B.R. (2001), 'Acceptable Risk Bases for Design of Structures', *Progress in Structural Engineering and Materials*, 3(2): 170–79.

Gollier, C. and N. Treich (2003), 'Decision-Making Under Scientific Uncertainty: The Economics of the Precautionary Principle', *Journal of Risk and Uncertainty*, 27(1): 77–103.

Haimes, Y.Y. (2002), 'Risk of Terrorism to Cyber-physical and Organizational-societal Infrastructures', *Public Works Management and Policy*, 6(4): 231–40.

Kaplan, S. and B.J. Garrick (1981), 'On the Quantitative Assessment of Risk', *Risk Analysis*, 1(1): 11–27.

Karpiloff, D.G. (2000), 'Protecting People and Buildings from Bomb Damage: Commercial Building Owners Perspective – The World Trade Center', *Proceedings of the Workshop on Protecting People and Buildings from Bomb Damage*, November 28–30, 2000, Washington, DC: National Academy of Sciences.

Keeney, R.L. and D. von Winterfeldt (1991), 'Eliciting Probabilities from Experts in Complex Technical Problems', *IEEE Transactions on Engineering Management*, 38: 191–201.

Little, R.G. (2002), 'A Probabilistic Approach for Protecting People and Buildings from Terrorist Attack and Other Hazards', *Proceedings of the International Conference on Protecting Structures Against Hazards*, Singapore: C.I. Premiere.

Little, R. (2004), 'A Holistic Strategy for Urban Security', *Journal of Infrastructure Systems*, 10(2): 52–9.

Mallonee, S., S. Shariat, G. Stennies, R. Waxweiler, D. Hogan and F. Jordan (1996), 'Physical Injuries and Fatalities Resulting from the Oklahoma City Bombing', *Journal of the American Medical Association*, 5: 382–7.

Mlakar, P.F., D. Dusenberry, J.R. Harris, G. Haynes, L. Phan and M. Sozen (2003), *The Pentagon Building Performance Report*, Reston, VA: American Society of Civil Engineers.

Morrall, J.F. (2003), 'Saving Lives: A Review of the Record', *Journal of Risk and Uncertainty*, 27(3): 221–37.

National Research Council (2002), *ISC Security Design Criteria for New Federal Office Buildings and Major Modernization Projects: A Review and Commentary*, Washington, DC: National Academy Press.

Office of Management and Budget (2005), *Guidelines and Discount Rates for Benefit-Cost Analysis of Federal Programs*, available online at http://www. whitehouse.gov/omb/circulars/a094/a94_appx-c.html accessed 16 July.

Paté-Cornell, E. (1994), 'Quantitative Safety Goals for Risk Management of Industrial Facilities', *Structural Safety*, 13(3): 145–57.

Paté-Cornell, E. (2002), 'Risk and Uncertainty Analysis in Government Safety Decisions', *Risk Analysis*, 22(3): 633–46.

Paté-Cornell, E. and S. Guikema (2002), 'Probabilistic Modeling of Terrorist Threats: A Systems Analysis Approach to Setting Priorities Among Counter-measures', *Military Operations Research*, 7(4): 5–24.

Reagan, R., F. Mosteller and C. Youtz (1989), 'Quantitative Meanings of Verbal Probability Expressions', *Journal of Applied Psychology*, 74(3): 433–42.

Rivkind, A. (2002), A Doctor's Story: Awaiting the Wounded', *Chicago Tribune*, 14 July.

Sevin, E. and R.G. Little (1998), 'Mitigating Terrorist Hazards', *Bridge*, 28(3): 3–8.

Technical Support Working Group (1999), *Terrorist Bomb Threat Standoff*, Washington, DC.

US Department of State (1999), *Report of the Accountability Review Boards on the Embassy Bombings in Nairobi and Dar es Salaam on August 7, 1998*.

US General Services Administration (2005), 'Leases in GSA/PBS Inventory as of June 3, 2005', available online at: http://www.gsa.gov/gsa/cm_attachments/GSA_BASIC/Lease_Report_for_public_6-3-05_R2-w-pC-b_0Z5RDZ-i34K-pR.xls 17 July.

Viscusi, W.K. and J.E. Aldy (2003), 'The Value of a Statistical Life: A Critical Review of Market Estimates Throughout the World', *Journal of Risk and Uncertainty*, 27(1): 5–76.

Washington Post (2004), 'The Choice: Homeland Security', 17 October.

Weightman, J. and S. Gladish (2001), 'Explosions and Blast Injuries', *Annals of Emergency Medicine*, 6: 664–78.

6. Optimal inspection strategies for Coast Guard operations

Niyazi Onur Bakir

The terrorism threat along the maritime borders has been widely pronounced as the nation has come to the realization that terrorists have the intention, sophistication and persistence to hurt the American economy and people in the homeland. The continuum of risks ranging from illegal weapon importation across the maritime ports to weapons of mass destruction (WMD) detonation at coastal targets has alerted the public to direct its effort more towards anti-terrorist thinking. The risk of illegal weapons and explosives importation in order to launch attacks against domestic targets has been compounded by the existence of multiple avenues to achieve this objective. In this chapter, the main focus is on the risk of illegal weapons and explosives smuggling in small vessels, that is, fishing boats and pleasure boats.

The Maritime Transportation Security Act (MTSA) of 2002 has assigned the maritime security enforcement responsibility to the United States Coast Guard (USCG), the Bureau of Customs and Border Protection (CBP) and the Transportation Security Administration (TSA) under the Department of Homeland Security (DHS) and the Maritime Administration (MARAD) under the Department of Transportation (DOT). The USCG has the lead responsibility in most MTSA assignments as well as the security of US waters and coastal targets. The agency has a long history of interdicting illegal drugs, other contraband and undocumented migrants. To this end, inspections are performed based on incoming intelligence and randomly to deter illegal activity and interdict weapon smugglers and terrorists. Terrorists may take a similar approach to drug and human smugglers operating in US waters, by using small vessels and boats for illegal importation of weapons and explosives.

This chapter seeks to determine optimal inspection schemes within a principal–agent framework where a risk-averse inspector sets the inspection frequency to deter a risk-averse inspectee from illegal activity. Principal–agent models (that is, Ross, 1973; Holmstrom, 1979; Shavell, 1979) are widely used in the context of law enforcement and regulation to derive incentive-compatible policies that minimize violations. Application of economic theory on law enforcement can be traced back to Becker (1968). Becker argued that criminal activities can be deterred effectively if either the penalties or the probability of prosecution are set at a maximal level. Since the prosecution is a costly activity, optimal fines should be maximal to minimize social costs of law enforcement.

Becker's results were verified by Epple and Visscher (1984) and Cohen (1987) in the context of pollution standard enforcement, which is a non-homeland security mission for the USCG. Epple and Visscher's model predicts that the level of effort by the vessel operator to prevent oil spills is an increasing function of the level of enforcement by the USCG. Cohen derives the optimal penalty as an inverse function of the probability of detection for a risk-neutral firm, and concludes that the USCG should increase the penalty level to increase the level of compliance if the resources devoted to inspection are reduced. However, as noted in Moffett et al. (2003), while the compliance rates are high, data on penalties levied do not seem to support these conclusions. Harrington (1988) investigated this apparent paradox between the theory of optimal law enforcement and actual penalty levels. Following the state-dependent law enforcement models in Landsberger and Meilijson (1982) and Greenberg (1984), Harrington developed a two-state enforcement model where the USCG and firms are engaged in a repeated game. In his model, firms are classified according to their history of environmental compliance. The main conclusion was that high levels of compliance can be maintained by low penalty levels if the USCG follows a state-dependent enforcement policy. Others have extended Harrington's model to introduce self-reporting of oil spills following Kaplow and Shavell (1994) (that is, Livernois and McKenna, 1999; Innes, 1999), and to relax the assumption of identical cost structure for the firms (that is, Raymond, 1999).

USCG inspections to detect illegal weapons and explosives smuggling certainly have different characteristics. Environmental damage is a stochastic externality in that the violation does not necessarily occur as a result of an intentional nefarious action. However, illegal weapons and explosives smuggling for terrorism purposes is an adversarial act. Since the intent is adversarial, the violator of the law is exposed to the risk of a long-term prison sentence. In this regard, the relationship between the USCG and the violator does not have a repetitive nature after detection. Furthermore, the consequences of a terrorism event are likely to be more harmful in economic terms and human fatalities. The deterrence level of USCG inspections should be high enough to minimize the incentives to launch a potentially catastrophic terrorist attack using illegally imported weapons and explosives.

In the context of arms control, models based on deterrence and threat games were widely developed to analyze the effectiveness of arms verification strategies. The players involved in this class of games are two rival nations selecting their commitment level to arms control agreements. Brams and Kilgour (1987, 1988) derive the deterrence equilibrium under a variety of settings in a two-person game that ensures full commitment to arms control agreement. Wittman (1989) introduced imperfect monitoring into detection games and concluded that the inspector should ignore the results of monitoring activity on occasion.

In this chapter, USCG inspections to interdict illegal weapons and explosives are studied in a principal–agent framework with a flavor of deterrence games. I explore the optimal inspection scheme for a homeland security mission with maximum deterrence and minimum cost possible. Frequent inspections and the prison sentence minimize the incentives to engage in a criminal activity as the expected utility of smuggling is reduced. However, inspection is a costly activity, and the USCG should allocate resources to maintain a given level of deterrence. Unlike some of the arms control and law enforcement models, the probability of detecting a criminal activity is assumed to be 1 if the inspection is performed on a criminal's fishing or pleasure boat. Two different cases are considered. In the first case, the USCG does not distinguish between the level of risk posed by each small vessel. In the second case, I assume that the USCG classifies small vessels into two different risk classes, and discuss how resources should be allocated between these two risk classes. This chapter also provides insights into the impact of risk tolerance on the level of inspection effort. To the best of my information, this is the first study to determine optimal level of effort exerted by a risk-averse USCG on a homeland security mission.

The chapter is organized as follows. The optimal fraction is computed assuming that vessels are identical in their risk exposure. A second risk type is then introduced, and the relation between the optimal fractions for both types is analyzed. The final section presents some concluding remarks.

INSPECTIONS WITHOUT A RISK CLASSIFICATION

The primary deterrence effort comprises the inspection operations performed by the USCG. Without further intelligence to classify small vessels based on their threat level, inspections are random. Let q be the fraction of small vessels inspected. Each inspection detects a smuggling attempt without an error. This fraction is determined by the level of resources allocated by the USCG. While the level of q may also depend on the daily workload of the USCG, it is assumed that a constant level of q can be maintained independent of the need to perform other missions. The cost associated with inspections is a function of q, and is denoted by $c(q)$. This function is assumed to be strictly convex (that is, $c'(q) > 0$ and $c''(q) > 0$). In other words, the shape of the cost function suggests that the marginal cost of inspections is increasing. Given the fleet size, maintaining a higher inspection rate is assumed to render a higher depreciation rate on the Coast Guard resources which implies that the marginal costs of maintenance and replacement is increasing.

Each vessel in US waterways is believed to be smuggling weapons and explosives for terrorist purposes with probability π. The terrorists' goal is to escape inspections and introduce illegal weapons and explosives into the US. If the mission is accomplished, then there is a probability p that the weapons and explosives will be used in a successful terrorist attack without any intervention. Thus, there is $1 - p$ probability that a terrorist plot will be discovered and terrorists will be arrested once they penetrate and introduce the contraband into the homeland. A successful terrorist attack is assumed to cost the economy $\$E$, and the disutility of this attack to the USCG is $v(E)$, where $v(0) = 0$ and $v'(E)$, $v''(E) > 0$. The objective of the USCG is to minimize the expected disutility of inspection efforts and a potential terrorist attack:

$$C(q, E, \pi, p) = c(q) + \pi p(1 - q)v(E) \qquad (6.1)$$

Terrorists are assumed to have a monetary pay-off of B from a successful smuggling attempt. B can be thought as a bribe paid to the owner of the boat, or monetary compensation to a terrorist who may have hijacked the boat. If illegal weapons and explosives are detected in a small vessel, then the inspectee is prosecuted and convicted of a terrorism plot, which leads to S years in prison. We assume that the disutility of S years of prison sentence is $f(S)$, where $f(0) = 0$ and $f'(S) > 0$. Since the probability of being detected is q, the expected utility from a criminal activity is:

$$D(B, q, S) = B(1 - q) - f(S)q \qquad (6.2)$$

The USCG's problem is:

$$\min_q C(q, E, \pi, p) \text{ s.t. } D(B, q, S) \leq 0, \quad 0 \leq q \leq 1 \qquad (6.3)$$

If the constraint is ignored, then the optimal level of q, q^*, is the solution to the equation $c'(q^*) = \pi p v(E)$, as long as $0 \leq q^* \leq 1$ exists. Let q^{**} be the solution to the problem in (6.3). A corner solution to the unconstrained problem may exist: $q^* = 0$ if $c'(0) > \pi p v(E)$ and $q^* = 1$ if $c'(1) < \pi p v(E)$.

Note that $dD(B, q, S)/dq < 0$, so $q^{**} = q^*$ if $q^* \geq B/B + f(S)$ and $q^{**} = B/B + f(S)$ if $q^* < B/B + f(S)$.

The optimal fraction of small vessels inspected, q^{**}, is increasing in B, whereas it is decreasing in S. As the monetary pay-off from a successful attempt to smuggle illegal weapons and explosives increase, there are more incentives to engage in this criminal activity. Hence, the USCG should increase the resources devoted to inspections for deterrence. On the other hand, an increase in prison sentence reduces q^{**}; a result consistent with Becker. B should be viewed as a policy parameter, in that the USCG solves the problem to deter all the smuggling attempts for which the monetary pay-off is at most B. The USCG should set the belief about the probability of a smuggling attempt based on B. In other words, π is the probability that terrorists offer a monetary pay-off higher than B to smuggle weapons and explosives. This probability depends on terrorists' perception of their expected pay-off from such an attempt. In this regard, π reflects the uncertainty of the Coast Guard about the utility of a terrorist attack for those who plan and execute the attack.

The model yields intuitive results for the relationship between the probability of attack and the fraction of small vessels inspected. The fraction of small vessels inspected is increasing in the probability of smuggling weapons and explosives and in the probability of using those weapons and explosives in a successful terrorist attack without intervention. If the USCG believes, based on incoming intelligence, that there will surely be an attempt to introduce weapons and explosives illegally, then every vessel should be inspected as long as $c'(1) < pv(E)$. Consider a scenario where the USCG receives intelligence about the possibility of a dirty bomb detonation by terrorists entering a port with a fishing boat. Then the probability of a successful attack is almost 1 if terrorists avoid USCG inspections, that is, $p \sim 1$. In this case, the model suggests that every vessel should be inspected, as the economic consequences may be significant. In this regard, the fraction of vessels inspected is also an increasing function of \$E.

Risk tolerance of the USCG towards potential economic losses of a terrorist event is a determinant of the optimal inspection policy. The following lemma states that q^{**} is increasing in the coefficient of absolute risk aversion under the stated assumptions.

Lemma 1 *Let $v_1(\cdot)$ and $v_2(\cdot)$ be two strictly convex disutility functions in economic losses such that $r_{v2} \geq r_{v1}$, $v'_2(0) > v'_1(0)$ and $v'_i(\cdot)$ $i = 1, 2$ is absolutely continuous. If q^{**}_1 solves $\min_q c(q) + \pi p(1 - q)v_1(E)$ and q^{**}_2 solves $\min_q c(q) + \pi p(1 - q)v_2(E)$, then $q^{**}_2 \geq q^{**}_1$.*
Proof: First, $v_2(x) \geq v_1(x)$. To see this, note that convexity implies $v_i(x) = {}_0\int^x v'_i(s) \, ds$, and by the absolute continuity of the first derivative $v'_i(x) =$

$v'_i(0) + {}_0\!\int^x v''_i(s)ds$. Let $z = \inf \{s : v''_2(s) < v''_1(s)\}$. By the continuity of $v''_i(\cdot)$, $v''_2(z) = v''_1(z)$, and $v'_2(z) > v'_1(z)$. Since $r_{v2} \geq r_{v1}$, $v'_2(s) < v'_1(s)$ for any s such that $v''_2(s) < v''_1(s)$. However, $\lim_{s \to z} v'_2(s) - v'_1(s) = v'_2(z) - v'_1(z)$ which leads to a contradiction. Hence, $v''_2(\cdot) \geq v''_1(\cdot)$, and this implies $v_2(\cdot) \geq v_1(\cdot)$. Since $v_2(E) \geq v_1(E)$, $q^*_2 \geq q^*_1$ where q^*_i solves $\pi p v_i(E) = c'(q^*_i)$. This clearly implies $q^{**}_2 \geq q^{**}_1$.

INSPECTIONS WITH TWO RISK TYPES

In this section, I assume that the USCG makes a risk classification based on incoming intelligence and previous experience. The probability of illegal weapons and explosives smuggling for type i vessel is π_i, where $\pi_1 > \pi_2$. A fraction t_i of vessels is of type i. Then if a fraction q_i of type i vessels are inspected and the total fraction of small vessels inspected is $q_1 t_1 + q_2 t_2$, with a cost of $c(q_1 t_1 + q_2 t_2)$, then the interaction between the amount of resources allocated on two types of small vessels can be modeled by this strictly convex cost function. The marginal cost of increasing the fraction of small vessels inspected in one risk type is negatively related to the level of resources allocated for inspecting the other type.

The assumption of identical utility function from smuggling is retained in this section. In this regard, B and S should be treated as policy parameters along with the fraction of small vessels inspected. While USCG inspections seek to deter a high fraction of potential smugglers, based on the level of B and S, there is still a probability π_i for each risk type i that a smuggling attempt is made.

In this new setting, the problem for the USCG is:

$$\min_q c(t_1 q_1 + t_2 q_2) + [\pi_1(1 - q_1) + ((1 - t_1)/t_1)\pi_2(1 - q_2)]pv(E)$$
$$\text{s.t. } B(1 - q_1) - f(S)q_1 \leq 0,$$
$$B(1 - q_2) - f(S)q_2 \leq 0$$
$$0 \leq q_1, q_2 \leq 1 \tag{6.4}$$

The first order conditions (FOC) for the unconstrained problem in (6.4) are

$$t_1 c'(t_1 q_1 + t_2 q_2) - \pi_1 pv(E) = 0$$
$$t_2 c'(t_1 q_1 + t_2 q_2) - t_2/t_1 \, \pi_2 pv(E) = 0 \tag{6.5}$$

The equalities in (6.5) cannot hold simultaneously because $\pi_1 > \pi_2$. This implies that at most one of the constraints in (6.5) should be binding. The solution to the program in (6.4) is stated in the following lemma:

Lemma 2 *The solution to the program in (6.3). $\hat{q}_1$ and $\hat{q}_2$, is as follows,*

Case 1: *If* $t_1 c'\left(\dfrac{B}{B+f(s)}\right) > \pi_1 pv(E)$, *then* $\hat{q}_1 = \hat{q}_2 = \dfrac{B}{B+f(S)}$

Case 2: *If* $t_1 c'\left(\dfrac{B}{B+f(s)}\right) \leq \pi_1 pv(E)$ *and* $t_1 c'\left(\dfrac{B}{B+f(s)}\right) > \pi_2 pv(E)$, *then*

$\hat{q}_2 = \dfrac{B}{B+f(S)}$ *and* $\hat{q}_1 =$

$$
\begin{cases}
\dfrac{1}{t_1}\left[c'^{-1}\left(\dfrac{\pi_1}{t_1}pv(E)\right) - t_2\dfrac{B}{B+f(S)}\right], & t_1 c'\left(t_1 + t_2\dfrac{B}{B+f(S)}\right) \geq \pi_1 pv(E) \\
1, & o.w.
\end{cases}
$$

Case 3: *If* $t_1 c'\left(\dfrac{B}{B+f(S)}\right) \leq \pi_2 pv(E)$, *then*

$$
\begin{cases}
\hat{q}_1 = \dfrac{1}{t_1}\left[c'^{-1}\left(\dfrac{\pi_1}{t_1}pv(E)\right) - t_2\dfrac{B}{B+f(S)}\right], \ \hat{q}_2 = \dfrac{B}{B+f(S)}, \\
\qquad\qquad\qquad\qquad\qquad t_1 c'\left(t_1 + t_2\dfrac{B}{B+f(S)}\right) \geq \pi_1 pv(E) \\[2mm]
\hat{q}_1 = 1, \hat{q}_2 = \dfrac{B}{B+f(S)}, \qquad t_1 c'\left(t_1 + t_2\dfrac{B}{B+f(S)}\right) \leq \pi_1 pv(E) \\
\qquad\qquad\qquad and\ t_1 c'\left(t_1 + t_2\dfrac{B}{B+f(S)}\right) > \pi_2 pv(E) \\[2mm]
\hat{q}_1 = 1, \hat{q}_2 = \dfrac{1}{t_2}\left[c'^{-1}\left(\dfrac{\pi_2}{t_1}pv(E)\right) - t_1\right], \ t_1 c'(t_1 + t_2\dfrac{B}{B+f(S)}) \leq \pi_2 pv(E) \\
\qquad\qquad\qquad and\ t_1 c'(1) \geq \pi_2 pv(E) \\[2mm]
\hat{q}_1 = \hat{q}_2 = 1, \qquad\qquad\qquad o.w.
\end{cases}
$$

Proof: See Appendix.

The solution has a complex form. The optimal fraction of small vessels inspected for high-risk types is at least as high as that of low-risk types. Net marginal benefit of increasing q_1 is higher for the USCG. Therefore, the USCG should allocate more resources to high-risk vessels. Further, both fractions are non-decreasing in π_i, p and $\$E$. As the probability or the level of harm from the terrorist attack increases, the USCG should increase resources devoted to this homeland security mission. Sufficiently high probability for a catastrophic consequence triggers inspection of every single small vessel sailing in US waters.

One implication of the model is an implicit lower bound on the fraction of small vessels inspected by setting parameters B and S. Allocating all resources to the high-risk small vessels and ignoring risks posed by low-risk small vessels may in the long run incentivize terrorists to shift their focus to low-risk small vessels. In reality, terrorists are adaptive to the new environment and will exploit any security gap with a carefully prepared smuggling plan that will evade inspections under the cover of a low-risk vessel, if the fraction of low-risk small vessels inspected is kept low.

CONCLUSION

In this chapter, the terrorism risk posed by importation of weapons and explosives in small vessels is considered within the principal–agent framework. The objective of the USCG is to minimize the expected costs from a terrorist attack originating from maritime borders, and the cost of implementing an inspection policy. Inspection of a higher fraction of small vessels is assumed to have a deterrence effect on terrorists as the expected utility from a smuggling attempt is decreasing in the fraction of small vessels inspected. First, small vessels are assumed to be identical in the level of risk they pose. In this case, the optimal fraction of small vessels inspected is calculated and this fraction is shown to be increasing with the degree of risk aversion for a particular class of utility functions.

The model for two risk types predicts that the USCG should allocate more resources to inspecting high-risk vessels. However, the fraction of small vessels inspected for both risk types should at least be at a level that provides a minimal level of deterrence from smuggling. While I recognize the implicit relation between π_i for $i = 1$, 2 and B, both variables of the model are assumed to be independent. In reality, if B is chosen high, it is expected that more potential smugglers are deterred by adjusting the fraction of small vessels accordingly in the model. However, the maximum amount that terrorist groups would be willing to pay for such a smuggling attempt is a function of the level of security along the entire border. If terrorists believe there are other avenues to import illegal weapons and explosives, then B is not likely to be high. In this regard, the USCG should evaluate the overall risk profile along the borders.

REFERENCES

Becker, G. (1968), 'Crime and Punishment', *Journal of Political Economy*, 6(2): 169–217.

Brams, S.J. and D.M. Kilgour (1987), 'Optimal Threats', *Operations Research*, 35(4): 524–36.

Brams, S.J. and D.M. Kilgour (1988), 'Deterrence versus Defense: A Game Theoretic Model of Star Wars', *International Studies Quarterly*, 32(2): 3–28.

Cohen, M.A. (1987), 'Optimal Enforcement Strategy to Prevent Oil Spills: An Application of a Principal–Agent Model with Moral Hazard', *Journal of Law and Economics*, 30: 23–51.

Epple, D. and M. Visscher (1984), 'Environmental Pollution: Modeling Occurrence, Detection, and Deterrence', *Journal of Law and Economics*, 27(1): 29–60.

Greenberg, J. (1984), 'Avoiding Tax Avoidance: A (Repeated) Game-Theoretic Approach', *Journal of Economic Theory*, 32(1): 1–13.

Harrington, W. (1988), 'Enforcement Leverage when Penalties are Restricted', *Journal of Public Economics*, 37: 29–53.

Holmstrom, B. (1979), 'Moral Hazard and Observability', *Bell Journal of Economics*, 10(1): 74–91.

Innes, R. (1999), 'Remediation and Self-Reporting in Optimal Law Enforcement', *Journal of Public Economics*, 72: 379–93.

Kaplow, L. and S. Shavell (1994), 'Optimal Law Enforcement with Self-Reporting of Behavior', *Journal of Political Economy*, 102(3): 583–606.

Landsberger, M. and I. Meilijson (1982), 'Incentive Generating State Dependent Penalty System', *Journal of Public Economics*, 19: 333–52.

Livernois, J. and C.J. McKenna (1999), 'Truth or Consequences: Enforcing Pollution Standards with Self-Reporting', *Journal of Public Economics*, 71: 415–40.

Moffett, M., A.K. Bohara and K. Gawande (2003), 'Governance and Performance: Theory-Based Evidence from US Coast Guard Inspections', Bush School Working Paper no. 406.

Raymond, M. (1999), 'Enforcement Leverage when Penalties are Restricted: A Reconsideration under Asymmetric Information', *Journal of Public Economics*, 73: 289–95.

Ross, S. (1973), 'The Economic Theory of Agency: The Principal's Problem', *American Economic Review*, 63: 134–9.

Shavell, S. (1979), 'Risk Sharing and Incentives in the Principal and Agent Relationship', *Bell Journal of Economics*, 10(1): 55–73.

Wittman, D. (1989), 'Arms Control Verification and Other Games Involving Imperfect Detection', *American Political Science Review*, 83(3): 923–45.

APPENDIX

Proof of Lemma 2: First note that $\hat{q}_i \geq B/B + f(S)$ for $i = 1, 2$. For Case 1, there is no incentive to increase q_1 and q_2 further from $B/B+f(S)$ because the marginal cost of increasing both exceeds the marginal benefit when $q_1 = q_2 = B/B+f(S)$. Thus, the result in Case 1 follows.

In Case 2, there is an incentive to increase q_1 further from the lower bound of $B/B+f(S)$, whereas it is not beneficial to do so for q_2. Thus, $\hat{q}_2 = B/B+f(S)$ and $\hat{q}_1 \geq B/B+f(S)$. We can increase q_1 until we hit the upper bound of 1. If the marginal cost of increasing q_1 at 1 is higher than the marginal benefit, then we have an interior solution where $t_1 c'(t_1 \hat{q}_1 + t_2 B/B+f(S)) = \pi_1 pv(E)$. Otherwise $\hat{q}_1 = 1$.

In Case 3, we may increase both q_1 and q_2 to achieve a lower objective value. Note that the net marginal benefit of increasing q_1 exceeds that of q_2 and the net marginal benefit of both variables decreases at the same rate when either q_1 or q_2 is increased. If net marginal benefit of increasing q_1 to 1 is negative, then we have an interior solution, $\hat{q}_1$, where $t_1 c'(t_1 \hat{q}_1 + t_2 B/B+f(S)) = \pi_1 pv(E)$. On the other hand, $\hat{q}_2 = B/B+f(S)$ because $\pi_1 > \pi_2$. If net marginal benefit of increasing q_1 to 1 is positive, keeping $q_2 = B/B+f(S)$, then $\hat{q}_1 = 1$. The optimum value, $\hat{q}_2$ depends on how $t_1 c'(\cdot)$ behaves with respect to $\pi_2 pv(E)$, keeping $q_1 = 1$. If $t_1 c'(t_1 + t_2 B/B+f(S)) > \pi_2 pv(E)$, then $\hat{q}_2 = B/B+f(S)$. We may increase q_2 to 1, if $t_1 c'(1) \leq \pi_2 pv(E)$. In other words, if the marginal cost of 100 percent inspections for both risk types is less than the marginal benefits for both types. An interior solution or $\hat{q}_2$ is obtained otherwise.

7. Balancing freedom and security after 9/11: risk management at the National Park Service

Larry Parkinson

The terrorist attacks of 11 September 2001 forced the US Department of the Interior and the National Park Service to confront a new reality: a number of America's most cherished landmarks were potentially in the cross-hairs of international terrorists. From the Statue of Liberty to the National Mall to the St Louis Arch and beyond – representing many of the nation's most powerful symbols of freedom and liberty – there was an immediate need to tighten security. Because these national icon sites were designed to attract millions of visitors in an open, welcoming environment, finding an appropriate balance between freedom and security has been an enormous challenge.

This challenge is exacerbated by fiscal realities. Because of federal budget constraints, increases in security generally require trade-offs in other programs. Consequently, before investing in new security measures, the Department of the Interior and the Park Service have engaged in a detailed risk assessment process, involving a series of critical questions, including the following. How real is the risk of a terrorist attack on a national icon? What are the likely consequences of a successful attack? What kinds of attacks are most likely, and which security precautions would be most effective in deterring and mitigating the threat? If we invest in enhanced security measures, is there a quantifiable level of risk reduction to be achieved?

This chapter sets forth the current public policy framework for national icon protection and the analytical framework for conducting risk assessments at key sites. It then describes the process of reducing risk through specific protective measures and prioritizing security investments. Finally, it describes two real-world examples at renowned icon sites to illustrate the difficult challenge of managing risks and achieving an appropriate balance of freedom and security.

PUBLIC POLICY FRAMEWORK FOR ICON PROTECTION

'National Monuments and Icons' Sector

Early in the process of developing a national infrastructure protection program, policy-makers recognized the unique status of national monuments and icons and the profound impact on national morale that would result from a successful terrorist attack on one of these resources. As stated in the *National Strategy for Homeland Security*: 'In addition to our critical infrastructures, our country must also protect a number of key assets – individual targets whose destruction would not endanger vital systems, but could create local disaster or profoundly damage our Nation's morale or confidence. Key assets include symbols or historical attractions, such as prominent national, state, or local monuments or icons.'[1] The February 2003 *National Strategy* amplified this point:

> Our national symbols, icons, monuments, and historical attractions preserve history, honor achievements, and represent the natural grandeur of our country. They also celebrate our American ideals and way of life – a key target of terrorist attacks. Successful terrorist strikes against such assets could profoundly impact national public confidence. Monuments and icons, furthermore, tend to be gathering places for large numbers of people, particularly during high-profile celebratory events – a factor that adds to their attractiveness as targets.[2]

Pursuant to the *National Strategies* and *Homeland Security Presidential Directive 7* (HSPD 7), the Department of the Interior ('Interior') is the sector-specific agency responsible for the 'national monuments and icons' sector. Interior has completed a Sector-Specific Plan for identifying, assessing, prioritizing and developing protective programs for critical assets within the sector. To date, Interior has focused on those National Park Service sites that are widely recognized both nationally and internationally to be symbolic of the United States, such as the Statue of Liberty, Independence Hall and the Liberty Bell in Philadelphia, and the principal memorials on Washington's National Mall.

Funding the Costs of Infrastructure Protection

The *National Strategy for Homeland Security* recognizes that the national effort to enhance homeland security will entail substantial costs. The strategy sets forth several fundamental principles to guide the allocation of homeland security spending:

- There must be a balance between benefits and costs.
- The government should only address those activities that the market does not adequately address.
- Federal, state and local governments, and the private sector must share homeland security costs.
- To the extent that homeland security objectives must be met by regulations, the federal government will provide regulatory incentives.

The strategy prescribes a cost–benefit analysis that accepts that 'it is not practical or possible to eliminate all risks', and that '[t]here will always be some level of risk that cannot be mitigated without the use of unacceptably large expenditures'.[3]

For the national monuments and icons sector, Interior faced three major challenges in addressing these costs. First, there had been very little investment in security prior to the September 11 attacks. The national parks, including the icon sites, traditionally have been freely accessible, open spaces, with little security beyond the ordinary law enforcement services provided by uniformed National Park Service rangers and United States Park Police officers. Consequently, at most locations, there was a minimal baseline level of security upon which an effective counter-terrorism security program could be built. Second, unlike the infrastructures at risk in virtually every other sector, the national monument and icon assets most likely to become terrorist targets are owned by the agency – in this case, the National Park Service – so there was little opportunity for cost-sharing. Third, federal agencies outside the Department of Homeland Security (DHS) are not eligible to receive homeland security funding from the DHS. Therefore, Interior has had to follow the ordinary federal budget process, and often find offsets in other areas to enhance its law enforcement and security programs.

ANALYTICAL FRAMEWORK: CALCULATING RISK

The government's infrastructure protection program is based on a philosophy of managing risk, informed by two fundamental realities: resources are limited, and elimination of risk in a free society is impossible. The challenge is to determine a reasonable level of risk in light of the terrorist threat and fiscal constraints:

> Because we must not permit the threat of terrorism to alter the American way of life, we have to accept some level of terrorist risk as a permanent condition. We must constantly balance the benefits of mitigating this risk against both the

economic costs and infringements on individual liberty that this mitigation entails . . .

Because the number of potential terrorist acts is nearly infinite, we must make difficult choices about how to allocate resources against those risks that pose the greatest danger to our homeland.

National Strategy for Homeland Security, at 2–3.

While Congress and the Department of Homeland Security have been criticized in the past for spending billions on 'homeland security pork'[4] that is not risk-based, there is currently a concerted focus on strategic risk analysis. As Secretary Michael Chertoff stated in announcing the results of a lengthy review of DHS activities, his first core principle is that the DHS 'must base its work on priorities driven by risk'.[5]

Risk analysis generally includes the consideration of three components: threat, consequence and vulnerability. Although there is a wide variety of public and private sector entities marketing somewhat different versions of risk assessment methodologies, there appears to be a rough consensus that risk is appropriately measured by the following formula:

$$\text{Threat} * \text{Consequence} * \text{Vulnerability} = \text{Risk}$$

This is the general framework used by the DHS and other public and private entities to assess critical infrastructure risks. One goal of the risk analysis process is to develop 'risk scores' that can be used to compare risks at individual facilities within a sector and, ultimately, to compare risks between facilities in different sectors. This will facilitate a more systematic and refined investment in risk-reduction strategies.

The Department of the Interior has developed this kind of risk assessment methodology and applied it at the National Park Service icon sites. Of course, the baseline level of security at the icon parks had been significantly enhanced long before the assessment methodology was formally applied. There was an immediate need following the September 11 attacks to bolster security, and Interior and the Park Service responded accordingly, often with temporary measures such as the installation of concrete Jersey barriers to restrict unauthorized vehicle access. Over time, and with the aid of additional funding from Congress, many measures became part of a permanent security package. While Interior and the Park Service informally conducted risk assessments throughout this process, the formal methodology was completed in 2004 as part of Interior's Sector-Specific Plan under HSPD-7.

Following is a brief discussion of the three components of the risk assessment methodology, beginning with an assessment of threat. Although others begin their risk assessments by analyzing consequences or vulnerabilities before turning to threat analysis, it is important to note that the costs of conducting assessments can be very high. A thorough assessment by independent experts at a major site can easily cost hundreds of thousands of dollars, but it is hardly money well spent if the site is unlikely to be a terrorist target. Consequently, Interior initially focused on the threat: Which locations are potential terrorist targets?

Threat

For most assets, it is far more difficult to reach an accurate assessment of threat than it is to analyze consequence or vulnerability. A threat picture is derived largely from intelligence, and it is rare that the intelligence available to US authorities includes specific targeting information. Instead, the available intelligence consists of bits of information derived from a wide variety of sources and methods, and more often than not, the information is non-specific and its credibility is undetermined. Even assuming a seamless information flow throughout the intelligence, law enforcement and security communities – a tall order, particularly in an environment in which much of the information is classified – those charged with protecting key assets are left with little actionable intelligence.

Because of this substantial intelligence gap, decision-makers must rely on threat assessments that analyze such factors as past practices of known terrorist groups, motivations, presence in the United States, available weapons and capabilities to carry out specific kinds of attacks. This must be an ongoing, evolving process that takes into account developments around the world – for example, the 2005 bombings in London demonstrate an increased possibility that future attacks in the US will involve suicide bombers.[6]

Immediately after the September 11 attacks, Interior and the Park Service compiled a list of those locations that would be most attractive to reasonably well-informed terrorists, keeping in mind that the September 11 attackers lived in this country, in some cases for years, and therefore were capable of making educated judgments about which locations held special significance for the American people. For a couple of locations, there existed pieces of specific and credible intelligence. For example, it has been publicly reported that the Bin Laden network had identified the Statue of Liberty as a potential terrorist target even before 2001. Beyond those locations specifically targeted, Interior and the Park Service had to decide which assets – in a National Park system of nearly 400 separate units – needed immediate security enhancements.

Two threshold questions needed to be answered in deciding where to devote scarce resources: (1) Who is the adversary that we are protecting against? (2) What are we protecting – landmarks, large groups of people, or both?

In response to the first question, Interior focused on the international terrorist threat posed by al-Qaida and its affiliates. Although there are dozens of other groups on the US list of designated terrorist groups, the al-Qaida threat is the most obvious and the most likely. Likewise, the al-Qaida threat is more compelling than the 'domestic terrorist' threat, notwithstanding the recognition that a terrorist attack can occur 'at any place, at any time'[7] and that 'Timothy McVeigh was a home-grown terrorist.' While there is a clear need to keep a watchful eye on domestic threats, the al-Qaida threat is simply a much higher priority, particularly when deciding how to spend limited security dollars.[8]

Narrowing the principal focus to an al-Qaida threat helps to answer the second question: What are we protecting? The history of al-Qaida clearly shows a preference to attack symbolic American targets, including the US Embassies in Kenya and Tanzania (1998), the USS *Cole* in the port of Aden, Yemen (2000), and the World Trade Center and the Pentagon (2001). Besides the White House and the Capitol Building, there are no more prominent symbols of America than landmarks like the Statue of Liberty, the Liberty Bell and Independence Hall, and the monuments on the National Mall. A successful attack at one of these sites would serve the dual purposes of damaging or destroying an American symbol and killing a large number of people. For these reasons, Interior focused on those symbolic sites at which an attack would resonate worldwide – and therefore likely would be near the top of al-Qaida's target list. Clearly, increasing security would also serve to provide added protection for the thousands of people present at these sites on any given day. However, for the multitude of other National Park Service sites that also attract thousands of daily visitors, but do not have a similar symbolic profile, Interior chose to address law enforcement and security needs with existing resources.

Consequences

Consequence assessment is intended to measure the overall impact of a successful terrorist attack on a particular asset. Depending on the asset under review, there are several categories of consequences that should be considered. In the case of the national icon sites, Interior first identified a narrow top tier of assets widely recognized both nationally and internationally to be symbolic of the United States. It then sent a team of law enforcement and security professionals to conduct an intensive, on-site evaluation. For several different attack scenarios, the team assigned a point value for the following consequences: (1) casualties and/or loss of life; (2) economic impact; (3) length of outage or disruption, or the length of time it would take to resume normal operations after an attack; (4) impact on other sectors; and (5) environmental impact. The cumulative point value produced an overall consequence value for each asset.

Vulnerability

Vulnerability assessment measures the likelihood of a successful terrorist attack on a particular asset. At each icon site, the Interior assessment team analyzed several different attack scenarios, including improvised explosive devices (both vehicle-borne and person-borne), airborne explosives, force-on-force, insider, cyber, chemical, biological and radiological. The assessment measured the effectiveness of existing security systems, including law enforcement countermeasures available to prevent or mitigate the attacks.

The resulting vulnerability scores necessarily reflect certain assumptions about the adversary's capabilities. Because al-Qaida in the past has been noted for being disciplined, well financed, well equipped, knowledgeable and patient, there is a natural tendency to assess vulnerabilities in that context. In fact, it is common for asset owners to engage teams trained in the special forces to simulate an attack in order to assess vulnerabilities. Predictably, the result for most attack scenarios is that few asset owners are able successfully to deter a sophisticated, well-planned attack, and the vulnerability scores invariably are high. As the United States and its allies are able to degrade al-Qaida's capabilities further by disrupting its leadership, interrupting the flow of terrorist financing, and other measures, it may be appropriate to adjust capability assumptions.

MANAGING RISK THROUGH SECURITY INVESTMENTS

By calculating threat, consequence and vulnerability, Interior's risk assessment methodology produced an ultimate 'risk value' – expressed as a numerical score – for each icon. The risk value provides a snapshot of the icon's security posture at the time the evaluation took place, and therefore can fluctuate as security measures are increased or decreased. By measuring the effectiveness of existing security systems, the risk assessments also identify security gaps. Interior can then determine what specific security enhancements would close the gaps and rerun the scoring methodology to quantify their impact. The next step, of course, is to decide whether the enhancements are worth the cost: how much risk reduction is actually achieved through which security investments? In addition to analyzing the potential impact at individual icon sites, a critical component of the risk assessment process is the ability to compare the benefits that can be achieved at one site versus another. This is an essential tool for identifying the highest-priority security needs within the Park Service and allocating scarce resources to meet those needs.

As expected, the icon site assessments identified numerous security enhancements that would yield a significant measure of risk reduction. These measures ran the gamut from low or no-cost steps such as strictly enforcing existing security procedures, to high-cost improvements such as permanent vehicle barriers around the perimeter of an icon site. Following are a few illustrative examples:

Enforcement of Existing Procedures

A significant challenge for any security program is ensuring that on-the-ground personnel do not become lax, particularly in an environment where the threat is not readily visible to those working at a particular site. Interior and the Park Service have had established security procedures at all icon sites, but there have been occasional lapses in compliance. For example, the Park Service, at considerable expense, installed a lift-gate vehicle barrier at one icon park's main entrance to protect against vehicle-borne threats, but park management discontinued its use during normal business hours after improper barrier deployment damaged several employee vehicles. By complying with existing barrier procedures, the park achieved an immediate risk reduction at no cost.

Training

Enhanced training is a low-cost way of reducing risk. In addition to specialized counter-terrorism training for the law enforcement and security officials working at the icon sites, Interior and the Park Service have promoted two additional kinds of training. First, all employees at an icon park – from the superintendent to the maintenance crew – should receive security awareness training to increase sensitivity to unusual or suspicious activities. Second, there should be some level of park visitor 'training' by incorporating security awareness messages into public information brochures and other public notices. The Statue of Liberty, for example, adopted the New York public transit authority's message – 'If you see something, say something' – as part of its public tour displays.

Visitor Screening

Visitor screening is a critical security component at nearly all of the icon sites, with the screening arrangements and equipment specifically adapted for each site. As one example, Interior concluded that the Statue of Liberty needed more sophisticated screening capabilities than those provided at other locations, primarily because of the unique characteristics of the statue itself. Therefore, since the statue reopened in the summer of 2004, all visitors who enter the monument itself are required to walk through an explosives screening portal. The portals are sophisticated, state-of-the-art devices with a high price tag, but they were deemed critical for this particular icon.

Technology

The icon risk assessments identified a need for technological enhancements to supplement the physical presence of law enforcement and security personnel. At some locations, there was a gap in camera coverage, resulting in blind spots that could be exploited by an experienced adversary. In addition, the assessment teams recommended upgrading several surveillance and monitoring systems to include better low-light and pan-tilt-zoom CCTV capabilities, alarm activation and intelligent monitoring software. Other technology improvements included such items as motion sensors, radiation detection devices and night vision equipment. Depending on the equipment being considered and the security gap that needs to be closed, technological upgrades can be expensive. It is also an area that requires close scrutiny by experienced security managers because of the wide range of technological 'solutions' being marketed in the post-9/11 environment. While enhanced technology is critical to our nation's homeland security efforts, much of the newly-emerging technology is expensive but unproven.

Barriers

The most important protection against the risk of vehicle-borne explosives is an appropriate stand-off distance. Therefore, the installation of permanent barriers to prevent unauthorized vehicles from approaching the icons is a top priority of Interior and the Park Service. Despite its high priority, it is one of the most difficult improvements to accomplish, largely because of the cultural preservation and aesthetic demands of erecting barriers on historic National Park Service sites. Most of the icons are in urban settings and any kind of significant structural changes, including vehicle barriers, require extensive community involvement and consultation. For example, in Washington, DC, the Park Service must obtain the approval of the National Capital Planning Commission before any such construction can occur. After years of discussion, the Planning Commission approved a design for a vehicle barrier at the Washington Monument and construction was recently completed. Construction is finally under way at the Lincoln Memorial and various options are still under discussion for the Jefferson Memorial, while the perimeter is secured temporarily by concrete jersey barriers.

Manpower

The National Park Service has significantly increased its law enforcement and security manpower at each of the icon sites since September 11. This is an expensive enhancement, particularly since each of the sites requires 24-hour coverage; to add one 24-hour post, the Park Service must retain approximately five officers. This component of the security program is constantly re-evaluated and readjusted depending on evolving needs, the deployment of other protective measures and budget changes. At two locations – the National Mall and Independence Park – the Park Service has supplemented its law enforcement and security force by adding contract security guards, which not only saves money but also frees up law enforcement officers to perform other duties.

BALANCING SECURITY AND FREEDOM

It is a relatively straightforward task to conduct risk assessments and develop plans for enhancing protection at the Park Service icons. However, there is nothing straightforward or simple about actually implementing a protection plan in the real world. As symbols of America, the icons stir strong emotions and any significant security proposal attracts keen attention from a variety of constituencies. Moreover, nearly all of the icon sites are in urban settings and have become an integral part of the fabric of city life. Consequently, in addition to developing security plans informed by sound risk management principles, the effort to build a post-9/11 security program for the Park Service has been marked by a continuous – and ongoing – dialogue with civic leaders, community groups, historic preservation officials, architects, media representatives, budget officials, congressional appropriators and vocal citizens. This is not to suggest that there is anything improper or unwelcome about this dialogue. It is a healthy debate that reflects the principles for which most of the icons stand. But it does present challenges, unique to this sector, in building an icon protection program that responds appropriately to the terrorist threat.

The core issue is finding an appropriate balance between security and freedom. Many of the icons themselves are shrines to liberty and freedom, and there is an understandable reluctance to erect barriers, add armed personnel and search visitors at these sites unless such measures are absolutely necessary. The range of opinion varies widely from those who advocate doing nothing to those who argue that the icons should receive a full panoply of available security measures. There is, of course, no single solution to this puzzle. In the end, Interior and the Park Service are working simply to find a reasonable balance that adequately protects these cherished American symbols while simultaneously keeping them open and accessible to the millions of visitors who come to the icons for inspiration.

This chapter presents two examples at renowned Park Service icon sites, to illustrate the challenges involved in searching for that reasonable balance. The examples are necessarily abbreviated, but highlight key public developments.

Statute of Liberty

The Statue of Liberty and Liberty Island were closed on 11 September 2001. Shortly after the closure, Interior and the National Park Service began a series of comprehensive security and safety assessments. On 20 December 2001, Liberty Island was reopened to the public and remained open, but the monument – consisting of three parts: the base, the pedestal and the statue itself – remained closed for two reasons. First, there were serious safety issues that needed to be addressed before the Park Service could responsibly invite visitors back into the structure. The safety measures included overhauling the fire detection and alarm systems, compartmentalizing interior spaces, enclosing existing stairwells to provide safe passage to exits, removing combustibles, upgrading lighting and developing additional exits. Second, there were a number of security enhancements required (informed by a series of security assessments), including screening for ferry passengers, increased US Park Police staffing, enhanced marine patrols, explosive detection canine support, a restricted water zone around Liberty and Ellis Islands, improved night-time surveillance capability, improved communications and radio equipment, and a new barrier at the Ellis Island service bridge.

These improvements began in the fall of 2001, but took a considerable amount of time to complete. The safety improvements, in particular, necessitated working closely with historic preservation officials, architects and others to modify the historic structure appropriately. As time went by, more and more people began to question why the nation's pre-eminent symbol of liberty remained closed, with some of the more vociferous voices proclaiming that the government had 'surrendered to terrorists'.

A brouhaha erupted in the fall of 2003 over the fact that a private support group, the Statue of Liberty-Ellis Island Foundation, was working with certain corporate sponsors, including American Express and Folgers coffee, to help raise money for the safety improvement projects. Although the Park Service has a long and proud history of partnering with others, including the foundation, to help support the Statue of Liberty and Ellis Island and welcomed the foundation's efforts, others took a more critical view of this effort. Some accused the Park Service of resorting to 'bake-sale fundraising' and used the occasion to attack the Bush administration and Congress for allegedly shortchanging the statue. Others demanded a federal investigation of the foundation and its president. In fact, both the administration and Congress had been very supportive of requested funding for the Statue of Liberty, and the Statue of Liberty-Ellis Island Foundation was simply continuing an admirable partnership effort that had begun in the 1980s.

Public controversy flared up again over the plan to reopen the monument. In March 2004, Interior Secretary Gale Norton announced a new visitor plan that would take effect in the summer of 2004, following completion of the safety and security improvements. Under the plan, visitors would receive a reservation-based guided tour through the base of the monument, the upgraded museum (which is housed in the base), the promenade at the top of the base, and the observation deck at the top of the pedestal. At the top of the pedestal, visitors would have the opportunity to see into the inner structure of the statue itself through a new glass ceiling, but they would no longer be able to climb through the statue to the crown because of serious safety and security concerns. Even before the plan was announced, many were loudly criticizing any reopening plan that did not allow a trip to the crown.

As things turned out, the monument reopened as planned on 3 August 2004, and nearly all of the controversy evaporated as it became clear that the visitor experience had become vastly improved. The Park Service eliminated the long waiting lines common before 9/11 through a timed reservation system, provided greatly enhanced guided tours, and permitted visitors to view the inside of the statue through a clear glass ceiling, guided by a park ranger and a new lighting and video system. The new security measures were well received, including a state-of-the-art explosives screening device commonly referred to as a 'puffer' because the machine 'puffs' the air around a visitor as he or she walks through the screening portal. The Statue of Liberty was one of the first locations at which this equipment was deployed; since then, the Transportation Security Administration has announced plans to deploy the machines at airports around the country.

All of the major components of the required security and safety programs at the Statue of Liberty are now in place, but some of those components remain on a temporary footing. For example, ferry passengers to

Liberty and Ellis Islands are still being screened at temporary facilities in Battery Park in Manhattan and Liberty State Park in New Jersey, and the Park Service is under substantial pressure to find permanent solutions. Similarly, one of the critical safety improvements at the statue was the construction of temporary stairs by which visitors exit from the statue's promenade. The state historic preservation officials approved this construction on the condition that the stairs would be temporary and that the Park Service would construct permanent new exits inside the monument, a difficult, time-consuming and costly endeavor. With respect to staffing, the law enforcement and security services are provided by the US Park Police (with the considerable assistance of contract security guards at the visitor screening sites), which had to redeploy significant resources to the Statue of Liberty and Ellis Island to address post-9/11 needs. Although the statue is now well protected, there is an ongoing need to assess the impact of that redeployment on other New York area parks that need Park Police protection.

Independence National Historical Park

There are two icons in Independence National Historical Park in Philadelphia – the Liberty Bell and Independence Hall (the birthplace of the Declaration of Independence and the Constitution).[9] They rest approximately 200 feet from each other on two city blocks in downtown Philadelphia, separated by a narrow two-lane city street named Chestnut Street. Because of widely divergent opinions on how to deal with Chestnut Street, the effort to find a reasonable post-9/11 balance at Independence Park has been particularly difficult.

Shortly after the September 11 attacks, the City of Philadelphia, with the strong support of the Park Service, closed the 500 block of Chestnut Street, which runs between the Liberty Bell and Independence Hall. Because the distance between the street and the two icons is approximately 50 feet, there was strong agreement at the time that vehicles needed to be kept off that block to protect the icons against vehicle-borne explosives. The Park Service commissioned an outside study by blast experts, whose report recommended unequivocally that Chestnut Street remain closed. In May 2002, the Park Service altered its existing screening operations to provide a secure two-block area with one screening location, so that visitors no longer had to go through magnetometers and package inspections at both the Liberty Bell Pavilion and Independence Hall. In order to maintain the secure zone, the Park Service also closed the sidewalk and restricted pedestrian traffic on the 500 block of Chestnut Street. In the meantime, the Park Service was working with security consultants and a design firm to develop a final security plan.

For the first year after 9/11, the Philadelphia community was reasonably receptive to the temporary security measures that had been installed at Independence Park. That patience began to wear thin in the fall of 2002, with some observers claiming that the Park Service was responding to the terrorist threat with heavy-handed security measures. The issue came roaring to a head in early December 2002 when Philadelphia's Mayor, without any prior notice to the Park Service or the community, announced that the 500 block of Chestnut Street would remain permanently closed. The announcement generated a public outcry, particularly from a number of business owners in the immediate area who argued that the street closure had had a serious impact on their businesses. A concerned group of citizens formed the 'Coalition to Free Chestnut Street' and began a skillful campaign to change the Mayor's position. In February 2003, the Mayor reversed his stance and announced that Chestnut Street would be reopened permanently on 1 April 2003. Interior and the Park Service, in coordination with the Department of Homeland Security, asked him to reconsider in March, particularly since the country had just gone to war in Iraq and the country was under an 'Orange' terrorist alert level. The Mayor, however, went forward as planned with the 1 April reopening. Since that date, Chestnut Street has remained open to all traffic.

The events between December 2002 and April 2003 polarized those who were working to find security solutions at Independence Park. The Coalition, members of the press, and others put strong pressure on the Mayor to change his Chestnut Street decision. The Coalition also retained its own security consultant, who attempted to rebut the Park Service experts. In one of the more unfortunate episodes during this period, someone intentionally leaked the security reports to the press, so that extraordinarily sensitive information – including detailed blast analyses of the icon sites – appeared in their entirety on the *Philadelphia Inquirer*'s website and became fodder for public discussion and editorializing. After the Mayor changed his position and agreed to reopen Chestnut Street, some in the media began attacking the Park Service mercilessly for not following suit. Despite this rough period, however, relations between the Park Service and the other stakeholders improved over time, due in large part to the efforts of a new Park Superintendent who arrived in early 2003 and immediately began forging strong working relationships with all interested parties.

Since April 2003, Interior and the Park Service have worked closely with the City of Philadelphia and many others to develop a security plan at Independence Park that includes an open Chestnut Street. Although Interior and the Park Service continue firmly to believe that the 500 block of Chestnut Street should be closed, both to improve security and to enhance the visitor experience in other ways, the fact remains that the City owns the street and can leave it open if it so chooses. The City's choice leaves the icons virtually defenseless if attacked with a vehicle bomb, but the City has concluded that it is an acceptable risk, particularly when balanced against other city needs and the symbolic nature of these particular icons.

The opening of Chestnut Street clearly reshaped the security discussion at Independence Park. One threshold question is whether it makes sense to invest in expensive security measures to protect against backpack bombs and other person-borne threats when the vehicle-borne bomb threat looms undeterred. Interior and the Park Service have concluded that it is essential to protect against person-borne threats, and have invested substantial resources to do so. Additional security measures have included a significant expansion of law enforcement and security personnel (including armed contract security guards), enhanced video surveillance, improved communications, and visitor screening for both sites. The current screening arrangement is a temporary solution that cannot be sustained in the long term, so considerable attention is being given to a permanent arrangement that will be acceptable to the Philadelphia community.

CONCLUSION

The tragic events of 11 September 2001 imposed upon the Department of the Interior and the National Park Service the formidable task of protecting America's national icons against a range of potential terrorist attacks. Starting with a near-blank slate, Interior and the Park Service have constructed and implemented a security program founded on strong risk management principles. Beyond the abstract application of such principles, however, lies a real-world challenge that is particularly acute for national monuments and icons: finding an appropriate balance between freedom and security. Wherever that balance lies, it is unique to each icon location and the effort to find it is complicated by history, tradition, aesthetics, community desires, budget constraints and symbolism. Consequently, this effort is a work in progress and is likely to remain so for many years to come.

NOTES

1. *National Strategy for Homeland Security*, at 30 (July 2002).
2. *National Strategy for the Physical Protection of Critical Infrastructures and Key Assets*, at 7 (February 2003).
3. *National Strategy for Homeland Security*, at 63–64 (July 2002).
4. 'Pork' or a 'pork-barrel project' refers to government money spent on unjustified projects, usually at the behest of a Senator or Representative in Congress. As an example Senator

Stevens of Alaska was able to get funds appropriated ($250 million) for the so-called 'Bridge to Nowhere', to an island occupied by less than 50 people.
5. 'Second Stage Review Remarks', DHS Secretary Michael Chertoff, 13 July 2005. Time will tell whether Congress will fully embrace this principle; current funding formulas are still designed to ensure that homeland security funds are spread throughout the country.
6. See *National Strategy for Homeland Security*, at 7 (July 2002): 'One fact dominates all homeland security threat assessments: terrorists are strategic actors. They choose their targets deliberately based on the weaknesses they observe in our defenses and our preparations. They can balance the difficulty in successfully executing a particular attack against the magnitude of loss it might cause. They can monitor our media and listen to our policymakers as our Nation discusses how to protect itself – and adjust their plans accordingly. Where we insulate ourselves from one form of attack, they can shift and focus on another exposed vulnerability.'
7. *National Strategy for Homeland Security*, at 1 (July 2002).
8. See *National Strategy for Homeland Security*, 'Executive Summary' at vii (July 2002). ('Al-Qaeda remains America's most immediate and serious threat despite our success in disrupting its network in Afghanistan and elsewhere. Other international terrorist organizations, as well as domestic terrorist groups, possess the will and capability to attack the United States.')
9. Independence Park includes many other historic structures and sites, but the Liberty Bell and Independence Hall are considered to have iconic stature.

REFERENCES

Homeland Security Presidential Directive 7 (17 December 2003)
National Strategy for Homeland Security (2002)
National Strategy for the Physical Protection of Critical Infrastructures and Key Assets (2003)
'Second Stage Review Remarks', US Department of Homeland Security Secretary Michael Chertoff (13 July 2005)

PART IV

Macroeconomic, sectoral and spatial impacts

8. The national economic impacts of a food terrorism event: initial estimates of indirect costs*

Thomas F. Stinson

Terrorist attacks create real losses for society. Quantifying those losses is a sobering, but important task since it provides vital information for policymakers to use as they choose how to allocate scarce public and private sector resources. Calculating the direct economic losses – the value of the lives and income lost and the business activity lost by firms in the industries and communities directly affected by any attack – is a relatively straightforward and useful first measure of the cost of the terrorists' actions. Those losses will be catastrophic for many affected individuals and firms. But, while substantial at the micro level, they are likely to be small when viewed against the entirety of the US economy.

Other losses will not be readily quantifiable. They include the psychological and emotional damage resulting from the attack. Those losses will be more widespread and are likely to extend well beyond the area immediately affected. In many instances those damages will be national in scope, for in the broadest sense we will all be victims of any future terrorist attack since each of us will lose some of the sense of security we once had. The psychological and emotional impacts that follow the attack are likely to influence consumer spending and business investment decisions and the performance of the entire US economy over an extended period.

Terrorism's follow-on impacts on the broader macro-economy are likely to be much larger than the losses suffered by those directly affected by the terrorist attack. A modest slowdown in national consumer spending, a slight increase in interest rates, a brief slump in the stock market, and a small increase in the value of the dollar will all slow the US economy only slightly in the short term. But even a small, temporary decline in the growth rate in an $11 trillion economy is likely to dwarf the direct losses caused by a terrorist act.

Looking to the longer term, any future terrorist attack also will force many firms to increase the resources they devote to security. The resources diverted to further security will not be available to produce market goods and services, and that will further restrict the long-term growth of the economy. In simple terms, terrorist acts produce negative technological change, adjusting production functions so that the amount of market output that can be produced from the economy's capital stock and labor supply is less than was possible before production processes were adjusted to secure products from deliberate contamination. Those productivity losses will be very costly, even after appropriately discounting future reductions in output to present values, since the amount lost will not abate over a few years but continue to grow, uninterrupted, into the future.

This chapter is a first attempt to provide a measure of the scale of the national economic losses resulting from a catastrophic terrorist event. Its focus is on the broad, spillover effects of such an attack on the national economy, not on the direct losses suffered by the victims of the attack. The research was motivated by concerns about the impact of a major food terrorism incident, but the value assigned to the indirect economic loss estimates by this study is indicative of the indirect economic impact of other large-scale, catastrophic terrorist events.

A terrorist act of the scale hypothesized would also create significant losses at the personal, firm and industry levels, but those losses are assumed to be outside the scope of this analysis. Only the short-term losses in national macroeconomic activity are covered in this study. No adjustments are made to reflect the value of the lives lost or the direct losses suffered by the food industry or those employed in the industry. Estimates of the productivity losses which would follow the attack, which would almost certainly be larger than the short-term indirect losses estimated, are also not included.

BACKGROUND ON THE FOOD SUPPLY CHAIN

Over the years America's food supply system has become more centralized and more dependent on large batch processing. For an increasing number of items the output from a single production run is distributed and consumed across large multi-state regions. This combination of large batch processing and widespread distribution has raised concerns about the security of the food supply chain since a single terrorist act could create simultaneous catastrophic events in several large population centers. The nature of America's food supply system combined with the fact that food is something that everyone consumes on a daily basis will extend the economic impact of a terrorist attack on the food system well beyond the direct impacts on the food sector.

The impacts of such an attack on the food supply chain would be national in scope. Learning that a terrorist group had successfully introduced a toxic agent into the nation's food supply would strike at the very heart of each American's sense of personal security. Thousands of Americans could consume fatal doses of a food-borne toxin before anyone was aware that terrorists had breached the security of the food supply chain. Those deaths would not all occur over a day or two, but more likely would accumulate over a period of two or more weeks. Depending on the product contaminated, the population at risk could be very large and spread across several large population centers.

The widespread geographic dispersion of the impacts of such an attack would also ensure that for the short term at least, Americans would feel less secure. Household spending patterns and business investment patterns would be adjusted and some purchases delayed or foregone entirely. In times of increased uncertainty the stock market typically declines and there is a flight to quality in the bond market and in foreign exchange. Each of those normal market reactions to the increased uncertainty and the short-term instability that would follow a terrorist attack would also affect national economic output. The changes brought on in macroeconomic variables would not necessarily be great. There is no reason, for example, to suspect that a terrorist attack would cause a recession. But any deviation from the growth path the economy would have followed in the absence of the terrorism event would be costly, and that loss in national economic output would not be recovered in the future.

APPROACH

The national economic impacts of a terrorist attack on the nation's food supply were simulated using a large-scale econometric model of the US economy. The model's structure is typical of Keynesian, large, open-economy, econometric models. In its simplest form the demand side of the real economy can be represented as below:

$$Y = C + I + G + NX$$

where: C = consumption, I = business investment, G = government, NX = net exports, and NFI = net foreign investment
and:

$$C = a + b(Y - T)$$
$$I = i_0 - i_1(r)$$
$$NX = e_0 - e_1 (FX)$$
$$NFI = n_0 - n_1 (r)$$
$$NFI = NX$$
$$(G \text{ and } T \text{ exogenous})$$

where: Y = income, T = taxes, r = the real interest rate, and FX = the value of the dollar.

The parameters a, i_0, e_0 and n_0 are shifters affecting consumption, investment, foreign trade and foreign investment decisions. The consumption demand shifters include consumer sentiment and household wealth. The investment shifter also includes stock market values.

When large-scale econometric models are estimated, the estimated value of a particular variable for the most recent period often does not equal that variable's observed value for the period. To ensure a better fit with the most recent historical data a special type of exogenous variable, often termed an add factor, is used. These add factors are specific to the independent variable of concern. For example, the simple aggregate consumption function shown above could be more completely represented as:

$$C = a_0 + a_1 CS + \alpha_1 CS + a_2 W + \alpha_2 W + a_Z Z + b(Y - T)$$

where CS is consumer sentiment; W, a measure of consumer wealth; Z, a vector of other consumer demand shifters and α_{CS} and α_W, add factors for consumer sentiment and wealth. Any shocks to the model needed to simulate alternative scenarios can also be introduced by adjusting the appropriate add factors.

To estimate the short-run economic losses caused by terrorism, an alternative scenario for the national economy was created by introducing changes to key parameters of the model. Parameters in four sections of the macroeconomic model were modified to produce the post-terrorist scenario. Exogenous shocks were applied to consumer sentiment, the S&P 500 stock market index, interest rates and the value of the dollar. Interest rate changes were made to both the benchmark 10-year Treasury yield and to both the Aaa Corporate – 10-year Treasury spread, and to the Baa Corporate – Aaa spread. Measures of the value of the dollar used included both its value compared to major trading partners and its value compared to other important trading partners. The consumer sentiment variable helps determine household spending in the model. The stock market variable affects both household spending through the wealth affect and business investment through the cost of capital. The 10-year Treasury bond affects both home mortgage rates and the cost of credit for business investment, while the credit spreads affect the level of business investment. The value of the dollar helps determine export demand for US-produced goods and services.

The exogenous shocks were applied as changes to the add factors for each of the major variables noted above. The add factors were adjusted for one year, then when necessary, tapered to reach the add factors used in the baseline forecast within eight quarters of the terrorist attack. The attack was assumed to occur at the start of the third quarter of 2005 and the simulation was run through 2010, at which point model results appeared to be in a stable long-run equilibrium.[1] Results from simulations using those shocks were then compared to the June baseline US economic outlook to determine the amount of economic activity lost due to the terrorist attack.

SPECIFYING THE SIZE OF THE SHOCKS

Specifying the values for each of the key variables in the post-terrorist attack scenario was the major modeling challenge. In this preliminary work the impact of the attack on the food sector is ignored. The study focuses solely on the larger macroeconomic variables. While the food sector would undoubtedly be affected, the question of food sector-specific impacts has been left for future study. The results from this study assume that the economic losses from any decline in food production and sales are included in the overall decline in consumption found by the model. Because some food consumption is essential to maintain life, the size of the decline in the sector would be limited, although some of the spending on food, particularly on food consumed away from home, would likely be diverted to other items. There would also likely be a significant, temporary drawdown of home food inventories as consumers limited the amount of all food purchases in the months after the event.

The size of the shock introduced into each key variable recalibrated for this simulation was based on changes actually observed following earlier geopolitical incidents directly affecting the United States. Data restrictions limited possible events to those occurring after 1970. Six events were chosen. Three were major events: the 11 September 2001 aircraft hijackings that led to the destruction of the World Trade Center's Twin Towers; Iraq's invasion of Kuwait in August 1990; and the Iranian Embassy hostage situation which began in October 1979. Three lesser events were also examined: the original World Trade Center bombing attempt in February 1993; the embassy bombings in July 1998; and the attack on the USS *Cole* in September 2000.

Monthly percentage changes were computed for 12 months following the terrorist shock for each variable used to drive the simulation. Percentage changes rather than the actual values were used since there were substantial differences in the starting level for those variables when the separate events occurred. The monthly mean changes for the three major events and for all six events were then calculated. The mean monthly changes were then converted into quarterly values and the quarterly values were used to determine new add factors for the model. Graphs showing the patterns of each of variable of concern following the shock are provided in the figures below.

Most variables used in the simulation showed only a modest response to the geopolitical shocks chosen. Typically, there was an immediate adverse reaction followed by a return to pre-attack levels within one year. Consumer sentiment, the stock market, the interest rate variables and the value of the dollar compared to the currencies of major trading partners all followed that pattern. The value of the dollar compared to the value of currencies of other important trading partners continued to increase throughout the entire 12 months, however. The pattern and size of the mean changes for both the three major events and all six shocks were generally very similar for each variable used in the simulation.

The University of Michigan's Consumer Sentiment Index typically fell quickly in the first six months after an attack, and then stabilized and recovered to pre-event levels within 12 months (Figure 8.1). But, even though the mean pattern was relatively smooth, the three major events showed substantially different responses with consumer sentiment recovering quickly after 9/11, but plunging dramatically following Iraq's invasion of Kuwait.

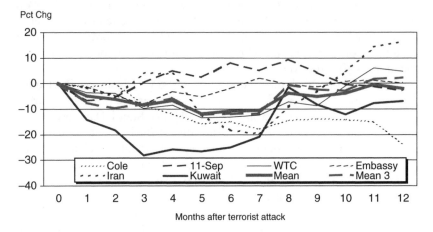

Figure 8.1   Monthly percentage changes in consumer sentiment index following selected geopolitical shocks

Average 10-year Treasury yields increased slightly during the first six months following the shock. The increased uncertainty following the event appears to have led investors to increase modestly the proportion of cash in their portfolios and shorten the maturities of their bond holdings. Treasury interest rates then fell slightly, then rose again in the last three months of the year (Figure 8.2). While those changes were not dramatic, even relatively small changes in interest rates have noticeable economic impacts. The spreads between Aaa corporates and the 10-year treasury showed almost no change (Figure 8.3), but the Baa–Aaa spread increased, also consistent with a shift to higher quality credits during a period of uncertainty (Figure 8.3).

The stock market also reacted negatively during the first six months after the shock. During the first three months following the three major geopolitical shocks the S&P 500 was down by more than 7 percent from the close in the month prior to the shock. After six months the market had recovered somewhat and was down just over 4 percent. After 12 months, the S&P average was again at the level observed just prior to the shock (Figure 8.4).

The dollar did not strengthen against the value of the currencies of other major trading partners following the US terrorist shocks. Instead, on average it weakened slightly (Figure 8.5). The substantial increase in the value of the dollar that occurred following 9/11 was more than offset by the decline in the value of the dollar following Iraq's invasion of Kuwait. The dollar did show a noticeable increase in value when compared to the

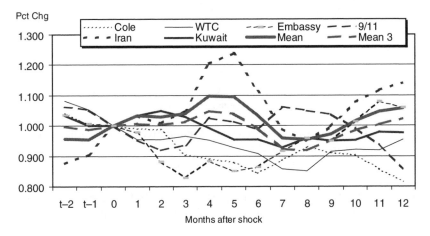

Figure 8.2   Monthly percentage changes in the 10-year treasury interest rate following selected geopolitical shocks

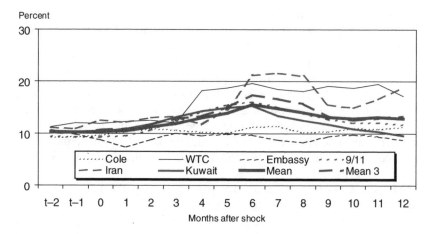

Figure 8.3   Baa–Aaa corporate interest rate spreads following selected geopolitical shocks

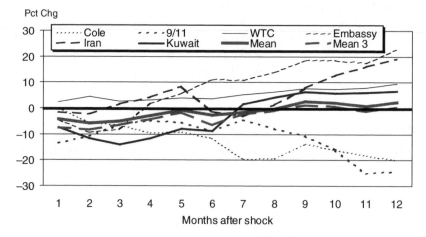

Figure 8.4   Monthly percentage changes in the S&P 500 following selected geopolitical shocks

value of other important trading partners, with both the three- and six-event averages showing an increase of more than 10 percent after 12 months (Figure 8.6).

Although there were only modest differences between the three- and six-event averages for each variable to be used in the simulations, there were

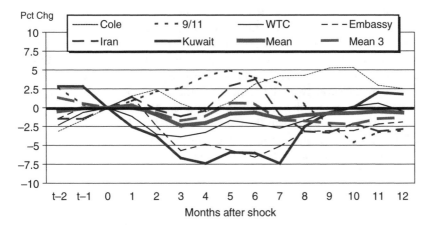

Figure 8.5   *Percentage changes in the value of the dollar compared to currencies of other major trading partners following selected geopolitical shocks*

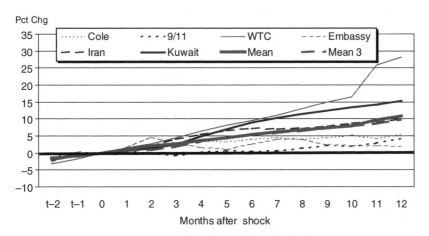

Figure 8.6   *Percentage changes in the value of the dollar compared to currencies of other important trading partners following selected geopolitical shocks*

often substantial differences in the shocks associated with particular events. For example, three months after the Iranian hostage crisis began the consumer sentiment index was nearly 4 percent higher than its pre-crisis level. But three months after Iraq's invasion of Kuwait, consumer sentiment was more than 28 percent below pre-invasion levels.

In general actual average responses to the geopolitical shocks examined were muted, and there were only modest differences between the three- and six-event averages of the shocks for each of the variables used to drive the simulations. The three major events did not show a consistent pattern of response for most variables, and there was no consistent ordering of the events by the severity of the response in the economic variables. Since the three-event averages showed a slightly smaller response to the shock, those values were chosen to form the scenario simulated. The resulting estimate of the national economic impact of a major terrorist event should be viewed as a conservative estimate of the short-term economic losses that would occur.

RESULTS

The scenario used in the post-terrorist simulation assumes that a terrorist attack occurred at the start of the third quarter of 2005. The only changes from the assumptions used in the baseline forecast were in the variables noted above. Policy parameters and other exogenous variables such as energy prices remained as in the baseline simulation.

Because the terrorist attack was assumed to occur midway through the year, its impact on real GDP growth in 2005 is muted. Baseline annual real GDP growth rate in 2005 was projected to be 3.56 percent; in the post-terrorist attack scenario real GDP growth fell only slightly to 3.48 percent. In 2006 the effects of the terrorist attack are more visible. The annual growth rate for real GDP was estimated to be 2.66 percent in the post-terrorist scenario, about one-third of a percentage point less than the 3 percent projection in the baseline (see Table 8.1).

When viewed on a fourth quarter over fourth quarter basis, baseline real GDP growth in 2005 was estimated to be 3.34 percent; in the post-terrorist alternative a 3.1 percent growth rate was projected. On a fourth quarter over fourth quarter basis, 2006 growth rates in the post-terrorist alternative were also about 0.3 percent less than the baseline scenario.

Even though the exogenously imposed shocks in the post-terrorist scenario were limited to the first four quarters after the hypothesized terrorist attack, real GDP growth rates were depressed for more than two years. On a quarterly basis the post-terrorist scenario produced a modest reduction in the US economic growth rate for nine consecutive quarters, through the third quarter of 2007. After that time the economic growth rate in the post-terrorist scenario moves slightly above the baseline rate. By 2010 the baseline and post-terrorist scenarios are roughly equivalent, with the post-terrorist scenario yielding about $10 billion less output at an annual rate.

Table 8.1   *Projected real GDP growth rates, baseline and post-terrorist scenarios, 2005–10*

Year	Annual		4Q/4Q	
	Baseline	Post-terrorist	Baseline	Post-terrorist
2005	3.56	3.48	3.34	3.10
2006	3.00	2.66	2.86	2.52
2007	3.10	2.84	3.32	3.25
2008	3.32	3.61	3.19	3.59
2009	2.97	3.27	2.91	3.11
2010	2.90	2.93	2.87	2.84

The cumulative loss in real GDP between mid-2005 and the fourth quarter of 2010, before discounting to present value, was estimated to be just over $190 billion. That lost output is never recovered, even though economic growth rates beyond 2010 are roughly equivalent in the baseline and post-terrorist scenarios.

Losses attributable to the decline in consumer confidence are concentrated in the first 12 months after the attack. They become negligible after another 12 months. Reductions in business activity due to higher interest rates, increased interest rate spreads, and the reduction in the stock market continue through the entire five-year scenario. The lost economic activity due to the increase in the value of the dollar is greatest in the second year after the attack; that impact then turns positive in years four and five as the dollar moves back to more normal levels against the currencies of other important trading partners (Figure 8.7).

The projected economic impacts of a terrorist attack shown above are based on mean levels of response to prior shocks. Should the terrorist attack create a larger than average shock to one or more of the key exogenous variables in the model, the national economic impact would be larger. Those larger shocks would also likely take longer to dissipate, delaying the economy's recovery to pre-attack levels. To illustrate the effect that differences in the size of the initial impact would have on both the size of economic losses and the timing of the recovery, several alternative simulations were run varying the consumer sentiment index assumptions, while using the same interest rate, stock market and foreign exchange assumptions as in the previous post-terrorist simulation. Results obtained when new shocks equal to the mean shock plus 0.5 standard deviation, one standard deviation, and two standard deviations were used are shown in Figure 8.8.

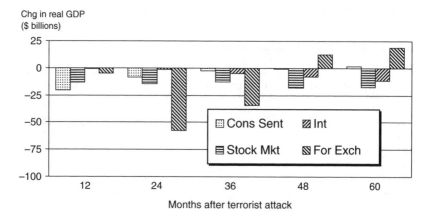

*Figure 8.7   Timing of GDP changes in post-terrorist scenario by type of
source of exogenous shock*

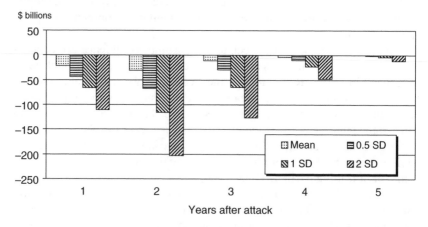

*Figure 8.8   Post-terrorist scenario losses in real GDP, alternative consumer
sentiment responses*

Not surprisingly, when larger shocks are assumed the losses in economic
output are greater. If the shock to consumer sentiment is assumed to be
equal to the mean shock plus one standard deviation beyond that shock,
real GDP falls by an additional $200 billion over the four years when com-
pared to the original post-terrorist scenario. Were consumer sentiment to
fall by two standard deviations more than the mean, real GDP would fall
by more than $400 billion between 2005 and 2010 compared to the post-
terrorist scenario constructed using mean shocks.

CONCLUSION

Policy-makers, as they seek to determine the appropriate amount of public resources to devote to anti-terrorist activity, must make crude cost–benefit calculations balancing the expected benefits from a reduction in the possible losses caused by terrorists against expected benefits from other private and public expenditures. Economic efficiency requires that for resources to combat terrorism to be appropriately allocated, the last dollar spent on anti-terrorist activities must reduce the expected value of losses by one dollar. The losses considered must, however, include both the more easily quantified measures of losses and those less easily measured. If only part of the losses are considered, too little will be allocated to defending against terrorism.

Calculations of the benefits from averting a catastrophic loss are difficult under the best of situations, and they are always based on limited information. Economic analysis can help improve policy by expanding and refining the quantifiable information available. This study attempts to add to the information available for decision-makers by providing an estimate of the national economic impacts of a catastrophic terrorist event.

The simulations of the short-term national economic impact of a catastrophic terrorist event indicate that even under conservative assumptions the annual real GDP growth rate would fall slightly during the year of the attack; they drop by about 0.3 percent below the baseline forecast in the following 12 months. Based on past responses of key driving variables for the US economy to geopolitical shocks, a current value loss of real GDP totaling more than $190 billion is projected. When larger shocks to key variables are assumed, the loss of real GDP is substantially larger. Under some combinations of assumptions current value losses in real GDP from a terrorist event could easily exceed $500 billion over a four-year forecast horizon.

These estimates of lost GDP do not include the impact of the productivity losses that would accompany any catastrophic terrorist attack in the US. Those losses, which would be ongoing and increasing over time, would exceed the short-term economic losses projected in this study. The short-term economic losses reported are losses in future national economic output. No adjustment was made for the lost earning capacity of those who die or are disabled by the terrorist action, nor are the costs of replacing or repairing any equipment or structures damaged or made unusable by the terrorists included. Those costs, while significant on a personal or firm level, would be small compared to the prospective losses in real GDP.

NOTES

*   This research was supported by the United States Department of Homeland Security through the National Center for Food Protection and Defense (NCFPD), grant number N-00014-04-1-0659. However, any opinions, findings, and conclusions or recommendations in this document are those of the author and do not necessarily reflect the views of the US Department of Homeland Security.
1.   During the summer of 2005 the US economy was thought to be growing at about a 3.5 percent annual rate. While energy prices were rising and the Federal Reserve was increasing the Fed funds rate at 'a measured pace' there were no serious economic problems on the horizon. A terrorist attack at a time when the economy was already facing potential problems would be likely to have a larger impact.

9. The economic cost of disasters: permanent or ephemeral?

Matthew P. Drennan

The general issue addressed in this chapter is whether a terrorist attack or a natural disaster with significant death and destruction will have long-term negative effects upon the local economy suffering such an attack. The specific case addressed here is the pre- and post-September 11 economy of New York City and the New York region. Terrorist attacks are only one type of the adverse shocks that have beset cities. More common are wars, civil disturbances and natural disasters such as Hurricane Katrina and the consequent massive flooding of New Orleans, and the tsunami that devastated some parts of South-East Asia in 2004. If a shock is defined as a sudden, unexpected, negative impact upon a local economy, then the negative impact upon some urban areas of industrial decline is not a shock. The adverse effects develop and accumulate slowly, often over decades. There is a simple economic connection between shocks and industrial decline. If a shock, natural (flood, earthquake) or unnatural (terrorism), destroys a non-trivial part of the capital stock of an urban area, then recovery, manifested by rebuilding and replacement, depends upon the expected rate of return of the new capital in the old location. If that is below the expected rate of return in other places, then the rebuilding and replacement will not occur, at least not by the unsubsidized private sector. The short, unqualified answer as to whether a shock to an urban economy has a permanent or temporary adverse effect depends upon expectations about returns to capital in that place. Where they are lower than in alternative places, the adverse effect will be permanent. Where they are competitive with alternative places, the adverse effect will be temporary.

In the next section I consider the macro environment of the New York economy, pre- and post-9/11. The transformation of that economy from producing and moving goods to producing and moving information has resulted in a stronger economy while at the same time increasing its vulnerability to terrorism. To almost no one's surprise, the post-shock economic data indicate recovery. That is followed by a more micro analysis of the relocation of displaced firms. Those choices throw light upon the current holy grail of urban economics: agglomeration economies. In the next section I review information on other urban areas that have suffered negative shocks, and attempt to sort out those that recover and those that do not. The firebombing of Tokyo and the nuclear bombing of Hiroshima in World War II are the most devastating of modern urban shocks, and yet those two places recovered (Davis and Weinstein, 2002). No shock we have seen in modern times has by itself caused permanent economic harm. Negative shocks can at worst accelerate economic decline already under way. A final section concludes.

NEW YORK THEN AND NOW

In the 1960s the economic activities of producing and moving goods, finance, and the corporate headquarters of manufacturing and mining firms, together dominated the New York region's economy, the Consolidated Metropolitan Statistical Area (CMSA). New York City (NYC), the core of the region, had 1.2 million jobs in manufacturing plus port-related transportation and wholesaling. Corporate headquarters in the city, including 128 of the Fortune 500 head offices, occupied 45 percent of the class A office space of midtown Manhattan (Drennan, 1991).

The port, with far fewer jobs, has shifted to New Jersey. Manufacturing, port activity and wholesale trade employment in the city has diminished to one-third of what it had been in the 1960s. The corporate headquarters have moved to the suburbs, other cities, or have downsized. Fewer than 30 Fortune 500 head offices are in NYC now (Drennan, 2002). Yet grass is not growing in the streets. The New York region, and New York City particularly, have become highly specialized in financial producer services and other producer services (law, accounting, advertising, public relations, business consulting, media, computer software, architecture, engineering and so on). The class A midtown office space, the supply of which is greater than when headquarters occupied 50 percent of it, is mostly (60 percent) taken by financial firms and law firms.

The transformation from an economy specialized in the production and distribution of goods to an economy specialized in information means that the major physical capital stock is comprised of office buildings, computers, telecommunication infrastructure and passenger transportation systems. The 11 September 2001 terrorist attack was a direct hit upon the human and physical capital of the modern information economy, if not the center then at least the icon, the symbol, of that economy.

In order to describe the macro trend of the New York regional economy prior to 9/11, I have split the region's earnings into those from traded goods and services industries and those from non-traded. For a full explanation of which industries are traded and which are non-traded, see Drennan (2002). Suffice it to say here that the sorting is not based upon the popular but flawed location quotient method. The earnings data are from the Regional Economic Information System (REIS) of the Bureau of Economic Analysis, US Department of Commerce. The area is the New York CMSA with the present geographical definition (27 counties in four states) fixed back over the full period, 1969 through 1999. Earnings have been converted to 2004 dollars using the New York region Consumer Price Index (CPI) for all items, all urban consumers. Although employment rather than earnings is more frequently used to measure economic activity in metropolitan areas, earnings convey the importance of any industry or group of industries for an area better than employment. Not all jobs are equal in terms of what they add to the economy.

Figure 9.1 shows the actual values of real earnings in both the traded and non-traded goods and services industries of the New York CMSA,

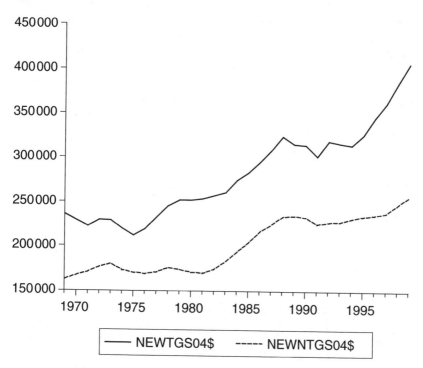

Source: Bureau of Economic Analysis, REIS (2005).

Figure 9.1   Earnings in traded and non-traded industries (millions of 2004 $, NY CMSA, 1969–99)

1973 to 1999. The region's economy is cyclically sensitive with clear dips in the 1973–75 and 1979–80 national recessions. The more recent 1989–90 recession stands out as corresponding to a big drop and slow recovery for the region. That reflects a severe stock market decline in 1987 that depressed earnings in the financial sector long after the national recession had passed, as well as the bursting real estate bubble that hit the two coasts particularly hard. However, as everyone knows and as Figure 9.1 makes clear, the latter half of the 1990s were boom years for the New York region. Although many other US metropolitan areas had faster growth in earnings than the New York region, that in part reflects population growth elsewhere. The population of the New York CMSA was up only 3 percent from 1990 to 1999 when the nation's population grew 12 percent.

More impressive than the growth in earnings has been the growth in the real wage. That growth reflects the transformation of the New York region's economy described above. Figure 9.2 shows the actual real wage from 1969 through 1999. From the early 1980s through 1999, the real annual wage of the New York CMSA was in a strong upward trend, rising from about $44 000 in 1981 to $57 000 in 1999. That is in sharp contrast with the national real wage, which was mostly flat until the late 1990s.

I have estimated a simple trade model in which the left-hand variable is the change of real earnings in the non-traded goods and services industries. The right-hand variables are current and lagged real earnings in the traded goods and services industries, the drivers of the economy, along with auto-regressive terms. The estimated trade equation is:

$$\Delta NTGS_t = -3{,}588 + 0.2826\,TGS_t - 0.2661\,TGS_{t-1} + 0.7172\,AR_{t-1} + -0.1421\,AR_{t-2}$$

(t statistics) (−0.4) (5.0)·   (−5.6)   (3.6)   (−0.7) (9.1)

adj. $R2 = 0.60$
$d.w. = 2.03$
$ADF = -2.37 > -2.62$, 10% critical value.

where $\Delta NTGS$ is the change of real earnings in non-traded goods and services industries in year t, and TGS is real earnings in traded goods and services industries in years t and $t-1$. The first difference form of $NTGS$ is used to remove the trend and make the variable almost stationary. The left-hand variable, $\Delta NTGS$, does not quite pass the augmented Dickey-Fuller unit root test at the 10 percent significance level. The AR terms are added to reduce autocorrelation. Coefficients on the traded goods and services variables are significant above the 0.01 level.

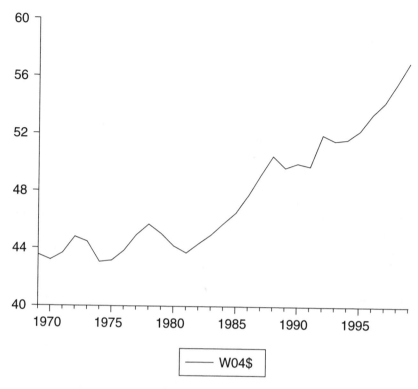

Source: Bureau of Economic Analysis, REIS (2005).

Figure 9.2   Annual wage (2004 $, NY, CMSA, 1969–99)

I have also estimated a wage equation in which the left-hand variable is the change in the annual real wage computed as total real earnings divided by total employment. Both are from the REIS data and both include the self-employed. The first difference form of the wage is used to remove the trend and make the variable stationary. The variable, $\Delta WAGE04\$$, does pass a unit root test at the 5 percent significance level. The right-hand variables are current and lagged values of the ratio of earnings in the financial and other producer service industries to the earnings in manufacturing. That is a variation on a measure of specialization developed by Au and Henderson (2002). The presumption is that the transformation of the region's economy from goods to information has raised the real wage. The estimated equation includes a second order autoregressive specification as shown below:

$$CHW04\$_t = 0.1217 + 7.5668\,PSRATIO_t - 7.8206\,PSRATIO_{t-1}$$

(t statistics)   (−0.4)   (3.1)   (−2.9)

$$+\,0.2613\,AR_{t-1} - 4364\,AR_{t-2}$$

          (1.4)   (−2.1)   (9.2)

adj. $R\,2 = 0.32$
$d.w. = 2.22$
$ADF = -3.35 < -2.97$, 5% critical value.

The *PSRATIO* coefficients are both statistically significant well below the 0.01 level.

I have used equations (9.1) and (9.2) to forecast the changes of non-traded goods and services earnings and the changes in the real wage for the years 2001 to 2003. The calculated forecasted levels compared with the actual levels are shown in Figures 9.3 and 9.4. To simplify the comparison, both actual and estimated values are shown as index numbers in which the actual value for 2000 is set to 100. Not surprisingly, the estimated values for non-traded real earnings, 2001–2003, are well above the actual values. The

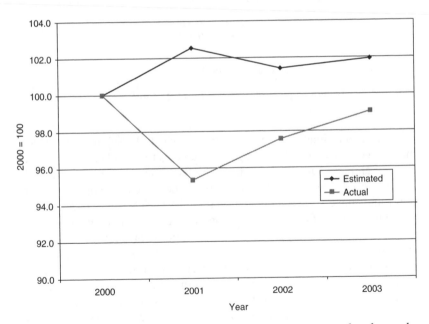

Figure 9.3   *Non-traded goods and services earnings, estimated and actual, NY CMSA*

actual earnings dropped about 5 percent from 2000 to 2001, and then increased in 2002 and 2003 but not enough to recover to the level of 2000.

The actual real wage fell in each of the three years after 2000, but the drop in 2003 is quite small. The 2003 real wage is 3 percent below the 2000 value. The forecasted real wage rose more than 5 percent for 2001, and then dropped somewhat for the next two years. Nonetheless it remained almost 4 percent above the 2000 level. It is impossible to determine how much of those visible negative divergences from the hypothetical trends represented by the estimated values of earnings and real wages are due to the shock of 9/11 rather than to the national recession and the stock market crash.

Turning from the region to New York City, the five years prior to 2001 constituted an unprecedented boom period for the securities industry. Employment growth in the securities industry, although strong, 20 percent, is a small part of the story. Securities industry earnings rose from $19 billion in 1995 to $45 billion in 2000, a gain of 135 percent. Those earnings represented 21 percent of all New York City earnings in 2000. Profits in the industry increased to $21 billion, a rise of 184 percent, while bonuses were up to almost $20 billion or 220 percent. Capital gains in New York City

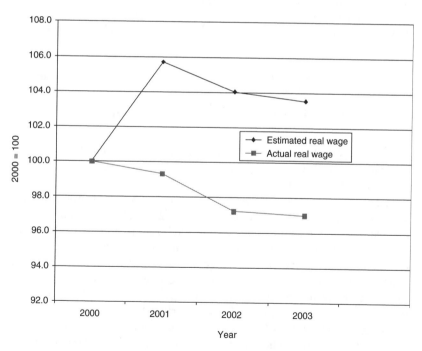

Figure 9.4   Real wage NY CMSA

*Table 9.1   Employment, earnings, profits and capital gains in securities
industry New York City, 1995, 2000, 2002*

Employment and earnings	1995	2000	2002	% change 1995 to 2000	% change 2000 to 2002
Securities industry employment (thousands)	162	195	170	20.4%	−12.8%
NYC total employment	3 339	3 723	3 584	11.5%	−3.7%
Securities employment as % of total	4.80%	5.20%	4.70%		
Securities industry earnings (millions $)	19 161	45 069	37 827	135.2%	−16.1%
NYC total earnings (millions $)	140 675	213 123	205 865	51.5%	−3.4%
Securities industry earnings as % of total	13.60%	21.60%	18.40%		
Profits, bonuses and capital gains					
Securities industry profits (millions $)	7 400	21 000	6 900	183.8%	−67.1%
Securities industry bonuses (millions $)	6 100	19 500	8 600	219.7%	−55.9%
NYC capital gains (millions $)	6 126	28 692	8 588	368.4%	−70.1%

Note: Securities industry is NAICS code 523, securities and commodities brokers and dealers as well as the stock and commodity exchanges.

Source: New York State, Office of the State Comptroller (2004), April.

went from $6 billion in 1995 to $29 billion in 2000 (Table 9.1). The city economy, as well as city and state tax collections, were awash in cash (New York State, 2004).

The bust came in the next two years. All of the measures shown in Table 9.1 suffered significant declines from 2000 to 2002, although none of them fell nearly as much as they had risen in the boom period. With the exceptions of the employment measures and total city earnings, positive changes resumed in 2003. Employment change in the city turned slightly positive in 2004 following three consecutive years of decline. Even the hard-hit securities industry posted a positive but small gain in jobs in 2004. Total job recovery accelerated in late 2004 and early 2005. As of August 2005, employment in New York City was 1.1 percent above the level a year earlier.

Rents for midtown office space fell from an average of $60 per square foot at the end of 2001 to $50 at the end of 2003. They have begun to recover and in mid-2005 were at $53. The midtown vacancy rate, about 8 percent in late 2001, moved up to 12 percent in 2003 and 2004. Since then it has fallen and was about 9 percent in mid-2005. The downtown office market, which includes the site of the World Trade Center, has not been as robust, but nonetheless is showing signs of recovery. The downtown vacancy rate, which was under 10 percent in the fall of 2001, rose to 17 percent in late 2002. It has since declined to 12 percent as of mid-2005. The historical premium of midtown office rent over downtown office rent is about $18 in 2005 (New York City, 2005), which has been the upper limit for that premium over the previous 15 years (Kelly, 2002).

It is impossible to say how much of the bust can be attributed to the terrorist attack rather than the stock market decline and the national recession. The beginning of recovery in 2003 for the securities industry's profits and bonuses plus capital gains, followed by broad employment growth along with falling office vacancy rates and rising rents in 2004–2005, all suggest a temporary impact. However, the relocation of firms and jobs displaced by the destruction and damage of so much of the downtown office stock can all be reasonably attributed to the terrorist attack. I now turn to that issue.

RELOCATION OF DISPLACED FIRMS

The central variables that underlie this empirical analysis of firm relocation are the stock of office space (capital) and its use prices (rents) in various locations. The neoclassical economic theory of production, in which capital, as well as labor, are perfectly mobile, the price of capital is everywhere the same, and capital can be replaced or added instantaneously, is less than useful. Office buildings are never moved, rents vary significantly by location, even within the same metropolitan economy, and new additions to the stock require three to five years or more from plan to opening, although conversions take less time.

The New York CMSA has far and away the largest concentration of office stock in the United States, and most of that stock is in the borough of Manhattan. With far less than 1 percent of the national population, Manhattan accounts for about 10 percent of the nation's office stock (Kelly, 2002). That concentration reveals 'how much the New York regional economy depends upon office functions as an economic driver' (Kelly, 2002, p. 6).

Partitioning the region's office market into the sub-areas employed by commercial real estate firms, it is clear that the four sub-parts of midtown, with 307 million square feet, dwarf the other parts (see Table 9.2). The next

Table 9.2　Stock of office space and office rents, New York region, 2nd quarter 2001

Market	Stock (millions sq. ft)	Rent ($per sq. ft)
Midtown		
Midtown core	155	$60
Midtown west	30	$58
Penn Station	28	$35
Midtown south	94	$39
All Midtown	307	
Downtown	108	$40
Total Manhattan	415	
New Jersey		
Urban New Jersey	35	$20
Suburban New Jersey	75	$24
Northern Suburbs	76	$28
Long Island & Boros	62	$24
Region ex Manhattan	248	
Total region	663	

Source:　Kelly (2002).

largest sub-part is downtown, the area south of Canal Street popularly known as Wall Street that includes the World Trade Center, with 108 million square feet. So the Manhattan office stock, midtown plus downtown, of 415 million square feet, is 63 percent of the region's total. These numbers are from the second quarter of 2001, and so they include the destroyed and damaged buildings of 9/11 (Kelly, 2002).

Rents were highest in the midtown core ($60) and midtown west ($58). Downtown rents were $40, reflecting the historical premium of the midtown core over downtown. The premium goes back perhaps 40 years or more. Rents in the four sub-parts outside Manhattan were well below the lowest Manhattan rents (Penn Station area). Note particularly that the lowest rents shown are for urban New Jersey, which includes the new office towers directly across the Hudson River from Manhattan and closest to downtown. At $20 per square foot, they are one-half the downtown level of $40.

Figure 9.5 shows office rents in constant dollars for midtown and downtown from 1969 through 2001. As noted, rents in midtown are above

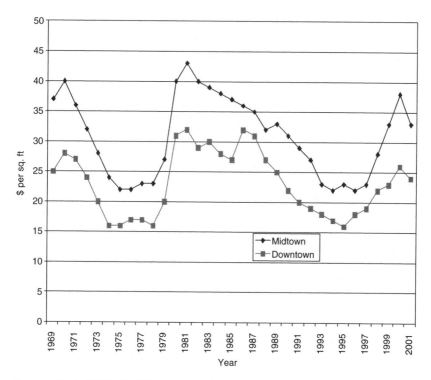

Source: Hugh F. Kelly Real Estate Economics.

Figure 9.5 Manhattan office rents, 1982 $, 1969–2001

downtown for all years shown. The rent trends, in constant dollars, in the two markets are almost mirror images of each other, reflecting the fact that they are close substitutes. The recent peaks of both series in 2001 are not as high as their previous peaks in 1981 for midtown and 1987 for downtown. The size of the midtown premium increases when rents are rising, and decreases when rents are falling. The existence of that premium reflects a number of factors. Midtown transportation links with suburbs are much better than downtown's links. Midtown is more convenient to two of the three major airports than downtown. Midtown is a mixed-use area with residences, theatres, museums, restaurants, hotels and entertainment embedded or nearby.

Downtown historically has been a 9 to 5 area that had been as deserted as downtown Houston or Los Angeles after 5 p.m. and on weekends. That had been gradually changing for the better over the past 25 years. Battery Park city, built on landfill west of the World Financial Center downtown, plus conversion of some obsolete downtown office buildings to condos, and the conversion of Tribeca to a residential neighborhood, have all stimulated an after-5 retail economy and the beginning of street life. The downtown buildings are on average older than the midtown buildings, making them less suitable for large employers. Developers have built far more office buildings in midtown than downtown in the past 50 years. Thus the newer stock is increasingly concentrated in midtown, attracting firms with large space requirements.

Destroyed or seriously damaged office buildings from the 9/11 attack add up to 34 million square feet. Almost one-third of the class A space in the downtown market was destroyed or damaged. Of the 34 million square feet, almost 25 million had been occupied by about 200 large private sector tenants, that is tenants occupying 10 000 or more square feet. Four hundred small tenants, leasing less than 10 000 square feet each, plus ten government agencies, had occupied the remaining 9 million square feet of destroyed or damaged space. The original amount of space rented in the destroyed or damaged buildings and the area of relocation for the 200 large firms is summarized in Table 9.3. The sub-areas are of midtown are not shown as in Table 9.2.

Large firms that collectively occupied 12.2 million square feet of the destroyed or damaged downtown space relocated downtown. That is, large firms that relocated elsewhere downtown accounted for half of the destroyed or damaged space, making downtown the top choice for relocation. The second-highest choice was midtown. Firms that had occupied 30 percent of the destroyed or damaged space relocated to midtown. Thus in terms of space originally occupied, large firms that collectively accounted for almost 80 percent of such space relocated downtown or in midtown.

Table 9.3   *Location choices of displaced large firms by market and square feet formerly occupied ('000)*

Market	Square feet formerly occupied	%
Downtown	12 197	49.1
Midtown	7 361	29.6
New Jersey	3 070	12.4
Northern suburbs	1 138	4.6
Soho to 14th St.	439	1.8
Long Island & Boros	381	1.5
Outside region	266	1.1
Total	24 852	100.0

Source: Hugh F. Kelly Real Estate Economics.

Far below in third place was relocation to New Jersey. Such firms accounted for 12 percent of the lost space. Of course the area of relocation may not be the same as a firm's first choice because of space availability. But the data on space availability, that is, vacancy by sub-market suggests that there was sufficient vacant space for displaced firms to get their first choice.

> Thus even with a regional vacancy rate of about 10% and an overall Manhattan vacancy of just 8.7% [immediately prior to 9/11], there was a volume of unused office space almost equivalent to three World Trade Centers in Manhattan alone, and nearly five World Trade Centers in the region. And this understated the available capacity . . . as a vast amount of 'sublet' space suddenly materialized when displaced tenants began to search the market after 9/11. (Kelly, 2002, p. 8)

The downtown sub-market had over 8 million square feet of available space on the eve of 9/11. How could it absorb displaced firms that had lost 12.2 million square feet (see Table 9.3)? The answer is a combination of increased availability through the canceling of sublets, renting less space then they had previously occupied, and sending some units to other sub-markets. In all the other sub-markets where large firms relocated, the available space far exceeded the space requirements of the relocating firms (Kelly, 2002).

If indeed displaced large firms got their first choice of sub-areas in which to relocate, then that massive relocation is a natural experiment on the value of agglomeration economies. Consider firms that chose to stay downtown rather than relocate in urban New Jersey. They opted for space that on average was twice as expensive as in urban New Jersey – $40 per square foot versus $20 (see Table 9.2). Firms requiring 100 000 square feet or more showed a tendency to relocate to urban New Jersey, which is mostly in Jersey City, directly across the Hudson River from downtown Manhattan. However, 'ten of the 24 locations represented by such firms in Urban New Jersey were classified as "temporary" as of March 2002' (Kelly, 2002, p. 23). The destruction of 9/11 freed firms from long-term leases as well as from the inertia associated with the high cost of moving a large operation elsewhere. They had no choice. Yet firms that occupied half of the destroyed or damaged space chose to remain downtown. Those choices provide a basis for estimating a lower limit for the value of the agglomeration economies perceived by the firms opting to remain downtown. Assume that a large firm requires 100 000 square feet of office space. In urban New Jersey the average annual cost would be $2 million ($20 per square foot × 100 000 square feet). Downtown, the cost would be $4 million ($40 per square foot × 100 000 square feet). By choosing to relocate downtown rather than to New Jersey such a firm reveals that it values the differential agglomeration economies of a downtown location at no less than $2 million annually. If the hypothetical firm valued the differential agglomeration economies at less than $2 million, relocation to New Jersey would be the rational choice. The relocation, 'voting with their feet', of large displaced firms primarily to downtown and midtown locations (see Table 9.3) attests to the perceived worth of those locations over alternatives in the region. The $2 million lower limit for the differential agglomeration economies in the example is actually too low because it ignores the significantly higher city and state business taxes faced by firms in Manhattan compared with firms in New Jersey.

Economists who have addressed the location consequences of 9/11 have overlooked the evidence for differential agglomeration economies conveyed by office rents in sub-markets. In 'Terrorism and the Resilience of Cities' (Harrigan and Martin 2002), the authors consider the impact of terrorism on large cities post-9/11 employing, first, a labor pooling model, which generates agglomeration economies. Lacking any data, the authors nonetheless present a strong conclusion from their labor pooling model. 'Any ongoing costs in coping with terrorism, however, can lead to a limited reduction in the size of the city' (Harrigan and Martin, 2002, p. 103).

Their second model is a core–periphery model, adapted from Fujita et al. (2001), which has only two sectors: agriculture and manufacturing. Although admitting the model is simple, 'the core periphery equilibrium does have features that suggest the real world'. One of those features is that 'some economic activity (manufacturing) is concentrated in a city while other activity is spread more evenly across space' (Harrigan and Martin, 2002, p. 104). The concentration of manufacturing in big cities, and even in some big metropolitan areas, has been in decline for at least 40 years. The real world that their core–periphery model suggests is the real world pre-1965. The economic activities concentrated in large cities are financial and other producer services as well as the top hierarchy of advanced consumer services (research universities, top medical schools, professional sports, opera, dance, theater and music). For those activities, information is a major input and output, products are non-homogeneous, and face-to-face interactions appear to be critical.

Glaeser and Shapiro, urban economists who are no doubt knowledgeable about agglomeration economies, appear to have overlooked them in considering the impact of terrorism upon New York City:

> We think that the impact of the bombing on the structure of New York is likely to be significant, and indeed that it should be significant.
> Our view is that while New York City itself is likely to be quite robust, the future of the downtown area is much less clear. This area once had a significant comparative advantage that came out of its proximity to the Port of New York. This advantage no longer exists. Within Manhattan, the only remaining

advantage of this area is its proximity to New Jersey and Staten Island. (Glaeser and Shapiro, 2002, p. 208)

That assertion contradicts the inference I would draw from the office rent data pre 9/11 for the New York region (see Table 9.2) showing downtown rents higher than in New Jersey and higher than in any sub-market except midtown. The assertion is based neither on a model nor on data. It is as valid a claim as that the only advantage of midtown is its proximity to Queens. Like Harrigan and Martin, they harken back to a vanished era when downtown New York developed serving the port, an era that is even further back in time than the era of manufacturing concentrated in cities. In addition to the rent data, other contemporary measures of the importance of the downtown area to the region's economy are in the movement of people and the movement of information. 'The destruction of the World Trade Center towers, for example, took out both a major subway transportation node in the basement and a concentration of wireless telecommunication nodes on the roof' (Mitchell and Townsend, 2005, p. 317). Moving massive numbers of people and massive amounts of information are modern central functions of downtown.

> But the attraction of the target to the terrorists was not only the concentration of human life and the powerful symbolism of the towers, but also the role of lower Manhattan [that is, downtown] as a key node in the global financial network – supported by an astonishing concentration of telecommunication infrastructure . . . The two main telephone switches in the financial district had more lines than many European nations. And there were more than 1500 antenna structures on top of the World Trade Center's north tower alone . . . the New York metropolitan area was at that point [9/11], the Internet's largest single international bandwidth hub, and several of its major switching centers (carrier hotels) were all within close proximity on the west side of lower Manhattan [that is, downtown]. (Mitchell and Townsend, 2005, pp. 320–21)

Glaeser and Shapiro argue that the disappearance of the port has signaled the slow death of downtown. Unburdened with any data on office space or rents, they conclude:

> In the absence of major government subsidies to the area, it seems reasonable to believe that downtown New York will continue its slide . . . Many of the businesses will move to midtown. Many others will move to nearby suburban office parks that are likely to be close enough to provide agglomeration economies that are probably not much less than those provided by downtown. (Glaeser and Shapiro, 2002, p. 221)

They do cite a source that claims large (over 50 000 square feet) displaced tenants signed leases in midtown (65 percent), New Jersey (17 percent), and places other than downtown. There are three problems with those data. First, if it is a count of tenants rather than square feet leased, then the percentage do not reveal in what sub-markets displaced large tenants leased the most and the least space. Second, the source (Heschmeyer, 2001) has a publication date only five weeks after 9/11. At such an early date it is difficult to imagine that a significant share of displaced tenants had made permanent location choices. Third, and most serious, we have no indication of what number or proportion of displaced large tenants are represented by that relocation data. The relocation data cited here from Kelly (2002) was current as of April 2002, seven months after 9/11, and it represents relocation choices of large tenants (205) that had been displaced from almost 25 million square feet (see Table 9.3). It is not a sample, it is the universe of displaced large (10 000 square feet or more) office tenants.

The picture of downtown painted by Glaeser and Shapiro is simplistic and too pessimistic. It has not been in absolute decline since the port disappeared in the 1960s:

> It must be remembered that the 1970s and 1980s represented the first major development cycle [construction of office buildings] for Lower Manhattan in a half century, and much of that stock has now been obliterated. What remains downtown is heavily weighted to office buildings constructed 75 to 100 years ago, hardly the most suitable workspaces for the 21st century. (Kelly, 2002, p. 44)
>
> The 1970s and 1980s office building boom downtown was a key factor in gradually changing the area from a 9 to 5 neighborhood to an area with residential and retail development nearby and considerable 'buzz'.
>
> The residential growth of lower Manhattan was made possible only by the vigorous growth of office-based jobs in the Eighties and Nineties. In 1980, when lower Manhattan had yet to see recovery take hold, the residential population below Canal Street was a paltry 7000 persons . . . By contrast, two decades of strong office job growth downtown have created a residential base of some 35000 in Community District One, with the area along the Hudson waterfront transformed from a dusty wasteland to a thriving example of exceptional urban planning spectacularly realized. SoHo and Tribeca, as neighborhoods, now stand for cutting-edge activities, galleries, shops, restaurants, and cinema, all leavened by residential conversions and new development fed by New York's economic vitality. (Kelly, 2002, p. 43)

That accurate portrayal is in contrast to Glaeser and Shapiro who note, 'In the 1980–2000 period, the general problems of downtown New York were hidden by the vibrant financial sector in which it specialized' (Glaeser and Shapiro, 2002, p. 221). Two of those general problems they note are that 'Downtown is far from the population centers of New York and is built around a port that no longer exists' (Glaeser and Shapiro, 2002, p. 222). Brooklyn, the most populous borough with 2.2 million people, is closer to downtown then to midtown by subway. Indeed the most upscale neighborhoods of Brooklyn are a few short subway stops from downtown, and Brooklyn Heights is walking distance from downtown. The vibrant downtown financial sector of the 1980s and 1990s drove the gentrification of Brooklyn neighborhoods. True, the port for ocean cargo is long gone, but the telecommunication port for information transmittal, critical for the office economy of Manhattan, is concentrated not just in midtown but in downtown too, as noted above. Finally, a key player in the vibrant financial sector, Goldman Sachs, recently announced its decision to build a new headquarters adjacent to the former World Trade Center site. The pronouncement of the death of downtown by Glaeser and Shapiro is premature.

Nonetheless, I do agree with Glaeser and Shapiro that the downtown office market has been in a long-term decline relative to midtown. The rent premium for midtown space has been persistent (see Figure 9.5). But judging from the rent data, a downtown office location remains the best substitute for a midtown location compared with the other sub-markets of the region.

PLACES THAT RECOVER AND PLACES THAT DO NOT

From the recent work of Davis and Weinstein (2002) we know that some urban places that suffered massive destruction in World War II, Tokyo and Hiroshima for example, have recovered. Glaeser and Shapiro (2002) show that over the past 50 years, Jerusalem has grown much faster than Tel Aviv despite the greater frequency of terrorist attacks in Jerusalem. Kobe, devastated by an earthquake in 1995, has reportedly been rebuilt and has resumed its role as Japan's major port. In a collection of pieces on cities that have recovered from wars, natural disasters, and terrorism, *The Resilient City* (Vale and Campanella, 2005), the editors conclude:

> We began this book with the observation that, at least for the last two centuries or so, nearly every traumatized city has been rebuilt in some form. This historical fact raises the question of whether it is possible for a city to be rebuilt *without* being resilient. What does the concept of a resilient city mean if every city appears to qualify? (Vale and Campanella, 2005, p. 335)

Although the editors do not answer their question, they hint at the answer in noting, 'the inertia of urban resilience is produced by a combination of undiminished geographic advantages, long-term investment in infrastructure, and place-dependent business networks' (Vale and Campanella, 2005,

p. 346). The first and third are correct I believe, while the second, investment in infrastructure, is a sunk cost of little importance. Geographic, or better, spatial advantages and place-dependent business networks are primary sources of the value of land zoned for industrial or commercial use. The value of land, however, can be discounted because of obsolete buildings. That is, if the land were vacant it could be worth more than the land plus obsolete building because of the demolition cost. A city is a snapshot of thousands of decisions about producing fixed capital, mostly structures, on that land spread over 100 years or more. Presumably they were economically rational choices for that parcel at that time. Market prices for land and improvements reflect present and expected future net income streams. If the expected rate of return from some replacement building on that site exceeds that of the present building after factoring in demolition or conversion costs, then the present building will be demolished or converted. But if there is no alternative use that would yield a higher return than the present use, and the present use is anticipated to yield diminishing future net income, then the present value, the price of the property, will be depressed. There is not a brisk market for such properties. Thus a negative shock to an urban economy that destroys and damages significant amounts of real property will have a permanent adverse effect if the expected return to capital there before the shock does not justify replacing or repairing what was lost. It is in the face of widespread destruction that replacement cost suddenly becomes central.

I now offer three cases of negative urban shocks: the Elmira, New York, flood of 1972 brought on by Hurricane Agnes, the devastation of Homestead, Florida, by Hurricane Andrew in 1992, and the massive flooding of New Orleans precipitated by Hurricane Katrina in 2005.

Elmira

The city of Elmira, New York, with a population of 31 000, is the central city of the Elmira MSA (Chemung County). The city has an area of grand old Victorian houses built in the early years of the twentieth century. According to a colleague in the Cornell University real estate program, a contractor of his acquaintance purchased one of those Elmira mansions for a pittance. He removed the paneling, sliding doors, leaded glass windows, chandeliers and stained glass, and sold them at a second-hand construction material warehouse outside of New York City for a profit.

In 1972, Hurricane Agnes brought double-digit inches of rain to the Elmira area. The Chemung River overflowed its banks, and downtown Elmira was in several feet of water. The city has never recovered. Many of the downtown stores were never reopened. Driving through downtown

Elmira one is reminded of a ghost town. The only new buildings one sees are health-related facilities, which are directly and indirectly financed by the massive inflows of public and private health expenditures. Of course many small cities in the US have experienced slow decline over the past 30 years or so as population and retail establishments have shifted to suburban locations. But Elmira's decline was not stretched over decades; it was sudden and unexpected. As argued above, the fact that the city of Elmira has not recovered is not due to the disaster itself but rather to the sluggish performance of the larger metropolitan economy, signs of which were evident long before the flood. Measuring from cyclical peaks, from 1956 to 1969, national employment rose 2.3 percent per year while employment in the Elmira MSA grew only 0.6 percent per year (Bureau of Labor Statistics (BLS), 2005).

The year of the flood, 1972, the metropolitan population was 102 000. By 2003 it was down to 90 000. Real per capita personal income was 95 percent of the US average in 1969, and since then its relative position has deteriorated, dropping to 77 percent in 2003. The real annual wage was above the US average by 10 percent in 1969, reflecting Elmira's historical specialization in manufacturing. That too has trended down, and in 2003 was 91 percent of the US average. Real income per proprietor, a crude measure of entrepreneurial performance, has dropped from 85 percent of the US average in 1969 to 37 percent in 2003. The one relative measure that has been trending up since the flood is real transfer payments per capita, a measure of dependency. It rose from 117 percent of the US average in 1972 to 132 percent in 2003. The employment to population ratio, a measure of labor utilization, was about the same as the national average in 1969, but since then it has declined (Bureau of Economic Analysis, REIS, 2005). The current picture for the city of Elmira from the 2000 census is even more grim.

Like many small cities away from the coasts, Elmira is predominantly white – 82 percent. Less than 15 percent of the adults have bachelor's degrees or higher. The national figure is 24 percent. Disability status among the population aged 21 to 64 is 26 percent, far above the national average of 19 percent. Labor force participation is 55 percent, considerably below the national average of 64 percent. When people believe that there are no jobs to be had or worth taking, they opt out of the labor force. Median household income is only 65 percent of the US average. As argued above, the value of real property conveys information about present and expected future income. That is true of residential property as well as commercial and industrial property. It appears that expectations in Elmira are low. The median value of single-family owner-occupied homes is $52 000, only 43 percent of the US average (Census Bureau, 2005).

The 1972 flood did not cause the depressed city of today. The failure to recover from the flood was caused by a stagnant metropolitan economy, which was evident before the flood and became worse over time.

Homestead

In 1992 the unusually powerful Hurricane Andrew made a direct hit on the small city of Homestead, Florida, in Dade County south of Miami. Much of the housing was destroyed, including trailers that represented a large part of the housing stock. The Homestead Air Force Base, the largest employer in the area, was completely destroyed and never reopened. According to the Mayor, the base had pumped $400 million annually into the local economy. Although the negative shock caused by the hurricane was far worse than what the flood caused in Elmira, Homestead appears to be rebounding. From 1990 to 2000, the population increased 19 percent or 1.7 percent annually, much faster than US population growth in that period.

Social and economic characteristics of Homestead, before (1990) and after the hurricane (2000), indicate that the effects of the shock were temporary. The population changed markedly in those ten years of rapid increase. The proportion of the elderly dropped from 11 percent to 8 percent, while the Hispanic population rose from 35 percent to 52 percent. Homestead was a very poor city in 1990 and continued to be so in 2000. Median household income was flat at under $30 000 in both years, compared with $46 000 for the nation in 2000. The poverty population was 30 percent of the total in 1990 and 32 percent in 2000. Although much poorer than Elmira, and with lower educational attainment (only 10 percent of adults in Homestead had a bachelor's degree or higher) the labor force participation rate was close to the US average in 2000. Given the large population increase and the massive destruction of housing, it is not surprising that the percentage of vacant housing units dropped from 13.5 percent to 9.6 percent. The median house value in 2000 was $88 000, 74 percent of the national average and much higher than in Elmira.

Although Homestead is much poorer, with lower educational attainment, and over one-half minority Hispanic, its population growth and high labor force participation suggests a stronger economy than Elmira. Homestead is part of the vibrant Miami metropolitan economy, and that is why it has recovered.

New Orleans

The media coverage of Hurricane Katrina focused upon the dramatic physical impacts: sudden death, human suffering, damage to the built environment and public disorder. Officials counted the dead, the injured, the evacuees, and are still estimating the cost for repairing buildings, and restoring water, sewer, road and electricity systems. What is absent from their calculations is not so tragic but quite substantial, namely the long-run economic impact. The question is, will New Orleans recover? The signs are not good, because the economy had been weak long before Katrina hit the city.

In the two decades following 1970, most large central cities of the United States lost population, including New Orleans. That pattern was reversed from 1990 to 2000 when most large central cities gained population, but New Orleans continued to decline (Drennan, 2002). From 2000 to 2004 it fell 4.6 percent, when New York City's population rose 1.2 percent. One sign of a vibrant city economy is the attraction of foreign immigrants. Net foreign immigration to New York city was 378 000 from 2000 to 2004, almost 5 percent of the city's population. The comparable figure was 3000 for New Orleans, only 0.6 percent of that city's population. The foreign-born share of New Orleans's residents is 5 percent, while New York City's share is 35 percent. New Orleans is a predominantly minority city (68 percent African-American) with a poverty rate ten percentage points above the national average, and median household income that is only 75 percent of the US average. The population decline noted above is mirrored in the pre-Katrina housing vacancy rate of 15 percent compared with 10 percent for the nation. Although the data suggests a city in decline, there are signs that before Katrina New Orleans had a much stronger economy than Elmira. Labor force participation of 63 percent was close to the national average of 66 percent. Median house value was almost 90 percent of the national median (Census Bureau, 2005).

Industries tied to oil, natural gas and petrochemicals are the strong specializations of the metropolitan economy, but only one-third of their earnings originate in the city. Much larger in the city is tourism – arts, entertainment and accommodations – which accounts for 8 percent of city earnings (Bureau of Economic Analysis, REIS, 2005). To put that share in perspective, it is double Manhattan's share of earnings from tourism. The city of New Orleans is more dependent upon tourism than it is upon energy and petrochemicals. The opposite is true for the remainder of the metropolitan area. With the exception of hotel chains, the tourism complex is probably dominated by many small firms lacking the resources and the access to credit typical of energy and petrochemical firms. Thus tourism might be depressed for a much longer period than energy and petrochemicals.

CONCLUSION

Agglomeration economies are apparently difficult to destroy. Although they have specific spatial domains, they are not physical but rather networks linking organizations and firms. Destruction of the World Trade Center and buildings nearby did not destroy the spatial advantages and the business networks linking downtown firms with each other, with midtown, the region and the world. That must be so because firms that had occupied half the destroyed space of all large tenants chose to relocate elsewhere downtown despite the fact that they could have paid much lower rents by relocating across the river in urban New Jersey.

But spatial advantages and place-specific business networks, agglomeration economies, can erode and even vanish because of changes in technology and shifts in national and international demand. In that sense they are fragile. The story of Elmira shows that a negative shock to a stagnant economy can have a permanent effect. The slow decline of New Orleans over the 25 years before Katrina may mean that the adverse economic effect of the flooding will be permanent.

REFERENCES

Au, C. and J.V. Henderson (2002), 'How Migration Restrictions Limit Agglomeration and Productivity in China', Working Paper No. w8707, NBER.

Bureau of Economic Analysis, Regional Economic Information System (REIS) (2005), website: (http://bea.gov/regional/reis/).

Bureau of Labor Statistics (BLS) (2005), 'Current Employment Statistics, Nonagricultural Establishment Employments, BLS website.

Census Bureau (2005), 'American Fact Finder', Census website: (http://census.gov/).

Davis, D.R. and D.E. Weinstein (2002), 'Bones, Bombs, and Breakpoints: The Geography of Economic Activity', *American Economic Review*, 92(5): 1269–89.

Drennan, M.P. (1991), 'The Decline and Rise of the New York Economy', in J.H. Mollenkopf and M. Castells (eds), *Dual City*, New York: Russell Sage Foundation, pp. 25–41.

Drennan, M.P. (2002), *The Information Economy and American Cities*, Baltimore, MD: Johns Hopkins University Press.

Fujita, M., P. Krugman and A.J. Venables (2001), *The Spatial Economy*. Cambridge, MA: MIT Press.

Glaeser, E. and J. Shapiro (2002), 'Cities and Warfare: The Impact of Terrorism On Urban Form', *Journal of Urban Economics*, 51: 205–24.

Harrigan, J. and P. Martin (2002), 'Terrorism and the Resilience of Cities', *Economic Policy Review*, Federal Reserve Board of New York, November, pp. 97–116.

Heschmeyer, M. (2001), 'Attack Magnified Existing NYC Office Trends', CoStar Group, 16 October, www.costargroup.com

Kelly, H.F. (2002), 'The New York Regional and Downtown Office Market: History and Prospects after 9/11', Report prepared for the Civic Alliance.

Mitchell, W.J. and A.M. Townsend (2005), 'Cyborg Agonistes: Disaster and Reconstruction in the Digital Electronic Era', in L.J. Vale and T.J. Campanella (eds), *The Resilient City*, Oxford: Oxford University Press.

New York City, Office of Management and Budget (2005), 'Monthly Report on Current Economic Conditions', 7 July.

New York State, Office of the State Comptroller (2004), 'The Impact of Wall Street on Jobs and Tax Revenues', Report 1-2005.

Vale, L.J. and T.J. Campanella (eds) (2005), *The Resilient City*, Oxford: Oxford University Press.

10. Analyzing catastrophic terrorist events with applications to the food industry*

Hamid Mohtadi and Antu Panini Murshid

'Forget the past: it's a war unlike any other', read one headline in the days immediately following the worst terrorist event in recent history.[1] The subject of John Kifner's column in the *New York Times* was Afghanistan; however, it could just as well have referred to the wider war on terror for it is an apt description of how 9/11 marks a watershed in the way many of us view the terrorist threat. It is rarely a good idea to ignore lessons from past experience, though in the aftermath of great tragedy rationality recedes and emotion-laden themes pervade much of our thinking. But was it all emotion?

The attack on the World Trade Center was unique in its ferocity. In isolation this event redefined the boundaries separating the realm of the 'possible' from the 'unthinkable'. To many, 9/11 broke from earlier forms of terrorism. It challenged old ways of thinking and called for fresher perspectives with new assumptions. Much of the discussion on the terrorist threat has embraced this approach. Thus attention has centered on what terrorists could do, rather than what they have done in the past, as a model for what they are likely to do in the future.[2]

Risk is therefore assessed on the basis of vulnerability. Accordingly the food sector has received considerable attention, since many concede that it is not only vulnerable to a chemical or biological attack, but that such an attack also offers the potential to inflict mass casualties. Yet, the fact remains that the food supply chain has not been a favorite target for terrorists, and unless one believes that a new strain of terror has evolved from a fresh paradigm disjointed from its past, it is difficult to ignore the failure of terrorists, thus far, systematically to target the food supply chain. As such it may be premature to equate vulnerability with risk, and doing so may lead to surprise when the pattern of terrorist activities plays out:

> I, for the life of me, cannot understand why the terrorists have not, you know, attacked our food supply, because it is so easy to do.[3]

So if vulnerability does not necessarily correlate with the pattern of terrorist attacks, what is the threat to the supply chain? Is it real or is this all merely speculation? To our knowledge, this simple, yet important, question has yet to be answered. This chapter takes a step toward this goal. We examine the risk of a catastrophic terrorist attack using chemical, biological or radionuclear (CBRN) materials. This focus reflects the goal of this research, which is to provide insights into the terrorist threat to the food sector. While the food supply chain can be attacked in a number of different ways, our focus on CBRN materials is warranted since their deliberate introduction into the civilian population is biased toward targeting the food sector's infrastructure, which provides reach over a wide region.

Assessing the risk of a major CBRN event is complicated by our limited experience with such events as well as by the quality of the data; the largest open-source dataset on terrorist activities (maintained by Pinkerton Corporation's Global Intelligence Services) records only 41 incidents involving weapons of mass destruction (LaFree et al., 2004). Clearly it is difficult to make any accurate statistical predictions from these data. Overcoming the paucity of these data however presents a significant challenge, as it becomes necessary to mine primary sources such as newspaper articles and Internet postings, in addition to an earlier literature on terrorism. Nevertheless in doing so we were able to compile a new, more comprehensive dataset on CBRN incidents composed of over 300 observations. Although the number of data points is still small, the process of extending these data is ongoing, and we expect to add several hundred more incidents to these data over time.

In addition to these quite severe data problems, assessing catastrophic risks poses conceptual problems since it entails extrapolating from observed levels in the data to unobserved levels. Classical statistical models are not well suited for this task; since emphasis falls on the modal behavior of the underlying stochastic process, the tails of the distribution are estimated imprecisely. But within the current context, of extreme risks, it is important to estimate these tails accurately. Fortunately, a statistical method known as extreme value theory (EVT) provides a framework for doing precisely that. EVT is therefore well suited for answering the types of questions that we are interested in.

Thus our contributions to this research are twofold. First, and most importantly, we develop a comprehensive data-set of CBRN incidents. Second, we apply a relatively novel statistical method to estimate the probability of terrorist activities involving CBRN weapons. Although extreme value analysis is well known to statisticians, to our knowledge this approach has not been utilized to assess the risk of catastrophic terrorist events.

The remainder of our chapter is organized as follows. First we describe our data in detail. Then we briefly discuss underlying patterns in terrorist activities, particularly those involving the use of CBRN material. We stress in particular the pattern of attacks on the food supply chain. Next, we outline our statistical methodology. We provide statistical evidence on the likelihood of a catastrophic event that involves the use of CBRN material and compare these results to the underlying pattern in the severity of terrorist attacks in general. Finally, we offer some conclusions. A separate data appendix, available from the authors, provides a case-by-case description of incidents in our data-set.

DATA

There are several existing databases that describe the incidence of terrorist activity. Perhaps the most well-known of these is the International Terrorism: Attributes of Terrorist Events (ITERATE) database. These data were originally compiled by Mickolus (1982) and spanned a period from 1968 to 1977. They were later extended to 2002 by Mickolus et al. (1989, 1993) and Mickolus and Fleming (2003). Included in these data are the date of attack, the type of event, the number of casualties (deaths or injuries), as well as various other characteristics of incidents; importantly however, only transnational terrorist events are considered. ITERATE defines an event as transnational along several criteria. These include the nationalities of the perpetrators, the location of the attack and the nature of the target (Mickolus et al., 1989).

A much more comprehensive database is maintained by Pinkerton Global Intelligence Services. These data are composed of roughly 74 000 terrorist events spanning a period from 1970 to 1997. While these data were compiled by Pinkerton Corporation's Global Intelligence Service (PGIS), they were coded through the efforts of Laura Dugan and Gary LaFree at the University of Maryland. The PGIS data-set is undoubtedly the most comprehensive source of terrorist event data compiled from open sources. It includes political, religious and economic acts of terrorism, and unlike ITERATE, PGIS data record instances of both domestic and international terrorism. However to our knowledge these data are still not publicly available.

Recently the Center for Nonproliferation Studies (CNS) at the Monterey Institute for International Studies has compiled a chronology of incidents involving the use of chemical, biological, radiological and nuclear agents dating back to 1900. Their Weapons of Mass Destruction database is perhaps one of the most comprehensive sources of data on such events. It is composed of approximately 1200 incidents relating to CBRN material. However, much of these data are comprised of hundreds of hoaxes and pranks and other events that do not necessarily relate to possession with intent or actual use. In addition, the Weapons of Mass Destruction database is unfortunately not in the public domain. Access is normally restricted to those with military or government IDs, except for a few years' worth of data which are reviewed in various studies by CNS staff (Cameron et al., 2000; Pate and Cameron, 2001; Pate et al., 2001; Turnbull and Abhayaratne, 2003).[4]

Another impressive source of data is the Terrorism Knowledge Base which is maintained at the National Memorial Institute for the Prevention of Terrorism (MIPT). These data begin in 1968 and continue to the present. Moreover the MIPT database is updated regularly; thus it is inclusive of the very latest incidents. Unlike ITERATE data these data include incidents of domestic as well as transnational terrorism. However prior to 1998, the MIPT data are less complete in this respect. While the data are in the public domain, full or partial versions of the data-set are not released to the public. Instead each recorded incident is posted on a separate webpage. Thus we were able to compile a data-set by visiting each of these (21 000 plus) webpages and recording the main characteristics of each event. Our data span a 38-year period from 1 January 1968 to 11 March 2005. Over this period, the MIPT Terrorism Knowledge Base records 21 095 incidents of terrorism that resulted in 27 573 fatalities and 70 434 injuries.

Despite the very large number of recorded terrorist incidents, very few of these have involved the use of nuclear, biological or chemical weapons. From the data we were able to compile from MIPT 56 incidents involved the use of biological or chemical agents. LaFree et al. (2004) conduct their analysis using the PGIS database. They record only 41 incidents that involved the use of nuclear, biological or chemical agents, or sophisticated explosives intended to inflict mass casualties. Clearly, we have rather limited experience with such forms of terrorism. However, there is a perception that terrorism involving the use of chemical, biological, radioactive or nuclear materials often goes unreported, either because of ignorance on the part of authorities or because of their attempts to suppress evidence (Douglass and Livingstone, 1987). Even when an incident is reported, depending on how we define 'terrorism', it may not be coded as such, or an incident may simply be missed. Thus for instance, the large-scale poisoning in 1984 by the Rajneeshee cult is not recorded in the MIPT database.

Given the scarcity of these data, we embarked on our own data collection effort. Our data-set comprises 314 incidents that have either involved the direct use of nuclear, biological or chemical agents, or that have implied a threat to their containment, by a group or individual. We compile these data by painstakingly gathering specific information about each event from various sources. These include databases such as the Terrorism Knowledge

Base as well as reviews of recent terrorist incidents that were culled from the Weapons of Mass Destruction database (Cameron et al., 2000; Pate et al., 2001; Turnbull and Abhayaratne, 2003) as well as the open literature, including fairly comprehensive sources of data on the use of chemical, biological or radiological weapons such as Jenkins and Rubin (1978), Livingstone and Arnold (1986), Douglass and Livingstone (1987), Hirsch (1987), Mullen (1987), Thornton (1987), Kellen (1987), Leventhal and Alexander (1987), Kupperman and Woolsey (1988), Kupperman and Kamen (1989), Mullins (1992), Purver (1995), Tucker (2000), Miller et al. (2001), Carus (2002) and Mize (2004). In addition, we consulted numerous newspapers and hundreds of websites. While our chronology currently includes 314 incidents, we expect this figure to increase significantly as more events that have yet to be cross-checked are added to these data.

Our chronology provides a general description of each incident, along with details on the type of agent employed and the number of casualties that resulted. The data cover a 45-year period from 1961 to 2005. Unlike the Monterey Institute's Weapons of Mass Destruction database, we focus only on those incidents that involved the use or possession of CBRN materials; we exclude all hoaxes. In addition, we include a number of attacks that involved a threat to containment of CBRN material. These include acts of sabotage, such as those at the SL-1 US Army reactor in Idaho Falls in 1961 reported in *Atomic Energy Insights*, 2(4), 1996 which led to three deaths. Also included are direct acts of violence committed on facilities containing nuclear, biological and/or chemical material, such as the attack on the nuclear facility near Lyon, France, when five stolen French army rockets were fired at the reactor (*West Australian*, 20 January 1982).

In our analysis of the use of CBRN weapons, we do not make a distinction between terrorism and criminal activity. First, because the nature of these materials is such that whatever the underlying motivation behind their use, these weapons have the potential to do significant harm, or create an atmosphere of fear and panic. Thus for instance, on 14 September 2002, when Chen Zhengping tainted his competitor's water supply and pastry dough with rat poison, the underlying motive may have been purely financial, but the incident caused 41 deaths and over 400 cases of hospitalization.[5] Similarly the Tylenol murders in 1982, which though not linked to terrorist activity, nevertheless created an atmosphere of alarm and panic. The second and critical reason why the distinction between criminal and terrorist activity may not be warranted is the fact that the use of biological, chemical or nuclear substances, even when they indicate acts of petty crimes such as the use of HIV-infected blood, betrays an increasing acceptance amongst the criminally inclined to resort to the use of previously exotic weaponry.

TRENDS IN TERRORISM

General Trends

According to MIPT's Terrorism Knowledge Base, the frequency of terrorist attacks has steadily increased since 1968. Furthermore, there has been an increase in the severity of terrorist attacks since the early 1990s. Thus, as we see in Table 10.1, almost all of the incidents where the number of people killed or injured exceeded 1000 occurred over the period from 1993 to 2004. This increasingly deadly pattern in the evolution of terrorism is clearly evident in Figure 10.1, which plots the logarithm of the maximum number of casualties (both fatalities and injuries) on any given day resulting from terrorist attacks. It is important to recognize that this trend is unlikely to be spurious. While the increasing frequency of terrorist incidents could merely reflect improved data collection efforts and better reporting in the media, this point cannot generally be made when we focus on a subset of data comprised of the worst terrorist events in a year. The argument here is that an attack of the same magnitude as that on the Tokyo subway system should generally not go unnoticed or unrecorded. Thus the inference that we are entering an increasingly deadly phase in the evolution of terrorism is not without merit.

Trends in the Food Chain

Equally disconcerting are the trends that we observe with respect to the choice of weaponry, targets and tactics. In recent years terrorists have focused more of their efforts on 'softer' targets. This switch simply reflects terrorism's best response to increased efforts to police against well-established threats. The diversification of targets has been a gradual effort on the part of terrorist organizations. In 1968 approximately three out of four terrorist attacks were aimed either at airlines, or at diplomatic, government and military targets. This concentration on 'high-profile' targets has diminished steadily. Now only one-quarter of terrorist attacks are aimed at airlines or government and military facilities. By contrast attacks on private citizens or private property have increased dramatically in the last few years (Figure 10.2).

To the extent that the food supply chain constitutes a softer target, the same trend is observed here as well. Thus, attacks on the food industry, for instance, have shown a dramatic rise since the 1960s, when there were no recorded attacks (Figure 10.3).

Most experts concede that the food chain, from production to processing and distribution, is highly exposed. In 1984 for instance, the

Table 10.1   Major terrorist events between 1968 and 2005

Date	Incident	Fatalities	Injuries
9/3/2004	A group of 35 Chechen separatists seized a school in the Southern Russian town of Beslan taking children, parents, and teachers hostage in the school gym. In the aftermath of the attack, the official death toll reached 338 although unofficial figures were higher. At least 727 people remained hospitalized, some in grave condition. The total number of hostages is believed to have been around 1200.	338	727
11/9/2001	Attack on the World Trade Center and the Pentagon, and the hijacking of United Airlines Flight 93.	2982	unknown
7/8/1998	A car-bomb exploded outside the US Embassy in Nairobi, Kenya.	291	5000
31/1/1996	The Tamil Tigers drove a massive truck-bomb into the Central Bank building in Colombo. The vehicle exploded, killing 96 people and injuring over 1400, amongst whom were 32 foreigners, including two US citizens, six Japanese and one Dutch national.	96	1400
20/3/1995	The Japanese extreme sect Aum Shinrikyo (Sublime/Supreme Truth), released sarin gas on the Tokyo subway resulting in 12 fatalities and thousands of injuries.	12	5000
12/3/1993	13 bombs exploded in Bombay within the space of three hours. At least 317 people died and 1200 were injured.	317	1200
26/2/1993	A bomb exploded in the parking garage of the World Trade Center in Manhattan, killing 6 and injuring 1042.	6	1042
10/4/1988	An attack on a weapons dump in Islamabad claimed the lives of over 100 people and caused over 1100 injuries.	100	1100

Source: MIPT, Terrorism Knowledge Base.

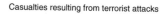

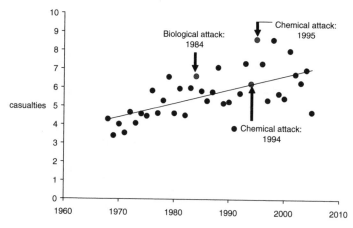

Casualties resulting from terrorist attacks

Notes: Casualties – the sum of fatalities and injuries – are measured in logs.

Source: MIPT, Terrorism Knowledge Base, and sources cited by the authors.

Figure 10.1 *An increasingly deadly trend in the evolution of terrorism*

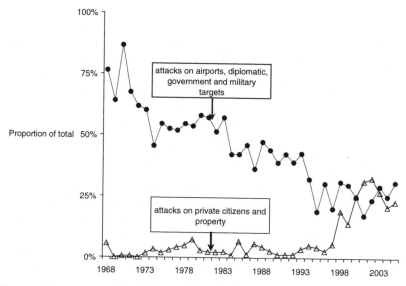

Source: MIPT, Terrorism Knowledge Base.

Figure 10.2 *Terrorist targets, 1968–2005*

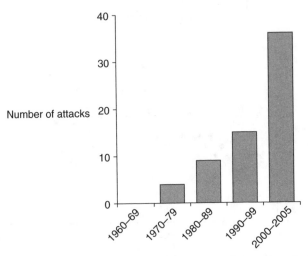

Sources: Based on authors' chronology of CBRN events and the sources cited by the authors.

Figure 10.3   Frequency of attacks on food or water supply

Rajneeshees – an Oregon-based cult – contaminated food at ten restaurants with *Salmonella typhimurium* causing 751 cases of illness (Carus, 2002). Court testimony suggests that cult members considered other more deadly pathogens including *Salmonella typhi* (which causes typhoid) and the AIDS virus (Carus, 2002). Since then there have been several serious attacks on the food chain (Table 10.2), many occurring in China where disputes have been settled through the use of Dushuqiang, a strong rat poison that has been banned since 1984. The most serious such attack occurred, as mentioned, in 2002 on a fast-food restaurant that led to 41 deaths and over 400 illnesses. In the US, the most serious attack on the food chain since the Rajneeshee incident occurred at the Family Fare supermarket in which Randy Bertram poisoned about 250 pounds of ground beef causing at least 111 cases of illness.

Yet importantly, while these cases of mass food-poisoning have led to large numbers of people becoming ill, in comparison to the September 11 attack, or any one of the major terrorist events in the last decade, the death toll has been relatively low. Thus the emphasis has often fallen on the potential economic costs of bio- or chemical terrorism, particularly the threat to agriculture. Pathogens affecting livestock such as foot-and-mouth disease (FMD) and Bovine Spongiform Encephalopathy (BSE) can cripple agriculture and cause widespread disruption to the food supply chain as recent events in the UK illustrate. Indeed an attack of this

Table 10.2 *The most serious attacks on the food chain: 1961–2005*

Date	Fatalities	Injuries	Incident
19/11/2003	0	50	About 50 people in more than 20 cities in Italy had to be treated for a variety of ailments including stomach pains, after they drank bottled water that had been injected with either bleach acetone or ammonia.
1/10/2003	0	64	Cao Qianjin threw 500 ml of a pesticide into the reservoir in Ruyang County, Henan. Province, China. Approximately 64 residents were poisoned.
23/9/2003	0	241	Several hundred (317) students and staff at an elementary school in Yueyang, Hunan Province, China, were sent to hospitals, after eating breakfast that had been laced with rat poison. Investigators stated that 241 students and staff showed some signs of poisoning.
31/12/2002	0	111	A supermarket employee in the US poisoned about 250 pounds of ground beef with an insecticide. At least 111 people fell ill after eating the meat.
June, 2002	0	60	In June 60 students and teachers at a school in Volgograd, Russia, were hospitalized after being poisoned with the salmonella typhi toxin.
19/5/2002	7	47	Seven members of the Johanne Marange Apostolic Church, a Christian fundamentalist group, died and another 47 were taken ill after drinking a tea that had been poisoned.
30/1/2002	Unknown	92	In Linxiang city, in China's Hunan Province, 92 children at the Yucai Private (primary) School fell ill after eating their school lunch which had been laced with rat poison. Of the 92, 40 were in serious condition.
8/8/2001	0	120	At least 120 patrons in 16 restaurants were made ill after eating noodles that had been contaminated with rat poison in Ningxiang, Hunan Province, China.
8/3/2000	2	60	Poisoned food was served to hundreds of students at a religious school in Jalaludin, Afghanistan. Two students died and 60 others lost consciousness.

Table 10.2   (continued)

Date	Fatalities	Injuries	Incident
3/11/1999	Unknown	48	Approximately 48 people fell ill after eating meat rolls that had been laced with rat poison at a fast-food restaurant in Deyang City, Sichuan Province, China.
8/3/1999	0	148	Five people were arrested in China, after putting nitric acid in a popular restaurant's specialty donkey meat soup, poisoning 148 people.
25/7/1998	4	60	Four people died and approximately 60 were hospitalized during a summer festival in Wakayama, Japan, in a case of mass food poisoning that possibly involved the use of cyanide.
1/1/1994	15	53	On New Year's day nine Russian soldiers and at least six civilians died after drinking champagne that had been laced with cyanide. The cyanide-laced champagne was being sold outside of the Russian compounds. Another 53 people, including 11 civilians, were hospitalized.
6/9/1987	19	140	Several fatalities resulted when members of the Philippine Constabulary were poisoned after accepting bags of iced water from an individual during a 'fun run'. As a result 19 people died and 140 fell ill.
Sep. 1984	0	751	Sometime early in September 1984, members of a religious cult known as the Rajneeshees contaminated salad dressing at ten restaurants in a small town in Oregon, USA. As a result 751 people became sick; there were no fatalities.

Sources: Based on authors' chronology of CBRN events and sources cited by the authors.

nature is not without precedent. In 1997, over 8 million pigs had to be slaughtered in Taiwan after the presence of FMD was confirmed in pigs. It is suspected that the disease was introduced deliberately. In that same year, rabbit hemorrhagic disease (RHD) was introduced into the rabbit population in New Zealand (Carus, 2002). As recently as 10 May 2005, a letter delivered to Prime Minister Helen Clark claimed that a vial of foot-and-mouth disease was released into the animal population in a farming community near Auckland, New Zealand.[6]

Chemical, Biological and Radionuclear Agents

While there have been attacks on our food and water supply that have involved the use of conventional weapons, there is no particular reason why terrorists should favor the food supply chain over other potential targets when using such conventional means of attack. The real threat as far as the food chain is concerned is likely to come from chemical, biological or radionuclear contaminants which can exploit an already present distribution network to maximize the potential for disruption. Of the 314 biological, chemical and radiological incidents that we recorded, 64 involved either a direct attack on, or a plan to attack, the food or water supply chains.[7] The majority of these attacks (50 altogether) involved the use of chemicals, eight attacks were carried out using biological agents and one suspected incident involved the release of plutonium into New York City's water reservoirs. In the remaining attacks the type of agent is unknown.

The use of biological weapons dates back to 700 BC, when the Assyrians employed rye ergot, an element of the fungus *Claviceps purpurea*, to poison the wells of their enemies (Eitzen and Takafuji, 1997; Phillips, 2005). Similarly ancient are the origins of chemical warfare, which date back to the fifth century BC during one of a series of wars between Athens and Sparta (Fries and West, 1921). Since then their effectiveness as a weapon has significantly improved. Improvements in technology have made these weapons much more accessible, leading to an increase in the frequency of their use in criminal and terrorist activity. Similar trends have also been observed in the use of radionuclear material (Figure 10.4).

That said, the incorporation of such weapons into the terrorist arsenal has been slow. While many groups are believed to possess limited stockpiles of dangerous chemicals or pathogens, or even radionuclear materials, their ability to deliver these agents effectively is questionable. Thus, for instance, the sarin attack on the Tokyo subway in 1995 was the culmination of several years of effort and trial and error by Aum Shinrikyo to perfect a weapon of mass destruction. During this time Aum experimented many times with the botulinum toxin and even considered the use of the Ebola virus. Earlier attempts in 1990 and 1993 to release the aerosolized variant of the botulinum toxin failed. Evidently the transition from conventional weapons to chemical, biological, radiological or even nuclear agents is not without costs. This could explain some of the

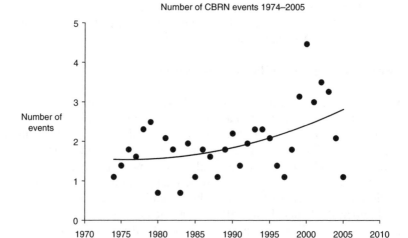

Notes: The number of events is actually the logarithm of (1+number of events).

Source: Based on authors' chronology of CBRN events.

Figure 10.4   Frequency of attacks using CBRN agents

inertia of terrorist organizations. Nevertheless, gradually the terrorist arsenal is expanding. Eventually the possibility exists that weaponized versions of these materials will be delivered against civilian populations. Aum Shinrikyo's attack on the Tokyo subway system is one example of this trend. Between 1960 and 2005 the number of casualties resulting from the deadliest attacks involving CBRN agents has gradually increased (Figure 10.5).

It is difficult to predict whether a continuation of these trends is likely or not. This will depend largely on the validity of the assumptions we make about terrorists' inclinations toward these new technologies and their ability to invest in the transition to weaponized forms of hazardous agents. It will also depend on the success of future efforts to tighten up controls on the distribution of such material. Nevertheless the pattern over the last four decades is clear.

METHODOLOGY

As with all statistical analyses, extreme value analysis makes the axiomatic assumption that we are dealing with random events. Thus, before we embark

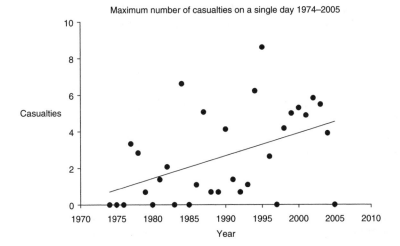

Notes: 'Casualties', which refer to both fatalities and injuries, are shown on a logarithmic scale. (The transformation log (1+casualties) was taken.)

Source: Based on authors' chronology of CBRN events.

Figure 10.5 Increasing number of casualties resulting from CBRN agents

on the description of our statistical methodology, we might ask whether or not terrorism is indeed a random event that would render itself to statistical analysis. There are at least three reasons why terrorism can be viewed as a stochastic or random event. First, even though some might view terrorism as an intentional, deterministic act to the individual terrorist, this view misunderstands the statistical concept of 'randomness' from a macro perspective. This stems from an inherent asymmetry of information between a terrorist on the one hand and the citizens, security forces and the government on the other. Thus while Mohammad Sidique Khan, one of four London bombers, may have known for sure that he was going to explode a bomb on the London Underground on 7 July 2005 from the perspectives of governments and the citizens, this is a stochastic event. The argument is analogous to the distinction between crime statistics and explaining criminal behavior.

Secondly, the effort to counter terrorism may succeed X fraction of the time and fail $1 - X$ fraction of the time. In this way a successful terrorist attack is the manifestation of a random 'system failure' in the sense of the operations risk literature. For example, the counter-terrorist activities in Europe over the past several years succeeded in disrupting numerous terrorist plots (PBS Frontline TV program, July 2005), but failed in the instances of Madrid and London. However, even from the perspective of the London terrorists, it was still not clear what the final outcome would be. It could have happened for instance that the bomb would fail to explode. Indeed, two weeks after the first multiple bombing of London's transportation system, four more suicide bombers attempted to replicate the events of 7 July 2005 and failed.

Finally, even when a terrorist successfully carries out his attack, the severity of the attack is clearly random. Why is it that 27 people died on the train between Russell Square and Kings Cross, but far fewer, seven people, died on the Edgware Road bombing? Ultimately there may be little that separates a catastrophic terrorist event from a minor act of terrorism, other than the final outcomes. The severity of terrorist incidents should therefore be viewed as random draws from some underlying stochastic data-generating process. This is precisely the approach that we adopt here. The approach towards quantifying the risk of terrorism in this probabilistic way is indeed quite consistent with the new direction of the Department of Homeland Security.[8]

Estimates of the probability of an event using traditional statistical methods strive for accuracy in the description of the modal-behavior of the underlying data-generating process. Such methods are apt for making inferences over regions where the bulk of the data lie. However they are ill-suited for the estimation of extreme quantiles. While knowledge of the underlying cumulative distribution function would make this a non-issue, such happy circumstances are rarely encountered in practice. When the underlying distribution is unknown, as is more often the case, small discrepancies in its estimation over the main body of the distribution can yield widely varying tail behavior.

Extreme value theory (EVT) is unusual in that it develops methods for accurately estimating the tails of distributions. At the heart of extreme value theory is the 'extremal types theorem', which states that if the maxima of sequences of observations converge to a non-degenerate law, then it must belong to one of three classes of distributions: (1) Gumbel distributions (light-tails); (2) Fréchet distributions (heavy-tails); or (3) Weibull distributions (bounded tails).[9] Through an appropriate re-parameterization of these three families of distributions, a unified representation, known as the generalized extreme value (GEV) distribution can be obtained. The GEV representation is particularly useful, since it bypasses the need to identify the type of distribution to which the extreme value limit law belongs. Instead standard statistical methodology from parametric estimation can be applied to identify the parameters of interest.

CATASTROPHIC TERRORIST EVENTS: HOW OFTEN AND HOW BAD?

In this section, we apply the above methods to estimate the likelihood of a catastrophic event that involves the use of CBRN agents. These results are then compared with trends in more conventional forms of terrorism. The severity of an attack is measured in terms of the number of fatalities or injuries it causes.

CBRN Terrorism

The variation in our CBRN data-set is rather limited. The overwhelming majority of attacks failed to cause death or injury. Nevertheless there is some structure in the tails of the distribution (Figures 10.6a and 10.6b). This coincides with the sarin attacks in Tokyo and Matsumoto, as well as a handful of other cases. To maximize the variation in our data-set, we model severity in terms of the total number of casualties, that is, the sum of injuries and fatalities. Ideally we would like to consider fatalities and injuries separately. However the number of deaths resulting from CBRN attacks is relatively low. This is clearly evident in Figure 10.6b: the tails of the distribution function underlying the severity of terrorist attacks shows much more structure along the axis measuring the number of injuries than fatalities. Thus it appears that chemical, biological and nuclear attacks have led to far more injury than death. The deadly sarin attack in Tokyo for instance claimed 12 lives, but injured over 5000. The largest number of

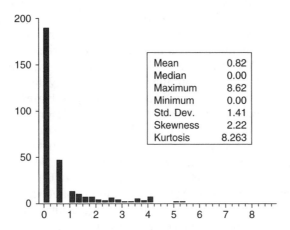

Figure 10.6a   Frequency distribution of casualties from CBRN attacks

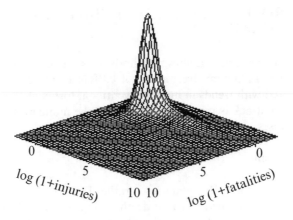

Notes: Injuries, fatalities and the total number of casualties are shown on a logarithmic scale. (The transformation log (1+casualties) was taken.)

Source: Based on authors' chronology of CBRN events.

Figure 10.6b   Frequency distribution, injuries, fatalities, from CBRN attacks

fatalities resulting from the use of CBRN agents (sulfuric acid) occurred in Uganda, when the cult Restoration of the Ten Commandments of God is suspected of poisoning its members. The total number of deaths in this poisoning attack is estimated at 200. However even this figure is relatively low when compared to the nearly 3000 people that died on September 11.

Clearly the limited variation in our sample is a concern. However, there nevertheless appears to be enough to derive an initial set of estimates of the incidence of extreme events. The application of extreme value theory typically involves 'blocking' the data into disjoint sub-periods of equal length and fitting a GEV distribution to the block maxima. In setting the block size researchers face a trade-off. Blocking too narrowly threatens the validity of the limiting argument made above, leading to biases in estimation. Wider blocks however will generate fewer maxima, leading to greater variability in our estimates. The choice of blocks of length one year has proved particularly popular. In part this decision has sometimes been forced onto researchers – for example when only annual maxima of daily data are available. However, this decision also reflects technical difficulties that arise in the presence of short-run dependence within high-frequency data: a one-year blocking window could bypass some of these difficulties. Given these considerations we choose a blocking length of one year.

Model Estimation

We restricted our sample from 1974 to 2005, since there were very few recorded CBRN incidents prior to 1974. We fit a number of plausible model specifications to these data. Diagnostic checks of the various models suggested the presence of non-stationary trend components in both the location and scale parameters characterizing the GEV distribution, and some of the extreme variation in the data can be explained by the heavy-tailed nature of the underlying stochastic model. This finding is not altogether surprising given the strong visual evidence of an upward trend in the number of casualties inflicted from CBRN attacks. We also considered more general specifications that allowed for quadratic trend components in either the location or scale parameters. However this usually led to 'over-fitting' in which the resulting models did not appear to explain the underlying structure of the data well.

Based on our estimated model, we can calculate the expected 'reoccurrence period' for a catastrophic event that entails large loss of life or injury. For instance an event on the same scale as Aum Shinrikyo's attack on the Tokyo subway could be expected to occur by 2009. In that attack there were a little over 5000 casualties. The reoccurrence period for an attack of this size however is continually decreasing (Figure 10.7). By 2020 an attack of that magnitude would be expected to occur approximately every 2.5 years. However these estimates assume a continuation of current trends, which may or may not be true.

While our estimates of the probability of attacks of various magnitudes summarize recent trends in the use of CBRN agents, there are a number of reasons why these figures should only serve as a rough guideline. First, the number of recorded incidents of CBRN attacks is relatively low. This has implications for the precision with which parameters in the model can be estimated. But it also involves drawing inferences as to the future likelihood of events based on patterns of behavior that are not necessarily well established. While the use of bio- and chemical weapons dates back many centuries, their effectiveness as a weapon in the terrorist arsenal is a recent phenomenon. Aside from Aum Shinrikyo's 'mastery' over delivery mechanisms for chemical and biological toxins, few terrorist organizations have managed to deploy these agents effectively. Even points of attack that have focused on fairly vulnerable sectors such as the food supply chain have usually failed. The injection of cyanide into grapes in 1978 failed because citric acid in the grapes broke down the cyanide. The Tylenol murders in 1982 by contrast caused seven fatalities, but even in this case damage was mitigated through preventative actions taken by the authorities. With some exceptions such as the Rajneeshee cult, which had access

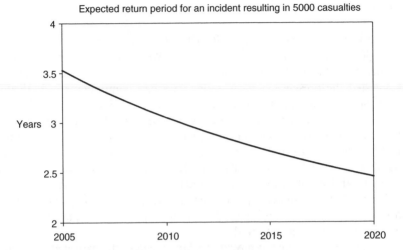

Notes: Based on the parameter estimates that indicate a linear trend in location and scale parameter of the distributions. Estimation was done in R using the ISMEV package. The ISMEV package is based on software written by Stewart Coles.

Figure 10.7   Reoccurrence period for a CBRN attack resulting in 5000 casualties

to their own medical facilities, terrorists have generally failed to introduce a bio-weapon that has been able to exploit the existing infrastructure in the food supply chain to cause catastrophic damage. While the sophistication of terrorists is likely to grow over time, it is apparent that the use of CBRN agents as a terrorist device remains in its infancy. Thus future trends in their use are necessarily difficult to predict.

Second, our estimate of the likelihood of future attacks assumes a continuation of current trends. However, post-September 11, the war on terror has taken on new meaning in government politics all over the world, which has made it increasingly difficult for terrorists to operate in a clandestine fashion. Moreover, terrorists have learned that inflicting mass casualties entails mass retaliation, which may act as a deterrent for future attacks.[10] It is not clear at this point if September 11 marks a structural break in the evolution of terrorism.

Given our limited experience with CBRN agents as a terrorist tool, an examination of the trends in terrorist activity more generally may help us shed more light on the future prospect of catastrophic terrorism. In the subsection below we examine these trends in more detail. Our analysis is based on the MIPT data, although these data have been expanded by including notable omissions in the dataset, such as the Rajneeshee food-poisoning case in 1984. Nevertheless, by far the bulk of these data relate to conventional forms of terrorism.

Conventional Terrorism: A Comparison

As with the use of chemical, biological and or radionuclear agents, the use of conventional terrorist methods has also increased in frequency. Moreover, with the increased sophistication of bombs and explosives, the death toll resulting from the most severe attacks has steadily risen. These trends are evident in a plot of (the logarithm of) the number casualties resulting from major terrorist attacks (Figure 10.1).

We take a similar approach here as in the previous subsection and consider a variety of different models that include the most parsimonious specifications based on the assumption of stationarity and allow for nonstationary trends in the parameters. Given the far wider variation within these data, we can measure severity as the number of fatalities, the number of injuries and the total number of casualties.

The tendency for the annual maxima in the number of injuries or fatalities caused by attacks to increase over time suggested nonstationary specifications. Our analysis confirmed this to be the case. The best-fitting models for the number of injuries and the total number of casualties (injuries and fatalities) are characterized by linear trend components in the location and scale parameters, with fairly light or bounded tailed behavior. Thus much of the increase in the severity of terrorist attacks can be described by deterministic linear trends in the underlying data-generating process, rather than excessively heavy tailed behavior.

Similarly the best-fitting distribution for the number of fatalities suggested a distribution with bounded-tails. However, importantly, the number of fatalities from terrorist attacks did not show the same dramatic increase as the number of injuries. As a result a linear trend component in the location parameter alone sufficed to describe these data well. While we also considered quadratic trend components in both location and scale parameters, the strength of the evidence in favor of these more complex model structures was not particularly strong. As a result the more parsimonious specification was preferred.

Based on our estimated models, we calculated the expected number of years for observing an attack of various magnitudes. Consistent with increasingly violent trends in terrorism, the expected number of years until the next major terrorist event is declining through time (Figure 10.8). The expected reoccurrence period for an event leading to 5000 injuries and fatalities is a little over four years. This estimate is very similar to that

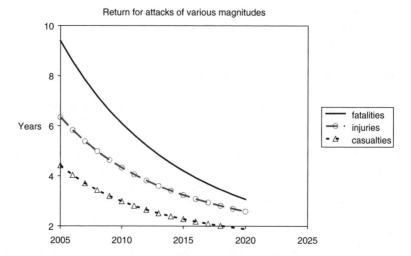

Notes: The reoccurrence period for injuries and total casualties that include fatalities are based on parameter estimates that indicate linear trends in location and scale parameters. The reoccurrence period for fatalities only was based on parameter estimates that indicate a linear trend in the location parameter only. Estimation was done in R using the ISMEV package and based on software written by Stewart Coles.

Figure 10.8   Reoccurrence period for attacks resulting in 5000 injuries or overall casualties or 1000 fatalities

based on the CBRN data. In fact the estimated reoccurrence period for such an event using the CBRN data was slightly shorter. The explanation for this is fairly straightforward. While terrorism using conventional means has had a long history, the use of chemical, biological or radionuclear agents is still relatively new, with limited consequences for public health. By far the majority of CBRN incidents cause no injuries or fatalities. Thus recent exceptions, such as Aum (1994, 1995), the Rajneeshees (1984), and the poisoning of Filipino police officers in 1987 and Russian peace-keepers in 1994, can only be explained within the confines of our statistical model by allowing the parameters of our extreme value distribution to be functions of time and by assuming heavy-tailed behavior. However when chemical, biological and radionuclear attacks are considered from a broader perspective that allows for various forms of terrorism, these nonstationary trends within the data become less prominent. Moreover, given the large numbers of fatalities and injuries arising from conventional forms of terrorism, catastrophic incidents such as the Tokyo gassing in 1995 can easily be described by statistical models characterized by fairly light tails.

Based on our statistical model of the annual maxima in the number of fatalities we were also able to calculate the expected reoccurrence period for a catastrophic event that results in a large-scale loss of life. While an attack of the same magnitude of September 11, one that causes approximately 3000 fatalities, is not expected soon, an attack that leads to 1000 fatalities could occur within the next ten years. Moreover, consistent with the non-stationary pattern in these data, the reoccurrence period for such an attack is decreasing steadily over time. By 2020 for instance an attack of this magnitude could be expected to occur roughly once every three years.

As noted above, at this moment there is not enough variation within the subset of incidents involving the use of CBRN agents to estimate accurately the risk of an attack of this (or any) magnitude. However, based on what has been observed to date, such an attack is unlikely to occur soon. Catastrophic terrorism that leads to a loss of life on a large scale is still more likely using conventional methods. As of yet, no terrorist group has demonstrated the potential to inflict a devastating attack using chemical, biological or radionuclear agents.[11]

CONCLUSION

This chapter is the product of ongoing research into the assessment of the risk of bioterrorism in the food sector. Our contribution in this chapter has been twofold. First, we have developed a fresh new data-set consisting of 314 observations from 1961 to 2005. This data-set focuses on past terrorist attacks that have involved chemical, biological or radionuclear agents, agents that are especially likely to be associated with the food sector as the channel for their dissemination. Second, we have adopted a statistical technique known as extreme value theory to assess the probability of terrorist events and even forecast the 'reoccurrence period' for events of certain magnitudes. We have also used another data-set (MIPT) consisting of over 21 000 observations as a benchmark to compare the risk of terrorism in the food sector with that at large.

Our results are somewhat alarming. For example, we have found that the frequency of catastrophic terrorist events, that is, those with large numbers of casualties, is on the rise. Correspondingly, the average reoccurrence period for such scale attacks is declining, so that by the year 2020, an attack leading to 5000 casualties could be expected to occur every 2.5 years. Similar trends underline our findings with respect to terrorist attacks more generally.

These finding have implications for calibrating the notion of risk assessment for private and public sector decisions involving risk avoidance and the costs and benefits of such decisions. These are some of the tasks ahead in this line of research that would be pursued in the coming year, but are outside of the scope of this chapter.

Additional extensions of the present work might include relating the CBRN data to the larger data-set on more conventional forms of terrorism by developing a conditional probability measure in which the probability of a CBRN attack is estimated, given that an attack of a certain magnitude has occurred. Other extensions in this line of research may include considering other specific pathogens with a potential to be used for bioterrorism. But that effort will depend on finding useful data on such agents.

NOTES

*   This research was supported by the US Department of Homeland Security (Grant number N-00014-04-1-0659), through a grant awarded to the National Center for Food Protection and Defense at the University of Minnesota. Any opinions, findings, conclusions or recommendations expressed in this publication are those of the authors and do not represent the policy or position of the Department of Homeland Security. A previous draft of this chapter was presented at the University of Minnesota, National Center for Food Protection and Defense (NCFPD). This chapter is a revised version of a second draft presented at the University of Southern California's CREATE symposium, 19–20 August 2005. We wish to thank Shaun Kennedy, Frank Busta and Jean Kinsey from NCFPD as well as the participants of the USC CREATE symposium for all their comments and feedback. The authors alone are responsible for any errors.

1. Kifner (2001).
2. It is important to stress that we are referring specifically to risk analysis. There is in fact a vast and impressive literature on terrorism and since at least Landes (1978) economists have been using both theoretical and empirical methods to examine various aspects of terrorism, from its implications for tourism (Enders and Sandler, 1991), to its effects on capital flows (Enders and Sandler, 1996; Blomberg and Mody, 2005; Abadie and Gardeazabal, 2005), and its consequences for economic growth (Abadie and Gardeazabal, 2003). However, as far as we know, there has been very little work on developing a systematic framework for assessing the risk of terrorist activity.
3. Speech by Tommy Thompson, former secretary of Health and Human Services on 3 December 2004.
4. We are grateful to Major Adam Wickersham, US Army, for his help in acquiring some of these data. It is our hope that in later versions of this study, we will be able to update our own database on CBRN through Major Wickersham's help.
5. 'China Deaths Blamed On Rat Poison', *CNN*, 16 September 2002; 'China Masks a Mass Poisoning', *The Guardian*, 16 September 2002.
6. 'Foot-and-mouth scare hits New Zealand', Associated Press, 10 May 2005.
7. We define attacks on the food or water supply as any attack that involves tampering with food and beverages with the potential to create large-scale casualties. Thus, for instance, simple targeted poisonings that are directed at one or perhaps a few specific individuals are not considered an attack on the food chain. However, the incident where contaminated water was handed to Filipino soldiers that led to 19 fatalities and 140 injuries is considered an attack on the food chain. We also regard attacks on livestock or the animal population in a separate category. Attacks on drugs and medication were also considered separately.
8. Thus, in his 13 July 2005 speech, Secretary Chertoff stated that, 'Although we have substantial resources to provide security, these resources are not unlimited. Therefore, as

a nation, we must make tough choices about how to invest finite human and financial capital to attain the optimal state of preparedness. To do this we will focus preparedness on objective measures of risk and performance.'

9. See for example Reiss and Thomas (2000).
10. For a game theoretic approach to understanding the action–reaction strategies of the governments and terrorists see for example Sandler and Enders (2004).
11. This statement may need some qualification. In 1984, Bhopal, India, was the site of one of the worst chemical disasters in history leading to approximately 3800 deaths and over 250 000 injuries following a gas leak in the fertilizer plant of Union Carbide. It was claimed by the engineering firm Arthur D. Little that the disaster may have been the result of a deliberate act of sabotage where someone placed water in the gas storage tanks that caused the chemical reaction. However, no independent inquiry has ever endorsed the theory of sabotage. The Indian government has always claimed that the disaster could be linked to faulty plant design and the claim that sabotage was involved was an effort on the part of the company to escape liability (see for instance Mehta et al., 1990 and 'Bhopal disaster deliberate act of worker, Carbide claims', *Houston Chronicle*, 11 August 1986). At this moment we do not feel there is enough evidence to indicate that the Bhopal incident was a deliberate act of sabotage. Thus we do not include it in our chronology.

DATABASES

Center for Nonproliferation Studies, Monterey Institute, 'Weapons of Mass Destruction Database'.

Johnston, R., 'Database of Radiological Incidents and Related Events', http://www.johnstonsarchive.net/nuclear/radevents/index.html

Mickolus, E.F. (1982), *International Terrorism: Attributes of Terrorist Events, 1968–1977 (ITERATE 2)*, Ann Arbor, MI: Inter-University Consortium for Political and Social Research.

Mickolus, E.F., T. Sandler, J.M. Murdock and P. Fleming (1989), *International Terrorism: Attributes of Terrorist Events, 1978–1987 (ITERATE 3)*, Dunn Loring, VA: Vinyard Software.

Mickolus, E.F., T. Sandler, J.M. Murdock and P. Fleming (1993), *International Terrorism: Attributes of Terrorist Events, 1978–1987 (ITERATE 4)*, Dunn Loring, VA: Vinyard Software.

Mickolus, E. and P. Fleming (2003), *International Terrorism: Attributes of Terrorist Events, 1992–2002*, Dunn Loring, VA: Vinyard Software.

MIPT Terrorism Knowledge Base, website, accessed 1–11 March 2005, http://www.tkb.org/Incident.jsp?incID=7467.

Authors' own compilation of CBRN data (for further information contact the authors).

REFERENCES

Abadie, A. and J. Gardeazabal (2003), 'The Economic Cost of Conflict: A Case Study of the Basque Country', *American Economic Review*, 93: 113–32.

Abadie, A. and J. Gardeazabal (2005), 'Terrorism and the World Economy', unpublished Working Paper.

Atomic Energy Insights (1996), 'What Caused the Accident? Plenty of Blame to Share', 2(4), (http://www.atomicinsights.com/ju196/SL-1cause.html).

Blomberg, B. and A. Mody (2005), 'How Severely Does Violence Deter International Investment?' unpublished Working Paper.

Cameron, G., J. Pate, D. McCauley and L. DeFazio (2000), '1999 WMD Terrorism Chronology: Incidents Involving Sub-National Actors and Chemical, Biological, Radiological, and Nuclear Materials', *Nonproliferation Review*, 7(2), 1–27.

Carus, S.W. (2002), *Bioterrorism and Biocrimes: The Illicit Use of Biological Agents Since 1900*, Fredonia, New York: Fredonia Books.

Douglass, J.D., Jr. and N.C. Livingstone (1987), *America the Vulnerable: The Threat of Chemical and Biological Warfare*, Lexington, MA: Lexington Books.

Eitzen, E.M. and E.T. Takafuji (1997), 'Historical Overview of Biological Warfare', in Frederick R. Sidell, Ernest T. Takafuji and David R. Franz (eds), *Textbook of Military Medicine: Medical Aspects of Chemical and Biological Warfare*, Washington, DC: Office of The Surgeon General, Borden Institute, Walter Reed Army Medical Center.

Enders, W. and T. Sandler (1991), 'Causality between Transnational Terrorism and Tourism: The Case of Spain', *Terrorism*, 14(1): 49–58.

Enders, W. and T. Sandler (1996), 'Terrorism and Foreign Direct Investment in Spain and Greece', *KYKLOS*, 49(3): 331–52.

Fries, A.A. and C.J. West (1921), *Chemical Warfare*, New York: McGraw-Hill.

Hirsch, D. (1987), 'The Truck Bomb and Insider Threats to Nuclear Facilities', in Paul Leventhal and Yonah Alexander (eds), *Preventing Nuclear Terrorism: The Report and Papers of the International Task Force on Prevention of Nuclear Terrorism*, Lexington, MA: Lexington Books, pp. 207–22.

Jenkins, B.M. and A.P. Rubin (1978), 'New Vulnerabilities and the Acquisition of New Weapons by Nongovernment Groups', in Shoko Evans and John F. Murphy (eds), *Legal Aspects of International Terrorism*, Lexington, MA: Lexington Books, pp. 221–76.

Kellen, K. (1987), 'The Potential for Nuclear Terrorism: A Discussion', with Appendix: 'Nuclear-Related Terrorist Activities by Political Terrorists', in Paul Leventhal and Yonah Alexander (eds), *Preventing Nuclear Terrorism: The Report and Papers of the International Task Force on Prevention of Nuclear Terrorism*, Lexington, MA: Lexington Books, pp. 104–22.

Kifner, J. (2001), 'Forget the Past: It's a War Unlike Any Other', *New York Times*, 21 September.

Kupperman, R.H. and J. Kamen (1989), *Final Warning: Averting Disaster in the New Age of Terrorism*, New York: Doubleday.

Kupperman, R.H. and R.J. Woolsey (1988), 'Techno-Terrorism: Testimony before the Technology and Law Subcommittee of the Judiciary Committee May 19, 1988', in *US Department of Justice*.

Lafree, G., L. Dugan and D. Franke (2004), 'Materials Prepared for Workshop on Non-State Actors, Terrorism, and Weapons of Mass Destruction', Center for International Development and Conflict Management Working Paper.

Landes, W.M. (1978), 'An Economic Study of US Aircraft Hijackings, 1961–1976', *Journal of Law and Economics*, 21(1): 1–31.

Leventhal, P. and Y. Alexander (1987), *Preventing Nuclear Terrorism: The Report and Papers of the International Task Force on Prevention of Nuclear Terrorism*, Lexington, MA: Lexington Books.

Livingstone, N.C. and T.B. Arnold (1986), *Fighting Back: Winning the War against Terrorism*, Lexington, MA: Lexington Books.

Mehta, P., A. Mehta, S. Mehta and A. Makhijani (1990), 'Bhopal Tragedy's Health Effects. A Review of Methyl Isocyanate Toxicity', *Journal of American Medical Association*, 264(21): 2781–7.

Miller, J., W. Broad and S. Engelberg (2001), *Germs: Biological Weapons and America's Secret War*, London: Simon & Schuster Adult Publishing Group.

Mize, K. (2004), 'Classical Radiological Dispersal Devices', Unpublished document, http://www.nlectc.org/training/nij2004/mize.pdf.

Mullen, R.K. (1987), 'Nuclear Violence', in Paul Leventhal and Yonah Alexander (eds), *Preventing Nuclear Terrorism: The Report and Papers of the International Task Force on Prevention of Nuclear Terrorism*, Lexington, MA: Lexington Books, pp. 231–47.

Mullins, W.C. (1992), 'An Overview and Analysis of Nuclear, Biological, and Chemical Terrorism: The Weapons, Strategies and Solutions to a Growing Problem', *American Journal of Criminal Justice*, 16(2): 95–119.

Pate, J., G. Ackerman and K. McCloud (2001), '2000 WMD Terrorism Chronology: Incidents Involving Sub-National Actors and Chemical, Biological, Radiological, or Nuclear Materials', Center for Nonproliferation Studies report, Monterey Institute of International Studies.

Pate, J. and G. Cameron (2001), 'Covert Biological Weapons Attacks Against Agricultural Targets: Assessing the Impact Against US Agriculture', Discussion Paper 2001-9, John F. Kennedy School of Government, Harvard University, August.

Phillips, M.B. (2005), 'Bioterrorism: A Brief History', *Northeast Florida Medicine*, 56(1): 32–5.

Purver, R. (1995), *Chemical and Biological Terrorism: The Threat According to the Open Literature*, Canadian Security Intelligence Service, June.

Reiss, R. and M. Thomas (2000), *Statistical Analysis of Extreme Values*, 2nd edn, Basel: Birkhauser Verlag.

Sandler, T. and W. Enders (2004), 'Transnational Terrorism: An Economic Analysis', Working paper, University of Southern California.

Thornton, W.H. (1987), 'Modern Terrorism: The Potential for Increased Lethality', Langley Air Force Base, VA: Army–Air Force Center for Low Intensity Conflict, CLIC Paper, November.

Tucker, J.B. (2000), *Toxic Terror: Assessing Terrorist Use of Chemical and Biological Weapons*, Cambridge, MA: MIT Press.

Turnbull, W. and P. Abhayaratne (2003), '2002 WMD Terrorism Chronology: Incidents Involving Sub-National Actors and Chemical, Biological, Radiological, and Nuclear Materials', Center for Nonproliferation Studies report, Monterey Institute of International Studies.

11. Simulating the state-by-state effects of terrorist attacks on three major US ports: applying NIEMO (National Interstate Economic Model)

Jiyoung Park, Peter Gordon, James E. Moore II, Harry W. Richardson and Lanlan Wang

The Department of Homeland Security recently issued *Planning Scenarios* (Howe, 2004) that included preliminary estimates of the losses from various hypothetical terrorist attacks on selected major targets. There are three problems with many of these estimates:

- The orders of magnitude are often much too vague to be useful, for example, 'millions of dollars', 'up to billions of dollars'.
- The range and types of targets are too limited: many more than a dozen or so scenarios pose a serious economic risk.
- The geographical incidence of losses is not made clear, probably on purpose because of a policy decision not to identify specific target sites. 'All politics are local' may be a slight exaggeration, but decision-makers have a keen interest in the spatial incidence of possible losses.

Our research addresses all three of these problems. We have created what we believe to be the first operational interstate input–output (IO) model for the United States. The National Interstate Economic Model (NIEMO) provides results for 47 major industrial sectors for all 50 states, the District of Columbia, and a leakage region: 'The Rest of the World'. In the application reported here, we use NIEMO to estimate industry-level impacts from the short-term loss of the services of three major US seaports – Los Angeles/Long Beach, New York/Newark and Houston – on the economies of all 50 states and Washington, DC, as a consequence of hypothetical terrorist attacks. The seaports of Los Angeles and Long Beach are treated as one complex, LA/LB. Seaports in New York and Newark are also treated as a single port, NY/NJ. We treat the attacks on the three port complexes as alternatives rather than as simultaneous events.

In pursuing our research goals, the choice of approaches involved difficult trade-offs. The use of linear economic models is justified by several factors, including the richness of the detailed results made possible at relatively low cost. NIEMO, for example, includes approximately 6 million input–output multipliers. The principal insight that drives our research is that, with some effort, it is possible to integrate data from the Minnesota IMPLAN Group (MIG), Inc.'s IMPLAN state-level input–output models with commodity flow data from the US Department of Transportation's Commodity Flow Survey and with data from other related sources, making it possible to build an operational multi-regional input–output model.

In the sections that follow, we describe the steps involved in reconciling the information content in these data sources and making them compatible, integrating them to build NIEMO, and applying it to the problem at hand. The application also required the necessary multiplicands: What shares of local final demand do the temporary losses of port services involve? Finally, we discuss the nature of our results and some of the possible implications for homeland security policies.

BACKGROUND TO MULTI-REGIONAL IO CONSTRUCTION

Many economists and planners are interested in evaluating the socio-economic impacts of business disruptions. Occasionally, they use geographically detailed input–output models. Isard (1951) demonstrated that traditional (national) IO models are inadequate because they cannot capture the effects of linkages and interactions between regions. To examine the full, short-term impacts of unexpected events such as terrorist attacks or natural disasters on the US economy, the economic links between states should be considered and accounted for. Multi-regional input–output models (MRIOs) include interregional trade tables and avoid some of the fallacies associated with aggregation (Robison, 1950). Building an operational MRIO for all the states of the US, however, requires highly detailed interstate shipments data.

Although Chenery (1953) and Moses (1955) had formulated a relatively simplified MRIO framework in response to the earlier discussions by Isard (1951), data problems persisted, and have stymied most applications. The non-existence or rarity of useful inter-regional trade data is the most problematic issue. Intraregional and inter-regional data must be comparable and compatible to be useful in this context, yet the currently available shipments data between states are only sporadically available and difficult to use.

It is not surprising, then, that few MRIO models have been constructed or widely used. The best known are the 1963 US data-sets for 51 regions and 79 sectors published in Polenske (1980), and the 1977 US data-sets for 51 regions and 120 sectors released by Jack Faucett Associates (1983), then updated by various Boston College researchers and reported in 1988 (Miller and Shao, 1990).

More recently, there have been two attempts to estimate inter-regional trade flows using data from the 1997 Commodity Flow Survey (CFS). The US Commodity Transportation Survey data on inter-regional trade flows have been available since 1977, but reporting was discontinued for some years. For the years since 1993, this data deficit can be met to some extent with the recent (CFS) data from the Bureau of Transportation Statistics (BTS), but these data are incomplete with respect to interstate flows. Based on the currently available CFS data, Jackson et al. (2004) used MIG, Inc.'s IMPLAN data to adjust the incomplete CFS reports by adopting gravity models constrained via distance and by making some additional adjustments.

Along similar lines and using the same basic data sources, we elaborate Park et al. (2004) who suggested a different estimation approach that relied on a doubly-constrained Fratar model (DFM). The Fratar model is an early transportation planning tool used to extrapolate trip interchange tables to reflect expected changes in trip ends. It is an intentionally naive numerical method requiring a minimum of assumptions. To proceed in this way, it was first necessary to create conversion tables to reconcile the CFS and IMPLAN (and other) economic sectors. This approach is elaborated in the sections that follow.

DATA

The primary requirements for building an interstate model for the US of the Chenery-Moses type are two sets of data:

- regional coefficients tables; and
- trade coefficients tables (Miller and Blair, 1985).

Models of this type can be used to estimate interstate industrial effects as well as inter-industry impacts on each state, based mainly on the two data sources:

- regional IO tables that provide intra-regional industry coefficients for each state; and
- inter-regional trade tables to provide analogous trade coefficients.

This implies the creation of three types of matrices:

- intraregional inter-industry transaction matrices;
- the inter-regional commodity trade matrix; and
- the combined inter-regional, inter-industry matrix, that is, a special case of an MRIO matrix, the core of the NIEMO model.

Before creating these matrices, however, the data reconciliation problem has to be addressed.

The main steps involved in building and testing NIEMO are shown in Figure 11.1. We developed a set of 47 industries, we call them 'the USC Sectors', into which many of the other economic sector classification systems can be converted. Figure 11.2 shows the state of our industrial code conversion matrix relative to the many data sources used in this study.

The detailed conversion processes occasionally involved case-by-case reconciliations of economic sectors. Inevitably, some conversions involved mapping one sector into more than one and vice versa. Some conversions required modifications with plausible weights extracted from ancillary data sources on a case-by-case basis.

Data for NIEMO Construction

The major problem in developing an interstate, inter-industrial model stems from the fact that it is difficult to obtain data describing trade flows between the states (Lahr, 1993). Since 1993, however, CFS data have been available for this purpose (Bureau of Transportation Statistics and US Census Bureau, 1999, 2000, 2003). Remaining problems with these data include high sampling variability or values omitted to avoid disclosure of individual company status. The existence of many unreported values has required relying on other data sources to approximate completeness of the CFS. It is not surprising, therefore, that there has been no comprehensive inventory of MRIO flows, since the work by Polenske (1980) and Jack Faucett Associates (1983).

The 1997 CFS reports trade flows between states for 43 SCTG sectors while the IMPLAN Total Commodity Output data-file includes their 509 sector values, available for all states. CFS includes the movement of foreign imports in its data as domestic movements. This means that all commodities coming into a US port are listed as outbound from that port

Table 11.1 *Economic Data Sources and Associated Sector Classification Systems*

Sector classification system	Economic data source					
	1997 Commodity Flow Survey (CFS)	2001 IMPLAN	1997 Bureau of Economic Analysis (BEA) Benchmark	2001 WISERTrade	2001 Waterborne Commerce of the US (WCUS)	2002 Economic Census
Standard Classification of Transported Goods (SCTG)	■					
Bureau of Economic Analysis (BEA)		■	■			
2001 IMPLAN		■				
North American Industry Classification System (NAICS)		■				■
Harmonized System (HS)				■	■	
Standard International Trade Classification (SITC)				■		
Standard International Trade Classification (SITCREV3-C)					■	
Waterborne Commerce of the US (WCUS)					■	

Source: Authors' construction.

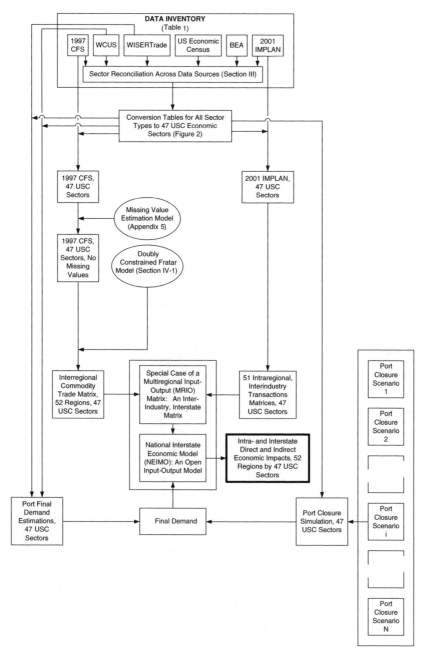

Figure 11.1   NIEMO data and modeling steps

Sector System	USC	SCTG	BEA	NAICS	IMPLAN (2001)	SIC	HS	SITC	WCUS
USC									
SCTG	C, E								
BEA	C, E	C, E							
NAICS	C, E	C, E	A						
IMPLAN (2001)	C, E	C, E	A	A					
SIC	C, W	P	P	C, W	P				
HS	C, E	C, E	A	C, E	C, E	P			
SITC	C, W	C, W	P	P	P	P	C, W		
WCUS	C, W	C, W	P	P	P	P	C, W	C, E	

Notes:

C: Complete mapping

A: Available from other sources

P: Possible to create mapping

E: Mappings constructed without any weights (Bayesian allocations)

W: Mappings constructed with plausible weights informed by additional data sources

214

Sector Classification Systems:
USC: USC sectors newly created
SCTG: Standard Classification of Transported Goods (http://www.bts.gov/cfs/sctg/welcome.htm)
BEA: Bureau of Economic Analysis (http://www.bea.doc.gov)
NAICS: North American Industry Classification System (http://www.census.gov/epcd/www/naics.html)
2001 IMPLAN: IMPLAN 509-sector codes
SIC: Standard Industrial Classification (http://www.osha.gov/oshstats/sicser.html)
HS: Harmonized System (http://www.statcan.ca/trade/htdocs/hsinfo.html)
SITC: Standard International Trade Classification available from WISERTrade (http://www.wisertrade.org/home/index.jsp)
WCUS: Waterborne Commerce of the United States (http://www.iwr.usace.army.mil/ndc/data/datacomm.htm)

Figure 11.2   Economic sector classification system conversions (current $)

and inbound to the next destination. Likewise, all commodities flowing to a port from anywhere in the US are outbound from the origin and inbound to the port. For these reasons, foreign imports in the 2001 IMPLAN data, which are available separately from domestic movements, are added to the IMPLAN Total Commodity Output tally.

NIEMO's inter-industry coefficient matrix is based on the commodity-by-industry version of the IMPLAN model. This is because the CFS trade matrix double- (or multiple-) counts commodities due to the movements of foreign imports to other states. We corrected these CFS multiple-counts by using the IMPLAN separate foreign imports movements values for commodities to improve the marginal distribution of the CFS matrix, and then re-estimated CFS entries to eliminate double- and multiple-counts.

In the current application, the 1997 CFS data were used as a baseline and updated to estimated 2001 values using 2001 IMPLAN data. The recent release of 2002 CFS data, to be matched to 2002 IMPLAN data, will simplify this approach in the near future.

Differences between industry classification systems from different data sources make data reconciliation especially difficult in the absence of standardized and tested conversion procedures. The estimation of 2001 trade flows from 1997 CFS, therefore, required several intermediate conversion steps between the SCTG code systems used in the 1997 CFS and the IMPLAN system of sectors, not always one-to-one matched pairs.

Figure 11.3 shows the data reconciliation steps enabling the aggregation of 509 IMPLAN sectors to 43 SCTG sectors. (The steps involved in data reconciliation, the definition of USC sectors and the quality of results are described are available on the CREATE website.)

Multiplicands and NIEMO Tests

After estimating all the values needed to invert the 2444-by-2444 matrix, NIEMO can be used to simulate the loss impacts from hypothetical attacks on any major US target. In this research, we considered attacks on the three top US ports: the combined ports of Los Angeles/Long Beach (LA/LB), the combined ports of New York/Newark (NY/NJ) and the port of Houston. Together, these three facilities account for 38.1 percent of all foreign goods exports and 48.5 percent for foreign goods imports (Table 11.2).

The trade activities for the three ports, foreign and domestic by USC sector, had then to be estimated. WISERTrade processes and supplies data on foreign waterborne exports and imports for each US port, based on raw Census data. They do not include information on domestic waterborne

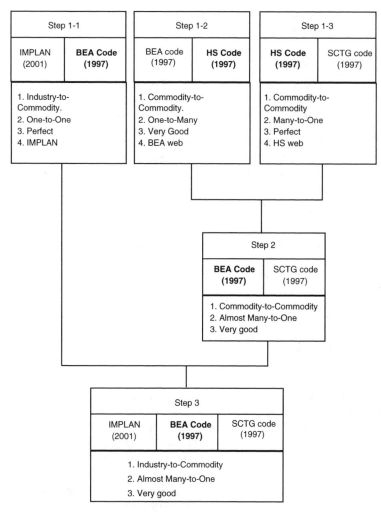

Notes:
Bold: Used as Reconciliation Code
1: Sector type
2: One = One sector, Many = Multiple Sectors
3: Quality of Reconciled Data
4: Sources and Abbreviations:
IMPLAN
BEA: Bureau of Economic Analysis (http://www.bea.doc.gov)
SCTG : Standard Classification of Transported Goods
(http://www.bts.gov/cfs/sctg/welcome.htm)
HS : Harmonized System (http://www.statcan.ca/trade/htdocs/hsinfo.html)

Figure 11.3   Data reconciliation steps, SCTG and IMPLAN

Table 11.2   Top ten US ports: foreign exports and imports (current $ millions), 2001

2001 Rank	Ports	Exports	Ports	Imports
1	Los Angeles / Long Beach, CA	33 222	Los Angeles / Long Beach, CA	164 578
2	New York, NY / Newark, NJ	21 378	New York, NY / Newark, NJ	64 009
3	Houston, TX	21 241	Houston, TX	23 539
4	Charleston, SC	12 836	Seattle, WA	23 209
5	New Orleans, LA	10 951	Charleston, SC	20 876
6	Norfolk, VA	10 892	Oakland, CA	16 021
7	Oakland, CA	9 194	Baltimore, D	15 686
8	Miami, FL	8 846	Tacoma WA	13 943
9	Savannah, GA	6 544	Norfolk, VA	13 052
10	Seattle, WA	5 483	Philadelphia, PA	11 877
	Top ten US ports	140 587	Top-ten ports	366 790
	All US ports	198 841	All US ports	519 607
	Total US goods trade	718 762	Total US goods trade	1 145 927

Sources: WISERTrade data for ports and Table 1277, 2002 Statistical Abstract of the United States for Total US Goods Trade.

exports and imports. Because WISERTrade uses SITC codes for its seaport data, it was necessary to reconcile the USC Sectors and the SITC Sectors. A USC–SITC conversion table was created on the basis of three other conversion tables: USC–SCTG, SCTG–HS and HS–SITC. The USC–HS conversion was easily accomplished because the USC–SCTG and SCTG–HS conversion tables were already available from the NIEMO construction process (see Figure 11.3 again). After obtaining a conversion table for five-digit SITCREV3_C codes and six-digit HS codes from the Waterborne Commerce of the US (WCUS), and modifying the SITCREV3_C codes to four-digit SITC codes for each port, we created a new, weighted table converting four-digit SITC codes to six-digit HS codes. This enabled us to complete and use the USC–SITC conversion table.

Domestic seaborne exports and imports data are available from the WCUS files, which use their own classification code system based on SITCREV3_C codes. A limitation of the WCUS data is that the units reported are in short tons instead of dollars. We first changed the kilogram magnitudes in the WISERTrade data to short tons. Second, we created a conversion between WCUS and SITC using short ton values. Third, we created dollars-per-ton conversion tables for each port. We were then able to reconcile all the necessary seaborne trade data.

The results of these various reconciliations can be corroborated through foreign trade data comparisons between WCUS and WISERTrade. We found foreign trade for each port to be almost the same for each USC sector, regardless of data source. The results of our efforts to document all goods trade for the three ports are shown in Tables 11.3 and 11.4. These are the bases for our final demand calculations for each port, before we return to the construction of NIEMO.

CONSTRUCTING NIEMO

As noted above, constructing NIEMO required two basic tables:

- tables of intraregional industrial commodity trade coefficients; and
- a table of regional inter-industry transaction coefficients, as shown in Figures 11.4 and 11.5 respectively.

While trade tables by industry are hard to create because of incompleteness or unavailability of data, inter-industry tables are relatively easy to identify because reliable data are available from IMPLAN at the state and industry levels. To estimate NIEMO, we used the 1997 CFS data plus missing value estimates (all updated to estimate 2001 values) that include interstate shipments data for the 43 SCTG commodity sectors; and the corresponding IMPLAN inter-industry coefficients tables for each state.

Constructing Interstate Trade Flow Coefficients

Estimated 2001 commodity trade flows among all 50 states plus Washington, DC and the rest of the world were developed from the original 1997 CFS for 29 USC commodity sectors. We had to deal with the unfortunate fact that the 1997 CFS includes unreported values for a variety of commodities, including some marginal values such as total shipments originating in state i and total shipments destined for state j, and matrix cells representing commodity trade flows between pairs of states. The 2001 IMPLAN data report total origin and destination values by state. Hence, it follows that the 2001 commodity trade flows could be estimated with a Fratar model. However, the missing values in the 1997 CFS must be estimated first. Excel Visual Basic was used to develop the model to estimate these missing values and to execute the Fratar updates. In the future, we will develop an updated version of NIEMO based on CFS and IMPLAN data for the same year (2002).

Table 11.3   Final demand estimates for three ports ($ millions)

USC sectors	Final demand losses for export		
	LA/LB	Houston	NY/NW
USC1	110.624	21.030	11.381
USC2	159.524	107.081	21.710
USC3	167.088	10.684	30.129
USC4	9.808	6.059	5.297
USC5	83.475	74.997	31.179
USC6	17.957	1.186	1.584
USC7	28.533	0.020	1.372
USC8	12.280	4.839	26.128
USC9	5.535	2.312	2.503
USC10	444.812	431.543	1388.771
USC11	217.227	581.027	138.793
USC12	42.581	17.722	32.541
USC13	2.205	3.137	0.886
USC14	237.746	383.748	366.643
USC15	288.688	188.017	132.205
USC16	75.518	14.911	124.903
USC17	50.345	13.302	38.216
USC18	64.813	11.630	112.296
USC19	138.581	28.803	110.335
USC20	214.835	65.322	178.686
USC21	47.451	28.101	54.134
USC22	94.798	83.030	117.701
USC23	438.116	458.650	322.004
USC24	329.556	113.974	344.952
USC25	206.774	71.162	183.343
USC26	110.942	22.128	183.762
USC27	193.418	63.437	359.330
USC28	60.535	21.956	111.678
USC29	260.899	311.011	261.775
Export total	4114.665	3140.819	4694.239

USC sectors	Final demand losses for import		
	LA/LB	Houston	NY/NW
USC1	288.754	13.098	111.216
USC2	70.167	20.270	114.113
USC3	25.924	5.003	36.580
USC4	18.155	2.366	33.683
USC5	94.350	66.335	283.289
USC6	48.996	32.410	154.150

Table 11.3 (continued)

USC sectors	Final demand losses for import		
	LA/LB	Houston	NY/NW
USC7	5.495	0.052	1.616
USC8	3.413	6.170	15.853
USC9	0.719	2.164	3.176
USC10	517.640	1131.517	1057.081
USC11	227.362	448.906	266.429
USC12	13.060	12.166	86.791
USC13	0.318	4.397	0.491
USC14	209.201	153.954	345.002
USC15	553.886	44.776	187.790
USC16	150.895	30.173	65.337
USC17	74.408	10.020	57.535
USC18	86.941	9.965	73.560
USC19	2904.049	43.955	918.190
USC20	216.420	38.831	140.534
USC21	145.305	154.038	91.427
USC22	538.601	148.629	147.485
USC23	1054.568	202.517	493.051
USC24	3438.119	170.468	352.015
USC25	1504.472	135.470	878.226
USC26	49.591	16.342	118.430
USC27	346.843	47.903	224.694
USC28	660.672	27.757	195.007
USC29	973.274	239.684	247.142
Import total	14221.599	3219.337	6699.895

Fratar models are useful for estimating updated commodity trade flows; the starting matrices include numerous estimated values for missing entries in the CFS data. However, the traditional Fratar model calibrates only off-diagonal inter-regional cells. In this application, new diagonal values accounting for intrastate trade flows had also to be estimated.

We developed the doubly-constrained Fratar model (DFM), a new formulation that updates the diagonal values in the CFS matrix, and used the traditional Fratar model to estimate the off-diagonal values. Combining these two operations, the DFM iteratively estimates all the updated CFS values simultaneously and consistently. The estimated values for each USC sector are the base values for the next iterative step of the DFM.

Define ETO_i and ETD_j as the estimated values of TO_i, the Total Origin (Output) value for state i, and TD_j, the Total Destination (Input) values for

Table 11.4 Sum of intra- and interstate effects: three ports, shutdowns one-month ($ millions)

State	LA/LB	NY/NJ	Houston
AL	26.96	19.97	28.25
AK	3.08	13.65	1.05
AZ	53.69	7.86	19.53
AR	25.52	11.39	24.38
CA	2641.24	115.76	146.24
Direct_Impact_EXPORT	4114.66	–	–
Direct_Impact_IMPORT	14221.60	–	–
CO	31.40	12.35	21.87
CT	16.04	47.97	8.79
DE	5.08	6.85	2.58
DC	0.63	1.64	0.28
FL	31.23	36.37	24.32
GA	25.92	35.00	23.61
HI	5.40	7.99	0.94
ID	12.31	12.16	3.51
IL	70.84	48.25	53.94
IN	53.17	36.55	44.96
IA	36.06	28.55	12.81
KS	31.99	9.26	17.80
KY	29.16	55.69	25.42
LA	77.95	105.94	96.59
ME	5.39	26.76	2.33
MD	11.43	42.75	6.87
MA	21.80	54.06	11.93
MI	54.99	95.82	40.50
MN	33.80	22.97	16.69
MS	14.68	12.14	28.79
MO	35.92	47.13	24.45
MT	16.27	5.72	3.34
NE	25.32	5.88	5.63
NV	13.08	2.33	1.68
NH	7.22	9.76	3.36
NJ	42.33	–	21.52
NM	6.62	4.68	21.85
NY	54.85	–	43.53
NY + NJ	–	2753.40	–
Direct_Impact_EXPORT	–	4694.24	–
Direct_Impact_IMPORT	–	6699.90	–
NC	33.14	45.19	22.98
ND	4.87	20.34	1.71

Table 11.4 (continued)

State	LA/LB	NY/NJ	Houston
OH	76.85	165.07	58.15
OK	26.99	24.61	70.97
OR	50.39	24.07	11.05
PA	61.80	247.67	44.13
RI	4.85	4.88	3.35
SC	16.76	33.23	14.49
SD	6.72	8.36	3.44
TN	33.69	28.18	25.43
TX	391.97	345.30	2233.28
Direct_Impact_EXPORT	–	–	3140.82
Direct_Impact_IMPORT	–	–	3219.34
UT	31.76	5.74	11.08
VM	2.41	11.75	1.64
VA	16.98	33.36	15.72
WA	79.50	16.21	17.98
WV	10.58	60.16	13.12
WI	52.77	65.68	28.46
WY	6.52	3.77	7.46
US Total	22766.18	16234.29	9733.92
Rest of World	492.02	589.97	316.02
World Total	23258.21	16824.25	10049.93

state j respectively. These estimates are provided by the procedure used to estimate missing values in the 1997 CFS data. Define IND_{ii} to be diagonal entries in a matrix consisting of IMPLAN's Net Domestic Products (NDP) plus Remaining IMPLAN Foreign Imports for each state i, the double subscript identifies diagonal entries.

$$IND_{ii} = NDP_{ii} + RIFI_i \qquad (11.1)$$

This makes it possible to define the variables shown in equations (11.2.1) through (11.5.2):

$$INTO_i = ITO_i - IFE_i \qquad (11.2.1)$$

$$= (IND_{ii} + IFE_i + IDE_i + OIFI_i) - IFE_i \qquad (11.2.2)$$

$$= NDP_{ii} + IDE_i + RIFI_i + OIFI_i \qquad (11.2.3)$$

$$= NDP_{ii} + IDE_i + AFI_i \qquad (11.2.4)$$

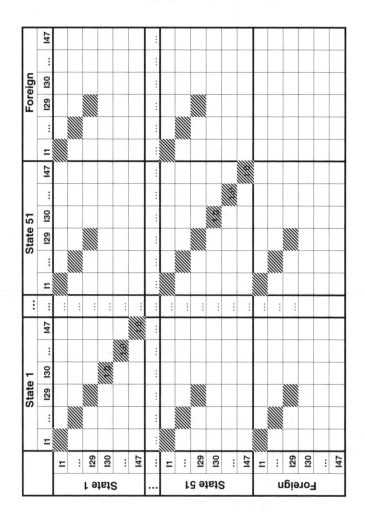

Notes:
1. White cells identify zero values.
2. Service sectors have no trade coefficients: Their Diagonal entries are 1.

Figure 11.4   Inter-regional trade coefficients based on commodity trade flows

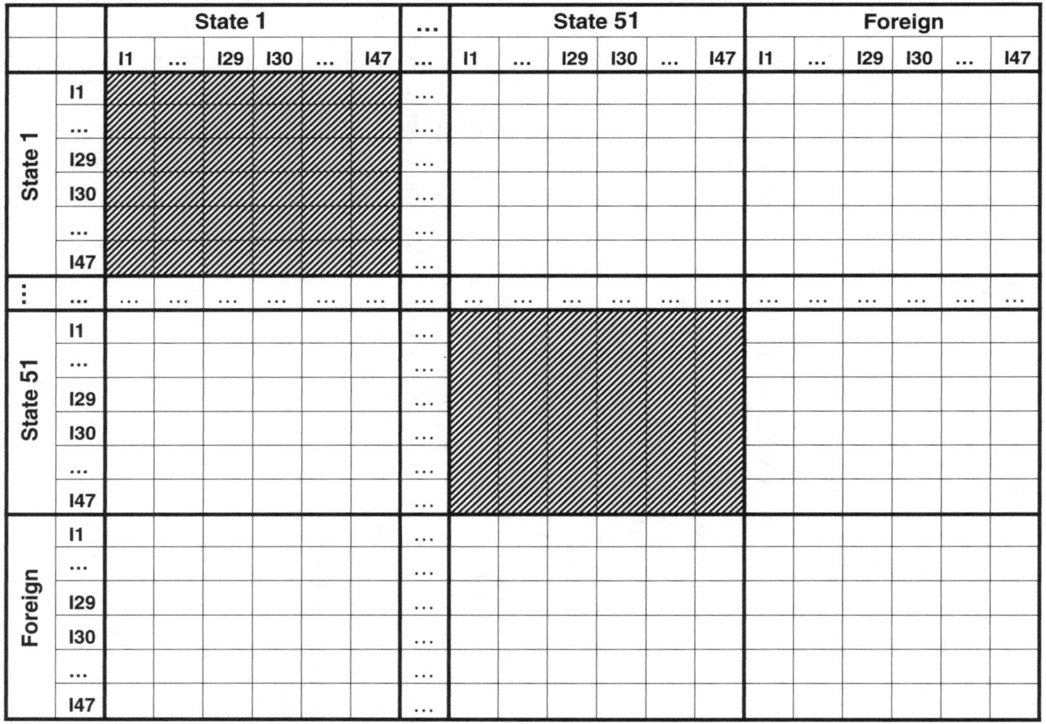

Note: 1. White cells identify zero values.

Figure 11.5 Inter-industry technology coefficients for 47 USC sectors based on IMPLAN

where: $INTO_i$ = 2001 IMPLAN Net Total (Outputs) Originating in state i;
$\quad\quad ITO_i$ = 2001 IMPLAN Total (Outputs) Originating in state i;
$\quad\quad IFE_i$ = 2001 IMPLAN Foreign Exports from state i;
$\quad\quad IDE_i$ = 2001 IMPLAN Domestic Exports from state i;
$\quad\quad OIFI_i$ = 2001 Outbound IMPLAN Foreign Imports
$\quad\quad\quad\quad$ (Transhipped) from state i; and
$\quad\quad AFI_i$ = 2001 IMPLAN Adjusted Foreign Imports to state i.

$$INTD_j = ITD_j - OIFI_j, \quad\quad\quad\quad\quad\quad (11.3.1)$$

$$= (IND_{ii} + IDI_j + IIFI_j) - IIFI_j \quad\quad (11.3.2)$$

$$= NDP_{ii} + IDI_j + RIFI_j \quad\quad\quad\quad (11.3.3)$$

where: $INTD_j$ = 2001 IMPLAN Net Total (Inputs) Destined for state j;
$\quad\quad ITD_j$ = 2001 IMPLAN Total (Inputs) Destined for state j;
$\quad\quad IIFI_j$ = 2001 Inbound IMPLAN Foreign Imports (Transhipped)
$\quad\quad\quad\quad$ to state j; and
$\quad\quad IDI_j$ = 2001 IMPLAN Domestic Imports to state j.

We did not account for foreign exports in the estimation of each trade flow in the definitions of $INTO_i$ and $INTD_j$. This is because the foreign exports data in IMPLAN identify foreign exports from each state. This presents two problems. First, it is not possible to separate out the quantities that go to the rest of the world from those that go first to the CFS 'outbound' category and then on to the rest of the world. And second, foreign exports directly to the rest of the world are associated only with the transportation services industry. Therefore, we assumed foreign exports are shipped directly from each state.

Net_INTO_i and Net_INTD_j exclude corresponding diagonal outputs IND_{ii} and IND_{ii}:

$$Net\_INTO_i = INTO_i - IND_{ii} \quad\quad\quad (11.4.1)$$

$$= IDE_i + OIFI_i \quad\quad\quad\quad (11.4.2)$$

$$Net\_INTD_j = INTD_j - IND_{jj} \quad\quad\quad (11.5.1)$$

$$= IDI_j \quad\quad\quad\quad\quad\quad (11.5.2)$$

Net_ETO_i and Net_ETD_j also exclude corresponding diagonal outputs IND_{ii} and IND_{ii}:

$$Net\_ETO_i = ETO_i - IND_{ii} \quad\quad\quad (11.6)$$

$$Net\_ETD_j = ETD_j - IND_{jj} \qquad (11.7)$$

The growth factors for origin states i and destination states j, G_i and G_j, are calculated from equations (11.8) and (11.9):

$$G_i = Net\_INTO_i / Net\_ETO_i, \qquad (11.8)$$

$$G_j = Net\_INTD_j / Net\_ETD_j. \qquad (11.9)$$

These growth factors are substituted into equations (11.10) and (11.11) to obtain balance factors L_i and L_j, which are used to update off-diagonal CFS entries iteratively:

$$L_i = \frac{Net\_ETO_i}{\sum_j (MV_{ij}^* \times G_j)}. \qquad (11.10)$$

$$L_j = \frac{Net\_ETD_j}{\sum_i (MV_{ij}^* \times G_i)}. \qquad (11.11)$$

The observed and estimated cell values MV_{ij}^* for the 1997 CFS data are the starting values to estimate the 2001 CFS off-diagonal flows ij, FV_{ij}^1. This is a standard application of the traditional Fratar model that relies on the calibrated factors provided by equations (11.8) to (11.11):

$$FV_{ij}^1 = MV_{ij}^* \times G_i \times G_j \times \left\{ \frac{(L_i + L_j)}{2} \right\} \quad \text{for all } i \neq j. \qquad (11.12)$$

Equations (11.13) to (11.14) define DG_i and DG_j, diagonal entry growth factors for origin states i and destination states j:

$$DG_i = ITO_i / ETO_i. \qquad (11.13)$$

$$DG_j = ITD_j / ETD_j. \qquad (11.14)$$

Equations (11.15) and (11.16) define DL_i and DL_j, the diagonal entry balance factors used to update the diagonal (intrastate) entries of the CFS matrix iteratively:

$$DL_i = \frac{ETO_i}{\sum_j (MV_{ij}^* \times DG_j)}. \qquad (11.15)$$

$$DL_j = \frac{ETD_j}{\sum_i (MV_{ij}^* \times DG_i)}.$$ (11.16)

Estimated Diagonal Values (DV_{ii}^1) are calculated via equation (11.17), which defines a second Fratar model estimating trade flows within each state i. These results also account for new foreign imports remaining within each state:

$$DV_{ii}^1 = MV_{ii}^* \times DG_i \times DG_j \times \left\{ \frac{(DL_i + DL_j)}{2} \right\}, \quad \text{for all } i=j. \quad (11.17)$$

These initial estimates of the updated diagonal values, DV_{ii}^1, the diagonal entry growth factors, DG_i and DG_j, and the Diagonal entry balance factors, DL_i and DL_j, are all updated iteratively until they converge to consistent values across equations (11.13) to (11.17).

$$DV_{ij}^T = DV_{ij}^{T-1} \times DG_i^{T-1} \times DG_j^{T-1} \times \left\{ \frac{(DL_i^{T-1} + DL_j^{T-1})}{2} \right\} \quad \text{for all } i=j.$$

(11.18)

DV_{ii}^T replaces IND_{ii} if and only if $DV_{ii}^T > IND_{ii}$. The final values DV_{ii} replace the diagonal values IND_{ii} in the CFS matrix if and only if $DV_{ii}^* > IND_{ii}$. The 2001 CFS totals for states i and j are reduced by the difference between the corresponding values DV_{ii} and the original diagonal values IND_{ii}.

These initial estimates of the updated off-diagonal CFS flows, FV_{ij}^1, the growth factors for origin states i and destination states j, G_i and G_j, and the balance factors, L_i and L_j, are all updated iteratively until they converge to consistent values across equations (11.8) to (11.12).

$$FV_{ij}^T = FV_{ij}^{T-1} \times G_i^{T-1} \times G_j^{T-1} \times \left\{ \frac{(L_i^{T-1} + L_j^{T-1})}{2} \right\} \quad \text{for all } i \neq j. \quad (11.19)$$

The stopping rule to identify the optimal values of FV_{ij}^T from equations (11.18) and (11.19) is shown in equation (11.20). The stopping condition is met by maximizing:

$$\sum_i \sum_j FV_{ij}^T$$ (11.20)

subject to:

$$0.999 < (\sum_i Net\_ITO_i / \sum_i \sum_j FV_{ij}^T) < 1.001, \text{ and} \qquad (11.21.1)$$

$$0.999 < (\sum_i Net\_ITD_j / \sum_i \sum_j FV_{ij}^T) < 1.001; \text{ or, alternatively,} \qquad (11.21.2)$$

$$0.999 < \sum_i \sum_j FV_{ij}^{T-1} / \sum_i \sum_j FV_{ij}^T) < 1.001. \qquad (11.22)$$

There is only limited information available about interstate trade in services. The 1977 MRIO inter-regional flow data-set on service sectors is reported to be problematic (Miller and Shao, 1990, p. 1652). Consequently, trade in services between states was assumed to be negligible. Further, given our focus on seaports, we also neglect foreign trade in services. The first step in constructing a NIEMO-type MIRO matrix is to create a set of 29, 52-state-by-52-state trade matrices, one for each of the various commodity sectors; and define 18, 52-state-by-52-state identity matrices, one for each of the various service sectors. These 47 final estimated trade flow matrices are combined into the MRIO format as shown in Figure 11.4. These trade values are producer values. To compare these matrices of estimated trade results with the original CFS trade tables, these producer values must be converted to purchaser values using the appropriate price ratios given in Appendix 1b, available on the CREATE website.

Denote the interstate flows appearing in the 1997 CDS data as V_{ij}. Denote the unreported value of total output originating in state i as TO_i, and the unreported value of total output destined for state j as TO_j. For each state for which 1997 CFS data have been estimated, the ratios, $\Sigma_i V_{ij}/TO_i$ (or $\Sigma_j V_{ij}/TD_j$), are close to unity. Also, referring to the DFM estimates, the state sums of updated trade flows between states ($\Sigma_i FV_{ij}^T$ or $\Sigma_j FV_{ij}^T$) and the IMPLAN total values ($INTO_i$ or $INTD_j$) are also very close to unity. These comparisons provide a basic quality check for the estimates presented here: all these estimates are plausible (Park et al., 2004). Detailed trade flow estimates by USC sectors are available upon request.

Constructing Inter-Industry Trade Flow Coefficients

The 47 USC Sector inter-industry input–output tables were created from the 509-sector 2001 IMPLAN inter-industry table, and then recombined as shown in Figure 11.5. These estimates required some intermediate to steps process the IMPLAN data, and are described in Appendix 6, available on the CREATE website.

ASSEMBLING NIEMO

The NIEMO version of an MRIO coefficient matrix is created by taking the product of the two matrices in Figures 11.4 and 11.5. The model includes no inter-industry data for trade between foreign countries, so the off-diagonal cells representing trade between locations in the rest of the world are necessarily zero. The coefficients for diagonal cells in the foreign-to-foreign region are equal to unity.

The NIEMO inverse matrix can be computed from this product as a special case of the Leontief inverse matrix ($= (I-CA)^{-1}$), as shown in equation (11.23). The structure of this inverse matrix is shown in Figure 11.6. In our applications, we used equation (11.23) to consider the impact of final demand changes, denoted as Y, occurring in any given state:

$$X = (I - CA)^{-1}Y, \qquad (11.23)$$

where X = the output vector,
$\quad Y$ = the final demand vector in a particular state,
$\quad A$ = the matrix of inter-industry technology coefficients, and
$\quad C$ = the matrix of interstate trade flows.

NIEMO accounts for the commodity effects of changes in trade within one region on services consumed only within other regions. Therefore, the cross-hatched cells in Figure 11.6 are the only ones that are non-zero.

Because A, C and Y are known, X can be calculated via NIEMO, the vector Y captures projected changes in final demand. For this study, we consider the direct impacts resulting from hypothetical attacks on three major US seaports. The Leontief inverse matrix will consist of $(52 * 47)^2 = 5,973,136$ cells. Given Y^*, hypothesized perturbations defined by interruptions in port services, new outputs X^* are then estimated. All of the required calculations were conducted using the MATLAB™ program.

SEAPORT FINAL DEMAND ESTIMATES

The trade activities by USC Sector for the Los Angeles/Long Beach, New York/Newark and Houston seaports are shown in Table 11.3. These figures are based on the reconciled data above. In the simulations reported here, we assumed that terrorist attacks would close the ports for one month. Because our data are for one year, we created one-month losses by dividing the elements of the sum column by 12. The hypothesized one-month final demand (direct) losses are shown in the fifth (FD LOSS) column. As expected, the

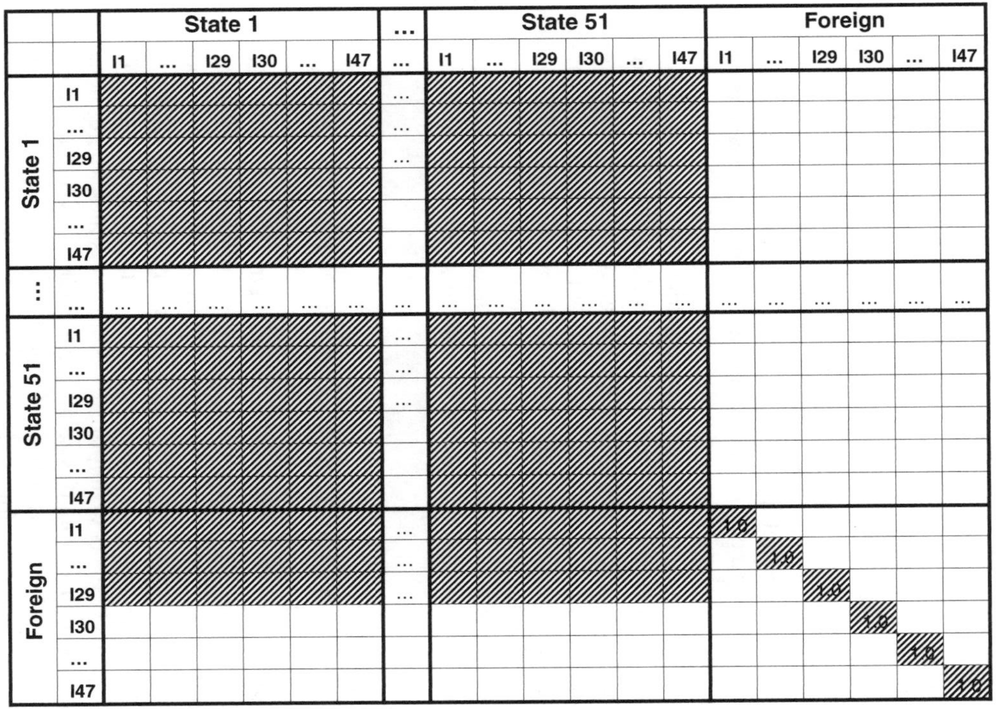

Note: 1. White cells identify zero values.

Figure 11.6   Final interregional inter-industry coefficients: inverse matrix $(I - CA)^{-1}$

LA/LB ports would experience the largest final demand losses ($18.3 billion), while the ports of NY/NJ and Houston incur $11.4 billion and $6.3 billion of direct losses respectively. NIEMO is a linear model and extrapolations to other time periods are straightforward. The caveat is that as the periods studied become longer, the assumption of constant, fixed coefficients becomes more problematic.

As inputs into the NIEMO simulations, FD LOSS data (Y^*) for each port were used as follows. Export losses are presumed to have the standard demand-driven multiplier effects. Import losses are less likely to have such effects and only their direct impacts are included in total effects. It could be argued that the loss of intermediate imports can initiate demand-driven multiplier effects, and that there could be substitutions from other domestic sources. Given the multiple assumptions underpinning this research, we prefer on this point to err on the conservative side. All the results are discussed below.

Because the New York/Newark ports straddle two states, we also tested an alternate 49-state NIEMO model that combines New York and New Jersey. We conducted simulations that compared the results generated by the two versions of NIEMO, with and without the two states combined. The outputs, shown in Appendix 7 available on the CREATE website, demonstrate that the results are approximately the same. This suggests that NIEMO accurately accounts for state-to-state commodity flows, even in circumstances in which flows are as difficult to separate as in the case of NY/NJ.

TERRORIST ATTACK SIMULATION RESULTS

Based on the export final demand losses shown in Table 11.3, the state-by-state indirect impacts from attacks on the three ports were estimated and are summarized in Table 11.4. Aggregate effects vary in direct proportion to port activity. The indirect effects are shown for each state. Direct as well as indirect effects are shown for the states directly impacted. We also include the direct effects of import losses for the states where the attack takes place. Examined from this perspective, multipliers summed across all states range from 1.24 (Los Angeles/Long Beach) to 1.98 (Houston). The differences are accounted for by the fact that LA/LB has the largest value of imports.

A one-month loss of the services of the Los Angeles/Long Beach port costs the US economy approximately $22.8 billion. Corresponding impacts for the ports of New York/New Jersey and Houston are $16.2 billion and $9.7 billion, respectively. If ports are unusable for longer periods, these losses would grow, although strict proportionality would be an overstatement of the impact because substitution options become more feasible and important as time passes. As expected, the overall state-by-state impacts are, in general, a function of state size and distance from the terrorist attack. Similar results are available from NIEMO simulations for all 29 USC commodity sectors (see the CREATE website for examples).

CONCLUSIONS

Several caveats must be attached to our results. We have several reasons to expect that they include both overestimates and underestimates. First, as already mentioned, linear, demand-driven models are more relevant to short-term impact analysis. In the longer run, markets drive a variety of substitutions and price adjustments that the version of the model adopted here cannot account for. Second, it is questionable that a cessation of imports would have demand-driven effects as large as would a cessation of exports. In the previous section, we focused on the full effects of export losses. Only the direct impacts of import losses were included. Third, our analysis omits induced effects transmitted via the household sector. In the short run, households do not adjust their labor force participation rates across state lines. Nevertheless, we believe that we have advanced the state of the art by identifying the approximate orders of magnitude of losses from these types of events.

Also, it is widely accepted that in a federal system, local decision-makers would benefit from information that includes the spatial incidence of losses from various terrorist attacks. Our model has made it possible to estimate these on a state-by-state basis, but for disaggregated intra-regional impacts there are advantages in applying a much more spatially disaggregated (3191-zone) model like the one we have developed for Southern California, SCPM (Southern California Planning Model). Few models with similar degrees of spatial disaggregation have been developed for other metropolitan regions.

NIEMO results have important political implications because the simulations show that the terrorist attacks in one state have significant economic impacts in other states. In the Congress, especially in the Senate where political power is evenly distributed among states, this conclusion could help to garner nationwide support for prevention measures in states where the terrorist threats are more probable even at more distant locations.

REFERENCES

Bureau of Transportation Statistics and US Census Bureau (1999), *1997 Commodity Flow Survey: United States*, Washington, DC.

Bureau of Transportation Statistics and US Census Bureau (2000), *Commodity Flow Survey 1997: CD-EC97-CFS*, Washington, DC.

Bureau of Transportation Statistics and US Census Bureau (2003), *2002 Commodity Flow Survey: United States (Preliminary)*, Washington, DC.

Chenery, H.B. (1953), 'Regional Analysis', in H.B. Chenery, P.G. Clark and V.C. Pinna (eds), *The Structure and Growth of the Italian Economy*, Rome: US Mutual Security Agency, pp. 98–139.

CREATE website: (http://www.usc.edu/create).

Howe, D. (2004), 'Planning Scenarios', http://132.160.230.113:8080/revize/repository/CSSPrototype/simplelist/Planning_Scenarios__Exec_Summary_.pdf

Isard, W. (1951), 'Interregional and Regional Input–Output Analysis: A Model of a Space Economy', *Review of Economics and Statistics*, 33: 318–28.

Jack Faucett Associates, Inc. (1983), 'The Multiregional Input–Output Accounts, 1977: Introduction and Summary, Vol. I (Final Report)', prepared for the US Department of Health and Human Services, Washington.

Jackson, R.W., W.R. Schwarm, Y. Okuyama and S. Islam (2004), 'A Method for Constructing Commodity by Industry Flow Matrices', Paper presented at the 2004 Southern Regional Science Association Conference, New Orleans, LA.

Lahr, M.L. (1993), 'A Review of the Literature Supporting the Hybrid Approach to Constructing Regional Input–Output Models', *Economic Systems Research*, 5: 277–93.

Miller, R.E. and P.D. Blair (1985), *Input–Output Analysis: Foundations and Extensions*, New Jersey: Prentice-Hall.

Miller, R.E. and G. Shao (1990), 'Spatial and Sectoral Aggregation in the Commodity-Industry Multiregional Input–Output Model', *Environment and Planning A*, 22: 1637–56.

Moses, L.N. (1955), 'The Stability of Interregional Trading Patterns and Input–Output Analysis', *American Economic Review*, 45: 803–32.

Park, J., P. Gordon, J.E. Moore II and H.W. Richardson (2004), 'Construction of a US Multiregional Input–Output Model Using IMPLAN', Paper presented at 2004 National IMPLAN User's Conference, Eastern Management Development Center, Shepherdstown, WV.

Polenske, K.R. (1980), *The US Multiregional Input-Output Accounts and Model*, Lexington, MA: DC Health.

Robison, W.S. (1950), 'Ecological Correlations and the Behavior of Individuals', *American Sociological Review*, 15: 351–7.

Statistical Abstract of the United States (2002), Table 1277. US International Trade Goods and Services, http://www.census.gov/prod/2003pubs/02statab/foreign.pdf

US Bureau of the Census, Current Business Reports, Series BW/96-RV (1997), *Annual Benchmark Report for Wholesale Trade: January 1987 Through February 1997*, Washington, DC.

12. Tourism and terrorism: the national and interregional economic impacts of attacks on major US theme parks

Harry W. Richardson, Peter Gordon, James E. Moore II, Soojung Kim, Jiyoung Park and Qisheng Pan

This chapter is one of a series of studies by members of the Economic Modeling Group at CREATE on the economic impact of a variety of terrorist attacks in the United States. These studies use either or both of two economic impact models, SCPM (the Southern California Planning Model) and NIEMO (the National Interstate Economic Model). This research uses only the latter model and traces the inter-regional economic effects of attacks on major theme parks (13, including two clusters) located in a modest number of states (eight). The theme parks are identified by state but not by metropolitan area to mask specific identity. It is important to note that our results are underestimates because our analysis, by focusing on the major theme parks, ignores some of the smaller parks. We have also omitted one park that would have passed the scale threshold. We left it out because the theme park was a relatively minor component of economic activities at the site.

NIEMO

The details of the model used in this analysis (NIEMO) are explained in a parallel paper, a version of which is published in this book (Park et al., 2007, Chapter 11 in this book) so only a brief description is offered here, just enough for the paper to stand independently. The model revives an approach adopted in the late 1970s and the early 1980s (Polenske, 1980; Jack Faucett Associates, 1983), the development of a MRIO (multi-regional input–output) model. Our version combines state-level data from the

IMPLAN input–output models with inter-regional trade flows based on the Commodity Flow Survey (CFS) aggregated to 47 economic sectors over 52 regions (50 states, Washington, DC and the 'Rest of the World'). This results in an MRIO matrix with almost 6 million cells. Construction of the model involved substantial data assembly and considerable data manipulation.

More recently, there have been two attempts to estimate inter-regional trade flows using data from the 1997 Commodity Flow Survey (CFS). Jackson et al. (2004) used IMPLAN data to adjust incomplete CFS information primarily by adopting gravity models constrained via distance. The second attempt (Park et al., 2007) is the foundation of this study. It uses the same basic data sources, but adopts a different estimation approach to update missing CFS data and a doubly-constrained Fratar model (DFM) to estimate the MRIO matrix.

Constructing NIEMO requires two basic kinds of tables: industrial trade coefficients tables and regional inter-industry coefficients tables. While trade tables by industry are difficult to construct because of incomplete information in the CFS data, the inter-industry tables present fewer problems because reliable data are available from IMPLAN at the state and industry levels. For details of the procedure used to estimate values for the empty cells in the trade flow matrix, see Park et al. (2007). A temporary problem is that the currently available 1997 CFS data had to be updated to match the 2001 IMPLAN data. The availability of the 2002 CFS data will permit a direct match with 2002 IMPLAN data, although because of sample size there are questions about the adequacy of the new data. Once initial trade flow matrices are estimated for sectors based on a reconciliation of CFS, IMPLAN and SCPM data, these can then be iteratively refined via a Fratar model. However, the conventional Fratar model cannot estimate the diagonal (intrastate flow) values, so NIEMO incorporates a DFM (doubly-constrained Fratar Model) to supplement the off-diagonal flow estimates from the standard Fratar model, providing consistent estimates for on- and off-diagonal values.

DIRECT AND INDIRECT BUT NOT INDUCED IMPACTS

Usually, input–output models measure the direct (final demand), indirect (intermediate input flows) and induced (secondary consumption associated with direct and indirect employment) effects of changes in economic activity. In applying NIEMO we have chosen to measure the direct and indirect impacts only, for several reasons. First, it is a convention in MRIO to ignore induced effects (Miller and Blair, 1983), presumably because induced consumption is less likely to cross inter-regional, for example interstate, boundaries. Second, although there are local induced impacts associated with local indirect effects, the local and the imported indirect impacts are typically allocated in a MRIO model via some assumption that falls short of the accurate allocations of the 'ideal' inter-regional input–output model. For example, imported inputs of an origin sector are allocated to a particular destination sector in the same proportion as local inputs. Third, in the specifics of the theme park application, there may be positive induced effects in origin states associated with negative direct effects in theme park states. In other words, if would-be visitors to the theme parks stay home they may spend some of their tourist money on additional consumption. This is not a conventional induced impact of the kind measured in input–output models because it is not a secondary consumption effect resulting from employment change. For these reasons, we chose not to measure induced impacts, even if the net effect is to generate under-bounded estimates.

The direct impacts in this research are not limited to theme park expenditures. Overnight visitors to theme parks spend money on accommodation and often on transportation (such as rental cars), and all visitors buy food and often shop. Our estimates include these expenditures. However, we do not include air transportation because of the difficulty of assigning impacts to individual states since most have major operations in several states, not merely the headquarters state. However, the maximum impact would be sizeable, about $11.85 billion over the 18-month recovery period assumed in our base scenario.

TERRORISM AND TOURISM

There has never been a major terrorist attack on any tourist site in the United States. The attack of domestic origin by Eric Rudolph in Centennial Park, Atlanta, during the 1996 Olympic Games is the closest approximation. Consequently, we have no domestic history on which to construct feasible scenarios, so we adopt international precedents as a template. We have chosen to analyze a relatively simple type of attack: a large conventional bomb attack at a major theme park. Our focus is on economic impacts, so we do not explore the potential deaths and injuries and damage to tourist facilities and infrastructure. The scale of attack that we have in mind might kill about 20 people, injure ten times as many, and destroy sufficient tourist attractions and facilities to close at least part of a theme park for a few months during reconstruction, and the park overall for perhaps the first month. Our best estimate is that in terms of human and infrastructure impacts, this would be a $250 million event, and thus relatively small in terms of potential terrorist events. In any event, our analysis is restricted to economic impacts, specifically business interruption. We leave it to others to estimate the human and physical infrastructure costs of terrorist events. In our view, the human and infrastructure costs would be swamped by the long-term blow to the theme park component of the tourist sector as visitors stayed away in droves out of fear. A major research task is to estimate the recovery period. We discuss this important but difficult task below.

Another key point is that the economic losses we report in our main findings would be gross, not net, losses. However, this may be based on an unreasonable assumption because tourists would not necessarily stay at home but would substitute other, presumably safer, destinations or alternatively (not examined here) spend vacation savings on other expenditures. To capture the possibility of diversion, we explore one scenario that is not meant to be very realistic, merely illustrative. We assume that all the daily visitors to the theme parks stay home while the overnighters substitute visits to national parks, broadly defined to include some national monuments, national historical parks and national resort areas. In this scenario, then, there are net losses but also some redistribution of tourist revenues from some locations and sites to others, often in different states.

Drakos and Kutan (2003) hypothesize a 'zero sum game' in which total tourist revenues remain the same, but tourists switch from destinations affected by terrorism to others that are currently considered safe. Their study looked at tourism in Greece, Turkey and Israel, with Italy included as a control destination not affected by terrorism in recent years. A terrorist incident in Greece was estimated to reduce the country's market share among the four destinations by 1 percent. Specifically, in our substitution scenario, we assume that the 55 percent of total visitors who are day trippers to the theme parks stay home while the 45 percent of overnight visitors to theme parks are allocated to a fairly comprehensive group of national parks and similar nationally designated destinations. These shifts are allocated in proportion to the national parks' most recent visitor rolls.

We explore a range of alternative attacks, not simultaneous attacks. In this chapter, we are not identifying specific theme parks, but are looking at some of the major theme parks distributed across eight states. Also, in a few cases several theme parks are located in the same metropolitan region; we refer to these as 'clusters'. We hypothesize that an attack at one theme park in a cluster will have more of an impact on other theme parks in the cluster than on theme parks outside the cluster, for example in other states. Our rationale for studying several attacks in several states is to illustrate the capacity of our national interstate model (NIEMO) to trace multi-regional economic impacts from any source of changes in final demand.

Our expectation is that the theme park sector of US tourism would take a long time to recover from a terrorist attack on a single theme park, and that the economic impacts would be nationwide in scope. There are several reasons for this view. One is the role played by theme parks in shaping the American psyche. Another is our focus on protecting children who form a sizeable share, perhaps the majority, of theme park visitors. A third is the concept of 'probability neglect'. This concept means that for psychological reasons we may suffer from fear that exaggerates risk and discounted harm, because this fear fails to take sufficient account of the low probability of being a victim. The same phenomenon explained some of the downward trend in air travel after 9/11. A fourth reason is the power of the 'displacement effect'. There are so many tourist substitutions available that it is easy to cancel (or postpone) a theme park trip and go somewhere else. We explore the national parks case that we justify in terms of the argument that lower densities reduce risk, but there are a wide range of alternatives to theme park visits such as a beach holiday, a motoring holiday, a foreign trip, and many others.

INTERNATIONAL EVIDENCE

In the absence of prior episodes in the United States, we decided to look at the evidence from international terrorist attacks on tourist sites. However, the previous literature on tourism recovery from terrorism is relatively thin (Aly and Strazicich, 2000; Pizam and Smith, 2000). Drakos and Kutan (2003) present evidence for a relatively short time period (1996–99) on the recoveries from tourist attacks in three countries: seven months in Greece and Turkey and four months in Israel. The shorter time period in Israel probably reflects a degree of immunity and reduced sensitivity for residents, and even for tourists, associated with the greater frequency of terrorist events. This raises a more general point: infrequency combined with a larger attack in the United States might make for a longer recovery period.

A related point to the scale issue is that what seems to count most in terms of impact is not the number of incidents but the number of fatalities. Moreover, the negative relationship between tourist revenues and the number of fatalities appears to be non-linear. Another approach, adopted by Enders and Sandler (1991), is to calculate the number of international tourists deterred by each terrorist incident. In their study of Spain, they calculated 140 000 tourists deterred by each Basque attack. This results in a second calculation that in 1988, with 5.392 million foreign tourists visiting Spain and 18 terrorist incidents, there would have been 50 percent more tourists without them. Finally, Frey et al. (2004) surveyed a range of studies with divergent results, with recovery periods as short as 2–3 months or as long as 18–21 months.

We decided to use the extreme attacks in Luxor (Egypt) in 1997 and in Bali (Indonesia) in 2002 as the best predictors of the recovery phase of a theme park attack in the United States. It is too early to evaluate the repercussions of the more recent attacks in Egypt in Taba in October 2004 and Sharma el Sheikh in July 2005, but we expect the recovery period to be broadly similar. The principal reasons for these choices are the scale of the attacks and the quality of the data. A monthly data series for international visitors is available in both cases. Moreover, the results of the two cases are broadly consistent with each other. In both cases, the number of visitors declined precipitously immediately after the attacks and then recovered very slowly over the next six months. The somewhat different example of the post-tsunami recovery of Phuket in Thailand after December 2004 is also consistent with this finding. This was the short-term impact. In the Bali case, annual tourism did not return to the pre-attack levels until 2004, and monthly data did not consistently (month after month) exceed the pre-attack levels until 18 months after the attack.

Of course, in the absence of a historical record, any scenario is little better than a hypothetical guess. Nevertheless, it is useful as an illustration, and the scenario we chose is consistent with the international evidence. The other key assumption is that if one theme park is attacked, attendance will suffer at all US theme parks.

Our working assumptions are as follows:

1. A cluster consisting of several theme parks in the same Consolidated Metropolitan Statistical Area (CMSA) or Primary Metropolitan Statistical Area (PMSA) and an individual (isolated) theme park are treated as equivalents.
2. A theme park (or cluster) attacked would be closed for one month, would then operate at 30 percent capacity for the next six months and approach normal (pre-attack) levels linearly through to the eighteenth month.[1]
3. The other major theme parks (our sample) in the country would operate at 50 percent of normal capacity for six months and then recover to normal (pre-attack) levels linearly through to the eighteenth month.[2]

Of course, theme park visits are subject to seasonal fluctuations (for example opening hours change during the year), as is international tourism. For example, the peak months in Bali are May and June. We chose to ignore this complication. However, any deviation from our assumptions is easily accommodated within the model.

RESULTS

We analyzed attacks on 13 theme park complexes in eight states. Two of the complexes were clusters of several parks within the same metropolitan region in Florida and California. We designate them Cluster A (FL) and Cluster B (CA) respectively. Table 12.1 presents a summary of the results. Recall our assumption about the spillover effects on other theme parks not under direct attack, namely that other theme parks in a cluster would suffer the same fate in terms of impacts as if they were directly attacked. A cluster attack would result in an economic impact of $23.62–24.92 billion. In comparison, the latest estimate of the cost of the 9/11 attack is $31.7 billion (*New York Times*, 10 July 2005), although it is unclear whether this estimate reflects the full costs of business interruption. Outside the clusters in Florida and California, the impacts would be smaller, in the $20.75–20.94 billion range, but still sizeable. Of course, this result is a consequence of our specific assumptions that an attack on any major theme park would have nationwide repercussions on all major theme parks. We report below on the most conservative of assumptions, that is, no spillover effects.

The foreign indirect impacts are in the $415–419 million range except for Florida and California, and $499 million and $472 million in these two states. Note that there are no foreign direct impacts because the direct impacts measure the effects on the theme park states. The term 'foreign' measures leakages to the rest of the world outside the United States, and these impacts are all indirect. Despite the importance of international tourism, the foreign impacts are quite small but consistent with the 2 percent estimate of international visitors at the theme parks.

The direct impacts are in the range of $11.82 billion to $14.19 billion and the indirect impacts fall within a range of $8.93 billion to $9.01 billion. The Florida and California clusters have somewhat larger impacts, whereas the impacts of attacks in other states are of similar magnitude.

THE NO-SPILLOVERS CASE

These results are very sensitive to the spillover effect assumptions. We do not believe that other theme parks in the country would be immune from the effects of an attack on a theme park in another State, but we can combine some of the data in Table 12.1 into another table (Table 12.2) to demonstrate the implications if this belief was incorrect. The data here show the results if the economic impacts are confined to the theme park(s) in the state subject to attack. This is the limiting case of minimal impacts, and is useful from that perspective even if not very realistic. As shown in

Table 12.1 Summary of theme park impacts, $m

Cluster	Direct			Indirect				Total
	Intrastate	Other theme park states	Total	Intrastate	All other states	Foreign	Total	
Cluster A (FL)	7622.3	6562.7	14185.0	3983.0	6253.8	499.1	10735.9	24920.9
Cluster B (CA)	5971.0	7499.1	13470.1	3312.3	6361.6	472.0	10146.0	23616.1
NV	681.2	11263.2	11944.4	326.8	8246.1	417.7	8990.7	20935.1
FL(i)	5321.6	6562.7	11884.3	2786.3	5770.5	417.2	8974.0	20858.3
CA(i)	4433.9	7499.1	11933.1	2488.9	6098.4	418.7	9006.0	20939.1
OH(i)	815.6	11070.2	11885.8	551.9	8018.3	417.7	8987.9	20873.6
OH(ii)	800.8	11070.2	11871.0	543.2	8015.1	417.1	8975.4	20846.5
NJ(i)	719.1	11147.0	11866.1	398.9	8134.3	416.2	8949.4	20815.5
CA(ii)	4400.0	7499.1	11899.1	2470.7	6092.6	417.5	8980.8	20879.9
NJ(ii)	704.3	11147.0	11851.3	391.6	8131.8	415.7	8939.1	20790.4
PA	361.6	11474.4	11836.0	286.9	8238.1	415.5	8940.5	20776.6
VA	308.9	11509.3	11818.1	204.0	8310.1	415.0	8929.1	20747.2
IL	371.5	11467.8	11839.4	315.8	8210.9	415.7	8942.4	20781.8

Table 12.2   Theme park impacts: limiting case, no spillovers, $m

Cluster	Direct	Indirect	Total	Multiplier
Cluster A (FL)	7622.3	3983.0	11 605.3	1.523
Cluster B (CA)	5971.0	3312.3	9283.3	1.555
NV	681.2	326.8	1008.0	1.480
FL(i)	5321.6	2786.3	8107.8	1.524
CA(i)	4433.9	2488.9	6922.8	1.561
OH(i)	815.6	551.9	1367.5	1.677
OH(ii)	800.8	543.2	1344.0	1.678
NJ(i)	719.1	398.9	1117.9	1.555
CA(ii)	4400.0	2470.7	6870.7	1.562
NJ(ii)	704.3	391.6	1095.9	1.556
PA	361.6	286.9	648.6	1.793
VA	308.9	204.0	512.9	1.661
IL	371.5	315.8	687.3	1.850

Table 12.2, the differences are very dramatic, with impacts varying from less than $0.5 billion in Virginia up to more than $11.61 billion in the Florida cluster. The economic multipliers are more or less very similar, in the 1.48 to 1.85 range. Remember that these may be underestimates because of the exclusion of induced impacts.

The overall conclusion is that, if there are no spillovers, the terrorist pay-off is maximized by attacking a large theme park or a park in a major metropolitan area with many theme parks, such as in Florida or California. On the other hand, if there are significant spillovers, an attack on any known theme park, even one of modest size with presumably less protection because the expense risks are lower, will result in similar nationwide economic impacts. Unfortunately, we do not and will not know which is the more likely scenario unless it happens.

On the other hand, it is a reasonable argument that the spillover scenarios are more plausible. It is our belief that a successful attack on any theme park in the country would have national repercussions. The reason is based on public perception of risks and behavioral adjustments. Given that a theme park visit is a deferrable event and has many attractive alternative vacation trip substitutes, why would a rational person not postpone such a visit by either going elsewhere or staying at home? This behavior is consistent with the hypothesis of 'probability neglect' mentioned above. If valid, any theme park attack would result in nationwide fear, if not panic, and a widespread if temporary shunning of all theme parks. Perception also influences the recovery period. In this research, we have used the Bali (2002) and the Luxor (1997) attacks as a template for the decline and recovery trajectory. This is probably conservative, given that an American family with children considering a visit to a theme park after an attack might react more cautiously than, say, Australian singles to a holiday in Bali after a bar attack.

A DIVERSION SCENARIO: THE NATIONAL PARKS

A standard objection to models of the kind used in this research is that, as noted above, declines in final demand are not necessarily net losses. For example, the business interruptions and structural damage associated with a natural disaster, such as an earthquake or a hurricane, are usually offset later by a revival of pent-up demand and an injection of reconstruction funds. There are losses involved, such as the opportunity costs of resources diverted to reconstruction, but there are offsets to many losses.

So it may be in this case. A decline in visitors to theme parks after a terrorist attack is likely to be partially offset by an increase in other, presumably considered safer, types of tourist activities. It is not reasonable to expect everyone to stay home. Thus, part of the change in the tourist scene will be a redistribution of tourist expenditures rather than a total loss. To illustrate this effect, we consider a single substitution scenario to measure the potential offset. Theme park visitors are divided into two categories: day trippers (55 percent) and overnighters (45 percent). We assume that the day trippers stay home. An alternative would be for them to spend the money saved on other items of consumer expenditure. We divert the overnighters to other tourist activities. In the example explored here, we assume – somewhat unrealistically – that they all go to national parks and similar nationally designated destinations. The results of this scenario are reported in Table 12.3.

We consider the maximum impact case, an attack on a theme park in Cluster A (Florida), and reallocate all the lost overnight visitors at all theme parks in the country over the 18-month recovery period to the designated set of national parks and resort areas in proportion to their current visitor levels. We excluded all parks with less than 0.5 million annual visitors, national highways and monuments in New York City and Washington, DC. The consequences are a marked geographical redistribution of tourist expenditures and their impacts because theme parks are typically located in densely populated urban settings while national parks are usually located in lower-density rural settings. Other substitution scenarios, such as a shift to beach holidays, would also have marked, but very different, geographical impacts, perhaps less consequential because of the

Table 12.3 Net impacts of National Parks Diversion Scenario ($m)

State	Direct Impacts			Indirect Impacts			Total Impacts		
	First year	Second year	Total	First year	Second year	Total	First year	Second year	Total
AL	0.0	0.0	0.0	-57.4	-7.1	-64.5	-57.4	-7.1	-64.5
AK	93.3	11.4	104.8	57.0	7.0	64.0	150.4	18.4	168.8
AZ	441.5	54.1	495.6	210.8	25.9	236.7	652.3	80.0	732.3
AR	126.7	15.5	142.2	54.8	6.7	61.5	181.5	22.2	203.7
CA	-2819.3	-343.2	-3162.5	-1463.5	-178.1	-1641.7	-4282.8	-521.4	-4804.1
CO	218.6	26.8	245.4	117.1	14.4	131.4	335.6	41.1	376.8
CT	0.0	0.0	0.0	-4.1	-0.5	-4.6	-4.1	-0.5	-4.6
DE	0.0	0.0	0.0	0.8	0.1	0.9	0.8	0.1	0.9
DC	120.4	14.8	135.2	52.9	6.5	59.4	173.3	21.2	194.6
FL	-6384.8	-786.7	-7171.5	-3308.4	-407.7	-3716.1	-9693.2	-1194.4	-10 887.6
GA	217.2	26.6	243.8	-28.7	-3.6	-32.3	188.6	23.0	211.6
HI	250.0	30.6	280.6	132.7	16.3	149.0	382.7	46.9	429.6
ID	0.0	0.0	0.0	-4.8	-0.6	-5.4	-4.8	-0.6	-5.4
IL	-218.9	-26.7	-245.6	-170.9	-20.9	-191.8	-389.8	-47.6	-437.3
IN	87.9	10.8	98.7	39.0	4.8	43.8	126.9	15.6	142.5
IA	0.0	0.0	0.0	-28.8	-3.5	-32.3	-28.8	-3.5	-32.3
KS	0.0	0.0	0.0	-12.8	-1.6	-14.3	-12.8	-1.6	-14.3
KY	136.8	16.8	153.6	64.3	7.9	72.2	201.1	24.7	225.8
LA	28.9	3.5	32.4	-20.7	-2.5	-23.2	8.2	1.0	9.2
ME	107.2	13.1	120.3	62.5	7.7	70.1	169.7	20.8	190.5
MD	97.2	11.9	109.2	53.2	6.5	59.7	150.4	18.4	168.9
MA	322.3	39.5	361.8	155.8	19.1	174.9	478.1	58.6	536.7
MI	55.0	6.7	61.7	4.3	0.5	4.8	59.2	7.3	66.5

Table 12.3 (continued)

State	Direct Impacts			Indirect Impacts			Total Impacts		
	First year	Second year	Total	First year	Second year	Total	First year	Second year	Total
MN	12.1	1.5	13.6	-6.7	-0.8	-7.5	5.4	0.7	6.1
MS	98.0	12.0	110.0	44.9	5.5	50.4	142.9	17.5	160.4
MO	198.9	24.4	223.3	101.5	12.4	114.0	300.4	36.8	337.2
MT	169.8	20.8	190.6	104.7	12.8	117.5	274.4	33.6	308.1
NE	0.0	0.0	0.0	-35.2	-4.3	-39.5	-35.2	-4.3	-39.5
NV	-116.5	-14.0	-130.6	-56.6	-6.8	-63.5	-173.2	-20.9	-194.0
NH	0.0	0.0	0.0	1.4	0.2	1.5	1.4	0.2	1.5
NJ	-250.8	-30.4	-281.2	-143.3	-17.4	-160.8	-394.1	-47.8	-442.0
NM	20.4	2.5	22.9	13.0	1.6	14.6	33.4	4.1	37.5
NY	359.4	44.1	403.4	154.4	18.9	173.4	513.8	63.0	576.8
NC	338.0	41.4	379.4	159.1	19.5	178.6	497.1	60.9	558.0
ND	0.0	0.0	0.0	-0.7	-0.1	-0.7	-0.7	-0.1	-0.7
OH	-412.8	-50.2	-463.0	-262.3	-31.9	-294.2	-675.0	-82.2	-757.2
OK	61.9	7.6	69.5	33.5	4.1	37.6	95.4	11.7	107.1
OR	0.0	0.0	0.0	-7.4	-0.9	-8.3	-7.4	-0.9	-8.3
PA	193.1	23.8	216.9	84.4	10.4	94.8	277.5	34.2	311.7
RI	0.0	0.0	0.0	-0.5	-0.1	-0.6	-0.5	-0.1	-0.6
SC	44.1	5.4	49.5	11.2	1.4	12.6	55.3	6.8	62.0
SD	173.2	21.2	194.4	103.4	12.7	116.1	276.6	33.9	310.5
TN	249.2	30.6	279.8	115.3	14.1	129.4	364.5	44.7	409.1
TX	218.5	26.8	245.3	-73.7	-9.1	-82.8	144.8	17.7	162.5
UT	365.6	44.8	410.4	213.0	26.1	239.1	578.6	70.9	649.5
VM	0.0	0.0	0.0	-1.2	-0.1	-1.3	-1.2	-0.1	-1.3

VA	168.8	20.8	189.6	91.6	11.3	102.9	32.1	292.5
WA	271.3	33.3	304.5	132.1	16.2	148.3	49.5	452.8
WV	55.9	6.9	62.8	31.9	3.9	35.9	10.8	98.6
WI	0.0	0.0	0.0	-33.3	-4.1	-37.4	-4.1	-37.4
WY	234.8	28.8	263.6	154.2	18.9	173.1	47.7	436.7
US subtotal	-4667.2	-572.4	-5239.6	-3166.2	-388.4	-3554.7	-960.8	-8794.3
Foreign	0.0	0.0	0.0	-155.1	-19.0	-174.1	-19.0	-174.1
Total	-4667.2	-572.4	-5239.6	-3321.3	-407.4	-3728.8	-979.9	-8968.4

Notes: * Unit: $ millions.
** Final Demand Losses are calculated by each MSA, but are aggregated by state to be used in NIEMO.

247

relatively high concentration of both theme parks and beaches in Florida and California.

More specifically, the big losers are Florida ($10.89 billion) and California ($4.80 billion), with Ohio a distant third ($0.76 billion). Although California, and to a lesser extent Florida, are well endowed with national park related facilities, their potential positive economic impacts are swamped by losses associated with theme parks. The top gainers are Arizona ($0.73 billion), Utah ($0.65 billion), New York ($0.58 billion), North Carolina ($0.56 billion), Massachusetts ($0.54 billion) and Wyoming ($0.44 billion). At least one-half of these are very low-density, sparsely populated states which presumably would be much safer in terms of the risks of death or injuries to visitors. Overall, the impacts are well dispersed so that no gainer is anywhere near the ballpark of the two main losers. Overall, given the assumptions, the diversion scenario still involves a net loss of $8.97 billion.

THE DISTRIBUTION OF GEOGRAPHICAL IMPACTS

One question is the sensitivity of the spatial distribution of indirect impacts to the location(s) of the direct impact. To test this, we assumed a $100 million decline in theme park revenues in each of the nine major theme park states. Note that for this simple test, we did not include the ripple effects of revenue losses at theme parks in states other than in the state attacked, so this analysis is somewhat distinct from the other scenarios discussed in this paper. The results are displayed in Table 12.4. They are not surprising. More than 90 percent of the impacts are intrastate, and the interstate impacts reflect a significant distance decay effect. In other words, the proportionate indirect impacts tend to be larger in states that are nearby to the state where the direct impacts occur.

CONCLUSIONS

This study reports on a preliminary analysis of the economic impacts of terrorist attacks on America's more prominent theme parks. A key assumption of the research is that in the public's psyche, an attack on one theme park will be perceived as an attack on all. However, we also report results of a more conservative assumption, specifically that of a 'no spillover' effect. We also recognize that even a major terrorist attack on a theme park will not ruin American vacation habits. Vacationers will probably switch to holidays considered safer. We examine one scenario: substituting visits to national parks, and their low-density environments, for theme parks.

The results can be easily summarized. In the spillover cases, even an attack on a moderately sized theme park will result in more than a $20 billion hit to the economy. An attack on a cluster could result in $25 billion of economic damages. In addition, the loss in airline revenues could run as high as almost $12 billion. These numbers combined are in the same neighborhood as the costs of the 9/11 disaster. On the other hand, if the repercussions are constrained in terms of spillovers, the impact could be as low as $513 million or as high as $11.6 billion, depending upon which theme park was attacked. In the diversion scenario, that is, substitution of national parks for theme parks, there still is an economic loss as some people will stay home, increase their savings and plan a vacation for the following year. However, there is a significant offset. Florida and California are net losers, because even though they have important national parks their economic impacts are modest compared with their theme parks. The big winners, that is, in terms of net gains, are sparsely populated states with rich natural and recreational resources, such as Arizona, Utah and Wyoming.

POLICY IMPLICATIONS

Because of the scarcity of both Department of Homeland Security and private sector resources, any study of the economic impact of a terrorist attack needs to consider the cost-effectiveness of the scale and scope of alternative prevention measures. It is somewhat easier to do this with economic impact analyses because they generate implicit guidelines on how much it is worth to spend. The economic impact estimates in this study are sizeable, yet are probably underestimates because of our exclusion of induced impacts and our focus on only the largest theme parks. They certainly justify significant expenditures on prevention, probably much more than those (based on anecdotal evidence) currently in place. The problem is the distribution of those expenditures among theme parks. In the spillovers scenarios, even the smaller theme parks are attractive terrorist targets because they are less protected, but may have nationwide economic impacts almost as damaging as in the case of a cluster attack. If such scenarios are considered more probable, there are certain implications.

For example, it may pay DHS to subsidize, or offer other incentives for, prevention measures in smaller theme parks. In no-spillovers scenarios, the implication is to focus on the larger theme parks, especially in the clusters. Also, if there is a case for subsidies in these cases, the providers should be local or state entities because the externalities will be more local than national. However, we suspect that, regardless of spillovers or not, the most

Table 12.4 Interstate impacts of a $100 m direct loss in theme park states, $m

								Total impacts								
State	CA	%	FL	%	IL	%	NV	%	NJ	%	OH	%	PA	%	VA	%
AL	0.26	0.1%	1.00	0.6%	0.31	0.2%	0.11	0.1%	0.29	0.2%	0.58	0.3%	0.18	0.1%	0.25	0.1%
AK	0.08	0.0%	0.02	0.0%	0.02	0.0%	0.02	0.0%	0.01	0.0%	0.05	0.0%	0.01	0.0%	0.06	0.0%
AZ	0.44	0.3%	0.10	0.0%	0.08	0.0%	0.21	0.1%	0.05	0.0%	0.07	0.0%	0.07	0.0%	0.08	0.0%
AR	0.44	0.3%	0.46	0.3%	0.43	0.2%	0.13	0.1%	0.16	0.1%	0.50	0.3%	0.40	0.2%	0.21	0.1%
CA	153.51	88.2%	1.28	0.7%	1.51	0.8%	5.27	3.2%	1.18	0.7%	1.25	0.7%	1.17	0.7%	0.91	0.5%
CO	0.34	0.2%	0.18	0.1%	0.60	0.3%	0.11	0.1%	0.14	0.1%	0.28	0.2%	0.14	0.1%	0.22	0.1%
CT	0.09	0.0%	0.15	0.1%	0.10	0.1%	0.09	0.1%	0.21	0.1%	0.11	0.1%	0.18	0.1%	0.15	0.1%
DE	0.04	0.0%	0.04	0.0%	0.03	0.0%	0.01	0.0%	0.18	0.1%	0.04	0.0%	0.14	0.1%	0.62	0.3%
DC	0.01	0.0%	0.01	0.0%	0.01	0.0%	0.01	0.0%	0.01	0.0%	0.01	0.0%	0.01	0.0%	0.05	0.0%
FL	0.24	0.1%	152.00	86.2%	0.24	0.1%	0.16	0.1%	0.34	0.2%	0.49	0.3%	0.36	0.2%	0.35	0.2%
GA	0.24	0.1%	2.46	1.4%	0.40	0.2%	0.14	0.1%	0.61	0.4%	0.67	0.4%	0.56	0.3%	0.79	0.4%
HI	0.11	0.1%	0.03	0.0%	0.04	0.0%	0.02	0.0%	0.02	0.0%	0.03	0.0%	0.02	0.0%	0.04	0.0%
ID	0.29	0.2%	0.09	0.1%	0.16	0.1%	0.06	0.0%	0.09	0.1%	0.17	0.1%	0.08	0.0%	0.06	0.0%
IL	0.87	0.5%	1.02	0.6%	155.75	87.2%	0.30	0.2%	0.64	0.4%	1.48	0.8%	0.87	0.5%	0.73	0.4%
IN	0.35	0.2%	0.39	0.2%	0.99	0.6%	0.19	0.1%	0.30	0.2%	1.03	0.6%	0.36	0.2%	0.69	0.4%
IA	0.78	0.5%	0.41	0.2%	1.42	0.8%	0.14	0.1%	0.37	0.2%	0.63	0.3%	0.38	0.2%	0.31	0.2%
KS	0.56	0.3%	0.18	0.1%	0.51	0.3%	0.15	0.1%	0.80	0.5%	0.52	0.3%	0.15	0.1%	0.60	0.3%
KY	0.20	0.1%	0.35	0.2%	0.46	0.3%	0.11	0.1%	0.18	0.1%	0.96	0.5%	0.31	0.2%	0.65	0.4%
LA	0.55	0.3%	0.71	0.4%	0.47	0.3%	0.19	0.1%	0.17	0.1%	0.26	0.1%	0.24	0.1%	0.28	0.2%
ME	0.08	0.0%	0.06	0.0%	0.08	0.0%	0.02	0.0%	0.06	0.0%	0.05	0.0%	0.12	0.1%	0.07	0.0%
MD	0.07	0.0%	0.08	0.0%	0.10	0.1%	0.05	0.0%	0.29	0.2%	0.10	0.1%	0.44	0.2%	1.21	0.7%
MA	0.14	0.1%	0.21	0.1%	0.15	0.1%	0.11	0.1%	0.26	0.2%	0.18	0.1%	0.21	0.1%	0.24	0.1%
MI	0.45	0.3%	0.56	0.3%	0.71	0.4%	0.31	0.2%	0.57	0.3%	1.68	0.9%	0.57	0.3%	0.80	0.4%
MN	0.55	0.3%	0.32	0.2%	0.90	0.5%	0.17	0.1%	0.32	0.2%	0.72	0.4%	0.39	0.2%	0.28	0.2%
MS	0.15	0.1%	0.34	0.2%	0.24	0.1%	0.06	0.0%	0.13	0.1%	0.23	0.1%	0.16	0.1%	0.16	0.1%
MO	0.39	0.2%	0.30	0.2%	0.73	0.4%	0.74	0.5%	0.40	0.2%	0.36	0.2%	0.34	0.2%	0.29	0.2%

MT	0.17	0.1%	0.03	0.0%	0.21	0.1%	0.03	0.0%	0.03	0.0%	0.04	0.0%	0.04	0.0%	0.02	0.0%
NE	0.68	0.4%	0.53	0.3%	0.55	0.3%	0.09	0.1%	0.27	0.2%	0.55	0.3%	0.54	0.3%	0.27	0.1%
NV	0.13	0.1%	0.03	0.0%	0.02	0.0%	146.93	89.7%	0.02	0.0%	0.03	0.0%	0.02	0.0%	0.02	0.0%
NH	0.05	0.0%	0.04	0.0%	0.04	0.0%	0.03	0.0%	0.03	0.0%	0.04	0.0%	0.06	0.0%	0.06	0.0%
NJ	0.31	0.2%	0.46	0.3%	0.41	0.2%	0.14	0.1%	149.39	88.2%	0.36	0.2%	0.70	0.4%	0.40	0.2%
NM	0.06	0.0%	0.07	0.0%	0.07	0.0%	0.04	0.0%	0.04	0.0%	0.08	0.0%	0.05	0.0%	0.03	0.0%
NY	0.42	0.2%	0.50	0.3%	0.49	0.3%	0.20	0.1%	1.54	0.9%	0.79	0.4%	1.57	0.9%	0.65	0.4%
NC	0.26	0.1%	0.77	0.4%	0.28	0.2%	0.13	0.1%	0.44	0.3%	0.60	0.3%	0.61	0.3%	2.11	1.2%
ND	0.10	0.1%	0.05	0.0%	0.17	0.1%	0.06	0.0%	0.06	0.1%	0.12	0.1%	0.11	0.1%	0.04	0.0%
OH	0.53	0.3%	0.71	0.4%	0.85	0.5%	0.54	0.3%	0.66	0.4%	158.75	86.4%	1.12	0.6%	0.86	0.5%
OK	0.31	0.2%	0.22	0.1%	0.21	0.1%	0.13	0.1%	0.16	0.1%	0.19	0.1%	0.14	0.1%	0.15	0.1%
OR	0.48	0.3%	0.12	0.1%	0.20	0.1%	0.18	0.1%	0.09	0.1%	0.20	0.1%	0.08	0.0%	0.10	0.1%
PA	0.47	0.3%	0.65	0.4%	0.59	0.3%	0.34	0.2%	1.86	1.1%	1.24	0.7%	157.60	87.9%	1.56	0.9%
RI	0.03	0.0%	0.05	0.0%	0.02	0.0%	0.03	0.0%	0.04	0.0%	0.05	0.0%	0.04	0.0%	0.04	0.0%
SC	0.11	0.1%	0.37	0.2%	0.14	0.1%	0.07	0.1%	0.12	0.1%	0.28	0.2%	0.20	0.1%	0.37	0.2%
SD	0.18	0.1%	0.07	0.0%	0.20	0.1%	0.04	0.0%	0.06	0.0%	0.22	0.1%	0.13	0.1%	0.07	0.0%
TN	0.29	0.2%	0.53	0.3%	0.30	0.2%	0.16	0.1%	0.38	0.2%	0.48	0.3%	0.39	0.2%	0.85	0.5%
TX	2.52	1.4%	3.50	2.0%	0.94	0.5%	2.01	1.2%	1.95	1.1%	0.99	0.5%	2.50	1.4%	1.21	0.7%
UT	0.29	0.2%	0.11	0.1%	0.08	0.0%	0.19	0.1%	0.04	0.0%	0.09	0.1%	0.07	0.0%	0.06	0.0%
VM	0.03	0.0%	0.04	0.0%	0.05	0.0%	0.01	0.0%	0.04	0.0%	0.03	0.0%	0.06	0.0%	0.03	0.0%
VA	0.13	0.1%	0.27	0.2%	0.30	0.2%	0.09	0.1%	0.27	0.2%	0.36	0.2%	0.47	0.3%	0.27	0.2%
WA	0.93	0.5%	0.25	0.1%	0.25	0.1%	0.27	0.2%	0.15	0.1%	0.22	0.1%	0.18	0.1%	157.67	86.7%
WV	0.05	0.0%	0.05	0.0%	0.06	0.0%	0.03	0.0%	0.06	0.0%	0.73	0.4%	0.26	0.1%	0.16	0.1%
WI	0.70	0.4%	0.63	0.4%	1.97	1.1%	0.26	0.2%	0.58	0.3%	1.00	0.5%	0.85	0.5%	0.80	0.4%
WY	0.06	0.0%	0.02	0.0%	0.17	0.1%	0.07	0.1%	0.02	0.0%	0.06	0.0%	0.03	0.0%	0.50	0.3%
															0.02	0.0%
US sub total	170.51	98.0%	172.85	98.0%	174.99	98.0%	160.97	98.3%	166.09	98.0%	179.95	97.9%	175.67	98.0%	178.20	98.0%
Foreign	3.45	2.0%	3.54	2.0%	3.63	2.0%	2.87	1.7%	3.33	2.0%	3.78	2.1%	3.59	2.0%	3.67	2.0%
Total	173.96	100.0%	176.39	100.0%	178.61	100.0%	163.84	100.0%	169.42	100.0%	183.73	100.0%	179.26	100.0%	181.87	100.0%

Note: * $100m are distributed according to sector proportions, which are adopted from the proportions in Cluster B.

visible theme parks, nationally and/or internationally, are the most vulnerable because of their symbolic value as representatives of American culture.

Rather than relying on government subsidies, a self-help strategy might be both preferable and more feasible, depending upon whether the Terrorism Risk Insurance Act is eventually abolished. Especially in the spillovers scenarios, there is a strong case for both co-insurance and collaborative joint-prevention programs whereby the association of theme park owners get together to pool both human and financial resources and expertise. This is particularly important for the smaller theme parks that may lack the internal resources to mount adequate prevention and mitigation programs or even to cover the insurance risks. It is rational for the large theme park owners to promote and participate in such an approach because a simultaneous attack on theme parks in more than one state is extremely unlikely on logistical grounds. So, even though an attack on an internationally known theme park is more likely because of its publicity effects, an attack on a much smaller theme park would be easier and less costly and would (on the assumption of spillovers) result in almost as much national economic damage.

NOTES

1. The calculation is as follows:
   Let the i month be M_i and the j year be Y_j, where $i = 1, \ldots, 18$ and $j = 1$ and 2.
   $M_1 = (\text{Raw\_Data})/12$.
   $M_i = M_i - M_i*0.3 = M_i*0.7$, where $i = 2, \ldots, 7$.
   Also, $M_i = M_i - M_i*0.3 - M_i*0.7*(i-7)/(18-7) = M_i*0.7*(1 - (i-7)/11)$,
   where $i = 8, \ldots, 18$.
   Hence, $Y_1 = \Sigma_{i=1}^{12} M_i = M_1[1 + 0.7*6 + 0.7*\{5 - (1 + \ldots + 5)/11\}]$ and $Y_2 = \Sigma_{i=13}^{18} M_i = M_1*0.7*\{6 - (6 + \ldots + 11)/11\}$.

2. Similarly to Note 1, by letting the j year be Y_j', $Y_1' = \Sigma_{i=1}^{12} M_i = M_1*0.5[6 + 0.5*\{6 - (1 + \ldots + 6)/12\}]$ and $Y_2' = \Sigma_{i=13}^{18} M_i = *0.5*\{6 - (7 + \ldots + 12)/12\}$.

REFERENCES

Aly, H.Y. and M.C. Strazicich (2000), 'Terrorism and Tourism: Is the Impact Permanent or Transitory?' Columbus, OH: Ohio State University, Department of Economics.

Drakos, K. and A.M. Kutan (2003), 'Regional Effects of Terrorism and Tourism in Three Mediterranean Countries', *Journal of Conflict Resolution*, 47(5): 621–41.

Enders, W.K. and T. Sandler (1991), 'Causality between Transnational Terrorism and Tourism: The Case of Spain', *Terrorism*, 14(1): 49–58.

Frey, B.S., S. Luechinger and A. Stutzer (2004), 'Calculating Tragedy: Assessing the Costs of Terrorism', Institute of Empirical Research in Economics, University of Zurich, WP 205.

Gordon, P., J.E. Moore II and H.W. Richardson (2005), 'The Economic Impact of Terrorist Attack on the Twin Ports of Los Angeles-Long Beach', in H.W. Richardson, P. Gordon and J.E. Moore II (eds), *The Economic Impacts of Terrorist Attacks*. Cheltenham, UK and Northampton, MA, USA: Edward Elgar.

Jack Faucett Associates (1983), *The Multiregional Input–Output Accounts 1977: Introduction and Summary, Vol. I (Final Report)*, prepared for the US Department of Health and Human Services, Washington, DC.

Jackson, R.W., W.R. Schwarm, Y. Okuyama and S. Islam (2004), 'A method for Constructing Commodity by Industry Flow Matrices', Paper presented at the 2004 Southern Regional Science Association, New Orleans, LA.

Miller, R.E. and P.D. Blair (1983), *Input–Output Analysis: Foundations and Extensions*, New Jersey: Prentice-Hall.

Miller, R.E. and G. Shao (1990), 'Spatial and Sectoral Aggregation in the Commodity-Industry Multiregional Input–Output Model', *Environment and Planning A*, 22: 1637–56.

Park, J., P. Gordon, J.E. Moore II, H.W. Richardson and Q. Pan (2007), 'Simulating the State-by-State Effects of Terrorist Attacks on Three Major US Ports: Applying NIEMO (National Interstate Economic Model)', Paper presented at the 2nd CREATE Symposium on the Economic Impacts of Terrorist Attacks, 19–20 August, University of Southern California.

Pizam, A. and G. Smith (2000), 'Tourism and Terrorism: A Quantitative Analysis of Terrorist Attacks and their Impact on Tourist Destinations', *Tourism Economics*, 6(2): 123–38.

Polenske, K.R. (1980), *The US Multiregional Input–Output Accounts and Model*, Lexington, MA: DC Heath.

PART V

The electric power sector

13. Worst-case electricity scenarios: the benefits and costs of prevention

Lester B. Lave, Jay Apt and Granger Morgan

WHY CARE ABOUT ELECTRICITY?

The US electricity system is vulnerable to human attack. Like virtually every part of the US economy, the US electricity system was not designed to foil sabotage. That is not surprising, since there was little threat when it was designed and built. We show that there are many benefits to the US economy from a thoughtfully designed system that would lessen the ability of terrorists to create major problems.

Why should we be concerned about electricity? (1) A blackout would paralyze nearly the whole economy in the affected region; (2) the electricity sector is particularly vulnerable to sabotage; and (3) a reliable, low-cost electricity supply is needed for the development of the US economy. When the electricity system fails, people find it difficult to commute (no traffic signals or trains), get up and down in buildings (no elevator), work (no lights, computers, copiers or faxes), cook (no microwave ovens, refrigerators, electric appliances, or solid state ignition to light natural gas stoves), and suffer a degraded living situation (no heating or air conditioning, TV, VCR or radio).

On 14 August 2003, 50 million people from Cleveland to Detroit to Toronto to New York City suddenly found themselves without electricity. Essentially all businesses, electric trains, water treatment facilities and other activities powered by electricity stopped. New Yorkers found themselves stranded in a city without subways or traffic signals. It was all but impossible to get up or down in tall buildings without walking, and all but impossible to drive in the city center. The blackout shut down the north-east, imposing costs estimated at $4–6 billion. This blackout, together with those in 1966 and 1977, showed the dependence of our economy and our lives on electricity.

Blackouts are hardly rare. Figure 13.1 shows the average customer loss of power for Long Island, New York from 1985 to 2000. Figure 13.2 gives comparable figures for five large utilities in California. Both understate the total

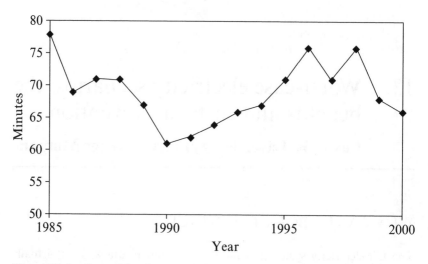

*Figure 13.1   Long Island power authority customer average interruption
              duration*

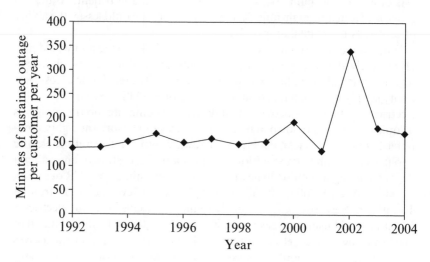

*Figure 13.2   System average interruption duration index, SAIDI
              (excluding storm-related outages) for PG&E*

outage time since they exclude outages due to major events, such as large
storms. Table 13.1 lists some of the major blackouts in the past few decades.
    Not only is electricity a tempting target because of the large costs asso-
ciated with disruption, but it is also easy to disrupt. Current systems are

designed to N −1 criteria, which means that they should not fail if the most critical component in the system fails. However, power parks with large amounts of generation make tempting targets, as do the long transmission lines that connect them to their customers. A single terrorist could dynamite transmission towers on several lines or several substations or use a rifle to destroy several high-voltage transformers, causing more damage than the N − 1 criteria is designed to handle. It is easier to cause blackouts than to hijack aircraft.

However, causing a blackout may not cause terror, given the frequency with which power is lost, as shown in Figures 13.1 and 13.2. In the US, the average customer loses power a few times per year. In areas prone to hurricanes or ice storms, outages of several days to several weeks are not uncommon.

The North American Electric Reliability Council logged 533 significant disturbances to the electric power grid in the US and Canada over the

Table 13.1   Major electricity blackouts

Date	Location	Population affected
11/9/65	Northeast	30 million people
6/5/67	PA-NJ-MD	4 million
5/17/77	Miami	1 million
7/13/77	New York City	9 million
1/1/81	Idaho-Utah-Wyoming	1.5 million
3/27/82	Western US	1 million
12/14/94	Western US	2 million
8/24/92	Florida	1 million
7/2/96	Western US	2 million
8/10/96	Western US	7.5 million
Jan 98	Quebec	2.3 million
Feb-Apr 98	Auckland	1.3 million
12/8/98	San Francisco	0.5 million
Dec 99	France	3.5 million
8/14/03	Great Lakes-NYC	50 million
8/30/03	London	0.5 million
9/18/03	Tidewater US	4 million
9/23/03	Denmark & Sweden	4 million
9/28/03	Italy	57 million
11/7/03	Most of Chile	15 million
7/12/04	Athens	3 million
9/26/04	Florida	1.5 million
8/25/05	Florida	1 million
8/19/05	Louisiana-Mississippi	2.1 million

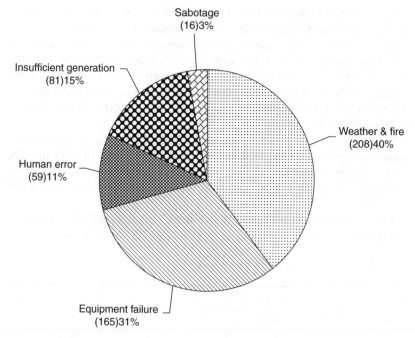

Source: Analysis of NERC DAWG data 1984–2000 by Jay Apt.

Figure 13.3   Causes of major disturbances

period 1984–2000. Approximately three each year cause a power loss of 1000 megawatts or more. As shown in Figure 13.3, eight blackouts were caused by criminal activity. Had these attacks been expertly designed, larger disruptions would have followed.

As shown in Figure 13.4, major blackouts are random events that occur between two and six times each year. They do not appear to be getting more – or less – frequent.

VALUING ELECTRICITY

Electricity has become essential to almost every aspect of our economy and our lives. Our transportation system depends on electricity, as do our stores and manufacturing plants. The US economy was designed assuming the availability of reliable, low-priced electricity. For example, we replaced pilot lights with solid-state ignition, and space heating systems that use convection to circulate hot water with hot air systems that require fans. We

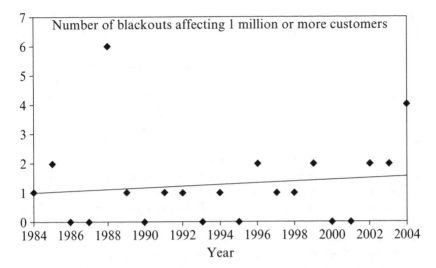

Source: Jay Apt analysis of NERC Distribution Analysis Working Group (DAWG) Database.

Figure 13.4 Are blackouts getting more frequent?

depend on electric elevators, electric trains and even electric toothbrushes. Electricity is needed to run the fan in your furnace. The immediate effects of losing power are devastating: we sweat – or freeze – in the dark.

Putting a dollar value on preventing a blackout requires putting a dollar value on: (1) losses to consumers and business customers from not having electricity; (2) losses to the economy; (3) increases in traffic congestion and other delays; and (4) injuries and deaths due to the blackout.

Customers pay electricity suppliers $250 billion per year, but this understates the value of electricity to the consumers. 'Consumer surplus' is a tool to quantify the value that customers enjoy above the price they pay. Most people would be willing to pay many times the 10 cents per kilowatt-hour price for electricity to run the furnace, air conditioner, computer and other appliances. A very rough, conservative estimate is that electricity customers get consumer surplus equal to perhaps $2.5 to $5 trillion or about 25 percent to 50 percent of GDP. More striking is the observation that almost all high-technology products require electricity during their production as well as in their use. Not having reliable electricity, sufficient electricity, or low-cost electricity would hamper innovation and economic growth.

The above cost is understated since it does not account for the large quantity of back-up power. Were it not for back-up generation, the outage costs would be much higher. Hospitals, financial institutions, communication centers and others spend about $5 billion dollars each year on back-up generation.

Taking the ratio of GDP to population gives a figure of $112 per person per day. Using this figure, if 50 million people lost power for a day, the cost would be approximately $5.6 billion, within the range of the official estimates for economic loss during the 14 August 2003 blackout.

When electricity is cut off, subways and other electric trains cease to run. Similarly, traffic signals fail. More people would try to use the street, resulting in intense congestion and even gridlock. The usual assumption in transportation economics is that additional time spent commuting is worth half the person's hourly wage rate (US Department of Transportation, Office of the Secretary of Transportation, 2003). The usual figure assumed is $12 per hour, although major cities, such as New York, are likely to have substantially higher wages.

The 1977 New York City blackout caused crime and riots, as well as mishaps, resulting in injuries and deaths. EPA estimates that individuals are willing to pay approximately $5.2 million per premature death averted (US Environmental Protection Agency, 1999).

Thus, the 14 August 2003 blackout affected 50 million people for 24 hours, caused perhaps one or more deaths, and perhaps 20 million hours of delay. Thus, we estimate the cost of the blackout as 50 million × $112 + 1 × $5.2 million + 20 million × $12 = $5.5 billion.

SOME 'WORST-CASE' SCENARIOS

We will sketch five 'worst-case' scenarios to show how vulnerable the US electricity system is and to start us thinking about how to prevent the damage that would result from these attacks. Some of the solutions cost little and could be implemented quickly. Others are difficult and expensive, but might be worth the trouble and expense.

1. A severe ice storm hits Southern Quebec–Northern New York State. A cylinder of ice 6 inches in diameter forms on all power lines, pulling down all transmission and distribution lines, as well as more than 770 transmission towers and thousands of distribution poles.
2. Three hurricanes strike Florida over a six-week period taking down thousands of distribution poles and some transmission towers. All three hurricanes travel similar courses, destroying much of the previous repair work.

3. A major earthquake strikes Northern California, collapsing part of the Bay Bridge and disrupting electricity service to San Francisco and much of the Bay area.
4. A shortage of reactive power leads to operator actions that trip a generator, and cause a cascade of failures resulting in 50 million people losing electricity for a day or more.
5. A category 4 hurricane hits New Orleans, flooding much of the city to a depth of 20 feet. The floodwaters contain sewage, industrial chemicals and fire ants. Since much of the city is 9 feet below sea level, the flood lasts for weeks. The electricity system is out since many of the poles and wires are submerged. Many of the houses not destroyed by the hurricane have to be demolished because of mold and other problems from being flooded.

All of these events happened: the first in 1998, the second in 2004, the third in 1989 and the fourth in 2003. The fifth event nearly happened in 2004 with Hurricane Ivan, and did happen in 2005 with Hurricane Katrina.

None of these events involve terrorists, but in each millions of people lost electricity, some for a month or more. In each case damage was in the billions of dollars and the economy was paralyzed for weeks. Katrina devastated New Orleans and surrounding areas. Hundreds of people drowned and property damage was hundreds of billions of dollars. Events as horrendous as these might easily have blacked out the affected areas for months or even years. Instead, nearly all the customers were reconnected in days, or a few weeks at the outside. Fortunately, our electricity system was built to handle catastrophic events and is managed to lessen damage and restore service quickly. However, for an event such as Katrina, damage is almost unimaginable and restoration can take months or years.

Note that most of these events occurred in the last few years and all occurred since 1989. A much larger hurricane or ice storm or earthquake that struck a large city could cause much greater damage. Perhaps some consolation could come from the damage being so great that the loss of electricity would not be the largest concern.

Human attacks mimic natural hazards in many ways, for example dynamiting a transmission tower is analogous to an ice storm taking down the tower. Human attacks do not differ qualitatively from problems caused by natural hazards and human error, but the timing and frequency can differ. In particular, terrorists could realize that they would have to mount two or more simultaneous attacks in order to go beyond the N − 1 criterion that the system is designed to withstand. High voltage transformers are rarely damaged by natural hazards or human error, but would be prime targets for terrorists; they could be destroyed from 1.5 miles away by a terrorist with a 50 caliber rifle. The longevity and unique design of most of these transformers means that utilities have limited ability to cope if one is put out of service – which makes them a more tempting target. Very high-voltage transformers are no longer manufactured in the US and so must be imported. Because of high global demand, delivery times are long. Many are too large to move in one piece or over normal roads or rail routes, further complicating replacement. While there have been discussions of producing smaller, lower-efficiency 'replacement' transformers for temporary emergency power, this has not happened.

Although the electricity system is most stressed at a time of peak demand, system operators are alert and ready to cope with emergencies. For example, 14 August 2003 was not a day of very high demand; system operators were not watching carefully to protect the system against overloading. In contrast, terrorists would strike during the period of highest demand so that extremely hot or cold temperatures would cause more discomfort and even death.

An attack on a transmission line is easy: the towers are essentially unprotected and their locations are obvious. During a heat wave or other period of high demand, taking out several transmission lines would lead to a blackout. Taking down transmission towers leads to a limited loss: the towers could be repaired in a week or so. If the attack destroyed several high-voltage transformers in the right substation, repairs could take months.

The cost, disruption and loss of life would be compounded if the terrorists could field a team of perhaps two dozen operatives. On the day of the blackout, 24 vans loaded with explosives could be driven into New York and instructed to arrive at their target at 4.45 p.m., when the lights were expected to fail. Operatives outside the city could blow up transmission towers on several major transmission lines going into the city. When the power fails, traffic signals would cease to work, quickly leading to gridlock. With gridlock, the police and fire departments would be unable to get their vehicles to problem areas, giving local control to terrorists. The terrorists could drive a vehicle into an underground garage or just park it next to the building and then detonate the explosives. The result would be explosions and fires at two dozen buildings. The fires could not be controlled because the gridlock would prevent the police and fire department vehicles from coming to the rescue. The result would likely be major damage at all 24 buildings, with possibly a few of them collapsing.

A terrorist-caused blackout would lead to some loss of life due to the heat, and major disruption. A blackout plus vans filled with explosives blowing up next to two dozen major buildings could cause thousands of deaths, billions of dollars in property damage and would certainly cause terror. We stress that our 'worst-case' scenarios begin with a loss of electrical power that takes out traffic signals, leading to gridlock. Terrorists would then be free to attack particular targets without worrying that police and firemen could get their trucks to battle the attack.

A centralized system is inherently vulnerable to a natural hazard, human error or terrorist attack. Attempting to protect this system against all terrorist attack becomes increasingly expensive, and cannot succeed. Nonetheless, there are changes that are cost-effective that would make it less vulnerable and help it to recover more quickly.

Ecologists use the term 'resilient' to describe a system that can absorb a major challenge and then recover quickly. We discuss how to make our electricity system more resilient.

HOW MUCH RELIABILITY DO WE WANT?

For outages of a similar duration, the direct costs of a power loss caused by a natural hazard or human error would be the same as the costs of a power loss caused by a terrorist attack, assuming that the same number of people are affected. Thus, society's goal should not be just forestalling blackouts caused by terrorists, but rather reducing the frequency of blackouts from any cause. It is helpful to state society's goal as fostering the reliability of the electricity system.

To formulate rational policy, we need to know the goal: How much reliability do we want? By spending more, we could construct an electricity system that was less vulnerable to terrorists, natural hazards or human error, for example, station armed guards around each substation or even around each transmission tower, or build multiple duplicative transmission lines. How much protection are we willing to pay for?

The US electricity system, while a marvel of technology, is not as reliable as it could be. In particular, it is less reliable than the systems of Japan, the UK and some other nations. There is no mystery about how to improve reliability, but it would increase costs and we have been unwilling to spend the additional money.

When the power fails for a few minutes or hours, residential customers grimly reset their clocks, vow to reset the blinking VCR some day, and bear the inconvenience. Manufacturing plants, some stores, hospitals, and others that find a loss of electricity much more than an inconvenience, get back-up generators. Providing back-up generators is now a major business in the USA.

Individuals can protect themselves against power failure by installing back-up generation. Whether this is a good investment depends on the

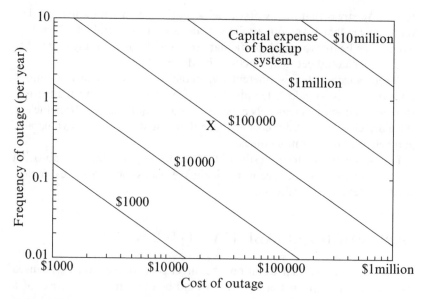

*Figure 13.5   Example analysis for back-up systems with 12 year
depreciation at 7% discount rate and annual O&M cost equal
to 2.5% of capital cost*

frequency of power failure and the loss if the power fails. Figure 13.5
shows the amount that a customer should be willing to pay for back-up
generation, given estimates of the frequency of blackouts and the cost if
the power fails.

PROTECTING THE ELECTRICITY SYSTEM

Protecting the electricity system against terrorists has much in common
with protecting it against natural hazards and human error. Measures to
protect against purposeful or unintended disruption could also be designed
to increase reliability. For example, building excess generating capacity in
different locations with the power transmitted by independent lines would
accomplish all three goals; a natural hazard or terrorist attack would be less
likely to take out all the generators or transmission lines; human error
might foul one generator or transmission line, but would be unlikely to foul
all of the generators or transmission lines.

Perhaps the major difference between natural hazards and human error
on the one hand, and terrorists on the other hand, is that guards and guns

might help to deter terrorists or lessen the damage if they attacked. The guards and guns do not help against hurricanes or operator error.

INCREASING RESILIENCY

We suggest 11 actions to increase the resiliency of the electricity system:

1. Improve operator training and communication.
2. Multiple transmission lines to deliver electricity.
3. For key substations, erect physical barriers for protection.
4. Diversified fuel supply and generation technology.
5. On-site fuel storage.
6. Decentralized generation with intelligent control.
7. Automate distribution for better control.
8. Back-up generators.
9. Ability to shed individual loads automatically, including greater use of autonomous agents.
10. Improved, secure information and control systems.
11. Inventory high-voltage transformers that are portable.

Many of the changes increasing resiliency would also increase reliability, lessen the damage from natural hazards and human errors, and deter terrorists, since they would not be able to cause so much disruption. We emphasize that careful project selection could make progress toward achieving all four goals. It is important to recognize these interactions or spillover effects since the contribution to achieving any one goal might not be sufficiently beneficial to justify the costs of the project. Accounting for the contribution to achieving all four goals might produce sufficient benefits to take much greater action. A corollary is that analyst attention ought to go to projects that achieve multiple objectives.

1. Improve Operator Training and Communication

This is an example of a change that would not require replacing expensive hardware. At relatively modest cost, improved operator training could prevent or lessen the damage if the system were under stress from natural hazards, operator errors or terrorists. The 14 August 2003 blackout, Three Mile Island core melt and many other mishaps could have been prevented by better operator training and communication. Similarly, improving communication among operators would be a modest expense that would have prevented blackouts such as the one on 14 August 2003.

2. Multiple Transmission Lines to Deliver Electricity

These are likely to be less vulnerable in getting the power from power parks to market. While having more than one transmission line would prevent a terrorist or natural disaster from disrupting the system by downing a single transmission tower, building additional lines is expensive. With current controls, having multiple transmission lines would do little good if there was not excess capacity in the system.

3. For Key Substations, Erect Physical Barriers for Protection

At present, many of the substations have no barrier beyond a chain-link fence. It would be difficult or expensive to raise the level of physical protection a notch.

4. Diversified Fuel Supply and Generation Technology

Having a more diverse fuel supply would prevent the difficulties that occurred in 1974–75 when the OPEC embargo threatened US oil supplies. Oil was then a major fuel for electricity generation, especially in areas such as California and New England. The embargo forced major reductions in electricity generation in some areas, creating disruption. The same problem occurred in California in 2000 when most generation used natural gas. An explosion and fire in a single gas pipeline caused a severe shortage in California in 2000, leading to electricity shortages. Until carbon separation and sequestration becomes an attractive technology and is accepted by the public, severely constraining greenhouse gas emissions could end the use of coal to generate electricity, cutting off half of generation capacity. Unfortunately, merchant generators, and even owners of large amounts of generation, have little incentive to invest in an array of fuels that are even slightly more expensive to achieve diversity of fuel supply.

Having a diverse mix of generation technology is important for the same reasons as having a diverse fuel mix. When natural gas prices climbed to $10 and even hit more than $50 per MCF in California in 2000, there was no ability to shift to other fuels since all the generation technology was hydroelectric, nuclear or natural gas.

5. On-site Fuel Storage

Fuel deliveries are vulnerable to disruption by natural hazards, human error or terrorists. If there is no local storage, which is generally true for natural gas, even a momentary disruption could lead to a blackout. Coal and nuclear fuel have the advantage that a great deal can be stored on site, meaning that the plant could keep running for weeks or even years without additional fuel deliveries. Wind turbines and photovoltaic cells could not have their fuel supply interrupted by terrorists, although a volcanic eruption could interrupt the solar energy or the wind could stop blowing for several days, requiring back-up generation. Fuel storage is especially important for distributed generation.

6. Decentralized Generation with Intelligent Control

Several power parks have more than 3 million kW of generating capacity, with huge high-voltage transmission lines transporting the energy to customers. These power parks are not resilient, since terrorists could put a large amount of generation capacity off-line by attacking the generators or the transmission lines or fuel supply. Perhaps the easiest way to protect the transmission and distribution lines would be not to build them, by putting the generation close to the customer. In addition, having many small generators rather than a few large ones would make generation less vulnerable to natural hazards, human error or terrorists. However, the system must be modified to provide intelligent control for these small, decentralized generators.

Decentralizing generation would increase diversity, but there are strong forces pushing greater centralization. People have become more reluctant to have generation plants located close to them, resulting in siting several generating plants at the same location. If carbon dioxide emissions were constrained, one option would be to gasify coal and separate and sequester the carbon dioxide. This technology is likely to have economies of scale that would move toward putting millions of kilowatts of generation in one location. Another push toward power parks would be construction of new nuclear generators. If the nuclear reactors are heavily guarded, the power parks are likely to contain a substantial amount of capacity to help pay the costs of the guards. Thus, there are several reasons for centralizing electricity generation, the effect of which would be to make the system less resilient and less reliable.

Decentralizing generation would begin with going from power parks to distributed generation with smaller units, perhaps going all the way to combined heat and power (CHP) units for each cluster of customers. Terrorists would find it difficult to do much harm if they had to attack each customer's CHP unit. Distributed generation lessens the need for transmission and distribution, including high-voltage transformers. With a completely decentralized system, knocking out all transmission and distribution lines would do little harm. There would be no high-value targets to attack.

Since small generation and CHP units run off natural gas or diesel fuel, the distribution of natural gas provides a point of attack for terrorists or natural hazards or human error. However, each consumer could have a large tank containing propane or diesel oil near the generator. If the tank had enough fuel to run the generator for a day or two, there should be time to restore the natural gas flow. The point is that it is difficult and expensive to store electricity, but cheap and easy to store propane or diesel.

Decentralized generators that could run off natural gas pipelines or stored liquids are a good illustration of resiliency. This technology would increase reliability as well as lower the potential damage from a natural hazard, human error or terror attack.

7. Automate Distribution for Better Control

The vast majority of power failures occur in the distribution lines. Control of these lines can be automated to give better control to prevent customers from losing power if a particular distribution line is compromised as well as locating the problem more quickly.

8. Back-up Generators

These could provide power if other generation or transmission lines fail. For customers requiring highly reliable power, there is no alternative to having back-up generators. The current system would have to be changed if back-up generators are to supply customers other than the owner with power. Most current regulations require a customer to disconnect from the network before turning on a back-up generator.

9. Ability to Shed Individual Loads Automatically, Including Greater Use of Autonomous Agents

At present a systems operator could shed load by getting interruptible customers to shut down or by blacking out particular substations. In the latter case, whole neighborhoods would lose power. An alternative would be to have each customer designate high- and low-priority power uses. A variety of devices, from power-line communication to radio broadcasts, could signal the low-priority uses to shut off. With several priority levels, the systems operator could shed from 10 to 90 percent of the load, quickly and automatically. If so, the sudden shutdown of one or more generators or interruption of one or more transmission lines would not necessarily cause a blackout. The major costs of disruption would be avoided because lower-priority loads could be shed instantaneously, protecting the high-priority loads. The use of autonomous agents would allow quick reaction to stop the spread of problems.

10. Improved, Secure Information and Control Systems

In the recent past, each utility had its own proprietary information technology. While some, perhaps most, of these had specific vulnerabilities, a hacker was unlikely to be able to use the same techniques to take control of more than a small part of one system. Today there is a trend towards standard systems, many communicating through the Internet. Manufacturers and users of control equipment have been slow to band together to recognize and fix vulnerabilities, but there are indications that this type of cooperation is beginning. Formalizing and expanding these early steps can certainly lessen the cyber vulnerabilities of the grid.

11. Inventory High-Voltage Transformers that are Portable

Perhaps the greatest vulnerability of the current system is losing a high-voltage transformer. A terrorist could destroy a transformer at a distance of 1.5 miles with a 50 caliber rifle. Since these transformers are no longer made in the US, we have little control over the priority of foreign manufacturers. The current high level of demand means that it would take months, or even years, to replace a transformer. These generators are so large that they are difficult to transport, and might need to be disassembled. An inventory of replacement units that are portable would do much to increase the resiliency of the electricity delivery system. This strategy was used to good effect in Argentina.

These 11 measures are only a few of the steps that could be taken to make the electricity system more resilient. If implemented, they would lead to large increases in system reliability, make the system less vulnerable to natural hazards and human error, and remove the electricity systems from the high priority list of terrorists.

SUMMARY AND CONCLUSION

American electricity users frequently experience power interruptions due to natural hazards or human error. Since the system is a tempting target for terrorists, we should expect terrorism to lead to more interruptions in the future. Even when terrorists decide to attack the electricity system, they are likely to cause less damage and fewer interruptions than the current hazards.

With thought and redesign, steps could be taken to accomplish simultaneously: improving reliability, protecting the system against natural hazards and human error, and protecting the system against terrorists. We stress the importance of interactions among the four types of threats since the benefits of improving any one might be too small to justify taking action, while the benefits of defending against all four threats might generate several times the benefit of any one and justify taking action. In particular, recognizing the interactions among the four would justify steps to improve the reliability of electricity delivery beyond the level currently prevailing.

The general goal is improving the resiliency of the US electricity system. We explore 11 ways of enhancing resilience. In general, each one of these would improve reliability while providing greater protection against natural hazards, human error and terror attack. We recommend that Department of Homeland Security (DHS) do a careful analysis of the costs and benefits of each of these 11 ways of improving resilience.

REFERENCES

US Department of Transportation, Office of the Secretary of Transportation (2003), 'Revised Guidance for the Valuation of Travel Time in Economic Analysis', February.
US Environmental Protection Agency (EPA) (1999), *The Benefits and Costs of the Clean Air Act 1990 to 2010, EPA Report to Congress*, November.

14. Risk and economic costs of a terrorist attack on the electric system*

Rae Zimmerman, Carlos E. Restrepo, Jeffrey S. Simonoff and Lester B. Lave

Understanding the costs of an attack on the electric power system is critical to developing policies and strategies to mitigate the consequences of terrorist attacks, given the very central role that electric power plays in the economy and the fact that it is a common target of terrorist attacks outside of the United States.

Since the mid-1980s, government and trade associations have documented over 400 electric power outages in the United States caused by natural hazards, operational circumstances, acts of vandalism, and other causes. Few, however, have been an indirect consequence of terrorism, and probably none of the events have been caused by direct attacks on the power system in the United States. In contrast, roughly 200 terrorist attacks on the power grid have been reported outside of the United States over the past few decades that point to a potential threat to the United States.

Estimates of the costs of such attacks can either be scenario-based or based upon statistical analyses of real events. Scenario-based efforts have ranged from configurations confined to the electric power system (Salmeron et al., 2004) to those of a more generalized nature incorporating generic interdependencies with other infrastructure connected to and dependent upon the electric power system (Apostolakis and Lemon, 2005). They usually are not based on real-event databases. Event-based analyses rarely extend to consequences of actual attacks or outages from other causes.

This chapter uses event-based analyses of electric power outages to identify where disruptions in electric power systems are likely to occur in an outage, and uses a wide variety of databases to project consequences of terrorist attacks on electric power and their costs. Three areas are used for estimates of economic and social costs: human fatalities and injuries, business loss, and transportation-related congestion. These approaches and cost factors can be extended to scenarios, events and conditions that differ from those illustrated.

APPROACH

The sequence of steps in estimating economic and social costs consists of identifying components in the electricity system vulnerable to disruption, areas within the United States where such vulnerabilities in such components are likely to exist, and for one of these areas, a quantification of selected economic costs on the basis of human fatalities and injuries, business loss (using inputs from regression analyses of event databases), and transportation-related congestion.

Both United States (n = 400) and international (n = 327) databases of electric power outages were constructed and used to obtain the most likely component to be disrupted in an attack or outage. The US database is from the Disturbance Analysis Working Group (DAWG) database, which is maintained by the North American Electric Reliability Council (NERC). The international database is from the National Memorial Institute for the Prevention of Terrorism's (MIPT) Terrorism Knowledge Base. Transmission lines and transformers were determined to be the critical links based on frequency of attack and, in the case of transformers, difficulty of replacement. Ninety percent of domestic outages involved transmission line disruptions and 60 percent of international outages due to terrorist attacks involved transmission lines. The actual distribution of components disrupted in each of the databases is shown in Table 14.1.

Once the most vulnerable component was identified from the databases, that is, transmission systems, scenarios were then developed on the basis of the degree of constraints posed by these components, that is, transmission routes. The alternative scenarios were combinations of: (1) only a few routes providing power to a city vs. many; and (2) a few sources of power feeding the lines through transformers vs. many sources of power (for example in-city generation). The most extreme scenarios are those where transmission runs along very few corridors, only a few power sources are connected to transmission via transformers (no in-city generation is available), and where both transformer substations and transmission lines would be cut.

Once the scenarios were defined, urban areas whose electric power delivery systems were characterized by the most extreme scenarios (very few transmission lines delivering power, connected to out-of-city or very limited numbers of power sources) were selected. It turns out that a number of major cities in the country, by virtue of their location near waterways,

Table 14.1   Distribution of disrupted electric power system components by type of component for the United States and Canada and international outage databases

Component disrupted	United States and Canada Number	International Number
Transmission lines and towers	182	122
Distribution lines	60	2
Circuit breakers	33	0
Transformers	29	7
Substations	21	19
Generation facilities	19	20
Switches and buses	15	0
Other	0	37

Note: The data in the column labeled 'United States and Canada' is compiled from a dataset that includes events in Canada (not included in the statistical analyses). Also, the total events implied in these tables are not equivalent to the original data-set totals for United States and Canada for two reasons. First, more than one component per event could be tabulated in this table, and that could yield totals that are higher than the original data-set. Second, component information was not indicated for a number of the cases, which would result in the total being lower than the total number of events in the original data-set.

Source: Zimmerman et al., 2005b, Table 1

have a high degree of vulnerability based on the criteria of constrained transmission systems and no or limited control over in-city generation capacity. Four major cities were selected and carried forward in the estimation of the cost of the potential outages: New York City, Chicago, San Francisco and Seattle. New York City's electric power is supplied through high-voltage transmission lines that enter the city from only two directions, north and west. Although New York City by regulation must generate 80 percent of its power within the city borders, in effect the city automatically shuts the generation system down to protect the equipment during an incident such as the blackout of 14 August 2003. Chicago obtains electricity from high-transmission lines coming in from the south-west and south, with some in-city generation. San Francisco has little or no in-city generation, and obtains its power from 500 kV lines connecting to the city from the south and smaller 161–315 kV lines from only two directions – from the south-south-east and across San Francisco Bay via San Mateo. Seattle has a major north–south transmission line running to the east of the city, which connects to the city via one line coming in from the east. Each of these cities is a large consumer of electricity.

The US database of non-terrorist events enables consequences to be identified from electric power outages, whereas international terrorist attack databases on electric power only allow an assessment of consequences to a much more limited extent. Moreover, extrapolations of consequences and their costs outside the US are difficult to apply to the US.

Human Fatalities and Injuries

Valuation of human life and injury has a very long history. Approaches include basing estimates on lost wages (the 'human capital approach'), risk-based estimates of occupations, expressions of 'willingness to pay' to risk one's life, and observations of what people actually do pay for protection against loss of life and injury. There are many variations on each of these approaches. Zimmerman et al. (2005a, p. 8) summarize these estimates more comprehensively as follows:

> The major sources for these estimates are government agencies, such as the US EPA estimates for value of a life in connection with air quality, insurance, jury awards, and reviews of regulatory decisions (Morall 1986). Estimates come in the form of per capita estimates, per unit of insurance purchased, and are often broken down by type of injury. The ranges as one would expect given the uncertainties and variations in condition are very wide. For example, Morall's now historical work gave a range for cost per life saved, as implied in 44 regulations, from $100 000 for steering column protection to $72 billion for formaldehyde regulation (Morall 1986: 30). The US EPA has summarized valuation estimates ranging from the mid-1970s through the early 1990s, and Viscusi and Aldy (2003) provide more recent estimates. The US EPA (1999: H-8) summary gives labor market based estimates ranging from $0.6 million to $13.5 million in 1990 dollars and contingent value-based estimates ranging from $2.7 million to $3.8 million in 1990 dollars.

Table 14.2 gives a few of these estimates, some of which are based on actual costs paid.

The estimated costs of deaths and injuries are portrayed generally according to the following formulation:

$$C(D, I) = (P_1)(D) + (P_2)(I) \qquad (14.1)$$

where: $C(D, I)$ = total cost of deaths and injuries (spatially and temporally specified)

$\quad\quad D$ = per capita estimate of the cost of deaths based on value of life estimates (for example, $5.8 million)

$\quad\quad I$ = per capita estimate of the cost of injury by type of injury

$\quad\quad P_1$ = estimated population at risk of dying

$\quad\quad P_2$ = estimated population at risk of being injured.

Table 14.2   Alternative estimates for value of life lost

Source	Measure	Value	Explanations and references
US Environmental Protection Agency (EPA) (1999)	Per capita for loss of life	$4.9 million ($5.8 million in 2005 dollars)	Developed for benefits of air quality
US Department of Justice (DOJ), Special Master (2004)	Per capita for loss of life	$250 000 to $7 million	Individual death compensation amounts. http://www.usdoj.gov/opa/pr/2004/April/04_civ_207.htm
RAND (Dixon and Stern, 2004)	Per capita for loss of life and injuries (civilians)	$3.1 million	Based on pay-outs to civilians following the 11 September 2001 attacks
US DOJ, Special Master (2004)	Per capita for injuries	$500 to $7.9 million	Compensation for physical injuries following the September 11 2001 attacks. http://www.usdoj.gov/opa/pr/2004/April/04_civ_207.htm
National Safety Council (2003)	Per capita for loss of life	$3.6 million	National Safety Council estimates

The term *I* for the cost of injuries can also be portrayed as a summation of different costs of injury, by type of injury, to reflect the considerable variability in these costs. Organizations that have developed estimates for health-related injuries include the National Safety Council (2003), the US Environmental Protection Agency (1999) and state agencies that oversee Workmen's Compensation. The estimated cost of death, however, usually overshadows the cost of injuries unless the size of the injured population and jury awards for such injuries are large.

Obtaining dollar estimates for fatalities and injuries directly from electric power outages is difficult, given that existing outages have produced few deaths and injuries in the US. The 1977 blackout in New York City that was accompanied by civil disorder, for example, resulted in two deaths and several thousand arrests. Thus, the approach is to use existing estimates of value of life and injury that are close to the estimates for those developed for environmental or terrorist causes. The US EPA (1999, p. 70) estimate for value of life based on benefit assessments for the provisions of the Clean Air Act is $5.8 million (increased from the original estimate in 1990 dollars using the Consumer Price Index). Higher values exist as well; for example,

Viscusi and Aldy (2003) estimate approximately $7 million per life lost. Using the $40 billion paid out and the total number of deaths in connection with the 11 September 2001 attacks (Dixon and Stern, 2004), the value of life lost estimated for civilians for those attacks was about $3 million.

Business Loss

Some estimates of business loss are available directly for specific electric power outages, but these are either anecdotal (based on surveys) or not easy to extrapolate from one area to another. A statistical regression analysis was conducted using United States outage data for the period 1990–2004. The resulting coefficients were then used to construct scenarios based on expected duration of outages and number of customers affected.

These estimates allow for calculations of business losses for outages in different seasons and geographical areas. A seasonal component was considered important for a number of reasons. First, the occurrence of outages may differ by season, since usage of electricity varies seasonally. For example, in summer there is a high demand for electric power for cooling, and in winter, there is a high demand for heating. Second, the impact of outages on business losses may differ seasonally. For example, industries that rely on refrigeration will be much harder hit in summer than in winter. Industries that rely on air conditioning to draw in more customers will be much more affected in summer than in winter. Outages are strongly influenced by weather, which is seasonal, so if we are trying to understand outages over time and in different parts of the country, looking at season is very important. Results by season allow the selection of a worst-case scenario, worst-case scenario for a particular cause (similar to terrorism), or alternatively, evaluating results for different scenarios.

The data used in the analysis is from the Disturbance Analysis Working Group (DAWG) database, which is maintained by the North American Electric Reliability Council (NERC). The events in the database contain information about the duration of the event, number of customers lost, megawatts lost, geographical location (state), utilities affected and the date of the event. Additional information related to the total number of customers served by the affected utilities and state population characteristics was also added.

The analysis used weighted least squares and logistic regression models. In examining the number of customers lost in an outage the modeling consisted of two parts. Many of the events in the database consisted of outages or disturbances to the electric sector that did not affect customers. Hence, the first part of the model consisted of examining the characteristics that determine whether an incident has zero or nonzero customers lost. The second part of the model provided analyses of the characteristics that help predict the number of customers lost, given that the number of customers lost for an event is nonzero.

The variables modeled in the regression analyses were customers lost, megawatts lost and duration of electric outages. The predictors used in the models include primary cause of the outage, season, total number of customers served by the affected utility, and state population density. From the information in the DAWG database the primary cause of an outage was coded as one of the following: capacity shortage, crime, demand reduction, equipment failure, fire, human error, operational error, natural disaster, system protection, third party, unknown and weather. Of these, weather and equipment failure were the most common causes of outages.

The results of the models suggest that for logged customers lost, the only variables that show a statistically significant association are logged total customers, primary cause and logged duration of the event. Customer losses are higher for natural disaster, crime, unknown causes and third party, and lower for capacity shortage, demand reduction and equipment failure, holding all else in the model fixed. In terms of duration, the analyses indicate that the most common causes of outages – weather and equipment failure – are associated with very different outcomes. Weather-related outages tend to be associated with longer durations than outages caused by equipment failure. The data also suggest that weather-related events are becoming more common and those caused by equipment failure less common. Season is also an important predictor of duration; holding all else in the model constant, these analyses suggest that winter events have an expected duration that is 2.25 times the duration of summer events, with autumn and spring in between.

The predictors that were used for estimating duration and customer loss, and those that were statistically significant are summarized below. (An asterisk (*) indicates predictors that were statistically significant at a 0.05 level.)

Predictors for duration:

- (Logged) population density*
- (Logged) number of customers serviced by the utility
- Primary cause of the outage*
- Season*
- Time index (days since 1990).

Predictors for customers lost:

- (Logged) population density
- (Logged) number of customers serviced by the utility*

- Primary cause of the outage*
- Season
- Time index (days since 1990)
- (Logged) duration.*

This kind of regression analysis constitutes a tool that can be used to construct scenarios for possible disruptions to the electric system caused by terrorist events. Given that there are different potential causes for an outage, a decision-maker can choose a cause based on its potential similarity to a terrorist event and then choose a geographical location through the state population characteristics and the utilities affected, as well as a time of year. The expected number of customers lost and duration of an event can then be used to estimate business losses for a specified scenario. This is shown in the following illustrative example, where these characteristics are estimated for the four cities described in a previous section, and for different seasons and causes of an outage. These scenarios show how this kind of model can be used to produce results for scenarios with diverse characteristics. A more detailed description of the regression model and predicted outcomes is described elsewhere (Simonoff et al., 2005).

In order to use the regression model for this purpose a number of steps were taken. First, a weighted least squares model was used to estimate the duration of an outage for the different causes and seasons in each of the four cities using the methodology described above. Table 14.3 gives 50 percent prediction intervals for duration of outage for the different causes

Table 14.3   Estimated duration of outages by cause of outage (in hours)

Causes	Low	Duration	High
Capacity shortage	8.72	19.21	42.34
Crime	7.06	19.62	54.54
Demand reduction	1.69	5.97	21.07
Equipment failure	3.04	9.74	31.20
Fire	5.23	15.04	43.20
Human error	0.77	2.03	5.37
Operational error	1.33	3.83	11.07
Natural disaster	2.16	10.99	55.84
System protection	9.02	25.10	69.86
Third party	23.46	29.71	37.62
Unknown	46.61	108.50	252.60
Weather	16.84	49.08	143.03

of outages in New York City during the winter months. These intervals give the central range within which there is a 50 percent chance of the duration falling in an individual incident. The causes given in the table are: capacity shortage, crime, demand reduction, equipment failure, fire, human error, operational error, natural disaster, system protection, third party, unknown and weather. Some causes are associated with higher estimated expected durations. Similarly, some causes are associated with more variable durations, as shown by wider prediction intervals.

The estimated expected durations obtained from the analysis described above were then used as an input to a logistic regression model to estimate the probability that there is zero customer loss for an outage. In a third step, a weighted least squares model was used to predict the number of customers lost given that there is nonzero customer loss. As with duration, 50 percent prediction intervals for customers lost were constructed. Table 14.4 shows 50 percent prediction intervals for the number of customers lost for the different causes of outages for New York City during the winter months. The expected number of customers lost is given by:

$$E(\text{Customers lost}) = (p)(0)$$
$$+ (1 - p)(E[\text{Customers lost given nonzero customer loss}]) \quad (14.2)$$

where p is the probability of zero customer loss.

Similar results to those shown in Tables 14.1 and 14.2 are applied to a number of scenarios and shown in Table 14.5.

Table 14.4 Estimated customer loss for outages by cause of outage

Causes	Low	Customers	High
Capacity shortage	21 775	30 434	42 536
Crime	1 003 612	1 604 029	2 563 650
Demand reduction	48 739	77 897	124 500
Equipment failure	29 627	96 036	311 300
Fire	56 593	142 076	356 679
Human error	59 434	97 244	159 108
Operational error	1 761 147	2 814 765	4 498 717
Natural disaster	68 343	132 135	255 473
System protection	30 077	153 071	779 017
Third party	556 194	888 941	1 420 755
Unknown	586 737	1 075 867	1 972 757
Weather	74 251	162 020	353 539

With the expected predicted duration in hours and predicted number of customers lost for a given city, cause of an outage and season, business losses are estimated with the following equation:

$$BL = (G)(C)(P)(D) \tag{14.3}$$

where: BL = business loss ($)
     G = GDP/person/day
     C = number of customers affected
     P = number of people per customer (assumed to be three) and
     D = duration (as a fraction of a 24-hour day)

The average per capita gross domestic product (GDP) can be computed for any region or for the nation as a whole by dividing the GDP by the applicable population. For the US as a whole, this comes to about $112 of GDP per person per day. This is based on dividing the July 2005 estimate of $12.1917 trillion (US Department of Commerce, Bureau of Economic Analysis, 2005) by 295 734 134, the US population as of July 2005 (US Central Intelligence Agency, 2005) for the per capita estimate, and dividing that by 365 days to obtain a per day estimate.

One way to validate the estimate is to apply it to the August 2003 black-out. Multiplying $112 by the 50 million people affected yields $5.64 billion in business losses, which is at the lower end of the estimates of economic impact of the outage, which were estimated to be between $6 billion and $10 billion (there were few other categories of loss, such as premature death) (various sources cited in Zimmerman et al., 2005b).

The number of customers affected in a blackout is not the same as the number of people affected. Utilities define a 'customer' as a meter. Therefore, the number of customers does not equal the number of people. In the case of a household with a single occupant a customer equals a person but for a family of five a customer would be equivalent to five people. In the case of a commercial or industrial enterprise a customer can represent thousands of kilowatts and hundreds of workers. In the applications presented in this chapter, an assumption of three people per customer on average was made. However, this assumption could be fine-tuned to local demographic and customer realities if more precise information were available.

The results show that depending on the geographical area, season and cause of outage the expected business losses can be quite substantial. In the examples chosen they range from $711 365 for an outage caused by human error taking place in the summer in San Francisco, to $245 225 986 for an outage caused by crime in the winter months in New York City (obviously, given the uncertainty associated with the various inputs to the model, these can be rounded considerably).

Table 14.5 Economic accounting: estimated business losses from predicted duration and customers lost

City	Cause of outage	Season	Predicted duration (hours)	Predicted # of customers lost	Expected business loss ($)
NYC	Crime	Winter	19.6	887028	245225986
NYC	Weather	Summer	21.8	134935	41491028
San Francisco	Natural disaster	Fall	5.6	132135	10437079
San Francisco	Fire	Spring	8.0	180631	20382402
Chicago	Human error	Summer	0.7	72048	711365
Seattle	Equipment failure	Winter	5.8	44661	3653671

It is important to note that these models are based on broad demographic characteristics of the individual cities and utilities (such as population density and customers served), and are not tuned to specific (unique to the city or utility) patterns of electricity use, structure of the power grid, and so on. Thus, the estimates in Table 14.5 are best viewed as representing (for example) the estimated expected business loss for an outage during the summer caused by crime in a city with characteristics like those of New York City, rather than in New York City itself.

Transportation-Related Congestion

One of the major outcomes of any unexpected event is congestion on the roadways surrounding the area. Such congestion often produces secondary effects that are far greater than the initial event. The costs of congestion or delay are expressed in terms of hourly costs of delay per traveler, per traveler by level of income or type of occupation, per vehicle or by size of city. Matching the unit costs with the magnitude of the effect (for example, number of travelers, income of travelers, number of vehicles by type, or city size) one can obtain the total cost of congestion for an area. Figure 14.1 portrays some of the choices available for making estimates of traffic congestion.

Given the wide variety of forms in which these costs appear, we use the most commonly referenced one, 50 percent of the hourly wage, which is for local personal travel (US DOT 1997, 2003).

We formulate the cost of congestion as follows:

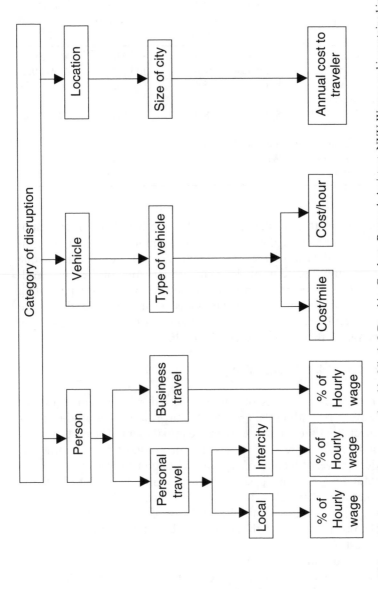

Note: This graphical presentation was produced by Nicole J. Dooskin, Graduate Research Assistant, NYU-Wagner and is contained in Zimmerman et al. (2005a).

Figure 14.1   Public service interruption: estimators for transportation-related congestion

$$C(T) = \left[\sum_{i=1}^{n} (X(i))(Y(i)) \right](Z)(T) \qquad (14.4)$$

where: $C(T)$ = the total cost associated with congestion for outage
duration T

n = the number of sectors for which wages are defined
X = sector for wage category i
Y = the number of workers in wage category i
Z = a congestion factor in terms of percentage of hourly wages
T = duration of congestion in number of hours

APPLICATION

The following is the application of the procedure to the New York City
area, which was chosen given its large size with respect to other cities in the
country. The application makes use of the three kinds of economic costs
described in this chapter – human fatalities and injuries, business loss and
transportation congestion.

Human fatalities and injuries are simply computed as a function of $5.8
million per life lost (as described in the section on 'Human Fatalities and
Industries' above) multiplied by number of people assumed dead.

Business loss is estimated using the regression model estimates for duration and customers affected under different conditions. For the New York
area, the number of customers lost was used for crime as a cause and winter
as a season. In spite of the fact that there are very few events caused by
crime in the database, crime is the cause closest to terrorism. Winter yielded
the longest estimated duration (autumn, spring and summer were associated with estimated durations for crime-caused events of 12.2, 12.8 and 8.7
hours respectively, while that for winter was 19.6 hours), and was thus a
'worst case' within the cause category of crime, though other causes, in particular weather, had longer durations.

Business loss estimates are calculated as follows (assuming that there are
three people per customer) based on equation (14.3): $112.84 × 887 028 × 3
× 19.6/24 = $245 225 986.

Transportation congestion costs are in costs per hour of delay per person.
Other estimates contained in the illustration were computed in the following way:

- Estimates of the total workforce were derived by Zimmerman et
  al. (2005b): 'The workforce of the New York Metropolitan Area in
  1990 was 9 346 645 (New York State Department of Labor (2005). This

represents about 48% of the total population. Considering that the total population of the New York Metropolitan Area in 2000 was 21 199 865 (US Census Bureau (2000): Census 2000 PHC-T-3. Ranking Tables for Metropolitan Areas: 1990 and 2000. Table 1: Metropolitan Areas and their Geographic Components in Alphabetic Sort, 1990 and 2000 Population, and Numeric and Percent Population Change: 1990 to 2000), the estimated total workforce is estimated to be 10 175 935.'

- Estimates for cost of delay nationwide were described above. A nationwide average hourly wage rate across all economic sectors of $16 per hour was used. This is somewhat lower than the 2004 New York City wage data for all occupations of $23.80 per hour based on a mean annual salary of $49 500 (New York State Department of Labor, 2005).
- The four hours of delay time is an assumption made by the authors for the amount of personal time the traveler would spend due to congestion during an outage. This is an estimate that can easily be changed by users as better information becomes available.

The final calculation for this illustration – a 19.6 hour blackout assuming 150 deaths (discussed in the conclusions section) – is as follows (based on equation (14.4)):

$C(T) =$

Estimated average business losses:

$112.84 (GDP/person/day) $\times$ 887 028 (customers) $\times$ 3 (# people/customer) $\times$ 19.6/24 (hrs): $245 225 986

+ Estimated cost of premature deaths:

$5.8 million $\times$ 150 deaths = $870 000 000

+ Public service disruption (transportation related for business travel): 10 175 935 workers $\times$ $16/hour (average wage) $\times$ 0.5 (cost of congestion per hourly wage for a business traveler) $\times$ 4 hours (extra delay time due to congestion) = $117 088 000

= $1 232 313 986

Note that the figures above retain the original numbers in order for the reader to be able to verify the calculations. In reality, we think the numbers are correct to one or two significant figures.

CONCLUSIONS

A general cost estimation approach and methodology based on actual events and other data is useful for estimating the cost of a terrorist attack against electricity. Databases of non-terrorist outages and statistical models applied to those databases provide a tool for estimating selected impacts of outages. These databases are also invaluable for identifying vulnerable grid scenarios and developing terrorism scenarios as a basis for selecting and prioritizing areas for the generation of cost estimates.

The illustration of the general methodology that is presented shows an estimated cost for an approximately one-day-long outage in a very heavily populated US urban area that is small relative to other major catastrophes (such as the 11 September 2001 attacks on the World Trade Center). For this outage and other events caused by terrorists or natural disasters, many social and economic costs are not quantified. For example, manufacturing establishments can suffer equipment losses when furnaces suddenly lose power. This has occurred in some blackouts. Many indirect costs are not captured here as well, and are critical to understanding the full extent of economic effects. Other than traffic delays, there are damages related to inconveniences that are very difficult to quantify; these might increase more than proportionally to the length of an outage (Richardson, 2005). Interdependencies between electric power and other infrastructure are an important foundation for the basis of quantifying indirect economic effects, and are beginning to be quantified, based on actual events (see for example, Zimmerman, 2004; Zimmerman and Restrepo, 2005).

About 70 percent of the estimated cost in the illustration is associated with the cost of lives lost. We assume that a blackout would result in 150 deaths, a number much larger than recent experience with blackouts, but one much smaller than other recent natural disasters, for example, Hurricane Katrina. In that hurricane, an estimated 154 elderly people alone died in hospitals and nursing homes, and many of these deaths are attributable to heat exposure due to air conditioning and life support equipment failure due to power outages: 'In the end, withering heat, not floodwaters, proved the deadliest killer, with temperatures soaring to 110 degrees in stifling buildings without enough generator power for air-conditioning' (Rohde et al., 2005). The estimate of 150 deaths could be smaller than what actually occurs if there is civil unrest or another attack associated with and taking advantage of the blackout. The latter is probably more likely to reveal the greater impact than the former, based on existing information. The tabulation of people killed in riots in the US from 1964 to 1971, for example, reveals a total of 228 killed and 12 741 injured (Collins and Margo, 2003).

Although sociological research has shown that under most circumstances people are not likely to panic and riot in instances of mass evacuation (see for example, Mawson, 2005), instances of evacuations from fires from areas with limited egress suggest the opposite. Moreover, the civil unrest in the aftermath of Hurricane Katrina involving the use of firearms also supports the fact that such behavior can accompany blackouts. In contrast to civil unrest, costs associated with another terrorist event that takes advantage of a blackout, however, are likely to be much greater. The deaths from international terrorist attacks on critical infrastructure and buildings, even without associated attacks directed at the electric power system, can far exceed those assumed in the illustration presented here for electricity alone. The second contributor to the size of the value of premature deaths is the per capita estimate for the value per life lost. The literature reveals quite a range, and the total cost of an outage is very sensitive to what is selected for that amount.

NOTES

* The authors acknowledge the contributions of Graduate Research Assistants Nicole Dooskin and Ray Hartwell for research on transportation congestion costs and value of life respectively. They also assisted in constructing the database along with Wendy Remington and Graduate Research Assistant Justin Miller.

This research was supported by the United States Department of Homeland Security through the Center for Risk and Economic Analysis of Terrorism Events (CREATE), grant number EMW-2004-GR-0112. However, any opinions, findings, and conclusions or recommendations in this document are those of the author (s) and do not necessarily reflect views of the US Department of Homeland Security.

REFERENCES

Apostolakis, G.E. and D.M. Lemon (2005), 'A Screening Methodology for the Identification and Ranking of Infrastructure Vulnerabilities Due to Terrorism', *Risk Analysis*, 25(2): 361–76.

Collins, W.J. and R.A. Margo (2003), 'The Labor Market Effects of the 1960s Riots', Nashville, TN: Vanderbilt University, Department of Economics, Working Paper No. 03-W24.

Dixon, L. and R.K. Stern (2004), *Compensation for Losses from the 9/11 Attacks*, Santa Monica, CA: Rand Institute for Civil Justice.

Mawson, A.R. (2005), 'Understanding Mass Panic and Other Collective Responses to Threat and Disaster', *Psychiatry*, 68(2), Summer: 95–113.

Morall III, J.F. (1986), 'A Review of the Record', *Regulation*, 10(2): 25–35.

National Safety Council (2003), 'Estimating the Cost of Unintentional Injuries', Itasca, IL: National Safety Council, available online at: http://www.nsc.org/lrs/statinfo/estcost.htm, accessed 21 October 2005.

New York State Department of Labor (2005), 'Average Wages by Industry', Available online at http://www.labor.state.ny.us/labor_market/lmi_business/eeo/nyjcnmsa.htm, accessed 12 August 2005.

Rohde, D., D.G. McNeil, Jr., R. Abelson, and S. Dewan (2005), 'Vulnerable, and Doomed in the Storm', *New York Times*, 19 September, available at http://www.nytimes.com/2005/09/19/national/nationalspecial/19victims.html, accessed 19 September.

Salmeron, J., K. Wood and R. Baldick (2004), 'Analysis of Electric Grid Security under Terrorist Threat', *IEEE Transactions on Power Systems*, 19(2), May: 905–12.

Simonoff, J.S., R. Zimmerman, C.E. Restrepo, N.J. Dooskin, R.V. Hartwell, J.I. Miller, W.E. Remington, L.B. Lave and R.E. Schuler (2005), 'Electricity Case: Statistical Analysis of Electric Power Outages', New York, NY: NYU-Wagner, ICIS for the USC Center for Risk and Economic Analysis of Terrorism Events (CREATE), May.

US Census Bureau (2000), 'Census 2000 PHC-T-3. Ranking Tables for Metropolitan Areas: 1990 and 2000. Table 1: Metropolitan Areas and their Geographic Components in Alphabetic Sort, 1990 and 2000 Population, and Numeric and Percent Population Change: 1990 to 2000', Available online at http://www.census.gov/population/cen2000/phc-t3/tab01.pdf, accessed 28 October 2005.

US Central Intelligence Agency (CIA), (2005), 'Field Listing – Population', *The World Fact Book 2005*. Available online at http://www.cia.gov/cia/publications/factbook/fields/2119.html, accessed 28 October.

US Department of Commerce, Bureau of Economic Analysis (2005), available online at http://www.bea.gov/bea/newsrel/gdpnewsrelease.htm.

US Department of Justice (DOJ), Special Master (2004), '9/11 Victim Compensation Fund Pays Over $2.6 Billion to Date', Available online at http://www.usdoj.gov/opa/pr/2004/April/04_civ_207.htm, accessed 28 October 2005.

US Department of Transportation (DOT), Office of the Secretary of Transportation (1997), *Guidance for the Valuation of Travel Time in Economic Analysis*, US Department of Transportation, April.

US Department of Transportation (DOT), Office of the Secretary of Transportation (2003), *Revised Guidance for the Valuation of Travel Time in Economic Analysis*, US Department of Transportation, February.

US Environmental Protection Agency (EPA) (1999), *The Benefits and Costs of the Clean Air Act 1990 to 2010, EPA Report to Congress*, November.

Viscusi, K. and J.E. Aldy (2003), 'The Value of a Statistical Life: A Critical Review of Market Estimates Throughout the World', *Journal of Risk and Uncertainty*, 27: 5–76.

Zimmerman, R. (2004), 'Decision-making and the Vulnerability of Critical Infrastructure', W. Thissen, P. Wieringa, M. Pantic and M. Ludema (eds), *Proceedings of IEEE International Conference on Systems, Man and Cybernetics*, The Hague: Delft University of Technology, pp. 4059–63.

Zimmerman, R., L.B. Lave, C.E. Restrepo, N.J. Dooskin, R.V. Hartwell and J.I. Miller, W.E. Remington, J.S. Simonoff and R.E. Schuler (2005a), 'Electricity Case: Economic Cost Estimation Factors for Economic Assessment of Terrorist Attacks', New York: NYU-Wagner, ICIS for the USC Center for Risk and Economic Analysis of Terrorism Events (CREATE), May.

Zimmerman, R. and C. Restrepo (2005), 'The Next Step: Quantifying Infrastructure Interdependencies to Improve Security,' *International Journal of*

Critical Infrastructures, Fall. UK: Inderscience Enterprises, Ltd. www.inderscience.com.

Zimmerman, R., C.E. Restrepo, N.J. Dooskin, R.V. Hartwell, J.I. Miller, W.E. Remington, J.S. Simonoff, L.B. Lave and R.E. Schuler (2005b), 'Electricity Case: Main Report – Risk, Consequences, and Economic Accounting', Center for Risk and Economic Analysis of Terrorism Events, May.

15. Regional economic impacts of a terrorist attack on the water system of Los Angeles: a computable general disequilibrium analysis*

Adam Rose, Gbadebo Oladosu and Shu-Yi Liao

Hurricane Katrina has dramatized how the lack of potable water contributes to human suffering. However, water is critical to the economy as well. Most businesses are directly dependent on water in some way, and others are dependent on water indirectly through their suppliers and customers. Water also is crucial to public safety. This has not only the obvious ramifications for businesses in the case of actual fires, but also the more widespread forced closing of high-rise office buildings, and hence many business operations, as a precautionary measure when sprinkler systems cannot be served and ordinary fire equipment would be ineffective because of its height access limit.

Estimation of economic impacts of utility lifeline disruptions has become more prevalent in recent years, though most of the literature has focused on electricity outages. Moreover, none of these analyses except Rose and Liao (2005) have factored in economic resilience, or the ability to mute the maximum impacts through inherent and adaptive responses at the level of the firm, industry or regional economy. Failure to consider resilience could lead to a gross overestimation of water outage risk (potential losses multiplied by the probability of occurrence). Mitigation, or the prevention of the occurrence of the threat, is typically the focus of risk reduction, but enhancing resilience may be a far less expensive alternative.

The purpose of this chapter is to estimate the direct and indirect economic impacts of an extended water service outage caused by a terrorist attack in Los Angeles, California. Given the ability of terrorists to target for maximum damage, the simulations pertain to a total outage over a two-week period. The analysis extends beyond the approaches prevalent in the recent literature, which have omitted resilience and often indirect economic effects as well. The simulations are performed with the use of a computable general equilibrium (CGE) model that addresses these oft-omitted factors and incorporates special features relating to natural and man-made disasters. The CGE framework has been successfully applied to water and electricity disruptions from natural hazards (Rose and Liao, 2005), as well as from technical and regulatory failures (Rose et al., 2004). It also has several advantages over other approaches in being applied to utility lifeline disruptions from terrorist attacks (Rose, 2005; Rose et al., 2005).

This chapter does not address all of the economic impacts of a water supply disruption but focuses on the major one – what is often termed 'business interruption'. We omit several considerations, such as the value of any lives lost, increased crime, psychological trauma, some infrastructure costs and property damage. Various cost estimating factors (see Zimmerman et al., 2005) might be used to complement our analysis. The advantage of our approach is that it involves a model that has behavioral content, so that we can examine a range of responses by individuals, businesses and markets to a water service outage. This not only sharpens the estimates but also helps to identify ways to reduce losses in the future utilizing relatively-low cost 'non-structural' approaches such as market price rationing, information clearing-houses, and various types of substitutes for water and other inputs. Our model is also grounded in the specification of water supply, storage, transmission and distribution systems (see, for example, O'Rourke et al., 2004), which enhances its accuracy and also helps identify appropriate mitigation and restoration options.

ECONOMIC IMPACTS

Partial Equilibrium Effects

Several approaches have been used to estimate the costs of utility lifeline outages. Direct, or partial equilibrium, effects of outages manifest themselves in four major ways: lost sales, equipment damage or restart costs, spoilage of variable inputs and idle labor costs. In addition, costs are incurred to reduce potential losses through the purchase of storage tanks, permanent changes in production processes, and water system capacity expansion to promote flexibility. At the margin, the cost of outages should be equal to the cost of these adaptive responses. For example, in the case of electricity, the most popular way of measuring outage losses recently has been tabulating expenditures on back-up generation rather than measuring damages directly (Beenstock et al., 1997). Still, measurement of just a single coping tactic, or single type of damage, is likely to understate the direct dollar loss.

Many regions of the US suffer significant water service disruptions for a variety of reasons, including pipe breaks, reservoir leaks, droughts or water supply contamination. While the costs have been nowhere as geographically extensive and costly as, for example, the 2003 north-east electricity blackout (see, for example, Graves and Wood, 2003; Zimmerman et al., 2005) the potential for large-scale economic damage and human suffering is quite evident from the Hurricane Katrina example.

General Equilibrium Effects

In this chapter, we utilize economic output losses as a common denominator for both partial and general equilibrium effects. This enables us to include some property damage and productivity losses into the measurement in addition to more conventional business interruption (Rose, 2004a). Overall, general equilibrium (GE) effects consist of several types. First is output loss to downstream customers of a disrupted firm through its inability to provide crucial inputs. This, and the other GE effects noted below, set off a chain reaction beyond the immediate or partial equilibrium (PE) effects, in this case in terms of customers of firms who have had their water service curtailed. Second is output loss to upstream suppliers of disrupted firms through the cancellation of orders for inputs. Again, this is transmitted through several rounds, though in this case in terms of suppliers. Third is output loss to all firms from decreased consumer spending associated with a decreased wage bill in firms directly affected by the water outage, as well as all other firms suffering negative GE effects. Fourth is output loss to all firms from decreased investment associated with decreased profits of firms suffering the water outage and other firms negatively impacted by GE effects. Fifth is output loss to all firms from cost (and price increases) from damaged equipment and other dislocations (including uncertainty) that result in productivity decreases in firms directly impacted.

The direct and indirect costs of water disruptions thus do not just take place during the period in which service is curtailed. Storage tanks or recycling equipment are purchased in anticipation of outages, and the carrying cost of increased inventories of water and of critical materials is incurred over a longer period as well. Equipment damage, spoilage, and idle labor costs may translate immediately into lost profits, but they may not be passed through in the form of price increases until a later date. The same is true of water utility cost and price increases that typically lag because they require adjustment by a regulatory body rather than being determined relatively automatically by the marketplace. The three time periods, which we designate as preparatory, crisis, and recovery, will vary in length depending on the context. For example, the length of a preparatory period would depend on the level of expectations prior to such an attack. For estimation purposes, however, they may all be simulated simultaneously in cases where there are no significant dynamic (that is, time-related) effects.

Note also that not all general equilibrium effects are negative. Some firms may benefit from the decreased prices associated with a shift in demand by other firms for various products. The analysis below indicates the existence of this possibility for several sectors, though the positive general equilibrium effects do not typically more than offset the negative partial equilibrium ones. In general, input–output (IO) models, the popular and simpler alternative to CGE models, are limited to unidirectional impacts. Unless modified or used judiciously (see, for example, Rose et al., 1997), they exaggerate indirect effects as being equal to multiplier values (in the range of two to three times the direct effects for a city like Los Angeles). CGE models can incorporate a wide range of offsetting effects.

Resilience

'Economic resilience' refers to the ability or capacity of a system to absorb or cushion itself against damage or loss (see, for example, Holling, 1973; Perrings, 2001). A more general definition that incorporates dynamic considerations, including stability, is the ability of a system to recover from a severe shock. We also distinguish two types of resilience in each context:

- Inherent: the ability under normal circumstances (for example, the ability of individual firms to substitute other inputs for those curtailed by an external shock, or the ability of markets to reallocate resources in response to price signals).
- Adaptive: the ability in crisis situations due to ingenuity or extra effort (for example, increasing input substitution possibilities in individual business operations, or strengthening the market by providing information to match suppliers without customers to customers without suppliers).

Resilience emanates both from internal motivation and the stimulus of private or public policy decisions (Mileti, 1999). Also, resilience, as defined in this chapter, refers to post-disaster conditions and response, which are distinguished from pre-disaster activities to reduce potential losses through mitigation (cf. Klein et al., 2003; Bruneau et al., 2003). In disaster research, resilience has been emphasized most by Tierney (1997) in terms of business coping behavior and community response, by Comfort (1999) in terms of non-linear adaptive response of organizations (broadly defined to include both the public and private sectors), and by Petak (2002) in terms of system performance.[1] These concepts have been extended to practice. Disaster recovery and business continuity industries have sprung up that offer specialized services to help firms during various aspects of disasters, especially power outages (see, for example, Salerno, 2003). Key services include the opportunity to outsource communication and information aspects of the business at an alternative site. There is also a growing realization of the broader context of the economic impacts, especially with the new emphasis on supply chain management. One company executive recently summarized the situation quite poignantly: 'In short, companies have started to realize that they participate in a greater ecosystem – and that their IT systems are only as resilient as the firms that they rely on to stay in business' (Corcoran, 2003, p. 28). Experience with Y2K, 9/11, natural disasters, and technological and regulatory failures, as well as simulated drills, have sharpened utility industry and business resilience (Eckles, 2003). Similar activities of public agencies have improved community resilience.

Resilience can take place at three levels:

- Microeconomic: individual behavior of firms, households or organizations.
- Mesoeconomic: economic sector, individual market or co-operative group.
- Macroeconomic: all individual units and markets combined, although the whole is not simply the sum of its parts, due to interactive effects of an economy.

Examples of individual resilience are well documented in the literature, as are examples of the operation of businesses and organizations. What is often less appreciated by disaster researchers outside economics and closely related disciplines is the inherent resilience of markets. Prices act as the 'invisible hand' that can guide resources to their best allocation even in the aftermath of a disaster. Some pricing mechanisms have been established expressly to deal with such a situation, as in the case of non-interruptible service premia that enable customers to estimate the value of a continuous supply of electricity and to pay in advance for receiving priority service during an outage (Chao and Wilson, 1987).[2]

The price mechanism is a relatively costless way of redirecting goods and services. Price increases, though often viewed as 'gouging', serve a useful purpose of reflecting highest-value use, even in the broader social setting. Moreover, if the allocation does violate principles of equity (fairness), the market allocations can be adjusted by income or material transfers to the needy.

Of course, markets are likely to be shocked by a major disaster, in an analogous manner to buildings and humans. In this case, we have two alternatives for some or all of the economy: (1) substitute centralized decree or planning, though at a significantly higher cost of administration; (2) bolster the market, such as in improving information flows (for example, the creation of an information clearing house to match customers without suppliers to suppliers without customers).

CHARACTERISTICS OF WATER OUTAGES

General Considerations

Terrorist attacks can damage the various components of a water service system, each with a different implication for the regional economy. At the most fundamental level, this involves destroying a reservoir or aqueduct, which reduces the supply of water, or contaminating the water itself. However, most cities are serviced by more than one source of water. Moreover, some cities have alternative sources of water (for example, adjoining rivers, or access to the water table through well drilling) for some emergency purposes, though this is not the case for LA. Extensive damage to or contamination of aqueducts or reservoirs will lead to a reduction of water availability to all customers across the board in a large geographic area.

The next level of the system is the pump station, which lies at the heart of a water subsystem area (WSA) (see, for example, O'Rourke et al., 2004). Destruction of a pump station, or major trunk line serving it, would also reduce water availability equally proportionally to all customers within a WSA. This, however, will not result in equal proportional cutback for all sectors in a city, since economic activity is not randomly or uniformly distributed within it. For example, some WSAs service industrial centers, while others service primarily residential or commercial customers. Thus, to model the economic impacts of damage to this component, and all downstream components of the system, it is necessary to have an economic model with spatial attributes.

Below the level of the pump station are regulation stations demarcating water pressure zones (WPZ). These are the terminals for local distribution lines that feed neighborhoods and that are hooked up to individual customers. This level of the system contains the most extensive amount of pipe in a densely populated area such as LA. Our geographic unit of analysis, however, will be the WSA rather than the WPZ, because at this stage of economic model development, we have the accompanying data for 15 WSAs but not thousands of WPZs.

On the demand (customer) side, resilience refers to implementing various inherent or adaptive coping measures for adjustment or adjustments, rather than passively carrying out business as usual. Some examples of resilient responses for dealing with water disruptions include:

- conservation – utilizing less water per unit of output;
- water substitution – utilizing bottled or trucked water;
- inventories – utilizing stored water;
- production rescheduling – making up lost production at a later date;
- water importance – utilizing the portion of a business that has no need for water.

In the case of water service disruptions, conservation is a limited option when the flow is completely shut off. Water source substitution is straightforward, but much more expensive and limited in many geographic areas where water is relatively scarce. Other input substitution involves using capital, labor or materials instead of water. Water is not typically stored in large quantities in LA by businesses, and water heaters and bottled water are limited to only a couple of days' supply for most residences. Production rescheduling is one of the most powerful options, even for a disruption as long as several weeks, and is applicable to all sectors whose output is not time-sensitive and that are not operating 24/7 at full capacity. 'Water importance' (ATC, 1991) is an adjustment for those aspects of production that do not require water (for example, sales and delivery services), and is thus a limited option for outages of short duration. All of these factors are important in designing simulations for the regional economic impact of a major water service outage caused by a terrorist attack or any disaster stimulus.

Simulation Parameters

Our simulations pertain to a total water service outage, as where all aqueduct connections and reservoirs are breached or contaminated. This is expected to have a duration of two weeks. As such, all sectors will be affected equally at first. As the system is repaired, sectoral differentials are in fact applicable, since only remaining portions of the county will be without water. So that we can focus on major considerations, we assume that recovery will take place all at once, thus abstracting from recovery issues. For a constant recovery pattern, simple geometry tells us that our total damage impacts will be cut in half.[3] This pattern, however, would have no effect on the strength of resilience as a whole or of its individual components.

Resilience options for businesses will include all of the options described in the previous subsection. We are not able to model household responses for any of our simulations at this time. Implicitly, our analysis also assumes there is no advance warning for the attack. We also hold the water utility service price constant, because water rates are set by regulatory bodies rather than the market and not in real time.[4]

THE LA CGE MODEL

CGE analysis is the state of the art in regional economic modeling, especially for impact and policy analysis (Partridge and Rickman, 1998). It is defined as a multi-market simulation model based on the simultaneous optimizing behavior of individual consumers and firms, subject to economic account balances and resource constraints (see, for example, Shoven and Whalley, 1992). The CGE formulation incorporates many of the best features of other popular model forms, but without many of their limitations (Rose, 2005). The basic CGE model has been shown to represent an excellent framework for analyzing natural hazard impacts and policy responses, including disruptions of utility lifeline services (Brookshire and McKee, 1992; Rose and Liao, 2005).[5]

Model Specification

We constructed a static, regional CGE model of the LA County economy consisting of 33 producing sectors. The sector classification was designed to highlight the sensitivity of production processes to water and electricity availability. Institutions in the model are households, government and external agents. There are nine household income groups and two categories each of government (state/local and federal) and external agents (rest of the US and rest of the world). Major features of the model include the following.

Production
Production activities are specified as constant returns to scale, nested (tiered) constant elasticity of substitution (CES) functions (see Appendix A for details). This reflects a hierarchical decision process and enables us to utilize different substitution elasticities between input aggregates. At the most fundamental level (4th tier), the decision-maker chooses the mix of capital and energy. In the 3rd tier, capital–energy aggregate is juxtaposed to labor. In the 2nd tier the capital–energy–labor aggregate is juxtaposed to materials. In the top tier, the decision-maker juxtaposes the KELM aggregate to water, that

is, chooses the optimal mix of water and other aggregate inputs. Water is included in the top tier so that utilization can be more clearly distinguished (see also Seung et al., 2000).

Supply and trade of goods and services
We specify transactions between LA County and the two external sectors in the model using the Armington function for imports and the constant elasticity of transformation function for exports. The former is specified as a CES function to reflect imperfect substitution between domestic goods and competitive imports in demand. The latter is also a CES function that reflects the revenue-maximizing distribution of domestic output between exports and domestic markets, respectively. Regional export and import prices are based on exogenous external prices plus percentage taxes and tariffs (for the 'rest of the world' sector) to reflect the open nature of the LA County economy.

Income allocation, final demand and investment
Households' production and consumption of goods and services are modeled using Cobb-Douglas expenditure functions.[6] Government consumption is specified as a Leontief expenditure function. Income elasticities are unity for both households and government, and price elasticities are one for households but less than one for governments. Savings by households and governments are fixed proportions of disposable income, while external savings balance out this account. Households, government and external entities also borrow from the capital account. Net savings by institutions, plus depreciation charges and retained earnings, are used to finance investment in capital goods. Investment in individual capital goods categories is a fixed proportion of total investment funding.

Equilibrium/disequilibrium conditions
Equilibrium conditions balance supply and demand in goods and services markets. Capital endowments in the economy are fixed to reflect the short-run nature of our simulations. In the labor market, the Keynesian closure rule is used to allow for unemployment even in equilibrium. This disequilibrium condition prevents the muting of impacts inherent in the forcing of an equilibrium by the application of the neoclassical closure rule (zero unemployment equilibrium).

Disequilibrium is introduced into the model in several other ways (see, for example, Rose and Liao, 2005). Most important are constraints on utility service supplies resulting from a terrorist attack. This causes a shift away from an efficient equilibrium to a second-best world. Because water rates in LA County are rigid, utility service markets cannot adjust in the usual manner. Price adjustment lags because regulation keeps prices constant at pre-attack levels, which does not allow markets to clear under what would otherwise be increasing price pressure from shortages. The model solves for the excess demand and with an opportunity cost loss for utility companies.

Another source of disequilibrium stems from temporary imbalances in trade and financial flows in and out of the county. An increased demand for imports will likely be required to offset the reduced production within the county. Trade imbalances are not as serious in a sub-national setting as at the international level, since they do not affect currency values. Moreover, lags in outside aid and insurance payments to pay for imports (or pay for intra-county products) can readily be handled by lags in the payments and expenditure of wages and capital-related income, as well as in tax revenues.

Finally, the model can incorporate fiscal imbalances. This would include debt, as well as other options (increased taxes, user fees or outside aid) to fund hazard mitigation, and deficit spending to fund recovery and reconstruction. These various alternatives are likely to have significantly different impacts on the regional economy. An infusion of outside aid will translate into an unfettered boon, and the economy might expand or contract depending on shifts in spending from one stream to another (fewer consumer goods and more public services from tax increases, or shifts from ordinary consumer expenditures to repair).

Model Construction

Los Angeles County has one of the largest regional economies in the US In 2002, total economic output in the county was about $647 billion, consisting of 57 percent net value-added (roughly equivalent to gross regional product), 39 percent intermediate inputs (including imports), and about 4 per cent indirect taxes. Exports from the county amounted to about $194 billion, 81 percent of which are shipped to the rest of the US, and 19 per cent of which are shipped overseas. Seventy-four per cent of the imports into the LA County economy comes from the rest of the US. Household income amounted to about $301 billion (MIG, 2005). The economy is highly developed, as exemplified by strong interdependencies between sectors, the prominence of manufacturing and service sectors, and a relatively high level of regional self-sufficiency.

Water is a key input into the LA County economy. In 2002, water utilities (Los Angeles Department of Water and Power, or LADWP) retail sales to end users were $551 million, and other government utilities (Metropolitan

Water District, or MWD) sales to municipalities in LA County were $352 million, including $131.6 million to the City.

Basic economic and utility data
The major source of the data for the model is a detailed Social Accounting Matrix (SAM) for LA County, derived from the Impact Planning and Analysis (IMPLAN) database (MIG, 2005).[7] The IMPLAN database uses a non-survey approach to downscale national and state economy indicators (output, income, employment) to the county level. Hence, it is important to verify the IMPLAN figures in key sectors for small area IO tables. The reconciliation of the data between region-specific sources (for example, LADWP and MWD) and the IMPLAN database are presented in Rose and Liao (2005).

Other data
Elasticities of substitution for regionally produced inputs and for imports were based on a synthesis of the literature (Rose and Liao, 2005),[8] and other major parameters were specified during the model calibration process. Spatial data on economic activity and the water system are discussed in the following section.

Note that the various types of resilience are incorporated into the model by modifying key CES production function parameters as discussed further below. This involves the use of a combination of survey data (Tierney, 1997) and simulation data (Chang, 2003), and an optimization method for parameter adjustment developed by Rose and Liao (2005).

WATER OUTAGE SIMULATIONS

Model Refinements

Although the basic LA CGE model includes fundamental economic aspects of the production and consumption of water, it lacks two important dimensions. The first relates to engineering considerations of storage, transmission and distribution. These affect the extent of possible disruptions, the resultant flow of water to various customers, and patterns of recovery. The second relates to the spatial dimensions of the water system. This helps pinpoint the direct effect on customers of various types, capturing differentials that arise because economic activity is not uniformly distributed geographically throughout the region.

The first dimension is included by working with LADWP staff and MCEER researchers to identify water system characteristics unique to the two main providers in the county, as well as general characteristics relating to water system engineering. The second is incorporated through GIS overlays of system components and economic activity. In essence, this amounts to specifying the sectoral employment composition by place of work onto a WSA map.[9] Essentially, adding these dimensions enables us to specify constraints on water availability to each sector of the model and to simulate reasonable recovery patterns. These patterns are entered into the model as economic sector water constraint changes over time.

Below we summarize some assumptions and refinements related to our simulation of a terrorist attack that causes a total water outage in LA County. In this case, all customers are initially cut off from service, so conservation is a limited resilience option. Some companies are also able to maintain some economic activity, because of the 'water importance' consideration – some parts of companies are not dependent on water for their operation (for example, delivery services). Other direct responses include substituting other factors of production for water and use of stored water. Production rescheduling, which takes place at a later date, should be deducted from the initial reduction in production so as not to overestimate the impacts of any disaster. There is often a cost of rescheduling, such as paying overtime work or the carrying cost of capital, though sufficient information was not available to estimate these costs.

With respect to indirect effects, all of the above adjustments are possible for suppliers and customers, both within and outside the WSA, of those companies initially disrupted by the attack. Companies within the county but outside the WSA need not make the direct effect adjustments, but they do need to cope with the reduced supplies of goods and services from those companies whose production was curtailed within the WSA. Note, however, that lack of availability of these products is really not the issue. Although the price of water in this case is held constant, the price of all other goods and services can adjust through the market mechanism, therefore representing a type of price-rationing. Even firms that have inventories of the products other than water in short supply will also bid up prices because of their concerns over inventory holdings; hence, it is not necessary explicitly to include inventory holdings in the calculation.

Other adjustments are made in the analysis. For example, since LA County is part of a large consolidated metropolitan area with much economic activity in close physical proximity, it is not unreasonable to increase the possibilities of substituting imports for goods whose production has been curtailed in the county. Increased transportation costs penalties in this case are likely to be minimal.

In Appendix Table 1, we summarize various parameter and water availability constraint adjustments in the basic CGE model for our simulations.

We note first an initial adjustment to convert our CGE model from a long-run equilibrium tool to reflect conditions in the very short run (two-week electricity outage durations). This involves reducing the substitution elasticities between all input combinations by 90 per cent of their initial values.[10] The only other major adjustment worth considering is the possibility of price change lags. However these are complex conceptually, and we have no information on which to base them empirically, so we have omitted them at this point.

Several countervailing factors to the more rigid economic structure just noted represent individual and market resilience. Conservation of water differs by sector, and we utilize the rates developed in the Rose and Liao (2005) Portland Water System study.[11] These rates range from 2 percent in water and sanitary services to 19 percent in construction, and are implemented by adjustment of the water input productivity term. In the case of indirect or general equilibrium effects we invoke the same parameters.[12]

Increased water substitution is a potential response and we model it by increasing substitution elasticities relating to non-durable manufacturing inputs by results from the Rose and Liao study again. These increases range from 184 per cent in health services to 402 per cent in construction.[13] We utilize the same parameter adjustments for water substitution in the indirect calculations of the model. As noted before, other factors of production can also be substituted for water; however, since we lack data on this response, we invoke a 10 per cent parameter increase for substitution between these factors in the direct and indirect portions of the model.

Inventories (storage) are only a minor option in the case of water in LA. Land prices affecting space for storage, as well as regulatory restrictions, limit the amount of water storage for nearly all customers. The only significant amount of water inventories are those that are in the pipeline system or end-user structures (for example, vats, water coolers, water heaters). End-use inventories are relatively trivial, but the pipeline system can represent several percentage points of a day's supply (though the volume depends on the location and extent of pipe breakage). We use the results of a fragility analysis of the LADWP system by O'Rourke et al. (2004) to estimate this inventory on a WSA basis, extrapolate it to the rest of LA County, and allocate it as a percentage of a two-week supply. Results average 3 percent for the county as a whole.

Water importance differs by sector, ranging from low levels of 15 per cent in mining to 100 per cent in water and sanitary services sectors. We have no basis for establishing an 'importance factor' for goods other than water as inputs.

Production rescheduling also differs by sector, with very high rates for those sectors whose deliveries are not time-sensitive (for example, durable manufacturing) and low rates for those whose are (for example, Hotels and Restaurants). We also assume that a two-week outage will not cause any permanent change in customer–supplier relationships. This resilience adjustment enters the model at both direct and indirect levels of analysis. As in the case of water importance, production rescheduling factors are considered reasonably accurate, and therefore sensitivity tests are not required.[14]

Finally, the price of water is fixed (see the discussion above). However, the price of all other goods is allowed to adjust to market conditions.[15]

Results

The results for a total water outage in Los Angeles County, with only inherent resilience associated with normal input and import substitution and without any adaptive resilience adjustments, can be quickly summarized. To begin, we have reduced direct delivery of water to all sectors by 99 per cent as an approximation of a total outage (reduction by 100 per cent involves some division by zero in the model and cannot be computed at this time). Inherent substitution is negligible, which is not surprising given that the elasticity of substitution between water and other inputs in our model, reflecting the very short run, is 0.02. Indirect (GE minus PE) impacts are very low because the economy is nearly shut down, and there is not much remaining economic activity to be impacted (see also Cochrane, 1997). The total, or GE, impact is a reduction of economic activity of 99.6 per cent, which translates into $20.7 billion, compared to base year gross output of $539.7 billion. The economic loss thus represents 3.8 per cent of one year's output in LA County. A basic IO model would yield a 100 per cent loss of output, because it omits all resilience (even inherent substitution). In this case too, there would be no standard multiplier effects of two to three times this amount, however, because there is so little remaining economic activity to be impacted. Hence, inherent resilience is approximately 0.4 per cent (100−99.6) according to metrics developed by Rose (2004b).[16]

Table 15.1 summarizes the results when several additional types of resilience are included. In this case, the 99 percent curtailment of water services results in only a 39.5 percent decrease in direct output once sectoral production functions are recalibrated. Aside from water and sanitary services, the sectors taking the greatest hit are primary metals, semiconductors, hotels and restaurants, and entertainment. The sectors least affected are mining, communications, and finance.

Indirect effects add another 2.2 percent loss, with the largest impacts on various types of transportation, education and business services. The implicit multiplier is thus only 1.056 [(2.2 + 39.5) ÷ 39.5] reflecting offsetting general equilibrium factors (primarily adjustments to price changes) in

Table 15.1   Economic impacts of a total water outage in Los Angeles County (includes all resilience adjustments)

Sector	Water input Baseline (million $)	Direct disruptions (%)	Output Baseline (million $)	Recalibrated direct (%) (Partial equilibrium, PE)	Indirect (%) (GE-PE)	Total (%) (General equilibrium, GE)	Total Loss (million $)	Total adj for rescheduling
1. Agriculture	0.56	99	1398	−53.0	−0.4	−53.4	−29	−7
2. Mining	1.13	99	2589	−13.2	−1.3	−14.6	−14	0
3. Construction	6.05	99	28770	−47.5	−1.0	−48.5	−537	−27
4. Food Processing	7.26	99	14744	−67.6	−0.3	−67.9	−385	−19
5. Petroleum Refining	5.42	99	11404	−47.8	−0.7	−48.5	−213	−2
6. Other Non-Durable Mfg	54.28	99	33435	−57.8	−0.4	−58.2	−748	−37
7. Primary Metals	12.58	99	3192	−87.1	−6.5	−93.6	−115	−1
8. Semiconductors	0.14	99	1133	−87.1	−0.2	−87.3	−38	0
9. Other Durable Mfg	15.86	99	63364	−72.4	−0.4	−72.7	−1773	−18
10. Local Private Transportation	1.04	99	1039	−18.2	−29.1	−47.2	−19	−13
11. Other Transportation	7.43	99	21407	−18.2	−37.0	−55.2	−454	−318
12. Communications	4.06	99	15674	−18.1	−1.3	−19.4	−117	−70
13. Private Electric Utilities	0.27	99	2349	−37.8	−1.0	−38.8	−35	−9
14. Gas Utilities	0.10	99	4738	−37.8	−1.0	−38.8	−71	−18
15. Water Utilities	0.00	99	381	−99.0	0.0	−99.0	−15	−1
16. Sanitary Services	5.00	99	1149	−97.0	0.0	−97.0	−43	−4
17. Wholesale Trade	12.90	99	35676	−18.3	−1.1	−19.4	−266	−3

305

Table 15.1 (continued)

Sector	Water input Baseline (million $)	Direct disruptions (%)	Output Baseline (million $)	Output change during 2-week water outage				
				Recalibrated direct (%) (Partial equilibrium, PE)	Indirect (%) (GE-PE)	Total (%) (General equilibrium, GE)	Total Loss (million $)	Total adj for rescheduling
18. Retail Trade	11.07	99	27761	−18.7	−3.5	−22.2	−237	−47
19. Real Estate	7.80	99	31230	−18.9	−0.5	−19.4	−233	−23
20. Banking & Credit	0.43	99	19759	−18.9	−0.5	−19.4	−147	−15
21. Security Brokers	0.25	99	8153	−18.9	−0.5	−19.4	−61	−6
22. Insurance	0.43	99	11733	−18.9	−0.5	−19.4	−88	−9
23. Hotels & Restaurants	23.03	99	14383	−77.4	−0.2	−77.6	−429	−172
24. Personal Services	4.74	99	4301	−18.5	−0.9	−19.4	−32	−13
25. Business Services	14.05	99	59026	−18.5	−13.1	−31.7	−719	−216
26. Computer Services	0.26	99	6035	−18.5	−3.6	−22.2	−52	−31
27. Entertainment	22.41	99	39098	−77.4	−0.2	−77.6	−1167	−817
28. Education	0.73	99	5015	−38.2	−14.7	−52.9	−102	−1
29. Health & Social Services	27.39	99	30138	−38.5	−0.3	−38.8	−450	−225
30. State & Local Electric Utilities	123.69	99	2425	−37.8	−1.0	−38.8	−36	−9
31. Local Public Transportation	1.94	99	1254	−18.2	−30.0	−48.2	−23	−16
32. Other Government	70.22	99	36916	−23.6	−12.4	−35.9	−510	−102
Total	486.53	99	5 39668	−39.5	−2.2	−41.7	−9157	−2250

Table 15.2   Relative prominence of resilience adjustments

Resilience factor	PE effect	GE effect
Water conservation	1.0	0.5
Adaptive water substitution	1.6	0.9
Water storage	3.0	2.0
Water importance	58.7	56.6
Production rescheduling	75.5	71.9
Total	91.0	89.8

contrast to the IO, or linear model, multiplier of about 2.5 increase over direct effects.

The total GE loss is a reduction of 41.7 percent, or $9.2 billion, but this does not include sizeable production rescheduling opportunities, which range from 30 percent to 99 percent across sectors. These reduce the sub-total general equilibrium losses by an additional $6.9 billion, or 75.4 percent, to $2.3 billion.[17] Hence, the total disruption is only a reduction of 10.2 percent of two weeks of economic activity, if we incorporate resched-uling actions into the post-disruption period. The sectors hit hardest in absolute terms (see the last column of Table 15.1) are entertainment, other transportation, and health and social services.

The relative influence of five resilience factors is presented in Table 15.2, including separate estimates of the partial equilibrium and general equilib-rium effects of each. Production rescheduling aside, the results indicate that conservation is the resilience factor with the weakest direct influence, and 'water importance' is the one with the strongest direct influence. The ranking does not change when indirect effects are considered. However, the total 55.7 percent $(99-43.3)$ resilience this option provides is still much lower than the potential of production rescheduling of 75.5 percent $[(41.7-10.2) \div 41.7]$.[18]

The combined effects of all resilience options to lower the potential neg-ative impacts of a total water outage in Los Angeles County is 88.8 percent $(99-10.2)$. This far exceeds the 5.6 percent $(2.2 \div 39.5)$ increase in impacts due to indirect, or net general equilibrium (total GE minus PE) effects. This indicates that resilience is a much greater force than net general equilibrium effects.

We can now measure inherent and adaptive resilience. Actually, water importance might be considered an inherent resilience factor since it is embedded in the economic structure. Thus, if we add this to the inherent resilience of water and other factor substitution, total inherent resilience is 56.1 $(0.4 + 55.7)$. Adaptive resilience, including its corresponding GE effects, is 32.7 percent $(99 - 56.1 - 10.2)$.[19]

How do our estimates compare to other estimates of the partial and general equilibrium economic impacts of water service disruptions from terrorist attacks? To date, there have been none. However, we can draw some inferences from studies of such attacks on electricity systems and from the literature on impacts of natural disasters on utility systems in general. Tierney (1997) conducted a survey of businesses following the Northridge earthquake, and Rose and Lim (2002) refined the data to arrive at a direct resilience estimate of 77 percent in relation to the ensuing electricity outage. Rose and Liao (2005) found direct economic resilience to be about 33 percent in a study of a water system outage in the aftermath of a hypothetical major earthquake in Portland, Oregon. However, the Rose–Liao analysis attributed all water system resilience to input substitution and conservation, subsuming water importance, but omitted production rescheduling, the likely major source of resilience. Estimates of resilience of the Los Angeles electric power system by Rose et al. (2006) were even higher than those presented here, owing to the much larger presence of utility independence, in that case from distributed generation (back-up generators, co-generation facilities, and own power plants in large manufacturing enterprises).[20] To date, however, this chapter is the first to evaluate the full range of resilience options and to assess their relative prominence.

We offer an important caveat in light of recent events. Our results are appropriate to outages of short duration and where the attack is focused on the water system. Events like Hurricane Katrina, with widespread devastation of buildings and other infrastructure and large duration of recovery, severely tax the resilience of businesses, markets and communities. Resilience estimates for such events are likely to be much lower.

CONCLUSIONS

This chapter summarizes the development and application of a computable general disequilibrium model to estimate the business interruption impacts of the terrorist attack on the water system serving Los Angeles County. The model has been especially designed to incorporate engineering and spatial aspects of this system in the context of the regional economy, to reflect the several types of disequilibria that a major water outage will bring about, to include the various inherent and adaptive resilience responses at various levels, and to capture both partial and general equilibrium effects. The simulation of a two-week total water outage in LA County amounts to a business interruption loss of $20.7 billion without any resilience adjustment and $2.3 billion with the inclusion of several types of resilience, most prominently the rescheduling (recapture) of production after water service is restored. The results indicate that inherent aspects of the water–economy relationship (for example, water importance) and adaptive behavioral responses (for example, conservation and production rescheduling) can reduce the potential disruption impacts by 88.8 per cent.

We emphasize two caveats of our analysis. First, many of our resilience factors are rough estimates, and more empirical work is needed to refine them. We also may have erred on the optimistic side by assuming decision-makers take advantage of all possible resilience options and that market and multi-market adjustments will take place in a relatively short period. However, our model serves the useful purpose of identifying the many important considerations affecting the impacts and the relative potential sensitivity of the results to these various factors. This provides a guide to setting priorities for further conceptual and empirical research. Second, we have measured only one, although likely the major, aspect of water outage – business interruption. Our next priority is to extend the model to be able to estimate the household impacts, given the sizeable portion of the market represented by this customer group. To complete the picture, however, it will be necessary to evaluate the costs associated with property damage, mortality and morbidity, and social dislocation and trauma. These estimates can be combined with fragility analyses to obtain probabilities of occurrence of various water service disruption levels in order to arrive at a standard measure of risk for the water system with respect to various types of natural hazards. Assessments of the risks of varying levels of terrorist attacks can be applied in an analogous manner.

One final conclusion has a great bearing on future policy and is especially poignant in light of Hurricane Katrina. In the aftermath of the September 11 terrorist attacks, no politician wanted to admit that the government could not protect us from a major threat. Likewise, in case of utility outages, no matter what the cause, we have looked to utilities to protect us. This chapter has indicated how customers can protect themselves and contribute to the national war on terrorism by enhancing resilience to disasters in general. It has identified several ways this risk reduction can be accomplished and the relative effectiveness of each type of resilience response at the individual, market and regional economy levels. There is a strong indication that people learn from disaster experiences, and that measures implemented for one type of disaster apply to others. Thus, there is some cause for optimism that resilience to disasters will increase over time.

NOTES

* The research in this chapter is supported by funding from the DHS Center for Risk and Economic Analysis of Terrorist Events (CREATE) and from the NSF-sponsored Multidisciplinary Center for Earthquake Engineering Research. The authors wish to thank Tom O'Rourke, Craig Davis and Brian Thomas for helpful input into this research. The views expressed in this chapter, however, are solely those of the authors, and not necessarily those of the institutions with which they are affiliated nor of their funding sources. Also, the authors are solely responsible for any errors or omissions.

1. Recently, Bruneau et al. (2003, p. 3) have defined 'community earthquake resilience' as 'the ability of social units (for example, organizations, communities) to mitigate hazards, contain the effects of disasters when they occur, and carry out recovery activities in ways that minimize social disruption and mitigate the effectors of further earthquakes'. Further, they divide resilience into three aspects, which correspond to the concepts defined above in an economic context. First is reduced failure probability, which we view as equivalent to mitigation in this chapter. Second is reduced consequences from failure, which corresponds to our basic static definition of resilience. Third is reduced time to recovery, which adds a temporal dimension to our basic definition. In sum, Bruneau et al. (2003) have offered a very broad definition of resilience to cover all actions that reduce losses from hazards, including mitigation and more rapid recovery. These refer to how a community reduces the probability of structural or system failure, in the case of the former, and how quickly it returns to normal in the case of the latter. We have focused on the essence of resilience – the innate aspects of the economic system at all levels to cushion itself against losses in a given period, or reduced consequences from failure. Bruneau et al. refer to this as the 'robustness' attribute of resilience but we emphasize that our definition is more consistent with the broader literature (see especially Klein et al., 2003). Also, in the infancy of conceptual and especially empirical analysis of economic resilience, we believe it is prudent to pin down fundamental considerations first. Dynamic aspects of resilience, including intertemporal trade-offs, system 'flipping', irreversibilities, and extreme non-linearities, are beyond the scope of this chapter.

2. Rose and Benavides (1999) have identified a potential flaw in non-interruptible service premia in a general equilibrium context because a given firm considers only its own benefits from continued service and not the benefits to its suppliers and customers.

3. Another consideration in evaluating the economic impact of water utility outages is the temporal and spatial pattern of system recovery. In the case where multiple aqueducts, reservoirs, pump stations or distribution lines are down, water service can be restored so as to minimize the disruption by sequencing restoration to favor customers who put the water to highest-value use (see, for example, Rose et al., 1997; Davidson and Cagnan, 2004; for examples in the case of electricity restoration). Moreover, this use would reflect not only the direct value to the water user but also the value to its suppliers and customers, thus adding to the list of advantages of using some form of applied general equilibrium modeling. Many utilities and municipalities have priority customers but more to maintain health and safety than to minimize negative regional economic impacts. This is reflected in priorities usually given to hospitals, fire and police protection, as well as residential customers in general. Moreover, restoration crews are frequently dispatched according to cost-engineering considerations (for example, priority is accorded to the node or link that can be returned to service most quickly or cheaply).

4. In other contexts, we have performed simulations for cases where water prices are flexible and respond to market demand and supply conditions (Rose and Liao, 2005). This provides insight into the efficient use of water and may be especially useful for rationing policy.

5. These advantages include the ability to model: multi-sector distinctions that facilitate the identification of specific targets; individual behavior (including bounded rationality); market behavior (including the optimal rationing feature of the price system); both stock

(property damage) and flow (business interruption) losses; non-market considerations associated with use of infrastructure services, iconic values such as national parks, and household activities such as additional time and inconvenience from utility outages; resilience to terrorist attacks; inclusion of the recovery process; economic disequilibria relating to critical input availabilities, labor markets, government budgets and trade balances; macroeconomic repercussions in the form of general equilibrium effects; the distribution of impacts across socio-economic groups; the spatial diffusion of economic impacts, though this adds great complexity to the model; and mitigation and its economic impacts. With respect to modeling considerations, CGE is operational (and in real time), can be constructed with readily available data, and is relatively low cost.

6. Incomes from labor and capital employment in the economy are shared among institutions after the following deductions are made. Governments collect profit taxes on capital and employer-paid social security taxes on labor income, while industries deduct depreciation charges and retained earnings before paying capital incomes. The remaining incomes are then distributed to households and external agents according to fixed shares. Institutions also receive inter-institutional transfers, such as subsidies, social security and income taxes.

7. The IMPLAN system consists of an extensive database of economic data, algorithms for generating regional input–output tables and social accounting matrices, and algorithms for performing impact analysis. IMPLAN is the most widely used database for generating regional IO models and SAMs in the US.

8. Sources of these elasticities include: Prywes (1986), Deardoff and Stern (1986), Reinert and Roland-Holst (1992), Li (1994) and McKibbin and Wilcoxen (1998).

9. This involves assigning employment data by Traffic Analysis Zone (TAZ) to the WSA in which it is located (see French, 1998; Rose and Lim, 2002). Various adjustments are needed for the location of employment for sectors such as agriculture and utilities (based on firm-specific data) because employment addresses are often assigned to a headquarters rather than a job site (for example, a sub-station).

10. The elasticity of substitution captures the ease of adjustment between input combinations in relation to changes in input price ratios. Such adjustment is easier for a longer time frame and visa versa. The elasticities in the basic model are first specified for a 'short-run' time frame (1–2 years) and are then reduced to reflect a very short time frame of our analysis. Unfortunately, we are not aware of any studies that have estimated elasticities for a kind of 'very short run' that we consider. Because electricity disruptions are hard constraints on water availability and because electricity prices need to be held fixed in some cases (reflecting institutional limitations or policy advantages) in future simulations, the reduced elasticities prevent unrealistic substitutions of other inputs for utility services. Only empirical estimation of very short-run elasticities would enable us to assess the implications of our approach to the accuracy of the results.

11. We have incorporated sectoral differentials into the analysis, but we were not able to include other major differences in the response by firms. For example, major differences exist between the ability of small and large businesses to cope with lifeline outages.

12. Conservation of other inputs is possible, but since we have no information on which to base this, we have omitted this consideration.

13. The existing substitution possibilities represent 'inherent' resilience, and the increased substitution possibilities (increased elasticity of substitution values) represent 'adaptive' resilience.

14. On-site alternatives to centralized water delivery from LADWP and MWD (for example, digging wells to tap groundwater) are not permitted in LA County. Thus, a popular response to electricity outages, distributed generation (for example, diesel-fired generators, co-generation facilities) is not applicable to the case of water.

15. Note that we confine our measurement of economic impacts to Los Angles County. Of course these impacts radiate to neighboring counties, as well as the nation as a whole, through price and quantity effects in various markets. The majority of these effects will take place within the boundaries of an 'economic trading area', a region in which the majority of firms do their majority of business with other firms in the area. In this case,

the trading area is more likely to be the five-county Southern California Association of Governments (SCAG) Region. Still, LA County will contain nearly all of the direct impacts and the majority of indirect ones.

Note also that, aside from the geographically spreading negative impacts, areas outside the disaster site are likely to incur positive benefits. Examples would be using branch plants, outsourcing critical aspects of businesses, and businesses in other areas producing goods now in short supply in the region hit by the terrorist attack. The sum total of all of these impacts needs to be considered to yield the net impacts to the nation as a whole.

16. We believe the fixed proportional result is a reasonable baseline for the empirical measurement of resilience. There are, however, rare cases, such as especially large disasters where losses bear a non-linear relation to input disruptions, but such cases also include other contributing factors, which, if modeled together, might not be non-linear.

17. Production rescheduling has been separated because it is the dominant resilience factor, and because it does not require any significant modeling refinements – it is simply a multiplicative factor.

18. We also test the effects of non-linearities and interaction effects in the model. Here we examine whether the whole of resilience is greater than the sum of its parts. We compare the simple sum of these options separately with the results of incorporating them into the model all at once. The difference between the two estimates represents a combination of interactions effects and non-linearities in our CGE model. In terms of PE effects, the results are nearly the same. However, the results do differ somewhat more significantly with the addition of GE effects.

19. General equilibrium effects might also be subtracted from the adaptive resilience estimate because they represent the inherent resilience of the price system.

20. The basic estimates of Rose et al. (2006) of economic impacts without resilience were consistent with the *per capita* economic impacts of a similar power outage in New York City conducted by Lave et al. (2007) using a less formal model, and one which omitted any estimates of resilience. This consistency check provides some validation of our model, as does the fact that some of our resilience parameters are based on survey research by Tierney.

REFERENCES

Applied Technology Council (ATC) (1991), *Seismic Vulnerability and Impacts of Disruption of Lifelines in the Coterminous United States*, report ATC-25. Redwood, CA: Applied Technology Council.

Beenstock, M., E. Goldin and Y. Haitobsky (1997), 'The Cost of Power Outages in the Business and Public Sectors in Israel: Revealed Preference vs. Subject Evaluation', *Energy Journal*, 18: 39–61.

Brooke, A., D. Kendrick and A. Meeraus (1988), *GAMS: A User's Guide*, South San Francisco, CA: Scientific Press.

Brookshire, D. and M. McKee (1992), 'Other Indirect Costs and Losses from Earthquakes: Issues and Estimation', in *Indirect Economic Consequences of a Catastrophic Earthquake*, Washington, DC: FEMA.

Bruneau, M., S. Chang, R. Eguchi, G. Lee, T. O'Rourke, A. Reinhorn, M. Shinozuka, K. Tierney, W. Wallace and D. von Winterfeldt (2003), 'A Framework to Quantitatively Assess and Enhance Seismic Resilience of Communities', *Earthquake Spectra*, 19: 733–52.

Chang, S. (2003), 'Evaluating Disaster Mitigations: A Methodology for Urban Infrastructure Systems', *Natural Hazards Review*, 4: 186–96.

Chao, H.P. and R. Wilson (1987), 'Priority Service: Pricing, Investment and Market Organization', *American Economic Review* 77: 899–916.

Cochrane, H. (1997), 'Forecasting the Economic Impact of a Mid-West Earthquake', in B. Jones (ed.), *Economic Consequences of Earthquakes: Preparing for the Unexpected*, Buffalo, NY: NCEER.

Comfort, L. (1999), *Shared Risk: Complex Seismic Response*, New York: Pergamon.

Corcoran, P. (2003), 'IBM Business Continuity and Recovery Services', *Disaster Recovery Journal*, 16: 38.

Davidson, R. and Z. Cagnan (2004), 'Restoration Modeling of Lifeline Systems', Research *Progress and Accomplishments, 2003–2004*, Buffalo, NY: MCEER.

Deardoff, A. and R. Stern (1986), *Michigan World Trade Model*, Cambridge, MA: MIT Press.

Eckles, J. (2003), 'Sungard Availability Services', *Disaster Recovery Journal*, 16: 5–6.

French, S. (1998), 'Spatial Analysis Techniques for Linking Physical Damage to Economic Functions', in M. Shinozuka, A. Rose and R. Eguchi (eds), *Engineering and Socioeconomic Impacts of Earthquakes: An Analysis of Electricity Lifeline Disruptions in the New Madrid Area*, Buffalo, NY: MCEER.

Graves, F. and L. Wood (2003), 'Economics Costs of the August 14th 2003 Northeast Power Outage: Preliminary Estimate', Cambridge, MA: Brattle Group.

Haimes, Y., N. Matalas, J. Lambert and B. Jackson (2003), *Assessment of the Vulnerability of a Water Supply System to Attack*, Center for Risk Management of Engineering Systems, University of Virginia, Charlottesville, VA.

Holling, C. (1973), 'Resilience and Stability of Ecological Systems', *Annual Review of Ecology and Systematics*, 4: 1–23.

Jiang, P. and Y. Haimes (2004), 'Risk Management for Leontief-Based Interdependent System', *Risk Analysis*, 24: 1215–29.

Klein, R., R. Nicholls and F. Thomalla (2003), 'Resilience to Natural Hazards: How Useful Is this Concept?' *Environmental Hazards*, 5: 35–45.

Lave, L., J. Apt and G. Morgan (2007), 'Worst-case Electricity Scenarios: The Benefits and Costs of Prevention', in H.W. Richardson P. Gordon and J. Moore (eds), *The Economic Costs and Consequences of Terrorism*, Cheltenham, UK and Northampton, MA, USA: Edward Elgar.

Los Angeles Department of Water and Power (LADWP) (2003), *Annual Report 2002–2003*, Los Angeles, CA, http://www.ladwp.com/ladwp/cms/ladwp006538.pdf.

Mileti, D. (1999), *Disasters by Design: A Reassessment of Natural Hazards in the United States*, Washington, DC: Joseph Henry Press.

Minnesota IMPLAN Group (MIG) (2003), *Impact Analysis for Planning System (IMPLAN)*, Stillwater, MN.

O'Rourke, T., T.Y. Wang and P. Shi (2004), 'Advances in Lifeline Earthquake Engineering', *Thirteenth World Conference on Earthquake Engineering*, Vancouver, Canada.

Partridge, M. and D. Rickman (1998), 'Regional Computable General Equilibrium Modeling: A Survey and Critical Appraisal', *International Regional Science Review*, 21: 205–48.

Perrings, C. (2001), 'Resilience and Sustainability', in H. Folmer, H.L. Gabel, S. Gerking and A. Rose (eds), *Frontiers of Environmental Economics*, Cheltenham, UK and Northampton, MA, USA: Edward Elgar.

Petak, W. (2002), 'Earthquake Resilience through Mitigation: A System Approach', paper presented at the International Institute for Applied Systems Analysis, Laxenburg, Austria.

Reinert, K. and D. Roland-Holst (1992), 'Armington Elasticities for United States Manufacturing', *Journal of Policy Modeling*, 14: 631–9.

Rose, A. (2004a), 'Economic Principles, Issues, and Research Priorities of Natural Hazard Loss Estimation', in Y. Okuyama and S. Chang (eds) *Modeling of Spatial Economic Impacts of Natural Hazards*, Heidelberg: Springer, pp. 13–36.

Rose, A. (2004b), 'Defining and Measuring Economic Resilience to Disasters', *Disaster Prevention and Management*, 13: 307–14.

Rose, A. (2005), 'Analyzing Terrorist Threats to the Economy: A Computable General Equilibrium Approach', in P. Gordon, J. Moore and H. Richardson (eds), *Economic Impacts of a Terrorist Attack*, Cheltenham, UK and Northampton, MA, USA: Edward Elgar Publishing Company.

Rose A. and J. Benavides (1999), 'Optimal Allocation of Electricity After Major Earthquakes: Market Mechanisms Versus Rationing', in K. Lawrence (ed.) *Advances in Mathematical Programming and Financial Planning*, Greenwich, CT: JAI Press.

Rose, A., J. Benavides, S. Chang, P. Szczesniak and D. Lim (1997), 'The Regional Economic Impact of an Earthquake: Direct and Indirect Effects of Electricity Lifeline Disruptions', *Journal of Regional Science*, 37: 437–58.

Rose A. and S.Y. Liao (2005), 'Modeling Regional Economic Resiliency to Earthquakes: A Computable General Equilibrium Analysis of Water Service Disruptions', *Journal of Regional Science*, 45: 75–112.

Rose, A. and D. Lim (2002), 'Business Interruption Losses from Natural Hazards: Conceptual and Methodology Issues in the Case of the Northridge Earthquake', *Environmental Hazards: Human and Social Dimensions*, 4: 1–14.

Rose, A., G. Oladosu and S. Liao (2006), 'Business Interruption Impacts of a Terrorist Attack on the Electric Power System of Los Angeles: Customer Resilience to a Total Blackout', in P. Gordon, J. Moore and H. Richardson (eds), *The Economic Impacts of Terrorist Attacks*, Cheltenham, UK and Northampton, MA, USA: Edward Elgar.

Salerno, C. (2003), 'Powered Up When the Lights Go Out', *Continuity Insights: Strategies to Assure Integrity, Availability and Security*, 1(6): 23–8.

Seung, C., T. Harris, J. Englin and N. Netusil (2000), 'Impacts of Water Reallocation: A Combined Computable General Equilibrium and Recreation Demand Model Approach', *Annals of Regional Science*, 34: 473–87.

Shinozuka, M. and S. Chang (2004), 'Evaluating the Disaster Resilience of Power Networks and Grids', in Y. Okuyama and S. Chang (eds), *Modeling Spatial Economic Impacts of Disasters*, Heidelberg: Springer.

Shoven, J. and J. Whalley (1992), *Applying General Equilibrium*, New York: Cambridge.

Tierney, K. (1997), 'Impacts of Recent Disasters on Businesses: The 1993 Midwest Floods and the 1994 Northridge Earthquake', in B. Jones (ed.), *Economic Consequences of Earthquakes: Preparing for the Unexpected*, Buffalo, NY: National Center for Earthquake Engineering Research.

US Energy Information Administration (EIA) (2002), Form EIA-412, 'Public Electric Utilities Database', http://www.eia.doe.gov/cneaf/electricity/page/eia412.html.

Zimmerman, R., L. Lave, C. Restrepo, N. Dooskin, R. Hartwell, J. Miller, W. Remington, J. Simonoff and R. Schuler (2005), *Electricity Case: Economic Cost Estimation Factors for Economic Assessment of Terrorist Attacks*, New York University, Wagner Graduate School, Institute for Civil Infrastructure Systems.

APPENDIX A: MODEL PARAMETERS

CGE models used for disaster impact analysis are likely to yield estimates of business disruptions for some if not all sectors of an economy that differ significantly from the direct loss estimates provided by empirical studies. This is because production function parameters are not typically based on solid data, or, even where they are, the data stem from ordinary operating experience (inherent resilience only) rather than from emergency situations. Hence, it is necessary explicitly to incorporate adaptive resilience responses into the analysis, for example, by altering the parameters in the sectoral production functions of the CGE model.

Inherent resilience is embodied in the basic production function for individual businesses. Adaptive resilience is captured by changes in the parameters. In the

Appendix A Table 1   Resilience parameter changes

Type	Parameter	Data	Modification (practical)	Modification (ideal)
Inherent factor substitution	σ	see text	none	none
Adaptive factor substitution	$\sigma \uparrow$	assumption	increase σ by 10% for all inputs	increase σ by Y_i% for input i
Inherent water substitution	σ_{WX}	see text	none	none
Adaptive water substitution	σ_{WX}[a] $\uparrow$	Tierney(1997) Chang(2003) Rose and Liao (2005)	increase σ_{WX} by 184–402% depending on sector	same
Inventories	I[b]	LADWP O'Rourke (2005)	loosen water constraints by 3% for each sector	values for each input i in each sector j
Water conservation	$A_{1W} \downarrow$	Tierney (1997) Chang (2004) Rose and Liao (2005)	decrease A_{1W} by 2–19% depending on sector	same
Water importance	A_{1W}	ATC (1991)	loosen water constraints	decrease A_{1W} by Y_j% for each sector j
Production rescheduling	ΔZ	FEMA (1997) Rose and Lim (2002)	multiplicative factor for each sector	same

Notes:
[a] Elasticity of substitution between water and other inputs (X).
[b] Refers to inventory (storage) of all inputs.

aftermath of a disaster, people behave in a more urgent manner and are more likely to bring forth ingenuity. For example, for short periods, maintenance can be skipped, water fountains can be turned off, water can be reused, etc. Also, in general, inefficient practices can come to light and new opportunities can be initiated. There is an extensive literature suggesting that managers can become more clever in emergency situations. There is additional literature, now very prominent in the energy and environmental fields, indicating a much greater range of conservation opportunities when one looks at the production process from a holistic view.

16. Two-sided electricity markets: self-healing systems

Richard E. Schuler*

Active customer participation in electricity markets, particularly charging buyers for the real-time actual cost of supplying their needs, may lead to a far more reliable system at lower cost than under current practice in the US. In effect, we still have a socialist system of supply that shields customers from the true cost consequences of their purchasing choices. Because like low gasoline prices, the reliable low-cost supply of electricity that is always available on instantaneous demand has become an entitlement for most consumers, it has been extremely difficult politically to institute true real-time retail markets for electricity, even though wholesale markets have been deregulated in many regions of the country for over five years. But since there exists an inverse relationship between system reliability conditions and the real-time price of electricity, raising each and every customer's awareness of those periodic stresses may not only save customers money, on average, but it may also increase the system's resilience to insults – both natural and terrorist-induced.

Much of the focus on terrorist attacks on the power grid imagines wide-spread areas of the country without electricity like during the north-east blackout of 15 August 2003. However, as outlined in a recent CREATE report (Zimmerman et al., 2005), unless prolonged over many days, the social impact of massive regional outages is small. Rather, it is extended widespread local outages that result from numerous physical breaks in the local electricity distribution system, each of which must be repaired individually, that can lead to substantial human harm. Examples are the consequences of hurricanes or ice storms that can leave many customers in areas larger than a state without electricity for more than a week, simply because there are not enough trained repair crews to restore the multitude of widespread downed lines more rapidly. By contrast, in most instances a multi-state regional blackout is usually precipitated by only one or two actual physical faults on the system that trigger wild swings in power flows (dynamic instabilities). Here a design aspect of the system, to preserve as much of the equipment on the high-voltage power grid from harm as possible, leads to the automatic isolation of supply equipment so that the system might be restored again rapidly after the outage without requiring the repair of many damaged pieces of equipment (see Schuler, 2006 for a detailed discussion of this design and operating philosophy). So while a sudden widespread regional blackout receives most of the headlines, it is only if coupled with the simultaneous physical damage of geographically dispersed supply equipment that the blackout might become prolonged. Historically, that widespread failure of equipment has not been the initiator of the blackout. Instead it has been the disconnection and isolation of equipment as a conscious automated protection strategy that when triggered in response to some large initial failure, expands the blackout but also paves the way for a speedy restoration – usually within a day.

If the rapid disconnection of crucial pieces of supply equipment is important for their physical protection, then in these highly unstable transient periods, it would also be helpful to have the users respond nearly as rapidly, since electricity cannot be stored and supply must closely approximate demand in every instant. Thus having load respond automatically to match the automated equipment disconnects might preserve and sustain electric service in many portions of the region that might otherwise be subject to a widespread blackout – if only customers could respond in time. Furthermore, because it is precisely because of shortages of generation supply that the cost of providing an additional kWh of electricity soars, confronting the buyers with those real-time prices might induce them to invest in equipment that might disconnect some of their equipment automatically, thus saving both money and the system.

AN EXAMPLE FROM AUSTRALIA

On Friday 13 August 2004 a transformer short-circuited and eventually exploded in a power station, leading to a sequence of automated responses that ultimately disconnected six generating units with a combined capacity of 3100 MW (see NEEMCO Final Report, 2005). As a result, the system frequency fell below 49 hertz (cycles per second), more than a 2 percent reduction from Australia's 50 hertz norm. Sixty percent of this drop in supply occurred instantaneously: the other two units tripped off-line 13 and 21 seconds afterward, as shown in Figure 16.1. This figure illustrates the precipitous fall in frequency within five seconds following the separation of the first three generators, and subsequent frequency drops after the separation from the system of each of the other two units. In between, other generation attempted to pick up some of the capacity deficit. However, in large part because the Australian system managers mandate that their

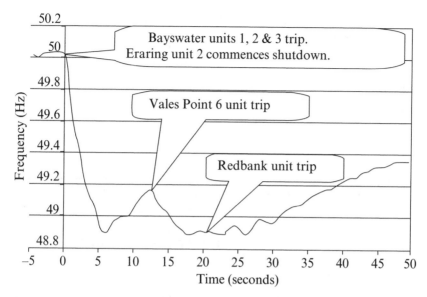

Source: National Electricity Market Management Company Ltd (2005).

Figure 16.1 *Australian generation-loss experience: system frequency over time*

load-serving entities (wholesale buyers) install frequency-sensing, automatic, load-shedding devices, 1500 MW of demand was available for automatic response, and another small portion of the loads had installed these devices in exchange for receiving payments for making this service available to the system. The net result, as illustrated in Figure 16.1, is that the system began to respond automatically to the initial disconnects within six seconds (far more rapidly than could have occurred in response to any human instructions), and within 31 seconds the system was on the path back to normal 50 Hertz operation.

Significant differences also exist in the wholesale market structures used in Australia, as compared to the US. There are only physical real-time energy markets in Australia, and the price cap is set at $14/kWh, 14 times higher than the largest price cap in the US. Thus customers are sensitive to shortage periods when the price of electricity can soar, and they therefore may be more willing to accept supply interruptions, particularly if those reductions can be channeled to less essential equipment. Furthermore, in a simulation of operations on a simple hypothetical power grid at Cornell University, Toomey et al. (2005) have demonstrated the relationship between system frequency (here 60 Hertz is the norm in the US) as an

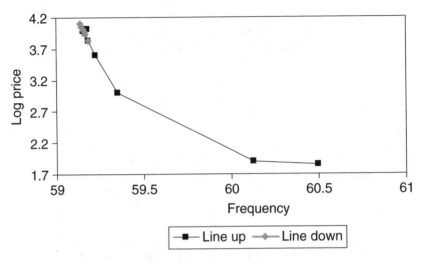

Source: Toomey et al. (2005).

*Figure 16.2   Relationship of price to system frequency in a simple three
bus simulated power system*

indicator of reliability and market price, as shown in Figure 16.2. Notice the
inverse relationship between price and frequency. This suggests that load
disconnect switches triggered by frequency-sensing detectors might be used
by customers to mute the effect of price spikes on the system. At the same
time, the customers' price-induced responses would help to maintain system
reliability. However, the sum of those market-driven responses by individual customers cannot be counted on to achieve the overall socially optimal
level of system reliability. Since all customers in a neighborhood are served
from the same electricity line, they receive the identical protection from
unanticipated interruptions – a public good that is subject to free-riding –
regardless of the differences in preferences among them. So, additional regulatory intervention beyond the individual responses by customers to prices
is required in order to achieve that socially optimal level of reliability.

INFERENCES FROM LABORATORY EXPERIMENTS

In fact there is virtually no experience in the US with the operation of large
power systems under market conditions where a substantial fraction of the
customers participate actively in the real-time market, in large part because
such practice is thought to be politically unacceptable. That is why a long

series of experiments have been conducted at Cornell University with human participants creating buyer and seller behavior, but where the actual power flows are governed by the laws of physics. A simple 30 bus system with six generators is used to replicate an alternating current network, and the buyers and sellers are located throughout this system.

A wide range of experiments have been conducted to explore the efficiency of alternative market-clearing mechanisms, and/or the effect of the number of different suppliers on their ability to exercise market power by exploiting system congestion. Other experiments have explored the effects of markets for generation reserves by location in combination with energy and VARs (value-added reseller) markets. The following analysis draws heavily on these experiments by examining the consequences of alternative structures for two-sided markets with active demand-side participation (Adilov et al., 2004). The implications for system generation requirements and line capacities were reported recently (Adilov et al., 2005). Thus this latest analysis should be instructive for inferring the implications that more active customer participation in real-time markets may have for the system's ability to withstand insults.

These experiments tested the efficiency of two alternative forms of active demand-side participation (see Adilov et al., 2004). As a base case for comparison, the typical utility pricing mechanism was tested where buyers pay a predetermined fixed price (FP) in all periods. In the second treatment, buyers were alerted prior to consumption periods when supply shortages were anticipated. In those periods, customers were given the opportunity of reducing their consumption below their normal benchmark purchases in similar periods, and by doing so they were able to earn a prespecified credit per kWh for each unit of reduced consumption. The third treatment was a simple real-time pricing (RTP) scheme where price forecasts were announced for the next-day and night periods, and based upon those forecasts, buyers decided how much electricity to purchase. However, buyers paid the actual market clearing price in each period for their purchases, and that price usually differed slightly from the forecasted price.

In each of these experiments, suppliers were free to engage in whatever offering behavior they liked, short of collusion with their competitors. The original purpose of these experiments was to understand the extent to which electricity markets might become more self-regulating, economically, were widespread customer participation to become prevalent (Adilov et al., 2004). However, the supply and demand allocations from these previous experiments have also been used to explore the physical implications for design capacities, the extent to which electricity flows become more predictable as the customers achieve greater involvement, and therefore the implications for the cost of providing reliability (Adilov et al., 2005).

Description of Prior Experimental Trials

Buyer problem

Each buyer was assigned a simple two-step discrete demand function with separate valuations for day and for night usage, as shown in Figure 16.3. In fact, these individual demand relationships are decomposed from an aggregate demand function that has a retail price elasticity of demand, at the mean price, of –0.3 (Faruqui and George 2002). Nineteen different buyers were included in each experiment, each with different assigned valuations. The aggregate demand function, ranging from very low prices to the reservation price, was given the inverted S-shape suggested by Schulze's work (reported by Woo et al., 1991) on the loss in consumer value for interruptible service.

Each customer's valuation differs between day and night, and there is an additional 'substitutable' block of energy that customers can choose to buy in either period (unused substitutable energy cannot, however, be carried over to the next day–night pair of periods). Typically, substitutable electricity purchases are valued less than the regular purchases in each of these periods. Furthermore, these induced valuations are increased substantially in pre-specified periods called 'heatwaves' to reflect the added value of electricity in extreme climatic conditions. The buyer's problem then is to maximize the spread between their assigned valuation for each quantity of

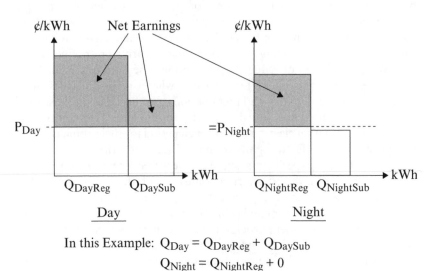

In this Example: $Q_{Day} = Q_{DayReg} + Q_{DaySub}$
$Q_{Night} = Q_{NightReg} + 0$
$Q_{DaySub} + Q_{NightSub} \leq Q_{SubMAX}$

Figure 16.3 Illustration of buyer's problem

electricity they buy, and the price they have to pay for it. Thus if all consumers behave optimally in these experiments, the total system load should be grouped around four distinct levels, representing combinations of normal, heatwave, day and night periods.

Seller's problem

Each of the six active suppliers was assigned three different generating units with different constant incremental production costs. In addition there was a fixed cost associated with each supplier's total capacity that was paid regardless of the supplier's level of activity. Each supplier is free to offer as much or little capacity into the market, up to the total capacity limit on their generation, as they wish, and they can specify a different price for each of the three different blocks of power. Offers may be made at prices lower or higher than the incremental production cost. The discretionary cost each supplier can incur is associated with whether or not and how much capacity they offer into the market. Each MW offered bears an opportunity cost of $5, regardless of having been selected to generate. This opportunity cost represents the commitment of resources and/or cost of foregone maintenance that is associated with planning to have those units available, as reflected in making an offer. The seller's problem is illustrated in Figure 16.4, and since the market in each period clears at the highest offer needed to meet the market demand, all suppliers with offered prices at or below

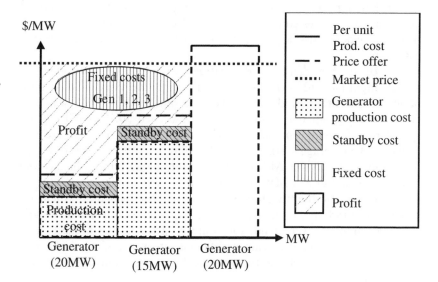

Figure 16.4   Illustration of seller's problem

that level are paid the identical last (highest) accepted offer. Each seller earns a profit in each period equal to the market price times the quantity they sell, minus the incremental cost of generating the electricity they sell, minus the $5 opportunity cost times all of the energy they offer into the market, minus their fixed costs.

Market structure and calibrations

In these two-sided markets, 19 buyers and eight sellers were included. Six suppliers were represented by humans; the seventh seller was the only generator subject to random outages, and its behavior was simulated numerically so that none of the six active participants would feel that their earnings were biased by a random phenomenon. A computer-simulated agent with a single 30 MW block of low-cost $20/MW generation was used to represent the outage unit and its capacity was always offered at $25/MW (including the $5/MW opportunity cost of making offers). The eighth supplier was a high-priced external source that was used only when internal supplies were not sufficient to clear the market.

Each of the buyers was assigned a different set of valuations for the energy they could purchase, and for approximately 80 percent of the buyers, those values were set very high, but realistically, based upon previous empirical work (see Woo et al., 1991). Therefore, the optimal quantity to be purchased did not change for the majority of buyers as prices varied unless the market-clearing prices reached levels many multiples higher than normally anticipated. Given the popular sentiment that most buyers are not interested in altering their electricity consumption or participating in demand-side programs, this assignment of values reflects that assertion.

Each of the three demand-side treatments was tested over the identical 11 day–night pairs (22 periods, total) with the same sequence of combinations of normal periods, heatwaves and unit outages. DRP was triggered by any predicted retail price that exceeded $0.106/kWh so that speculative behavior on the part of suppliers might also initiate this program. The average market demand in these experiments was designed to be approximately 200 MW (lower at night, higher during the day and in heatwaves), and 330 MW of active supply was available, plus the 30 MW provided by the numerically simulated base-load unit, when not subject to a random outage. The wholesale market was cleared at, and all accepted suppliers were paid, the uniform price of the highest (last) accepted offer. Demand was always met, despite withholding, because of the availability of purchases from external sources, about which all participants knew.

Market sequence

Each market period began with the auctioneer (ISO/RTO) providing fair load forecasts (quantities) for the upcoming two (day–night pair) periods. All buyers and sellers were told before each day–night pair whether the upcoming period had normal or heatwave conditions, and whether or not a unit outage had occurred. Next the suppliers submitted their price-quantity offers for both of the day–night periods. Then, either price fore-casts or firm prices and/or anticipated market conditions were given to the buyers. Under FP, the retail price was always set at $0.085/kWh, which included a $0.04/kWh wires charge, regardless of wholesale market condi-tions. Under the DRP treatment, the same fixed price of $0.085/kWh was charged for all purchases, but when DRP was announced to be in effect, a $0.079/kWh credit for purchases below each buyer's announced benchmark consumption level was provided. Under the RTP treatment, a fair forecast of market clearing prices for the next day–night pair was announced, based upon market conditions and the suppliers' offers. The buyers then made their quantity purchases, suppliers were committed and the market-clearing wholesale prices were declared. In the case of RTP, buyers were told the actual price they were assessed for their purchases in each of the previous day–night periods, which however did not vary more than 20 percent from the forecast prices for those periods. Finally, each seller was told their earn-ings, and each buyer was apprised of the net value of their purchases, including DRP credits where applicable. The process was then repeated for the next day–night pair until all 11 pairs were completed.

Summary of Experimental Results for Two-Sided Markets

These experiments were repeated for two different groups of participants, and the resulting total market efficiencies are summarized in Table 16.1 for the DRP and RTP treatments as a percentage of the wholesale rev-enues under the FP treatment. As a benchmark, the theoretical socially optimal levels of efficiency are also presented. The combined data indi-cate that it is possible to gain 6.75 percent in overall efficiency, compared to a FP system, without regulatory controls on suppliers. Experiments on both DRP and RTP also provide welfare gains to consumers, but in the case of DRP the offsetting loss to suppliers is so great that there is a net welfare loss; whereas with RTP, a combined gain of 2.02 percent is obtained. In many instances, the large price spikes generated under the FP system are muted by the RTP and DRP treatments, as shown elsewhere (see Adilov et al., 2004).

Most of the substantive differences in the quantities purchased between the different pricing schemes are statistically significant. As shown in

The electric power sector

Table 16.1   Two-sided experimental results: overall efficiency for combined trials

1. Deviations as % of FP revenues without regulation:

	% added consumer value	% change in supplier profit	Combined change
RTP	9.02	−6.99	2.02%
DRP	13.86	−17.52	−3.67%
Social optimum (as comparison)	29.32	−22.57	6.75%

2. Statistically valid differences in behavior from FP results (@ 0.95 level):

	RTP vs. FP		DRP vs. FP	
	Consumers	Sellers*	Consumers	Sellers*
Value/profit	+	−	+?	−
Quantities bought/sold:				
Days	−	−?	−	−
Nights	+	+?	−	+?

Note: * With fewer sellers, statistical significance is harder to attain.

Table 16.1, buyers consume less electricity in all periods under DRP, as compared to FP; whereas under RTP customers buy more electricity at night and less during the day than under FP. Furthermore, the last column emphasizes the overall conservation effect of DRP since it results in a statistically significant reduction in purchases both during the day and at night, as compared to RTP. Unfortunately, there is too much conservation under DRP, as highlighted by the separate quantity comparisons between both DRP and RTP and the socially optimal level of consumption where RTP results in the smallest difference.

In a poll that was conducted for both groups of subjects that participated in this experiment, there was a reversal of stated preferences from selecting DRP to preferring RTP as experience was gained with both regimes. The first group switched from 74 percent preferring DRP initially to 64 percent preferring RTP afterward, a statistically significant reversal. The second group's reversal was less appreciable, moving from only 53 percent preferring DRP ahead of time to 68 percent preferring RTP after having tried both. However the final fraction that preferred RTP was similar in both groups.

Implications for Flows on Individual Lines

The market-clearing supply by each generator and the usage by each customer were assigned to specific nodes on the PowerWeb simulated 30 bus electrical network shown in Figure 16.5. The locations of generators remained fixed, but since the flows on individual lines differ depending on the demand characteristics at each bus, and the assigned valuations for electricity purchases varies widely among different participants, 15 different randomly selected spatial allocations of the buyers were made for each of the two different sets of participants in the experimental trials. Since each trial was comprised of 22 time periods (11 day–night pairs), the period with the maximum line flow was selected as the surrogate for required installed capacity for each 22-period trial. In every case, the line flows were computed using an AC, non-linear optimal power flow procedure to minimize the total cost of meeting the demand, and these maximum line flows are summarized in Table 16.2 by market treatment and customer assignment.

In addition to the three market-based treatments (FP, DRP and RTP), the line flows were computed for the socially optimal conditions (cost-based offers and optimal purchases by buyers), and the former regulatory regime was simulated under fixed-price purchases by buyers. In this simulation of regulation, the actual purchases by each customer under the FP

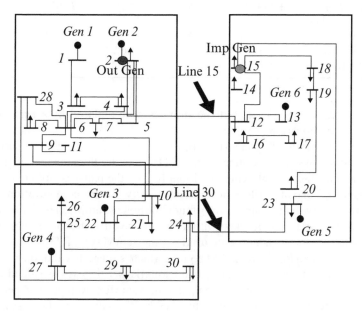

Figure 16.5   PowerWeb simulated electricity network with monitored lines

Table 16.2   Implied line and generation capacity requirements by market treatment

Regime	FP	DRP	RTP	REG	SO
Sum across all lines in the system of maximum absolute value in flow (MW) across 22 time periods for each of 39 lines					
Average all trials 1–30	649.57	588.74	604.03	645.15	604.76
% Difference from REG	0.7%	−8.7%	−6.4%	0.0%	−6.3%
Avg. difference from REG	4.42	(56.41)	(41.12)	–	(40.40)
Paired T-statistic	2.32	(6.93)	(10.33)	–	(20.48)
P-value	0.027	0.000	0.000	–	0.000
Summary of system load (MW)					
Average system load all trials 1–30	178.58	158.56	172.43	178.58	176.14
% Difference from REG	0.0%	−11.2%	−3.4%	0.0%	−1.4%
Max system load all trials 1–30	275.00	275.00	254.01	275.00	252.00
% Difference from REG	0.0%	0.0%	−7.6%	0.0%	−8.4%

market regime were used, but the supplies were replaced by a least-cost, cost-based allocation.

For each of the 30 trials (that is, different power systems) the sum of maximum flows across all lines under RTP is smaller than for the regulated regime. This fact is highlighted in Table 16.2 by the pair-wise differences in this sum of maximum line flows. Under every system configuration, the difference between the sum of maximum line flows (SumMax) under regulation with FP and under markets with RTP is positive. Furthermore, Table 16.2 notes that across all system configurations, the SumMax for RTP averages 6.4 percent less than for the regulated regime, which is suggestive that on average less line capacity might be required under markets if they are two-sided with active customer response. By comparison, SumMax averages 0.7 percent greater flows for market-based systems with FP than for regulated systems with the same FP signals to buyers. However, the market regime simulated here has no price caps or restrictions on capacity withholding, as compared with markets actually implemented in the US, so suppliers in these experiments are free to speculate wildly under the market regime; whereas the regulated regime is simulated with cost-based supplies throughout.

Table 16.2 also shows that the DRP demand-side mechanism is effective (as is RTP) in moderating speculative behavior by suppliers, since for every customer configuration the difference in SumMax between FP and DRP is positive (as it also is for FP-RTP), and SumMax for DRP is also smaller than for the regulated regime in all but one of the 30 configurations. In fact, on average across all configurations, DRP results in an 8.7 percent smaller SumMax than for a regulated regime, suggesting how effective active demand-side participation might be in moderating peak line flows, and in the long run in reducing investment in facilities.

The maximum system loads are also tabulated for each of these market regimes in Table 16.2 where RTP is shown to result in a 7.6 percent reduction in peak load, as compared with the regulated regime under FP (peak loads under regulation might also be lower if RTP were inaugurated under regulation, but that scenario cannot be fairly simulated with the available experimental data). Finally, note that the maximum flows are also computed for socially optimal power exchanges, and Table 16.2 indicates that on average across all 30 system configurations the RTP market system comes closest to this ideal, both in terms of the sum of maximum line flows across each system, and in terms of peak loads. In fact, t-tests were conducted on the pair-wise differences in SumMax across all combinations of regimes (where SumMax for each configuration is considered an observation). Both DRP and RTP simulations yield statistically significantly lower line flows than under a FP regulatory regime, and only the FP market regime results in slightly higher, but significant, line flows as compared to the FP regime under regulation. (None of the simulations for the regulatory regime consider differences in unit costs that might arise because of different incentives.)

Line Flow Predictability

In previous experimental analyses of the single-sided electricity markets (no active demand-side participation) used throughout the US, the simulated line flows are directly proportional to system load when the dispatch minimizes total system cost and is based upon the actual cost of generation (for example simulations of perfectly regulated or perfectly competitive markets). But, when that least-cost dispatch is based upon offers from deregulated suppliers who are free to speculate, that highly correlated simulation of physical relationship breaks down and is highly erratic (see Thomas, 2002). Thus it is interesting to explore the physical line flows that might be inferred from these recent experiments on full two-sided markets with active demand-side participation. One indication of the facility with which the system might be operated under various market regimes is suggested by the relationship between overall system load and the flows on any individual line.

In a preliminary analysis using the line flows derived from the PowerWeb 30 bus electrical transmission network shown in Figure 16.5, two lines were selected to illustrate the possibilities. The location of all generators is shown, including the import generator that cleared the market when insufficient internal supplies were offered. Two of the lines were selected for analysis (line 15 with the greatest variability and the more typical line 30), but the flows for only one of the 30 random allocations of buyers to busses is used in this illustration. Statistical tests were performed on the correlation between system load and line flows on those two links for the different market regimes. These regression results are summarized in Table 16.3. Because of the location of

Table 16.3   Statistical Relation Between Line Flows and System Load

	Social optimum	(Reg. regime) Fixed price with regulated sellers	Results with active participants		
			Fixed price	Demand reduction program	Real-time pricing
Regression results for tie line 15					
Intercept	40.1779	39.1761	17.9780	29.9462	33.0568
Std Err	3.0375	2.1514	3.1385	3.8662	3.5013
Slope Coefficient	(0.1982)	(0.1901)	(0.1025)	(0.1789)	(0.1909)
Std Err	0.0167	0.0116	0.0168	0.0236	0.0197
R-Squared	0.7701	0.8657	0.4695	0.5777	0.6906
F-Statistic	140.6651	270.7614	37.1714	57.4517	93.7394
P-value	0.0000	0.0000	0.0000	0.0000	0.0000
Regression results for tie line 30					
Intercept	(17.5262)	(18.5527)	(9.1573)	(13.9666)	(17.5818)
Std Err	1.5631	1.7259	2.4566	3.0202	3.1587
Slope Coefficient	0.0751	0.0753	0.0437	0.0802	0.1024
Std Err	0.0086	0.0093	0.0132	0.0184	0.0178
R-Squared	0.6449	0.6111	0.2079	0.3104	0.4409
F-Statistic	76.2617	66.0048	11.0260	18.9069	33.1193
P-value	0.0000	0.0000	0.0019	0.0001	0.0000

Note: The following linear regression equation was estimated with OLS.
Line Power Flow = Bo + B1 × System Load
N = 44 for all regressions

the generators and specific buyers, there is actually a negative correlation between system load and the flow on line 15 (due to changes in the optimal system dispatch), but that negative relationship exists under all five regimes. What is different is the magnitude and the degree of statistical significance of that relationship. The relationships are nearly identical under the socially optimal, previously regulated and RTP regimes; the association is weakest under the FP market case, but improves somewhat under DRP.

In the case of a more typical transmission link like line 30, where there is a positive relationship between system load and line flow in all five cases, once again the socially optimal and former regulated regimes yield almost identical results. Here, the relationship is much weaker under the FP market regime; compared to regulation, it becomes almost identical in magnitude but not in statistical significance under DRP, and it is even stronger under RTP, although still not as significant statistically. Thus operators of electrical systems may also find value in the widespread implementation of demand-side participation in market exchanges if it strengthens the predictability of flows on any particular line.

SUMMING-UP

This series of anecdotes, academic results derived from theoretical, experimental and numerical exercises, and real-world incidents can be combined to formulate a sequence of hypotheses and inferences:

1. If we allow markets to reign in supplying electricity, real-time price can be a very good indicator of the emerging status of system reliability. In particular, there appears to be a nice inverse correlation between price and system frequency which in turn is a good indicator of system stress.
2. Facilitating customer participation, although politically unpopular with respect to what is perceived as an entitlement, confronts many more buyers with the cost consequences of their behavior – and indirectly, therefore, their impact on reliability, a public good shared by neighboring customers.
3. Automatic frequency detection devices may offer low-cost, low-hassle ways for many customers to respond to price; thus making customer participation more palatable.
4. In the earlier 'Float Together/Sink Together?' paper (Schuler, 2006), the desirability was shown of having portions of large electric systems operate autonomously and of allowing them to separate under duress. That isolation can reduce damage to essential equipment and permit the system to be reassembled far more rapidly than if it crashed everywhere.

Widespread customer participation in markets may expand and disperse that 'islanding' capability to a local micro-level.

5. The Australian experience of the summer of 2004 demonstrates how mandated frequency response by large blocks of users can save the electric system from collapse in the face of large disturbances automatically. How much greater would those salutary consequences be were the customers' responses scattered widely over the system?

6. Incidentally, these analyses suggest that the system might be easier to operate, and its overall capacity requirements might be reduced (costs might be lower), were all customers to be actively encouraged to confront the consequences of real-time prices.

CONCLUSIONS

Just as 'distributed generation' (more numerous, widely scattered, but smaller units) is thought to enhance overall system reliability and resilience, so too it is illustrated here how devising methods to have many more customers engaged as active participants in electricity markets ('distributed buyers') may also enhance their reliability. These conclusions follow regardless of the source of the initial insult on the system: random equipment failure, natural disaster or terrorist assault. In fact an extremely successful coordinated terrorist assault on the power system might be no greater than the random sequence of outages the Australians experienced on 13 August 2004. In that case, decentralized automated demand response, mostly by large blocks of load, effectively muted the consequences of the initial shock and led to the rapid automatic restoration of the system. How much greater might the system's resilience be if many small customers also responded? Note, however, that it is important not to have all of these response mechanisms tied together tightly through a common information delivery system. In that case the electricity system may become more vulnerable through a cyber-attack.

The best way to involve a large number of widely dispersed customers is simply to provide each with a meter capable of detecting electricity system characteristics, like frequency, that are highly correlated with the price they are to pay. Who is to pay for the installation of that metering? Is it in the public interest to have it installed? Perhaps we should take our cue from a substantial infrastructure investment of 50 years ago in the National Defense Interstate Highway System. Is what we need today the 'Nationwide Anti-Terrorism Electricity Metering Network'? This analysis describes the salutary benefits of getting the customers into the game.

NOTE

*   Work on this analysis was supported through NYU by the Center for Risk and Economic Analysis of Terrorism Events, funded by the US Department of Homeland Security at the University of Southern California. I am grateful to the continued collaboration by my colleagues and students at Cornell University who worked with me on many of the analyses contained in this chapter. They include Nodir Adilov, Tom Light, Tim Mount, Bill Schulze, David Toomey, Bob Thomas, Jim Thorp and Ray Zimmerman. I would also like to express appreciation for support on related projects provided by the Power Systems Engineering Research Center (PSERC), an NSF-supported industrial consortium, and the Consortium for Electricity Reliability Technology solutions (CERTS), funded by the US Department of Energy.

REFERENCES

Adilov, N., T. Light, R. Schuler, W. Schulze, D. Toomey and R. Zimmerman (2004), 'Self-Regulating Electricity Markets', presented at the Advanced Workshop in Regulation and Competition, Rutgers Center for Research in Regulated Industries 17th Annual Western Conference, San Diego, 24 June.

Adilov, N., T. Light, R. Schuler, W. Schulze, D. Toomey and R. Zimmerman (2005), 'Differences in Capacity Requirements, Line Flows and System Operability under Alternative Deregulated Market Structures: Simulations Derived from Experimental Trials', Proceedings of IEEE Power Engineering Systems 2005 Conference, San Francisco, 12–16 June.

Faruqui, A. and S. George (2002), 'The Value of Dynamic Pricing in Mass Markets', *Electricity Journal*, July: 45–55.

National Electricity Market Management Company Ltd. (2005), 'Power System Incident Report – Friday 13 August 2004', NEMMCO Final Report, Australia, 28 January.

Schuler, R. (2006), 'Float Together/Sink Together? The Effect of Connectivity on Power Systems', in H. Richardson, P. Gordon and J. Moore *The Economic Impacts of Terrorist Attacks*, Cheltenham, UK and Northampton, MA, USA: Edward Elgar.

Thomas, R. (2002), 'Markets and Reliability', Report to Consortium on Electricity Reliability Technology Solutions, Washington, DC, January.

Toomey, D., W. Schulze, R. Schuler, R. Thomas and J. Thorp (2005), 'Public Goods and Electric Power: A New Look at the Role of Markets', Cornell Report to PSERC, Ithaca, NY, August.

Woo, C.-K., R. Pupp, T. Flaim and R. Mango (1991), 'How Much Do Electric Customers Want to Pay for Reliability? New Evidence on an Old Controversy', *Energy Systems and Policy*, 15: 145–59.

Zimmerman, R., C. Restrepo, N. Dooskin, R. Hartwell, J. Miller, W. Remington, J. Simonoff, L. Lave and R. Schuler (2005), 'Electricity Case: Main Report – Risk, Consequences, and Economic Accounting', CREATE Preliminary Report, NYU, New York, 6 June.

Index